KANT AND MILTON

SANFORD BUDICK

Kant and Milton

HARVARD UNIVERSITY PRESS

Cambridge, Massachusetts, and London, England
2010

Library of Congress Cataloging-in-Publication Data

Budick, Sanford, 1942–
    Kant and Milton / Sanford Budick.
        p. cm.
    Includes bibliographical references (p.   ) and index.
    ISBN 978-0-674-05005-1 (alk. paper)
    1. Kant, Immanuel, 1724–1804.   2. Milton, John, 1608–1674.   I. Title.

B2798.B765 2010
193—dc22   2009037575

To
Stanley Cavell,
Michael Kaufman,
and the memory of
Wolfgang Iser

Contents

Acknowledgments

It is a pleasure to express my gratitude for the unstinting help of the staffs of the rare book collections at the Bayerische Staatsbibliothek (Munich), the Staatsbibliothek zu Berlin, the British Library, the Warburg and Courtauld Institutes, and at the universities of Göttingen, Halle, Konstanz, Marburg, and Münster. Special thanks are due for the hospitality and instruction of Werner Stark in making it possible for me to explore the Kant Archiv of the University of Marburg; to Sabine Volk-Birke, Hans-Joachim Kertscher, and Günter Schenk, who admitted me to the riches of the G. F. Meier holdings of the Franckesche Stiftung (Halle); to Marvin Spevack, who generously facilitated my access to the collections of the University of Münster; and to Dorothea Barfknecht, Bibliotheksamtsrätin in the Handschriftenabteilung of the Preußischer Kulturbesitz, Staatsbibliothek zu Berlin, who was my guide and decoder in the Herder Nachlass. I am especially grateful to Jakob Hessing and Dafna Mach for checking and improving my translations of German texts.

It is difficult to express the depth of my appreciation to the National Endowment for the Humanities. Without the freedom and means afforded by the endowment's fellowship, the principal work required by this undertaking would scarcely have been begun, much less brought to even a provisional close.

At various stages of my work I have benefited greatly from the encouragement and stimulation of Rachel and Shaul Almakies, Lawrence Besserman, Marshall Brown, Arthur Budick, Burton Budick,

Stanley Cavell, Bernhard Fabian, Dieter Henrich, Annette and Steven Hochstein, the late Lore Iser, Dennis Kurzon, Shlomo and Lynndy Levin, Zephyra Porat, Ayelet and Yuval Sharon, Karlheinz Stierle, Patricia Stierle, Tzachi Zamir, and the late Moshe Barasch, as well as from the creative insights and loving faith of my wife, Emily Miller Budick.

At Harvard University Press Lindsay Waters immediately grasped the significance of investigating Kant's relation to Milton. He was supportive throughout. Phoebe Kosman guided my work on the manuscript with rare intelligence and tact. Cheryl Lincoln's copyediting was a model of helpfulness and clarity.

I am particularly indebted to Wolfgang Iser and Michael Kaufman for the care they lavished on my manuscript, even if—and especially because—their searching comments necessitated recasting it entirely. Wolfgang Iser's passing opens an irreparable wound in the community of those who reflect on, and inhabit, the relation between philosophy and literature.

Last, I must emphasize that the imperfections in the finished product are my responsibility alone.

Notes on Citations and the Term *Succession*

Citations of Kant in German are from *Kants Werke: Akademie-Textausgabe* (Berlin: de Gruyter, 1968). Unless otherwise noted, quotations from Kant given in English are from the following texts: *Immanuel Kant's Critique of Pure Reason,* trans. Norman Kemp Smith (London: Macmillan, 1993); *Groundwork of the Metaphysics of Morals* and *Critique of Practical Reason* in Immanuel Kant, *Practical Philosophy,* trans. Mary J. Gregor (Cambridge: Cambridge University Press, 1996); *The Critique of Judgement,* trans. James Creed Meredith (Oxford: Clarendon, 1973) or, as indicated, *Critique of the Power of Judgment,* trans. Paul Guyer and Eric Matthews (Cambridge: Cambridge University Press, 2000); *Religion within the Boundaries of Mere Reason and Other Writings,* trans. and ed. Allen Wood and George di Giovanni (Cambridge: Cambridge University Press, 1998); *Observations on the Feeling of the Beautiful and Sublime,* trans. John T. Goldthwait (Berkeley: University of California Press, 1960); *Anthropology from a Pragmatic Point of View,* trans. Mary J. Gregor (The Hague: Nijhoff, 1974); *Correspondence,* trans. and ed. Arnulf Zweig (Cambridge: Cambridge University Press, 1999); and *Universal Natural History and Theory of Heaven,* trans. Ian C. Johnston, www.mala.bc.ca/~johnstoi/kant/kant1.htm. (I have sometimes slightly modified Johnston's translations.) In the case of *Observations on the Feeling of the Beautiful and Sublime,* an additional page reference, marked *Obs.,* is given after the English translation and refers to Goldthwait's volume. References to the *Critique of Pure Reason* are given to the A or B texts;

those for the *Groundwork,* the *Critique of Practical Reason,* and the *Critique of Judgment* are to the *Akademie-Textausgabe* page numbers, which Meredith and Gregor give in the margins of their translations. All page number references to Kant's texts are given in parentheses immediately after citations. Page numbers of the *Akademie-Textausgabe,* the *Critique of Pure Reason,* the *Groundwork of the Metaphysics of Morals,* the *Critique of Practical Reason,* the *Critique of Judgment, Religion within the Boundaries of Mere Reason,* and *Anthropology from a Pragmatic Point of View* are, except where noted otherwise, usually preceded by the abbreviations *AA, CPR, GMM, CPrR, CJ, Rel,* and *Anth,* respectively, though references to the *Critique of Pure Reason* are most often given simply to the A or B texts. If not mentioned above and not otherwise indicated, translations are mine. All underlining, whether in my text or in quotations, indicates my added emphases.

Citations of Milton are from John Milton, *Complete Poems and Major Prose,* ed. Merritt Y. Hughes (New York: Odyssey, 1957). I have used this text rather than excellent newer editions because it preserves the capitalizations that generally remained standard in eighteenth-century editions of Milton's poetry. References to the writings of Johann Gottfried Herder (preceded by the abbreviation *SW* in my text) are to *Herders Sämmtliche Werke,* ed. Bernhard Suphan, 33 vols. (Berlin, 1877–99).

Throughout this book I have adopted the rendering "succession" for *Nachfolge* that has recently been offered by Guyer and Matthews at 5:283 in their translation of the third *Critique.* This translation of *Nachfolge* suggests far more accurately than Meredith's translation, "following," the independence achieved in this exceeding of imitation by a special kind of imitation. Yet the terms *Nachfolge* or *succession,* like the terms *Nachahmung* or *imitation,* are still subject to confusion because they do not by themselves make clear whether they refer to a process or an achieved condition (or product). In addition to the term *succession* by itself, I have therefore frequently employed the phrases *procedure of succession* and *succession procedure* or, alternatively, *condition of succession,* as the context requires. We have Kant's direct warrant for speaking of the "procedure" of succession (*CJ,* 5:253). In making this my normative form of reference, I have also followed the example of John Rawls, "Themes in Kant's Moral Philosophy," in *Kant's Transcendental Deductions: The Three Critiques and the Opus postumum,* ed. Eckart

Förster (Stanford: Stanford University Press, 1989), pp. 81–113, who suggests that Kant's term *categorical imperative* is clarified by referring to it as "the procedure for applying the categorical imperative" or "the CI-procedure" (p. 81). In fact, the need for appending the term *procedure* to both the *categorical imperative* and the *succession* reflects, as I will explain in due course, a significant relationship between these activities in Kant's thought.

KANT AND MILTON

Succession which has reference to a precedent, and not imitation, is the proper expression for all influence which the products of an exemplary *author* [*originator*] may exert upon others. . . . [They] serve as a model, not for *imitation,* but for *succession.* The possibility of this is difficult to explain.

—Kant, *Critique of Judgment* (1790)

Such a painting, designed with freedom, is cause for admiration. This, Milton executes preeminently.

—Kant, anthropology lecture (1788–89)

Aesthetic ideas are those representations that contain a wealth of thoughts which *ad infinitum* draw after it a succession of thoughts. Such ideas draw us into an immeasurable prospect, e.g. Milton's saying, "Female light mixes itself with male light, to unknown ends." Through this soulful idea the mind is set into continuous motion.

—Kant, anthropology lecture (1792–93)

The will is thought as independent of empirical conditions and hence, as a pure will, as determined *by the mere form of law,* and this determining ground is regarded as the supreme condition of all maxims. The thing is strange enough, and has nothing like it in all the rest of our practical cognition.

—Kant, *Critique of Practical Reason* (1788)

Introduction

Over the course of three decades Kant was repeatedly drawn to Milton's poetry for aid in reflecting principally on one question: How can one achieve a mental life that is characterized by *independence and spontaneity*—the *originality (Originalität)* of the poetic genius, preeminently—and at the same time inherit one's given world, one's past, through the mere *imitation,* which, says Kant, underlies all learning?[1] Directly and indirectly, he spent his life searching for an answer. To be sure, this same question has preoccupied innumerable other individuals over many centuries in many parts of the globe. Indeed, the ways in which we answer this question may be said to constitute culture itself, perhaps even what is considered to be human. Yet Kant's attempts at an answer are of special interest. In the history of thought no one else has so powerfully described the independence of the individual human mind. And, undeniably, whether or not one agrees or disagrees with this or that aspect of his descriptions, no one else's account of that mental independence has more significantly shaped the ways in which countless individuals, in the West and well beyond, think of their independence, even, indeed, of what their minds are.

This book tells the previously untold story of how Kant's reflections on this question crystallized into a concrete answer in the years 1785–90. At the core of this story is a scene of the relation of moral philoso-

---

1. Kant, *Critique of Judgment,* §47: "Every one is agreed on the point of the complete opposition between genius and the *spirit of imitation.* . . . Learning is nothing but imitation" (5:308). In Chapter 6 I will show that these statements are preamble to the claim for originality that, in §49, Kant actively derives from Milton's poetry.

1

phy to the experience of a certain kind of poetry, namely, Milton's poetry of the sublime. Almost eighty years ago René Wellek published a book about the early impact of Kant on British philosophy and British literature entitled *Immanuel Kant in England, 1793–1838*.[2] For the present book an alternative, accurate title would be *Milton and Miltonism in Immanuel Kant, 1764–95, with Special Emphasis on 1785–90*. Whether or not I have been adequate to the telling of the story laid out here, its inherent excitement is that it shows one of the greatest of all philosophers in the act of discovering his freedom and moral feeling by encountering the poetry of one of the greatest of all poets. It shows concretely how poetry functioned for Kant as the co-worker of philosophy.

Kant said that what "can be called *poetry*" encompasses everything that provides experience of art: "poetic art includes the arts of painting, horticulture and architecture, as well as the arts of composing music and verse *(poetica in sensu stricto)*." But he added that *poetry in the strict sense* provides the most significant kind of artistic experience: "poetry wins the prize . . over every other fine art. . . . A good poem is the most penetrating means of stimulating the mind" (*Anth*, 7:246–247). "*Poetry,*" he asserts at the heart of the *Critique of Judgment*, "holds the first rank among all the arts. It expands the mind by giving freedom to the imagination" (5:326). For him the poetry that was of special philosophical interest because of its "painting, designed with freedom" *(in freyheit entworfenes Gemälde)* was exemplified by "Milton preeminently" (*Milton vorzüglich: AA*, 25.2:1494). Milton's poetry projects freedom in its representation of the experience of the sublime. I will argue that during Kant's most intense and creative years of writing moral philosophy, 1785–90, his engagements with the experience of the sublime, especially in Milton's poetry, repeatedly made possible—for Kant himself—what he regarded as the highest achievement of "practical rea-

---

2. René Wellek, *Immanuel Kant in England, 1793–1838* (Princeton: Princeton University Press, 1931). This is a good place to mention Stephen Fallon's highly informative *Milton among the Philosophers: Poetry and Materialism in Seventeenth-Century England* (Ithaca: Cornell University Press, 1991). Fallon's interest, like Wellek's, is in the impact of philosophers on poetry. My interest here is in the integral role of poetry in philosophy: how Milton's poetry is an active partner in Kant's philosophical work, and, equally, how the grounds of that joint work give us a new understanding of the nature of Milton's poetic enterprise.

son": "the grand disclosure" of freedom and moral feeling (*CPrR*, 5:94).

Understanding the way Kant grasped Milton's poetry is no less significant for our appreciation of Milton than of Kant. Better than anyone else since Milton, Kant understood why Milton has no anxiety of influence.[3] Milton, Kant saw, *imitates* no one. In 1792–93 Kant characterized Milton's poetry as an art of "succession." In 1790, with one eye already firmly fixed on Milton's poetry, he had explained why the poet who engages in the procedure of succession is freed from the relation of dependency that is entailed by imitation: "*Succession* which has reference to a precedent, and not imitation, is the proper expression for all influence which the products of an exemplary *author* [*originator*] may exert upon others. . . . [They] serve as a model, not for *imitation,* but for *succession.* The possibility of this is difficult to explain" (*CJ,* 5:283, 309). Kant hits upon the proper expression for Milton's and his own way of succeeding to an effectively endless line of *a special kind of influence,* that is, of exemplary representations by exemplary authors. Those who achieve this procedure of *succession* can experience influence in the condition of freedom. The efficacy of this procedure is not self-evident. In fact, Kant's qualifier to the above explanation—"the possibility of this is difficult to explain"—has been the occasion for this book.

Kant's way of experiencing the influence of Milton on his own thought is, I maintain, the source and the occasion for his explanation of the difference between influence by succession and influence by imitation. This is to say that in the act of theorizing and giving examples of the procedure of succession, Kant, too, is in a relation of influence-in-freedom to his immediate exemplary author, Milton. At highly important junctures of Kant's moral philosophy, Milton's poetry provides Kant with experience of an effectively endless line of sublime representations. In its fully developed form, Kant's Milton-derived and Milton-applied concept of influence-in-freedom has significance far beyond Kant's relation to Milton. This concept can explain any in-

---

3. In using the phrase *anxiety of influence,* I refer, of course, to the wide currency given to the phrase by Harold Bloom's *The Anxiety of Influence: A Theory of Poetry* (New York: Oxford University Press, 1973), where Bloom's great exemplar of a writer who occasions this anxiety in later writers is Milton.

fluence within which—and as a function of which—the successor achieves creative freedom.

The Kantian-Miltonic idea of influence certainly applies to the effect of Milton's poetry not only on poets and philosophers but on the attentive general reader. Largely lost in oblivion, Kant's Miltonic aesthetics and Miltonic moral reason, firmly linked to his direct comments on Milton, constitute the most penetrating account ever written of the inner workings, and the inner impact on the reader, of Milton's poetry. Kant provides nothing less than a formal explanation of how that poetry discloses moral agency. Aside from Kant, in three and a half centuries of Milton criticism no one else has come to grips with this fundamental issue at this fundamental level.[4] My chapters accord-

4. A recent study that locates a point of departure for thinking about moral agency in Milton's poetry is Stanley Fish's *How Milton Works* (Cambridge, Mass.: Harvard University Press, 2001), with its thesis that "Milton works from the inside out" (p. 23). The economy of argument in my chapters has led me to avoid, in general, entering into the debates of contemporary Milton criticism, especially since these debates lately revolve around issues different from the ones that Kant sees in Milton. It will be evident, however, that though I have a different view of what goes on in the Miltonic "inside," I am strongly in agreement with what might be called the directionality of Fish's thesis. My disagreement is with his blanket assertion that there is no "evidentiary procedure" (p. 10) in Milton's representation of what occurs in the inside of ethical thinking. Fish's assertion blocks the possibility of seeing, and experiencing, the poetic-moral procedure—the *procedure of succession* identified in Milton's poetry by Kant—that Milton pervasively follows. Not surprisingly, Fish's *en passant* remarks about Kant's interest in "public knowledge" leave out of account Kant's profound acknowledgment of the always subjective re-discovery of the maxims of the categorical imperative. Fish's statement that Milton is different from Kant because in Milton's "epistemology . . . the circuit of communication goes from one regenerate heart to another" (p. 59) is in fact an apt restatement of the workings of the Longinian line of sublime inspiration that Addison applied to Milton's poetry and that (we will see) Kant inherited from Addison and the constellation of German Miltonism. I will be showing that for Milton, knowledge of the "inside" is demonstrably earned—as it is for Kant following Milton—by a formalism in the mind that the formalism of poetry discloses. Kant engages the feature of Milton's poetry that the eighteenth century, at least, viewed as most profoundly Miltonic: the ethically productive (not merely eliminative) power of poetry of the sublime. For Fish "conversion . . . must come *first*"; that is, it must already be in place before a state of moral enlightenment can be represented or recognized (p. 59). We will see that for Kant, and for what Kant saw in Milton, achieving a moment of rational "conversion," "revolution," or "rebirth" is the principal work of achieving "sublimity" and its effects (*Rel*, 6:47–48, 73; *CPrR*, 5:71,

ingly contain direct analyses of those central aspects of Milton's poetry that Kant's thought illuminates. The proportion of my discussion of the way Kant's philosophical system is interwoven with Milton's poetry greatly exceeds, however, my direct analyses of that poetry. In more general ways, I have had my detailed say about some proto-Kantian or Kantian aspects of Milton's poetry on a variety of occasions.[5] Here I have limited, though I hope also deepened, such discussion in laying out the necessary components of a book on Kant and Milton.

It is certainly surprising that Kant's relation to Milton, even his interest in Milton, has not been studied before. One of the reasons for this omission is undoubtedly that the extant evidence of Kant's engagement with Milton has only recently become more or less readily available. This has been made possible by the publication or databasing of the surviving transcripts of Kant's anthropology lectures, where many of his most important comments on Milton are to be found.[6] Partly due to the nature of lecture transcripts, perhaps even more to Kant's lecture style, Kant's Miltonic reflections almost always come to us in telegraphic, even if densely contextualized, form. Yet only a handful of philosophers of the first rank have left us such a rich collection of reflections on any poet. We are now in a position to appreciate the depth of these reflections by seeing them in relation both to each other as well as to the philosophical issues that drive them.

86–88). To be sure, the Kantian-Miltonic sublime is also partly eliminative, in that it suspends that which encumbers the mind, thereby uncovering the innate human capacity for free choice of the good. Yet the work of this sublime is not antinomian but rather an active interior journey to the disclosure of freedom and moral feeling. For both Milton and Kant, we pursue this journey in company with others and their interior journeys and disclosures (as in a Kingdom of Ends).

5. These discussions, exploring some Kantian dimensions of Milton's poetry, appear in *The Dividing Muse: Images of Sacred Disjunction in Milton's Poetry* (New Haven: Yale University Press, 1985) and *The Western Theory of Tradition: Terms and Paradigms of the Cultural Sublime* (New Haven: Yale University Press, 2000). In writing these books, however, I was not yet aware of the depth of these Kantian dimensions, nor of the role of Milton's poetry in eighteenth-century German Miltonism in general and in Kant's own thought specifically.

6. See *Kants Gesammelte Schriften*, XXV, 2 vols., *Kants Vorlesungen über Anthropologie herausgegeben von der Akademie der Wissenschaften zu Göttingen*, ed. Reinhard Brandt and Werner Stark (Berlin: W. de Gruyter, 1997). A number of the extant transcripts of Kant's lectures have not yet been published but are available in the Kant Archiv of the University of Marburg.

My chapters are woven both from Kant's direct responses to Milton's poetry and from reconstructions of Kant's prominent place within the constellation of eighteenth-century German Miltonism. With regard to a methodology for engaging in such reconstructions, I have been instructed by Dieter Henrich's expositions of the *Konstellationsforschung* (constellation research) that is needed to reassemble the *Konstellationen* of post-Kantian Idealist philosophy (not least in relation to a poet: in Henrich's cases, to Hölderlin). Henrich uses the term *constellation* as a metaphor for the object of a rigorous research method. His method confronts the hard fact that the innovations of post-Kantian philosophy emerged from within mappings of dense interchange between both major and apparently minor thinkers. By recovering the extensive reciprocal illuminations within a given constellation, Henrich is able to reconstruct otherwise lost "dynamic" or dialogic meanings in the work of even the best-known philosophers, since they, too, developed their positions as intellectual differentiations within a given constellation. Henrich has shown that in some cases it even becomes possible to bring to greater completeness ideas of major philosophers of which they themselves may have been only partially aware. In addition, this mode of deduction from the constellation lends far greater subtlety and, at the same time, greater force to arguments for the impact of a given idea on a given thinker. These gains are made possible by realizing that each idea in the constellation was sustained and made accessible by the matrix of the entire constellation.[7] All of these aspects of Henrich's *Konstellationsforschung* find operative counterparts in the chapters of my Kantian-Miltonic story.

Indeed, what I am describing here in Kant's engagement with pre-Kantian constellations of philosophical interpretation of Milton's poetry may even strike us as an uncanny forerunner of some of the phenomena of constellation that Henrich has discovered among the

7. Henrich has worked out and applied his model in a multitude of publications. My references here are to his latest descriptions of his model in "Konstellationsforschung zur klassischen deutschen Philosophie" and "Weitere Überlegungen zum Programm der Konstellationsforschung" in *Konstellationsforschung*, ed. Martin Muslow and Marcello Stamm (Frankfurt am Main: Suhrkamp, 2005), pp. 15–30 and 207–218. See also, especially, Henrich's exposition in *Konstellationen: Probleme und Debatten am Ursprung der idealistischen Philosophie (1789–1795)* (Stuttgart: Klett-Cotta, 1991), pp. 29–46.

Jena and Tübingen post-Kantians. This anticipation of post-Kantian *Konstellationen* is especially vivid in the expositions of "aesthetic light and shadow" that were at the heart of German Miltonism. We will see that this network of expositions principally formed the Miltonic constellation in which Kant was embedded. But whether there may be a phenomenon of anticipation linking these earlier and later constellations is not my concern here. Rather, my story is focused on Kant's procedure of succession to Milton's poetry. This procedure of succession emerged from Kant's engagement with the constellation of German Miltonism. My ultimate concern is the disclosure of freedom and moral feeling, both in Kant and Milton, which becomes apparent in that procedure of succession. My six chapters build to a description of a culminating moment of crystallization in Kant's relation to Milton. This occurred in §49 of the *Critique of Judgment* (1790). At that moment Kant made his deepest discoveries concerning the mind's access to freedom and moral feeling. In Chapters 3, 4, and 5 we will see, moreover, that he had in practice made his way to those same Miltonic discoveries already in the *Groundwork of the Metaphysics of Morals* (1785) and the *Critique of Practical Reason* (1788).

Kant's interest in Milton's poetry was always focused on its formalisms and thematics of freedom. Certainly these aspects of Milton's poetry were rendered more vivid by the fact that Milton was, in his life, a legendary champion of liberty against tyranny of all kinds. In Kant's lectures he frequently expressed his deep admiration for Milton's self-sacrificial devotion to the Cromwellian Revolution.[8] Within the constellation of German Miltonism, Milton's regicidal writings were even

8. Here, for example, is Kant in a lecture in 1772–73: "The great poet Milton was a supporter of Cromwell's side. When the king's side became stronger, most of Cromwell's supporters quit Cromwell's side and sided with the king. Milton, however, did not do this. . . . Thus he was offered the position of a secretaryship and many thousand pounds sterling annually if he would join the king's side. But Milton was so convinced of the dignity of a Republican . . . form of government that he remained immovable. [Der große Dichter Milton hatte die Parthey des Cromwells gehalten, als nun die Parthey des Königs gewaltiger wurde, so traten die meisten von der Parthey des Cromwells ab, und auf die Seite des Königs, Milton aber that es nicht . . . so both man ihm, wenn er zur Parthey des Königs treten würde, die Stelle eines Secretairs an, wo er jährlich viele 1000 Pfund Sterling erhalten hätte. Milton aber der von der Würde einer Republikanischen . . . RegierungsForm zu überzeugt war, blieb unbeweglich.]" (Marburg Kant Archiv, Parow, 168).

represented as a prominent feature of his poetic identity. In the Prussia of Friedrich II or Friedrich Wilhelm II, however, open admiration of this political Milton could not be unproblematic. Precisely because of Milton's importance to progressive thought in eighteenth-century Germany, any public engagement with his writings had to be carefully conducted. Kant's special interest in Milton's poetry dates at least from the early 1760s. Precisely in 1789 a great many aspects of Kant's quest for freedom, including the light shone upon it by the fall of the Bastille, came together in his explications of Milton's painting designed with freedom. Upon hearing of the declaration of the French republic, Kant famously exclaimed (echoing Luke 2:29–32), "Now let your servant go in peace to his grave, for I have seen the glory of the world."[9] Experienced in a kindred spirit, his disclosures of freedom and moral feeling in his engagement with Milton's poetry are, I contend, the climax of his own revolutionary philosophical activity in 1789–90. It is partly because of the politically dangerous tilt of this intellectual intimacy with a revolutionary and regicidal poet that Kant strikes an appearance of balance and correctness in his otherwise inexplicable citation, in §49, of verses of the poetaster "great king." Despite this camouflage, we will see that three works of poetry that were of deep significance for Kant's quest for freedom in the years 1785–90 are Milton's *Paradise Lost, Samson Agonistes,* and the great sonnet on his blindness. Kant read *Paradise Lost* for its formalisms of *a priori* freedom, just as he read *Samson Agonistes* for the mind's resistance to coercion and its disclosure of an inviolable, inner, personal freedom. Remarkably, as I believe Kant strongly sensed, the deepest layer of Milton's sonnet on his blindness is a disclosure of just this human freedom and moral feeling even vis-à-vis the power and expectations of the heavenly king (beyond all earthly kings) Himself.

By way of commencement I wish to add some preliminary remarks about the experience of the sublime. We have insufficiently faced the fact that the operations of the sublime that Kant describes, and that he himself systematically experiences within his own system, must in significant part take place in the region of the subliminal or of what is

9. On Kant's openly expressed admiration for the French Revolution, see Manfred Kuehn, *Kant: A Biography* (Cambridge: Cambridge University Press, 2001), pp. 340–343.

concealed from full consciousness. In the "Analytic of the Sublime" he explicitly describes this state of affairs in the "aesthetic idea," which he tells us stands at the interface of the empirical and the *a priori* as well as of the aesthetic and the moral:

> By an aesthetic idea I mean that representation of the imagination which induces much thought, yet without the possibility of any definite thought whatever, i.e. *concept,* being adequate to it, and which language, consequently, can never get quite on level terms with or render completely intelligible. (*CJ,* §49, 5:314)

I will recur to Kant's aesthetic ideas repeatedly in many of the following chapters, finally reaching something like a systematic discussion of them (at least within the parameters of this book) in Chapter 6. Yet we can already say that the above passage does not mean that for Kant discursive language must despair before the challenge of increasing the intelligibility of these partially subliminal, even partially occluded, representations of aesthetic ideas and the experience of the sublime. It does mean, however, that we must develop strategies for obtaining evidence, and reflections of evidence, of such representations. Only then can we try to stand with Kant at the threshold of consciousness, where he experiences representations of this kind in others and where he himself represents them.

One such strategy is to try to understand the complementary elements of aesthetic shadow and aesthetic light that have a central place in Kant's mature theory of the sublime and that he experienced in Milton's poetry of sublime light and shadow, "disciplin'd / From shadowy Types to Truth" (*Paradise Lost,* XII.302–303). We will see that Kant's ideas of aesthetic light and shadow inform the "discharge [of energy] all the more powerful" after the "check to the vital forces" (*CJ,* 5:245) that came to define the Kantian sublime and its function within the moral sublime. In the *Critique of Pure Reason* he had written of the interface between the empirical and the *a priori* that there is "an art concealed in the depths of the human soul, whose real modes of activity nature is hardly likely ever to allow us to discover, and to have open to our gaze" (A141/B180–181). His mature grasp of the experience of the sublime—as represented not only in nature but especially in works of art and in the art of the mind—would make it possible for him to change his mind (beginning in 1785) about what is concealed and what can be made accessible at that interface. The aim of this book is to show that his fully developed idea of aesthetic light and shadow gave him access *in concreto* to the conditions, meanings, and uses of concealment in the art of the sublime. In the four or five years leading up to the *Critique of Judgment,* he discovered (in contradiction to explicit assumptions in the *Critique of Pure Reason*) not only "the *unconditioned*"— or freedom—"in the series of causal connection" (*CPrR,* 5:3) but also an *a priori* causality that was exercised by this freedom.[10] He discovered this in what he called the procedure of "succession" (the *Nachfolge*) represented in Milton's art of the sublime and of "aesthetic ideas" (*AA,* 25.2:1561). It is characteristic of this Miltonic art that it partly represents the concealed and the act of concealment. As I have said, Kant's own succession to this art necessarily, partly, also represents the concealed and the act of concealment. Yet in this art and its successions, the shadows or concealments are eminently compensated by light and disclosures.

We must turn, then, to Milton's poetry and Kant's experience of it to understand the procedure of succession. Here we will be directly challenging the misinformed notion that Kant had no substantial experience of works of art. This erroneous idea has in our time been reinforced by the misguided proposition that his aesthetics even excludes experience of art.[11] Kant repeatedly said that poetry (empiri-

10. Martin Heidegger, *The Essence of Human Freedom: An Introduction to Philosophy,* trans. Ted Sadler (New York: Continuum, 2002), pp. 13–22, questioned whether Kant had found a way to understand the *a priori* causality of freedom. I will return to this question in my Conclusion.

11. This is the burden of frequently echoed comments in Hans-Georg Gadamer's *Truth and Method,* 2nd ed., trans. Joel Weinsheimer and Donald G. Marshall (New York: Continuum, 1989), pp. 42–44ff. The surprisingly superficial character of Gadamer's comments here is especially apparent in his vague statement "In the realm of aesthetic taste models and patterns certainly have a privileged function; but, as Kant rightly says, they are not for imitation but for following [*Nachfolge*=succession]" (p. 42). It is already clear in Kant's statement at *CJ,* 5:309, which Gadamer is citing, that Kant is trying to identify the special kind of *Nachfolge* of "ideas" that can "arouse [*erregen*] like ideas" in a line of artistic genius (genius, which Gadamer argues becomes the distinctive concern of the philosophical generation after Kant). Kant makes this identification unmistakable in §49, where this *Nachfolge* is seen as central to the genius's achievement of "aesthetic ideas," and his or her being "aroused" (*aufgeweckt*) to "exemplary originality" in the exercise of "freedom" (*CJ,* 5:317–318).

cally encountered poetry) was for him the highest form of aesthetic experience, and he made clear which kind of modern poetry he regarded most highly: namely, English poetry, most notably the poetry of Milton. In the *Critique of Judgment* Kant gave us what is, by consensus, "without question the most influential work of aesthetic theory ever written."[12] To a significant extent, the fantasy that he had no substantial experience of works of art and the persuasion that his aesthetics excludes experience of art may well be the result of lack of familiarity, even among highly cultured modern readers, with the most demanding and most stimulating poetry that Kant experienced. His principle at the opening of the *Critique of Pure Reason*, "With experience all our knowledge begins" (B1), cannot be bypassed in considering his reflections on poetry and aesthetic ideas. To begin to understand the depth of those reflections and to see how his experience of art is even integral to his aesthetic-moral philosophy, we must build from his experience of Milton's poetry.

Curiously enough, Gadamer says that Kant is "old-fashioned" in being closer to French classicism and further from a concern with originality such as Lessing showed in the case of Shakespeare (pp. 56–57). These statements slight Kant's profound exposition of "exemplary originality" as well as his repeated, explicit identification with German Miltonism, which set itself totally against the French classicism of Gottsched. It is hard to understand, in any case, why Gadamer thinks that Kant's distinction between imitation and following can be understood as self-evident, given Kant's rider, "The possibility of this is difficult to explain." The difficulty broached here by Kant, and for which his entire theory of the experience of the sublime begins to provide an explanation, is at the heart of his insight about the experience of art. It is also about the route to aesthetic ideas that leave the empirical behind. Gadamer may have been relying on Heidegger here as authority for disregarding the importance of Kant's *Nachfolge.* As mentioned above, I will have a word to say about Heidegger in my Conclusion.

12. *Critical Theory since Plato*, 3rd ed., ed. Hazard Adams and Leroy Searle (Boston: Thomson Wadsworth, 2005), p. 418.

CHAPTER 1

Kant and Milton

Fundamentals and Foundations

With self-assured authority Kant repeatedly invoked what he considered to be Milton's exemplary genius. Both Milton and Shakespeare are Kant's usual modern examples of genius, but Milton is far more important to him than Shakespeare. For Kant, and for Germany hardly less than England in the mid-eighteenth century, Milton is the greatest modern genius of the sublime. More than any other work, Edmund Burke's *Philosophical Enquiry into the Origin of Our Ideas of the Sublime and Beautiful* (1757) occasioned the German philosophical investigation of the experience of the sublime. When Burke called upon "our great poet" of the sublime, there could not be a moment's doubt that Milton was meant even before a single verse was cited.[1] In Kant's subsequent *Observations on the Feeling of the Beautiful and Sublime* (1764), Milton is the first and most extensively invoked exemplar. For Kant, Milton's poetry represents what he would come to call the "exemplarity" of the sublime. Contemporary readers of the *Critique of Judgment* (1790) would have been able to recognize as a commonplace, albeit a commonplace of exemplarity, that "the poet" to whom he refers in §49 of the "Analytic of the Sublime" has a unified and distinctive identity. Kant speaks here of "representations of the imagination [that] may be termed *ideas* . . . partly because they at least strain after

1. Edmund Burke, *A Philosophical Enquiry into the Origin of Our Ideas of the Sublime and Beautiful*, ed. Adam Phillips (Oxford: Oxford University Press, 1990), section XIV, p. 73. Moses Mendelssohn's detailed précis of Burke's book already appeared in the year after its publication, in *Bibliothek der schönen Wissesnschaften und der freyen Künste* 3 [*sic*] (1758): 290–320.

something lying out beyond the confines of experience." The particular list of such "ideas" that he draws up for "the poet" tells us that Kant has Milton near the center of his thinking: "The poet essays the task of interpreting to sense the rational ideas of invisible beings, the kingdom of the blessed, hell, eternity, creation, &c." (*CJ*, 5:314). Only Milton—not Homer, Virgil, Dante, or Tasso, and certainly not Milton's German imitator, Friedrich Gottlieb Klopstock (consistently held in low regard by Kant)—can fit Kant's bill.[2]

In fact, in a lecture in 1781–82 Kant had already made the following parallel, direct comment on aesthetic ideas in Milton's poetry:

> Poetry offers many materials in the world of invisible beings, so that Milton in his *Paradise Lost,* one of the most magnificent poems, has delivered such things, about which one would otherwise know nothing. When one [otherwise] tries to think of a sublime invisible being or of a malevolent character opposing the Lord of the world and the supreme governor, what kind of ideas can emerge? (*AA,* 25.2:991)

> [In der Welt der Geister giebt die Poesie vielen Stoff, so daß Milton in seinem verlorenen Paradiese Eines [*sic*] der herrlichsten Gedichte geliefert hat, weil man von solchen Sachen nichts weiß. Wenn man sich einen erhabenen Geist denkt, und einen andern mit einer feindseeligen Gesinnung gegen den Regierer der Welt, und gegen den obersten Beherrscher, was können da für Ideen hervorgebracht werden!][3]

We will soon see that Kant had even more explicit things to say about how Milton's poetry exemplifies aesthetic ideas. And we will gradually see as well that the significance of recognizing that he is thinking of Milton in the *Critique of Judgment,* §49—one of the most important runs of pages in all of Kant's writings on aesthetics—is markedly double. Seeing this connection both opens one more way for grasping Kant's understanding of Milton's poetry of sublime experience and provides an expanded, deepened access to many of Kant's chief terms in §49. But I return here to introductory matters.

---

2. At the beginning of Chapter 6 I will have more to say about this particular identification without a name.

3. The syntax of the transcription seems partially corrupted.

Despite Kant's apparent cultural or linguistic distance from Milton, he unhesitatingly rated Milton's poetry (and Pope's, too) higher than any German poetry.[4] Kant's differentiation of Milton's excellence was not a matter of deciding a cultural competition but rather of keeping clear the qualities that constitute that which is truly exemplary in poetry: "One must distinguish expressions [verbalisms] from thoughts and even so the poet from the writer or versifier. . . . *Milton* was a true poetic genius, as is clear from reading just his *Paradise Lost.* . . . Klopstock does not represent the [poetic] case. . . . Read *Milton* in his description of the journey of the angel [i.e., *Paradise Lost,* V.247–287]."[5] It was because of Kant's reflection on Milton's extensively com-

4. For reasons that I will touch on later, Kant did not hold in high regard the early artistic productions of either Goethe or Schiller, that is, at least up to the time of the publication of the *Critique of Judgment,* 1790.

5. Here are Milton's verses:

> nor delay'd the winged Saint
> After his charge receiv'd; but from among
> Thousand Celestial Ardors, where he stood
> Veil'd with his gorgeous wings, up springing light
> Flew through the midst of Heav'n; th' angelic Choirs
> On each hand parting, to his speed gave way
> Through all th' Empyreal road; till at the Gate
> Of Heav'n arriv'd, the gate self-open'd wide
> On golden Hinges turning, as by work [255]
> Divine the sovran Architect had fram'd.
> From hence, no cloud, or, to obstruct his sight,
> Star interpos'd, however small he sees,
> Not unconform to other shining Globes,
> Earth and the Gard'n of God, with Cedars crown'd [260]
> Above all Hills. As when by night the Glass
> Of *Galileo,* less assur'd, observes
> Imagin'd Lands and Regions in the Moon:
> Or Pilot from amidst the *Cyclades*
> *Delos* or *Samos* first appearing kens [265]
> A cloudy spot. Down thither prone in flight
> He speeds, and through the vast Ethereal Sky
> Sails between worlds and worlds, with steady wing
> Now on the polar winds, then with quick Fan
> Winnows the buxom Air; till within soar [270]
> Of Tow'ring Eagles, to all the Fowls he seems
> A *Phœnix,* gaz'd by all, as that sole Bird
> When to enshrine his reliques in the Sun's

plex representations of this kind (which I will soon analyze) that he was certain that *"Milton* was a true poetic genius. [*Milton* war ein wirkliches dichterisches Genie.]"[6] This kind of concrete exemplification of Milton's exemplary genius was of the utmost importance to Kant, because he viewed the phenomenon of exemplary genius as the surest indication of the universal human potential for freedom, originality, individuality, and even moral feeling. In other words, Milton's genius was for Kant the exemplification of the inimitable uniqueness of every human being. We will see more and more clearly that this is why poetic "originality" matters so much to Kant. Here, still framed in general terms, is another example of his probing of this Miltonic exemplary uniqueness:

> The characteristic of the genius is that what he performs cannot be performed by many others, but could only have come from him; the contrary phenomenon is called *vulgare* [common, usual]. Idiosyncrasies are assumed manners through which one sets oneself apart, and which others could imitate should they wish to. The fanatical [enthusiastic] way of writing is that of the eccentric but has no originality, because many can imitate it. The originality of the genius comes from a

---

> Bright Temple, to *Egyptian Thebes* he flies.
> At once on th' Eastern cliff of Paradise [275]
> He lights, and to his proper shape returns
> A Seraph wing'd; six wings he wore, to shade
> His lineaments Divine; the pair that clad
> Each shoulder broad, came mantling o'er his breast
> With regal Ornament; the middle pair [280]
> Girt like a Starry Zone his waist, and round
> Skirted his loins and thighs with downy Gold
> And colors dipt in Heav'n; the third his feet
> Shadow'd from either heel with feather'd mail
> Sky-tinctur'd grain. Like *Maia's* son he stood, [285]
> And shook his Plumes, that Heav'nly fragrance fill'd
> The circuit wide.

6. This is translated from the Hamilton transcript of Kant's anthropology lectures in the semester of 1772–73, now in the database of the Marburg Kant Archiv (Ham., pp. 110–111, 188): "Man muß Ausdrüke von Gedanken und eben so Dichter von Schriftsteller und Versemacher unterscheiden. . . . *Milton* war ein wirkliches dichterisches Genie, man lese nur sein verlornes Paradies. . . . Klopstock stellt die Sache nicht so vor. . . . Man lese *Milton* in der Reise des Engels."

special disposition of talents which can very seldom be met in another person yet is [in itself] harmonious. Klopstock can be imitated very well, but Milton only with difficulty because his images are original. (*Reflection* 914, *AA*, 15.1:399–400)

[Das Eigenthümliche des genies ist [das], wenn das, was iemand leistet, [auch] nicht auch von vielen anderen hätte geleistet werden könen, sondern von ihm allein hat geschehen könen; daß andere heißt das *vulgare*. Eigenheiten sind angenommene Manieren, durch die man sich unterscheidet, und die andre, wenn sie wollen, auch nachmachen können. Die Schwärmende Schreibart ist die des Sonderlings, aber hat keine originalitaet. Denn viele könen sie nachmachen. Die originalitaet des genies kommt auf einer besonderen Stimmung der talente an, die nur selten bey einem anderen angetroffen wird und doch wohllautend ist. Klopstock kann sehr gut nachgeahmet werden, aber Milton schweer, weil seine Bilder original sind.]

I will return to this passage further on in this chapter, but I continue first with the historical placement of Kant's engagement with Milton.

For us it has become almost impossible to grasp the extent and significance of Milton's centrality to eighteenth-century poetry not only in England but in Germany as well. This was the case to a spectacular degree during the entire period in which Kant was reaching intellectual maturity and, indeed, in the decades when he was at the height of his powers. During that period Germany turned especially to England no less for literary than for philosophical inspiration.[7] We no longer have any significant philosophical, or, indeed, even literary, access to

---

7. Curiously enough, when commentators on Kant and his contemporaries mention the impact of Edward Young's "Night Thoughts" or Alexander Pope's *Essay on Man* or *The Rape of the Lock*, they show no awareness of the dominant Miltonic features, even Miltonic mythologies, which significantly underpin these works, to say nothing of the reiterated awareness of these writers themselves both that they were Milton's inheritors and that they were painfully inferior to him and the "divine harmony (how justly join'd!) of *Milton, Greece*, and *Rome*." For this last point see Young, following Addison, in a work that had a large role in forming the opinions of Kant and his contemporaries on the question of what a *Nachfolge* rather than a mere imitation might be: *Conjectures on Original Composition*, ed. Edith J. Morley (London: Longmans, 1918; first published 1759; German translation 1760), pp. 26–27. Otto

the fact that, as James Thorpe put it, there never was before and proba-
bly will never be again a dominance of an entire age by any other poet
as total as was Milton's of the English eighteenth century. In this pe-
riod not even Shakespeare rivaled Milton's sway.[8] Kant's Germany di-
rectly reflected the facts of this Miltonic centrality.[9] As late as 1796
Johann Gottfried Herder would ask, "Where is Milton . . . paid warmer

---

Schlapp, *Kants Lehre vom Genie und die Entstehung der 'Kritik der Urteilskraft'* (Göttingen:
Vandenhoeck & Ruprecht, 1901), pp. 52n, 61n, 305–306, 344n, and 417, notes
Young's impact on Kant's concept of the *Nachfolge*. I will return to this in Chapter 2.

8. James Thorpe, ed., *Milton Criticism: Selections from Four Centuries* (London:
Routledge, 1965), p. 8: "There were over a hundred editions of *Paradise Lost* during
the [eighteenth] century—more than twice as many as of Shakespeare's plays, fifteen
times as many as of the *Faerie Queene*. Milton was the most popular subject in the peri-
odicals; he was talked about (and even read) by all classes of people; and perhaps a
majority of eighteenth-century verse can be said to have been modelled on, imitative
of, or influenced by Milton. It would be difficult to imagine a more exalted poetic
reputation, and the attitude of the eighteenth century toward Milton will probably
never be duplicated in favor of any writer."

9. How this centrality of Milton in Germany came about is not my subject here, but
I will note briefly that it was apparently inaugurated in the discovery of Milton's sub-
lime poetry—for German use—by Jacob Bodmer. Bodmer used Milton as a lever to
pry German poetry from the rule-tight grip of French Neoclassicism. In this, Bodmer
was bitterly opposed by Gottsched. The ensuing famous struggle, the so-called
"Bodmer-Gottsched Streit," was decisively won by Bodmer and the Miltonists, not
least by Klopstock ("the German Milton," Herder called him), whose epic poem *Der
Messias* was extensively derived from *Paradise Lost*. On these matters see Johannes
Crüger, *Joh. Christoph Gottsched und die Schweizer J. J. Bodmer und J. J. Breitinger* (Berlin,
1883). In the history of German literature of the eighteenth century, Milton was the
powerful second wave of British influence, the first being that of Pope, the third—at-
taining a dominant position just after Kant completed his major writings on aesthet-
ics and ethics—that of Shakespeare. In this sense, Kant's aesthetic formation is both
strongly Miltonic and largely (though not totally) pre-Shakespearean.

With the exception of Hans-Dieter Kreuder's *Milton in Deutschland: Seine Rezeption
im latein- und deutsch-sprachigen Schrifttum zwischen 1651 und 1732* (Berlin: Walter de
Gruyter, 1971)—which deals with the period prior to the burgeoning of German
Miltonism that begins with Bodmer—none of the studies of Milton's impact on Ger-
man writings is systematic or detailed. What is available, besides Tisch's 1968 essay
mentioned below, are Gustav Jenny, *Miltons Verlornes Paradies in der deutschen Litteratur
des 18. Jahrhunderts* (St. Gallen, 1890); G. L. Robertson, "Milton's Fame on the Conti-
nent," *Proceedings of the British Academy* 3 (1909): 1–17; and Enrico Pizzo, *Miltons
Verlornes Paradies im deutschen Urteile des 18. Jahrhunderts* (Berlin: Felber, 1914). Though
Milton's poetry was far less fortunate than Shakespeare's in finding talented transla-

homage than in Germany?"[10] When it came to taste in art, Kant's Germany, and Kant no less than the cultured Germans around him, were more open to non-German cultures than later periods in German history would be. The leverage of Milton's poetry—in the *Bodmer-Gottsched Streit,* in the apishly Miltonic *Messias* of Klopstock, in so-called "Seraphic" poetry, and in the fascination with the experience of the sublime in all its manifestations—was a primary factor in the eighteenth-century revolution in German poetry and poetics. In particular, as I have begun to suggest, no other modern poet in English, German, or, indeed, world literature generally was so directly and fully identified with the sublime. J. H. Tisch noted that in Kant's Germany the adjectives *Miltonisch* and *erhaben* (sublime) were frequently synonymous.[11] Because philosophical reflection and reflection on poetry were so often profoundly integrated in Kant's time, it is hardly surprising that eighteenth-century German philosophers—Kant chief among them because of his unsurpassed engagement with the experience of the sublime—focused intensely on Milton's poetry. Yet it is a strange fact (which I will soon try to place historically) that Kant's interest in Milton has never been canvassed even superficially, much less studied.

~

In the Elsner transcript of Kant's anthropology lectures of 1792–93, we hear his response to a passage in Book VIII of *Paradise Lost.* (I will later show that Kant knew that Hume had also responded to this particular passage.) In Milton's verses the angel Raphael instructs Adam in the

---

tors, it was widely available both in English and in German. In fact, with the inspiration of Kant's friend and philosophical correspondent Georg Christoph Lichtenberg, a complete two-volume edition of Milton's poetry, in English, was published in Göttingen in 1784 (not 1785, as Pizzo, p. 104, mistakenly says of volume two), that is, a year before Kant published the *Groundwork.*

10. *SW,* XVIII.119: "Wo ist dem Milton . . . wärmer gehuldigt worden, als in Deutschland?"

11. J. H. Tisch, "Milton and the German Mind in the Eighteenth Century," in *Studies in the Eighteenth Century,* ed. R. F. Brissenden (Canberra: Australian National University Press, 1968), p. 227. The synonymy of sublimity and Milton is, of course, also a prominent British phenomenon. Tisch is in fact borrowing and extending a statement to this effect by Raymond Dexter Havens, *The Influence of Milton on English Poetry* (Cambridge, Mass.: Harvard University Press, 1922), p. 8 and n. Both in England and (directly and indirectly) in Germany, this synonymy is most especially the effect of Addison's famous *Spectator* essays (beginning 1712) on *Paradise Lost.*

need to keep open the possibility of an extensive grouping of stars in our own immediate neighborhood of the cosmos. Such a constellation of reciprocating luminaries may be constituted, says Raphael, by celestial bodies—including the planet on which we stand—that we do not usually think of as luminaries, much less as stars. This constellation may even extend, he suggests, endlessly outward and it may reflect the di-polar microstructure of all life:

> What if that light
> Sent from [Earth] through the wide transpicuous air,
> To the terrestrial Moon be as a Star
> Enlight'ning her by Day, as she by Night
> This Earth? reciprocal, if Land be there,
> Fields and Inhabitants: . . .
> . . . ; and other Suns perhaps
> With thir attendant Moons thou wilt descry
> Communicating Male and Female Light,
> Which two great Sexes animate the World,
> Stor'd in each Orb perhaps. (*Paradise Lost*, VIII.140–152)

The angel adds that these possibilities remain "obvious [open] to dispute" (VIII.158), so that the value of reflecting on them is solely, but significantly, in their capacity to expand and inspire the mind. In his lecture Kant invokes this passage not only in the verses that he cites directly but in every element of his lecture comment:

> The creative imagination is the true root of genius and the basis of originality. Spirit is the preeminent constituent [lit., piece].
> Aesthetic ideas are those representations that contain a wealth of thoughts which *ad infinitum* draw after it a succession of thoughts. Such ideas draw us into an immeasurable prospect, e.g. Milton's saying, "Female light mixes itself with male light, to unknown ends." Through this soulful [ingenious] idea the mind is set into continuous motion. (*AA*, 25.2:1561)

> [Die schöpferische Einbildungskraft ist die wahre Wurzel des Genies und der Basis der Originalität. Geist ist das vorzüglichste Stück.
> Ästhetische Ideen sind solche Vorstellungen, die eine Fülle von Gedanken enthalten, die bis ins Unendliche eine Folge von Gedanken

nach sich ziehen. Solche Ideen ziehen uns in einen unabsehbaren
Prospekt, z. E. Milton's Ausspruch: Weibliches Licht vermischt sich
mit männlichem Licht zu unbekannten Endzwecken. Durch diese
geistvolle Idee wird das Gemüt in einen continuierlichen Schwung
versetzt.]

Underlying this comment on a Miltonic "succession of thoughts"—*eine
Folge von Gedanken nach sich ziehen*—is Kant's entire theory of the moral
sublime, which he had set out a few years earlier in the *Critique of Judg-
ment.*[12] Here, as in Milton, it is not certainties and answers but the rep-
resentation and the succession of thinking that count. Kant's idea of

---

12. On the term *succession* or *procedure of succession,* see my "Notes on Citations and
the Term *Succession*" in the front matter. I have assembled the elements of my descrip-
tion of Kant's term primarily from statements in the *Critique of Judgment* but also from
the *Critique of Practical Reason.* For the reader's convenience I will note here that these
elements amount to the following propositions :
  1. Empirically or heteronomously the mind follows an effectively endless pro-
     gression of representations (*CJ,* 5:318) that is "evoked by a particular repre-
     sentation" (*CJ,* 5:250).
  2. Each representation in the progression that admits of *Nachfolge* (as opposed
     to *Nachahmung,* imitation) represents "its own inadequacy" to represent (*CJ,*
     5:252–253).
  3. The act of following a progression of examples of this kind issues in the sub-
     lime (*CJ,* 5:255) and in exemplarity (*CJ,* 5:309, 318).
  4. This heteronomous procedure of succession discloses an isomorphic, au-
     tonomous ("self-maintaining") succession procedure that also issues in the
     sublime, thence in freedom and moral feeling (*CJ,* 5:313, 318). This disclo-
     sure is closely related, perhaps identical, to what Kant calls "the grand dis-
     closure" of freedom and moral feeling in the *Critique of Practical Reason*
     (5:94).
  5. Parallel to this isomorphism of the heteronomous and the autonomous
     Nachfolgen, a *transfer* takes place, in the sublime (*CJ,* 5:266–267, 352–353),
     from the sensible (and the example, the individual) to the supersensible
     (and exemplarity, the universal). In both procedures of succession, reason
     "transfers" (a) that which "can . . . be . . . exhibited by actions in the sensible
     world in accordance with the formal rule of a law of nature" into (b) the
     realm of the "supersensible" (*CPrR,* 5:71).
There are slippages in Kant's descriptions of these terms for the transfer. One of
the principal aims of this book is the unraveling, with Milton's help, of the isomor-
phic elements of the transfer, which Kant tends to leave jumbled. We can already
state the results of this unraveling this way: (a) the transfer that ultimately interests
Kant is only the mind's inward, autonomous transfer between sensible and super-
sensible standpoints that issues from an inward *Nachfolge* (this is seen most clearly in

the *Nachfolge* is of a "succession" or more precisely of a *procedure of succession* in an infinite progression of representations, such as the *Folge von Gedanken nach sich ziehen*, both *within* and *following* Milton's verses, superlatively exemplifies.[13] The succession procedure draws the reader infinitely onward into an immeasurable prospect, which produces the "soulful idea" in the experience of the sublime. Kant calls this idea "soulful" *(geistvoll)* because, though it is occasioned by empirical experience, it arouses the mind to a corresponding idea that is *a priori*. This procedure of succession to sublime representation necessarily occurs, at least to a large extent, in the region of the subliminal. Yet the philosopher who experiences it can distinguish traces of its activity and even record its leap to a moral maxim.

According to Kant's theory of the moral sublime (which I will set out in detail hereafter), the occasioning, empirical experience of the succession has a number of key components: It is of an effectively infinite *Progressus* or line of repetition of the same basic representation (in this case, the female and male light emanating from female and male stars); it is an encounter of *a particular representation* that puts us in mind of following out and succeeding to the *Progressus;* its initially

---

the mind's incremental humiliations of self-conceit that are described in the second *Critique*); (b) the autonomous transfer is disclosed by an isomorphic, heteronomous *Nachfolge* of representations, each of which also effects a transfer between the two standpoints (as in the representations of *Samson Agonistes* that, I will propose, Kant is following in the second *Critique*).

13. To a great extent what I have to say in this book is a clarification of a set of connections that works concretely and extensively in Kant's writings but which he nonetheless leaves largely unspecified, sometimes vague, and at times even confusing: namely that his idea of the *unendlichen Progressus* of representations (5:83) in the *Critique of Practical Reason* or *Progressus ohne Ende* of representations (5:255) in the *Critique of Judgment* is not only the same for him as the *Fortschritte ins Unendliche* of representations (*CJ*, 5:250) that he names in his first formal definition of the sublime, but that these terms can already be equated in the *Critique of Practical Reason* with the endless *Nachfolge* of examples that provide access to the archetypal or exemplary (5:85, coordinated with the *unendlichen Progressus* of representations at 5:83) and then, more explicitly, with the *Nachfolge* of examples that discloses the exemplary in the *Critique of Judgment* (5:309, 318). As part of this clarification, I have explored the connections that he makes between this *Progressus*—and thus with the *Nachfolge*—and aesthetic ideas (*CJ*, 5:314). I will show that Kant imbibed his detailed association of a *Nachfolge* of Milton's sublime poetry with aesthetic ideas from the German Miltonist line that flowed from Addison's association and exemplification of a Longinian sublime *Nachfolge* with Milton's sublime poetry.

encountered representation, as well as each of the representations in the line of this *Progressus,* shows its own incompleteness as a representation (within this Miltonic example itself, it is a tracing of points of light against interstellar darkness); the experience of this *Progressus* causes "a momentary check to the vital forces" when the mind cannot bring together (a) the imagination's projection of the infinite extensibility of the progression with (b) reason's requirement of a defined whole that would delimit the progression. Precisely in that moment of loss of power the mind experiences a freedom from all encroaching pressures or needs, so that (Kant believes he has shown) we succeed to the moral feeling that can only be felt in freedom. The temporal duration of the experience of the succession procedure is as uniquely compressed as that of the sublime. In Kant's mature thought whenever we encounter one of his experiences of Milton's poetry of the sublime, it is clear that the groundwork that has been laid for the procedure of succession is extensive and deliberated, yet the moment of effectuation is a flight to infinity and a lightning transaction. Very likely, the effectively incalculable velocity of the culmination of this procedure is one of the reasons for Kant's (and other writers') reaching for an analogical language of "aesthetic light." (In Chapter 4 we will see that the instantaneous nature of this event is consonant with Kant's comments on the pinpointed "rebirth" or "*revolution* in the disposition of the human being" [*Rel,* 6:47–48].)

Kant's lecture comment on the Miltonic procedure of succession echoes and opens up a key moment of the succession procedure in the *Critique of Judgment,* §49. I will describe that moment in detail in Chapter 6. We will then be able to see how Kant clarified in both theory and practice the succession procedure to which he had already made his way in practice in the *Groundwork of the Metaphysics of Morals* and the *Critique of Practical Reason.* At this stage my proposal is more limited. My contention here is that Kant finds his explanation for the mind's access to spontaneity by considering what happens to consciousness when the *Progressus* and the mind's successive reflection on it are not complete and finite but incomplete and infinite ("a wealth of thoughts which *ad infinitum* draw after it a succession of thoughts [eine Fülle von Gedanken . . . die bis ins Unendliche eine Folge von Gedanken nach sich ziehen]"). This imagining of succession in the infinite *Progressus* is the procedure of succession that is most fully described, indeed, in the third *Critique* and that we encounter as well in the lecture passage about Milton quoted above. In later chapters I will show that, as we expect of any complex idea in Kant's thought, there was much that led up to this crystallization. I will suggest that the "Schematism" in the first *Critique* and the "Typic" in the second *Critique* are the forebears of the procedure of succession in the third *Critique*. Each of these terms describes the imagination's "procedure" of representation precisely and extensively in a procedure of succession.[14] In addition, each of these procedures locates a "third," or mediate, zone that makes possible the mind's bridging of the *a priori* and the empirical. Yet only the procedure of succession of the third *Critique* is directly linked to freedom and the systematic disclosure of moral feeling.

In the Davos disputation between Ernst Cassirer and Martin Heidegger, two of the main points of difference concerned (a) the limitations and potentialities of the Kantian Schematism and Typic and, separately, (b) the human imagination of the infinite. Yet neither Cassirer nor Heidegger saw the emergence, in Kant's writings, of a conjunction between these topics such as his account of the Miltonic succession procedure allows us to see or at least glimpse.[15] I suggest that in the procedure of succession Kant builds upon and goes beyond the Schematism and the Typic. He goes decisively further by describing

14. The Schematism is explained as "a universal procedure of imagination" at A140/B179–180; the Typic as "a universal procedure of the imagination" at *CPrR*, 5:69. In the "Analytic of the Sublime" of the *Critique of Judgment*, Kant spells out, once again, its link with succession: "In the successive aggregation of units requisite for the representation of magnitudes the imagination of itself advances *ad infinitum* without let or hindrance—understanding, however, conducting it by means of concepts of number for which the former must supply the schema. This procedure belongs to the logical estimation of magnitude, and, as such, is doubtless something objectively final according to the concept of an end (as all measurement is), but it is not anything which for the aesthetic judgment is final or pleasing" (5:253).

15. The "Davos Disputation between Ernst Cassirer and Martin Heidegger" (1929) is given as Appendix IV to Heidegger's *Kant and the Problem of Metaphysics*, 5th ed., trans. Richard Taft (Bloomington: University of Indiana Press, 1997). See especially pp. 194–195. With regard to Kant's focus on "progress *ad infinitum*" (*CJ*, 5:250), it is interesting to note that soon after the first publication of Heidegger's book, Heinrich Levy, "Heideggers Kant-Interpretation," *Logos* 21 (1932): 1–43, commented that Heidegger had given too much power to the transcendental imagination—that is, to "the structure of the Kantian *infinite intellectual intuition* and the *infinite intuitive understanding* [die Struktur der Kantischen *unendlichen intellektuellen Anschauung* und des *unendlichen anschauenden Verstandes*]"—to be consistent with Heidegger's own theory (25).

the productive imagination (not merely the reproductive imagination) of succession toward the infinite. In the *Critique of Judgment* he calls this a "progress *ad infinitum*" of representations that is generated by the imagination (5:250). This is the infinite succession—seen above in his procedure of succession to Milton's poetry—that in the *Critique of Judgment* he names as part of his first formal definition of the sublime. The effect of infinite succession, I am proposing, is also the key to the explanation of how it is possible to achieve *a condition of succession* that is not *imitation*. Kant indeed seems to give up on being able to provide this explanation when he says, "The possibility of this is difficult to explain" (*CJ,* 5:309). Yet the effect of following the infinite succession begins to explain how the succession—the achieved final-stage *condition of succession* itself—is not imitation but rather that which can prepare the mind for disclosing the spontaneity of *a priori* "exemplary originality" (*CJ,* 5:318).

Kant, that is, directly explains how the experience of the sublime, as interim experience, discloses freedom (and therefore the possibility of spontaneity):

> The sublime . . . is a feeling of imagination by its own act depriving itself of its freedom by receiving a final determination in accordance with a law other than that of its empirical employment. In this way it gains an extension and a might greater than that which it sacrifices. But the ground of this is concealed from it, and in its place it *feels* the sacrifice or deprivation, as well as its cause, to which it is subjected. . . . Acting in accordance with principles of the schematism of judgment [now described as part of the succession procedure] (consequently so far as it is subordinated to freedom), it is at the same time an instrument of reason and its ideas. But in this capacity it is a might enabling us to assert our independence as against the influences of nature. . . . It is only through sacrifices that this might makes itself known to us aesthetically (and this involves a deprivation of something—though in the interests of inner freedom . . .). (*CJ,* 5:269–271)

In other words, Kant now sees the necessity of a succession to an infinite *Progressus*—in the experience of the sublime—so that we can even begin to exercise freedom and spontaneity.

For Kant the access to the condition of freedom and spontaneity is both empirical and *a priori*. Thus in the Transcendental Deduction he specifies that "the occasioning causes" of the "production" of *a priori* concepts must be empirical (A86). This can seem self-contradictory, but it is only a refinement of his saying, in the opening sentences of the introduction to the first *Critique* (which I cited, in part, in my introduction), that *a priori* understanding must always be *aroused* by experience: "There can be no doubt that all our knowledge begins with experience. For how should our faculty of knowledge be awakened into action did not objects affecting our senses partly of themselves produce representations, partly arouse the activity of our understanding to compare these representations, and by combining or separating them, work up the raw material of the sensible impressions into that knowledge of objects which is entitled experience? In the order of time, therefore, we have no knowledge antecedent to experience, and with experience all our knowledge begins" (B1). In this vein I am proposing that the effect which Kant attaches to the originality of the art of a genius is only a special case of his explanation of the potential freedom for originality in every human being. The succession procedure is in the first instance an empirical following not merely of one "product" of one predecessor (*CJ*, 5:309) but of an extended plurality that he calls the "succession [*Nachfolge*] by others . . . for a continually progressive culture" (*CJ*, 5:319). This empirical following occasions an awareness of an *a priori* succession. In each case this infinite line of following the "succession by another . . . arouses [another] to . . . a sense of his own originality in . . . freedom" (*CJ*, 5:318).

In other words, in his exposition of the succession procedure in the experience of the sublime, in the *Critique of Judgment,* the procedure of succession takes on a function and meaning that were not envisioned in the extensive comments on succession in the Second Analogy and the Schematism of the first *Critique*. In the *Critique of Judgment* succession is also and especially understood to be the original product of following the effectively infinite line of succession. This product is triggered by imitative following but, because of the sublime experience that ensues, becomes original and totally different from imitation.

Here it is worth putting side by side passages that we have already seen separately. In the first *Critique* Kant memorably wrote that the "schematism of our understanding, in its application to appearances and their mere form, is an art concealed [*eine verborgene Kunst*] in the depths of the human soul, whose real modes of activity nature is hardly likely ever to allow us to discover" (A141/B180–181). In the third *Critique* he discovered the connections between the succession procedure and the sublime "[that] is a feeling of imagination by its own act depriving itself of its freedom by receiving a final determination in accordance with a law other than that of its empirical employment. In this way it gains an extension and a might greater than that which it sacrifices." "But," he immediately adds, "the ground of this is concealed from it [*deren Grund aber ihr selbst verborgen ist*]" (*CJ*, 5:269). Kant, I am saying, has in fact now discovered at least the place and connections of this art concealed in the depths of the human soul, an art that he sees laid out in Milton's poetry of the sublime.

〜

Thus I am proposing that we need to put together Kant's statements about (a) the status of Milton's "images" as "original" or *exemplary* of "originality" and which therefore (unlike Klopstock's images) can be "imitated . . . with difficulty" and (b) Milton's aesthetic ideas, produced by the experience of the sublime, which are "representations that contain a wealth of thoughts which *ad infinitum* draw after it a succession of thoughts." These two kinds of statements are complementary components of the same theory and its language for originality. This is also the language for the spontaneity that is enabled, first of all, in the experience of the sublime. The condition of being original in Milton's images cannot be that these images have not been made before by anyone else. It does not make sense to say that a new image, in this sense, would be any harder to copy than a copy of a copy. Instead, the "originality" that interests Kant is that of the artist's, or any individual's, spontaneous synthesis of a unity from a manifold of representations. It is not accidental that we find these components of Kant's theory, working in these special senses, in his reflections on Milton's poetry. For Kant, Milton's poetry preeminently *(vorzüglich)* offered the exemplification of the succession procedure in its fully evolved form. I resume my analysis of that exemplification.

〜

Two features of Milton's poetry are crucial for Kant's Miltonic exemplifications, though Kant grasped them fully only in his mature theory of the sublime. Both features ultimately become integral to his

Miltonic succession procedure of aesthetic light. These are the follow-
ing of an endless progression, and sublime representation of light and
shadow as representation, per se, of the inadequacy to represent.

Kant came to identify in Milton's poetry an endless progression of
representations—an open-ended typology—that was indispensable to
the experience of the sublime. He had earlier missed this even in his
focused remarks on the Miltonic sublime in his *Observations on the Feel-
ing of the Beautiful and Sublime,* yet it is worth lingering on those re-
marks to see how they point toward Kant's mature understanding of
Milton's poetry. Here is Kant at the opening of his discussion of the
sublime in the *Observations:*

> The sight of a mountain whose snow-covered peak rises above the
> clouds, the description of a raging storm, or Milton's portrayal of the
> infernal kingdom, arouse enjoyment but with horror. . . . In order that
> [this] impression could occur to us in due strength, we must have a *feel-
> ing of the sublime.* . . . Tall oaks and lonely shadows in a sacred grove are
> sublime. . . . Temperaments that possess a feeling for the sublime are
> drawn gradually, by the stillness of a summer evening as the shimmer-
> ing light of the stars breaks through the brown shadows of night and
> the lonely moon rises into view, into high feelings of friendship, of dis-
> dain for the world, of eternity. The shining day stimulates busy fervor
> and a feeling of gaiety. The sublime *moves,* the beautiful *charms.* The
> mien of a man who is undergoing the full feeling of the sublime is ear-
> nest, sometimes rigid and astonished. . . . The sublime is in turn of
> different kinds. Its feeling is sometimes accompanied with a certain
> dread, or melancholy. (p. 47)

> [Der Anblick eines Gebirges, dessen beschneite Gipfel sich über Wol-
> ken erheben, die Beschreibung eines rasenden Sturms, oder die Schil-
> derung des höllischen Reichs von Milton erregen Wohlgefallen, aber
> mit Grausen; . . . Damit jener Eindruck auf uns in gehöriger Stärke ges-
> chehen könne, so müssen wir ein Gefühl des Erhabenen . . . haben. . . .
> Hohe Eichen und einsame Schatten im heiligen Haine sind erha-
> ben. . . . Gemüthsarten, die ein Gefühl für das Erhabene besitzen, wer-
> den durch die ruhige Stille eines Sommerabendes, wenn das zitternde
> Licht der Sterne durch die braune Schatten der Nacht hindurch bricht
> und der einsame Mond im Gesichtskreise steht, allmählig in hohe
> Empfindungen gezogen, von Freundschaft, von Verachtung der Welt,

von Ewigkeit. Der glänzende Tag flößt geschäftigen Eifer und ein Gefühl von Lustigkeit ein. Das Erhabene **rührt,** das Schöne **reizt.** Die Miene des Menschen, der im vollen Gefühl des Erhabnen sich befindet, ist ernsthaft, bisweilen starr und erstaunt. . . . Das Erhabene ist wiederum verschiedener Art. Das Gefühl desselben ist bisweilen mit einigem Grausen oder auch Schwermuth . . . begleitet.] (*AA,* 2:208–209)

References not only to *Paradise Lost* but to "Il Penseroso" and "L'Allegro" and, to a somewhat lesser degree, to *Samson Agonistes* were common in mid-eighteenth-century Germany. The extraordinary, Europe-wide success of Handel's *L'Allegro, il Penseroso ed il Moderato* and *Samson,* both employing a poet's—Milton's—texts to an extent that is virtually unique among eighteenth-century libretti, no doubt had something to do with this familiarity. Yet in the *Observations* Kant's Miltonic references are of an uncommon order both of specificity and of generalizing power. To show the *differentia specifica* of experience of the sublime, Kant adheres, in detail, to the oppositions that Milton has set up between "Il Penseroso" and "L'Allegro." Clearly Kant felt he could trust his German reader to recognize his detailed Miltonic references and to follow his analysis of Milton's poetry, even without naming Milton's poems. They could follow him here in his pursuit of the power of the sublime to move the soul, the mind, which is what most interests him in Milton's poetry. When he says, "the sublime *moves,* the beautiful *charms,*" we know which counts more for him. His evocation of the beautiful, "the shining day stimulates busy fervor and a feeling of gaiety [Der glänzende Tag flößt geschäftigen Eifer und ein Gefühl von Lustigkeit ein]," is a somewhat thin and, we may say, Prussian invocation of the setting of "L'Allegro," where "young and old come forth to play / On a Sunshine Holiday" (97–98). His identification with the Miltonic sublime of "Il Penseroso," however, is strong and deep: "Tall oaks and lonely shadows in a sacred grove are sublime. . . . Night is sublime. . . . Temperaments that possess a feeling for the sublime are drawn gradually, by the quiet stillness of a summer evening as the shimmering light of the stars breaks through the brown shadows of night and the lonely moon rises into view, into high feelings of friendship, of disdain for the world, of eternity" (*Obs,* 47). We should note how carefully Kant was scrutinizing—and thinking with the aid of—

the following passages of "Il Penseroso." I reproduce the first passage from "Il Penseroso" with Kant's allusions in brackets. I give the second passage (also from "Il Penseroso") followed by Kant's transfer from the sensible to the supersensible, which he effects by running the gamut of Milton's representations of the same transfer:

> me Goddess [*heiligen*] bring
> To arched walks of twilight groves [*Haine*],
> And shadows brown [*braune Schatten*] . . .
> Of Pine or monumental Oak [*Hohe Eichen*] (132–135)

> missing thee, I walk unseen
> On the dry smooth-shaven Green,
> To behold the wand'ring Moon,
> Riding near her highest noon,
> Like one that had been led astray
>
> . . . . .
>
> Where I may oft outwatch the *Bear* [i.e., the stars of Ursa Major],
> . . . or unsphere
> The spirit of *Plato* to unfold
> What Worlds, or what vast Regions hold
> The immortal mind that hath forsook
> Her mansion in this fleshly nook (65–92)

wenn das zitternde Licht der Sterne . . . hindurch bricht und der einsame Mond im Gesichtskreise steht, allmählig in hohe Empfindungen gezogen, von Freundschaft, von Verachtung der Welt, von Ewigkeit.

as the shimmering light of the stars breaks through the brown shadows of night and the lonely moon rises into view, into high feelings of friendship, of disdain for the world, of eternity.

In these remarks Kant's very placement of Milton's poetry—a mere human artifact—together with sublime objects of nature anticipates an important crux in the *Critique of Judgment*. Kant there at first restricts to objects of nature the stimuli that cause the feeling of the sublime, but then, as if inadvertently, changes his mind (cf. *CJ*, 5:252–

253). In the *Observations* Kant shows that this double focus of sublime seeing—on nature and art—was early a distinct option for him. But this is not all. Remarkably enough, if we follow the explicit, citation-bound referentiality of his language, we see that his focus on art, specifically on Milton's poetry, is actually, as Kant would say, "anteced-ent"—or preparatory—"in the order of time." This is to say that Kant follows verses of Milton not only to exemplify the act of representing the sublime of art but to exemplify the act of representing (in the mind) the sublime of nature as well. In fact, the former is unmistak-ably seen to disclose the latter. How this is possible, or what it might mean, is by no means self-evident; and it was presumably not yet clear to Kant himself. Only his later linkage between the experience of the sublime and the succession procedure would explain this possibility and, indeed, make it central to his thinking of aesthetic ideas.

∽

Yet the grounds for this linkage, too, were waiting in readiness from an early date in Kant's accustomed ways of regarding Christian typology. The idea of a succession or *Nachfolge* of representations into the in-finite, the unknown, and the soulful (or spiritual or supersensible) must have been associated by Kant, at some level, with the pattern of Thomas à Kempis's *Nachfolge Christi*. For German Pietism (such as that of Kant's home) Thomas's famous work placed complex ideas of imitation at the center of the Christian's life.[16] In the spirit of that kind of *imitatio*, Kant will make explicit, in *Religion within the Boundaries of*

16. Martin Gammon, "'Exemplary Originality': Kant on Genius and Imitation," *Journal of the History of Philosophy* 35 (1997): 563–592, has remarked that to some ex-tent "Kant follows the familiar sense of *Nachfolge Christi*, the imitation of Christ, in which the divine life serves as an archetype of virtue rather than a pattern for imita-tion" (584). In addition, one must keep in mind that the terms *Nachahmung* and *Nachfolge*, and the refinement of distinctions between kinds of imitation (and disci-pleship) of divine models, have a vast theological history. See, for example, Anselm Schulz, *Nachfolgen und Nachahmen: Studien über das Verhältnis der neutestamentlichen Jüngerschaft zur urchristlichen Vorbildethik* (Munich: Kösel-Verlag, 1962); Hans Dieter Betz, *Nachfolge und Nachahmung* (Tübingen: J. C. B. Mohr, 1967); and Hans Kosmala, "Nachfolge und Nachahmung Gottes," I and II, in *Studies, Essays and Reviews*. Vol. 2, *New Testament* (Leiden: E. J. Brill, 1978), pp. 139–231. Kant's attempt to grasp the meaning of *Nachfolge* was thus itself inevitably part and parcel of an effectively infinite *Nachfolge* of such attempts, in which Milton stands out among the latest of the great *Nachfolgern*.

Mere Reason, a typological "succession" *(Nachfolge)* "*in infinitum*" *(ins Unendliche)* in an "infinite progression" *(Fortschritt . . . ins Unendliche)* toward the archetype *(Urbild)* of Christ (6:62–67). To Kant it had to be obvious, late as well as early, that Milton's Puritan-pietist typology of imagination and his idea of reason "disciplin'd / From shadowy Types to Truth, from Flesh to Spirit" *(Paradise Lost,* XII.302–303) lay at the center of his entire poetic enterprise in his masterwork, that is, from the very beginning, where Milton announces that the range of his subject is typologically defined, from "Man . . . till one greater Man" (I.1–4).[17] Yet in Kant's exposition of aesthetic ideas, his identification of Milton's poetry with the "wealth of thoughts" that is created by the "succession" "into the infinite" represents a conceptual breakthrough because now Kant has found its place in the moral sublime. The formalism of this Miltonic typology (which, we will see, he called a *"Typik"* in the second *Critique* [*CPrR,* 5:67–71]) became, I submit, Kant's central concern in the experience of the sublime.

In a similar way, it was only at a late date that Kant significantly deepened the German line of inquiry into Miltonic "aesthetic light" *(aesthetisches Licht)* and "light and shadow" *(Licht und Schatten).* This inquiry, even in Kant's hands in the *Observations on the Feeling of the Beautiful and Sublime,* does not yet yield major insights. But Kant's continuation of this inquiry (we will see in detail in Chapter 2) was to become of central, creative importance to his formulation of aesthetic ideas, precisely as a Miltonic point of departure from, or advance upon, the Miltonic goal of Idealist transcendence. The "disdain for the world" of Kant's *Observations,* closely observing Milton's "Il Penseroso" (with its description of "Plato" and "the immortal mind that hath forsook / Her mansion in this fleshly nook"), required a further Miltonic ingredient, namely, a poetics of blindness.

Of vital importance for Kant's way of putting together his succession

17. On the specifics and contexts of Milton's typology, see R. H. MacCallum, "Typological Symbolism and the 'Progress of the Soul' in Seventeenth-Century Literature," in *Literary Uses of Typology from the Middle Ages to the Present,* ed. Earl Miner (Princeton: Princeton University Press, 1977), pp. 103–104; Barbara Lewalski, *Protestant Poetics and the Seventeenth-Century Religious Lyric* (Princeton: Princeton University Press, 1979), pp. 111–144; and Sanford Budick, "Milton and the Scene of Interpretation: From Typology toward Midrash," in *Midrash and Literature,* ed. Geoffrey H. Hartman and Sanford Budick (New Haven: Yale University Press, 1986), pp. 195–212.

procedure of sublime representations and for clarifying his concept of aesthetic light was, indeed, the Miltonic poetics of blindness that he likely first appreciated after Lessing pointed it out in the *Laokoon*, two years after the publication of the *Observations*. In its Kantian incarnation this is the feature of Milton's poetry that, we will note, Herder particularly attacked in Kant when he saw what Kant was making of it. Moreover, we will see that Herder mounted his attack on Kant in a Miltonic guise, as if for Kant's sins against Milton. Kant's Miltonic idea is that each representation in the endless progression of the experience of the sublime must represent "its own inadequacy" to represent (*CJ*, 5:252–253). In Milton's poetry this idea is expressed as a poetics of represented negativity. Inspired by, but more cogent than, Burke and Lowth in the same vein, Lessing described Milton's poetics of blindness this way:[18]

> Count Caylus . . . would make the test of a poem its usefulness to the painter. . . . The contemptuous judgment which Caylus passes on [Milton] was the result as much of national taste as of his would-be rule. The loss of sight, he says, may well be the strongest point of similarity between Milton and Homer. Milton cannot fill picture galleries, it is true. But if the range [*Sphäre*] of my physical sight must be the measure [*Sphäre*] of my inner vision, I should value the loss of the former in order to gain freedom from the limitations on the latter. . . . *Paradise Lost* is . . . the finest epic after Homer.[19]

In Lessing's diction the repetition of the word *Sphäre* (suggesting eyeballs) vividly reinforces the idea that in Milton's poetry it is the nega-

---

18. I described many of the elements of Milton's poetics of deficited imaging in *The Dividing Muse: Images of Sacred Disjunction in Milton's Poetry* (New Haven: Yale University Press, 1985), and even mentioned various parallels between Miltonic and Kantian concepts, but at the time I had only a vague awareness of Kant's interest in Milton. Correlations between Kant's and Milton's ideas of representing negativity, as well as between Kant's sublime and Milton's, began to emerge in my *The Western Theory of Tradition: Terms and Paradigms of the Cultural Sublime* (New Haven: Yale University Press, 2000), yet here, too, the extent of Kant's Miltonic culture and the impact of Milton on Kant's aesthetics and ethics were not yet apparent to me.

19. Gotthold Ephraim Lessing, *Laocoön: An Essay on the Limits of Painting and Poetry* (1766), trans. Edward Allen McCormick (Indianapolis: Bobbs-Merrill, 1962), chap. 14, p. 74.

tion of or within sensory representation that produces the supersensible presentation.

It tells us a good deal about German culture in the 1760s that Lessing could assume that there were fit German readers who would readily understand the logic of his assertion, which is based (like Kant's way of proceeding cited above) on an unnamed but obvious reference to specific verses of Milton. Lessing's reference is to *Paradise Lost,* III.40–55. There we find Milton's acceptance of his blindness coupled with his apostrophe to light, in which he formulates the principle of the emergence of the supersensible presentations of "Celestial Light" exactly from the *expunging* and *purging* of the merely sensory, that is, the purging of earthly light seen in representations of "Nature's works":

> Thus with the Year
> Seasons return, but not to me returns
> Day, or the sweet approach of Ev'n or Morn,
> Or sight of vernal bloom, or Summer's Rose,
> Or flocks, or herds, or human face divine;
> But cloud instead, and ever-during dark
> Surrounds me, from the cheerful ways of men
> Cut off, and for the Book of knowledge fair
> Presented with a Universal blanc
> Of Nature's works to mee expung'd and ras'd,
> And wisdom at one entrance quite shut out.
> So much the rather thou Celestial Light
> Shine inward, and the mind through all her powers
> Irradiate, there plant eyes, all mist from thence
> Purge and disperse, that I may see and tell
> Of things invisible to mortal sight. (*Paradise Lost,* III.40–55)[20]

As I began to suggest earlier, Kant's idea of Miltonic aesthetic light and shadow is itself a feedback function of the succession procedure insofar as the deficited (light and shadow) structure of each representation in the endless progression that produces experience of the sub-

---

20. Lessing's reference to these verses was noted, timidly, in *Lessing's Laokoon,* ed. Albert Hamann and Lewis Edward Upcott (Oxford, 1892), p. 262. I have commented on the poetics of blindness embodied by this passage in *The Dividing Muse,* pp. 72–73.

lime is itself produced by the "momentary check to the vital forces" and "discharge all the more powerful" (*CJ*, 5:245).

Kant himself traces these connections. More than is at first obvious, in his lecture comment on *Paradise Lost*, VIII.140–152, he saw a projection "to unknown ends" of a line in effectively infinite succession, that is, in Milton's extrapolation to "other Suns and . . . Moons . . . Communicating Male and Female Light." In Kant's account of the Schematism in the *Critique of Pure Reason*, he described a vital element of any such succession: namely, the alteration or alternation, he says, "between reality and negation ['cessation in nothingness (=0=*negatio*)'], or rather a transition from the one to the other, which makes every reality representable as a quantum. The schema of a reality, as the quantity of something in so far as it fills time, is just this continuous and uniform production of that reality in time as we successively descend from a sensation which has a certain degree to its vanishing point, or progressively ascend from its negation to some magnitude of it." In the *finite* line of succession these representable quanta form "the successive apprehension of an object" (A143–145/B183–184). In the *infinite* Miltonic line of succession, we can now add, these representable quanta form, no less, the represented object. In Kant's lecture comment on the *Folge von Gedanken nach sich ziehen* of Milton's poetry, the passage that he chooses is a representation of a continuum of points of light. More precisely, it is a representation of the *aesthetisches Licht* (aesthetic light) or, even more precisely, the *aesthetisches Licht und Schatten* (shadow) that (as I will show in some detail in the next chapter) was definitive of the constellation of German Miltonism.

We can see the ground of these Kantian-Miltonic connections in suggestive passages of the Dohna transcription of Kant's anthropology lectures, probably given in the winter semester of 1791–92. The transcript is somewhat disjointed, but we can nonetheless follow Kant's route to the exposition of an "exemplary originality" under the heading "*Of the dimness and clarity of representations*" (*Von der Dunkelheit und Klarheit der Vorstellungen*) (p. 11). He proceeds to his destination by comparing the representations of "points [and] lines" in mathematics, in philosophy, and in poetry, in Milton's poetry in particular:

In mathematics the simple concepts of points [and] lines are the easiest; in philosophy they are the hardest. In philosophy the **concrete** goes before the **abstract;** in mathematics the **abstract** before the **concrete.**

In philosophy one cannot think a thing **in the abstract,** but rather one must first take it **in the concrete** case. . . . A poet must be able to substitute shadow for things, since he can create shadow. This is to be seen in **Milton's** journey of the angel. In the poet is found only the manner, mode, and method of things—the shadow-images of things—not however things themselves. . . . One calls the exemplary ideal when it can serve others as a rule, when it is worthy of imitation. . . . **Genius** is . . . established in freedom from the constraints of rules. . . . That is **original** which cannot be imitated; but that is exemplary which is worthy of imitation. Therefore exemplary **originality** is the best.

[In der Mathematik sind die einfachen Begriffe von Punkten Linien die leichtesten, in der Philosophie die schwersten. In der Philosophie geht das **concretum** vor dem **Abstracto,** in der Mathematik das **Abstractum** vor dem **Concreto.** In der Philosophie kann man sich nicht eine Sache **in abstracto** denken, sondern muß immer erst einen Fall **in Concreto** annehmen. . . . Ein Poet muß an die Stelle der Sachen Schatten setzen können, denn Schatten kann er erschaffen. Man sehe **Miltons** Reise des Engels. Beim Poet kommt nur Manier, Art und Weise der Sachen vor, nicht aber die Sachen selbst[,] es sind nur Schattenbilder derselben. . . . Man nennt das exemplarisch musterhaft, was andere [*sic*] zur Regel dienen kann, was nachgeahmt zu werden verdient. . . . **Genie** wird . . . gesetzt in der Freiheit vom Zwange der Regeln. . . . **Original** ist das was nicht nachzuahmen ist, exemplarisch aber das, was nachahmungswürdig ist. Daher ist die exemplarische **Originalitaet** die beste.] (pp. 109–116)]

At least provisionally, we can fill in what is implicit here. To Kant and his informed auditor, it was clear what is meant by instancing "**Milton's** journey of the angel" (i.e., Raphael), the exemplum which had already been cited at length (as we will see in the next chapter) by Georg Friedrich Meier. For Kant the element of special relevance in these verses of Milton is the angel's *linear* journey from heaven to earth, "down thither prone" (*Paradise Lost,* V.266), in which the abiding, underlying reality is represented by "light" (250) that is *veiled, shaded, shadowed* (250, 277, 284).[21] This exemplary poetic representation of a

---

21. Milton invokes the picture of the "seraph" (*flame*) with its shading wings famously drawn by Isaiah (6:2).

line that extends beyond our tracing is effectively infinite. The exemplary originality of Milton's talent amounts to genius. The Miltonic representation that interests Kant (here, too, following Meier, but actually with less clarity of distinction, as we will also see in the next chapter) is of aesthetic light and shadow. In Kant's most perspicuous, integrated expositions of the sublime and of aesthetic ideas, the representation of light and shadow is seen as a successive flaring out of *energeia* in an endless *Progressus*. *Energeia* of this kind is represented in the continuous oscillation (descent and ascent) between light and shadow, between "reality" that is sensory content and "negation" of that sensory content. Exemplary form emerges from the relation, in oscillation, between that sensory reality and its negation.

In the intertwining of Longinian and Miltonic traditions of the sublime, such as we find in Addison and Young and their German inheritors, we will see that this kind of transmission of light, or *taking fire*, is already of considerable importance to a procedure of succession. These accounts anticipate and complement Kant's account of the succession to the sublime line of representation and of genius. Kant contemplated his conception of aesthetic light and shadow in the chiaroscuro qualities of Milton's poetry. For Kant this is the aesthetic light and shadow that are at the heart of the "aesthetic ideas" that in the anthropology lecture he characterizes as Miltonic. For Kant aesthetic light involves an epicyclic and vertiginous reflexivity. The light and shadow structure of each representation in the endless progression produces the experience of the sublime in the "wealth of thoughts which *ad infinitum* draw after it a succession of thoughts. Such ideas draw us into an immeasurable prospect." This procedure is identical with that which Kant describes in the "Analytic of the Sublime" as producing the "momentary check to the vital forces" and "discharge all the more powerful" (*CJ*, 5:245). This momentary blackout, produced by following the endless progression of representations of light and shadow, stamps each representation with an additional partial eclipse of representation itself.[22]

∿

22. It may be that the idea of an energetic model of the *Nachfolge* was for Kant a development from his early ideas of an *"Auswickelung* [*sic*] *der Natur,"* an "unwrapping of

In the passage from *Paradise Lost,* VIII.140–152, that Kant cites in the Elsner anthropology lecture, the module of representation that is endlessly repeated is a bi-polar structure called "Female" and "Male" light. As described by Kant, the *following* of the progression of this bi-polar light initially consists of imitation or repetition of empirical representations. Ultimately, however, the *following* achieves the condition of *succession* by transferring the mind to a thinking of "exemplarity," which for Kant is a representation of *a priori* universals. Without reference to a procedure of succession in the sublime, Henry Allison has pointed to formal isomorphisms between the heteronomous and the autonomous in Kant's aesthetics.[23] Building upon Allison's insight, I propose that in Kant's view the formal isomorphism of a heteronomous succession procedure makes possible an "unbounded expansion" (*CJ,* 5:315) of the mind so that reason can become conscious of an autonomous succession procedure. In the autonomous succession procedure, reason is liberated by "the sublime as a presentation of an indeterminate concept of reason" (*CJ,* 5:244) to achieve freedom and moral feeling. This achieved consciousness entails a transfer from the sensible to the supersensible. We will see that in Kant's view a transfer takes place within a heteronomous (or artistic) as well as an autonomous procedure of succession.

The "succession of thoughts" that, Kant says, is drawn after the

---

nature" (1:226), and, following Leonhard Euler's theory of light, of the "propagated" (*propagatam*) "motion of waves" (*in motum undulatorium*) in the *"materia ignis,"* matter of fire (1:376, 378), that we meet, respectively, in Kant's *Allgemeine Naturgeschichte und Theorie des Himmels* (1755) and in his doctoral dissertation, *Meditationum Quarundam De Igne Succincta Delineatio* (*Succinct Exposition of Some Meditations on Fire,* 1755). Kant revived the term *Auswickelung* in the *Critique of Judgment* (5:418, 423). Kant's dissertation is available in English in *Kant's Latin Writings: Translations, Commentaries, and Notes,* trans. and ed. Lewis White Beck et al., 2nd ed. (New York: Peter Lang, 1992), pp. 11–35.

23. Henry E. Allison, *Kant's Theory of Taste: A Reading of the Critique of Aesthetic Judgment* (Cambridge: Cambridge University Press, 2001), pp. 256–261. In this formal isomorphism the unconditioned relation of the heteronomous to the autonomous is clearly crucial for Kant. Allison (focused on what he believes is the centrality of beauty rather than the sublime in Kant's aesthetic ideas) puts it this way: "In expanding the mind and 'prompting much thought,' (albeit of an indeterminate kind) aesthetic ideas lead the mind . . . from something sensible to the supersensible" (p. 260). In Chapter 6 I turn, in greater detail, to Allison's views of aesthetic ideas and of formal isomorphism.

"wealth of thoughts" in the *"ad infinitum" Progressus* is prepared by the constellation of interpretation of Milton's poetry that Kant encountered.[24] (In Chapter 5 I will discuss the importance that Kant attaches to heteronomous "preparation"—*"Vorübung"*—in the second *Critique.*) Preparatory experience of such constellation remains, in itself, heteronomous, whereas the procedure of succession culminates in an experience of the sublime and a transfer between the heteronomous and the autonomous. In fact, however, Kant's engagement with the constellation of German Miltonism strongly shares features of *following* with the Miltonic procedure of succession and even provides access to that procedure. As a result it is sometimes impossible to say where Kant's following of this constellation (of both its German and its British discursive participants) leaves off and his procedure of succession (directly to Milton's poetry) commences. It is thus definitive for Kant's Miltonic succession procedure that the aesthetic idea comes into being in the tracing of a complex constellation that is a representation of a line of light as well as a line of interpretation. For Kant this continuous line extends from the constellation of German Miltonism to the constellational form of Milton's poetry, which, indeed, itself represents a procedure of succession.

We observe signs of this continuous line in the case of Kant's lecture comment, that is, in the background of his encounter with, and in his present interpretation of, the Miltonic verses that are his chosen exemplification. In 1755 he had opened the third part of his *Universal Natural History and Theory of the Heavens (Allgemeine Naturgeschichte und Theorie des Himmels)* with this citation from Alexander Pope's *Essay on Man:*

> Wer das Verhältniß aller Welten von einem Theil zum andern weiß,
> Wer aller Sonnen Menge kennet und jeglichen Planetenkreis,
> Wer die verschiedenen Bewohner von einem jeden Stern erkennet,
> Dem ist allein, warum die Dinge so sind, als wie sie sind, vergönnet,
> Zu fassen und uns zu erklären.
> *Pope. (AA,* 1:349)

---

24. See Henrich, *Konstellationen: Probleme und Debatten am Ursprung der idealistischen Philosophie (1789–1795)* (Stuttgart: Klett-Cotta, 1991), pp. 42–43, for his differentiation of two types of constellation that operate simultaneously and in partnership.

Here are Pope's verses, which Kant's citation faithfully follows:

> He, who thro' vast immensity can pierce,
> See worlds on worlds compose one universe,
> Observe how system into system runs,
> What other planets circle other suns,
> What varied being peoples ev'ry star,
> May tell why Heav'n has made us as we are.
>   (*Epistle,* I.23–28)[25]

Pope proposes that he who would attempt to understand the plan of the cosmos must consider the possibility that planets (like the earth) and suns might all be, from a valid point of view that we cannot readily access, *stars;* and that each of these stars might be inhabited like the earth-star. When Kant later cited and focused minutely on Milton's verses that describe, in detail, the same possibility, even set (in the angel's challenge to Adam) in very much the same framing of a challenge, he could not have failed to recognize that, in the verses that he (Kant) had already cited from Pope, Pope was self-consciously following these same verses of Milton (in addition, no doubt, to following later writers such as Fontenelle in the *Pluralité des mondes*).[26] Here are Milton's verses once again:

>   What if that light
> Sent from [Earth] through the wide transpicuous air,
> To the terrestrial Moon be as a Star
> Enlight'ning her by Day, as she by Night
> This Earth? reciprocal, if Land be there,

25. I cite Pope's verse from *The Poems of Alexander Pope,* ed. John Butt (New Haven: Yale University Press, 1963).

26. Pope certainly realized that Milton was himself thinking of the accounts of these matters in Galileo's *Sidereus Nuncius* and Kepler's *Somnium.* (On these matters see Marjorie Hope Nicolson, *A World in the Moon. A Study of the Changing Attitude toward the Moon in the Seventeenth and Eighteenth Centuries. Smith College Studies in Modern Languages,* 17 [1936].) With Kant's expert knowledge of the history of astronomy, both Pope's and Milton's backward glances were surely obvious. It is important to note, however, that Kant's citations of Pope's and Milton's verses collectively trace points of the specific line that Kant follows in his Elsner comment. I will lay out more of Kant's citations of Milton's verses as we proceed.

Fields and Inhabitants: . . .
. . . ; and other Suns perhaps
With thir attendant Moons thou wilt descry
Communicating Male and Female Light,
Which two great Sexes animate the World,
Stor'd in each Orb perhaps. (*Paradise Lost,* VIII.140–152)

For anyone who cited these verses of Milton, as well as Pope's invoca-
tion of these verses of Milton, this linkage had to be obvious, since
seven lines earlier Pope famously trumpeted his aim to follow Milton's
chief aim in *Paradise Lost,* namely, to "justify the ways of God to men"
(I.26). Pope here sets out to "vindicate the ways of God to Man" (*Epis-
tle,* I.16). Pope's following of Milton's verses is only one point in the
constellation of interpretation that Kant encountered before he laid
out and enacted his procedure of succession to Milton's verses in his
lecture comment. The procedure of succession that Kant produced,
here and elsewhere, can even be understood as a higher order of
the phenomenon of interpretive constellation that Dieter Henrich
describes. Yet its aesthetic impact is significantly different because
(among other things) the procedure of succession traces a progres-
sion that must be effectively infinite and because each of the represen-
tations in the progression must represent its inadequacy to represent.

At the risk of getting ahead of my story, it is worth expanding on this
last point at this juncture. Although Kant follows constellation and suc-
cession in a continuous line that contains many kinds of language, in
the procedure of succession the role of the language of poetry—de-
fined in Kant's particular way—is unique and indispensable. Only in
the language of this kind of poetry does the example come to repre-
sent exemplarity. Here exemplarity is the effect of following, instanta-
neously and in a single partially eclipsed representation, the projected
infinite progression of such representations. In the resulting experi-
ence of the sublime, the example is freed of its impingements in the
individual's self-referential world and instead represents the universal,
or exemplarity, in the example. This transfer from the sensible to the
supersensible is the ground of the transfer between points of view that
is required by moral reason (specifically in the categorical imperative
procedure, as we will see in Chapter 3). Here the thinking and willing
of the individual for the individual's well-being are transferred to the

individual's thinking and willing of the well-being of all rational be-
ings. In Kant's experience, the language of poetry that enables this
aesthetic and moral transfer is preeminently found in Milton's poetry
of the sublime. This is Milton's poetry of infinite progressions of light
and shadow, including, indeed, the tracing of astronomical constel-
lation.

~

In fact it is not surprising that Kant would one day apply something
very like a process of tracing astronomical constellations to the proce-
dure of succession, especially in his succession to a poetry that traces
astronomical constellation. Already in 1755, in the *Universal Natural
History and Theory of the Heavens,* the tracing of stellar configurations
was for him no whimsical pastime. Rather, it was instrumental in for-
mulating his now famous theory that nebulous stars were themselves
galactic systems composed of multitudes of individual stars.[27] Kant
long retained his interest in this early thinking. In fact, at the time of
writing the third *Critique* he allowed the chief contents of that work to
be republished in abstract form by Georg Michael Sommer. This was
the *Auszug aus Kants Naturgeschichte und Theorie des Himmels* (König-
berg, 1791). The cosmological parallels between elements of Kant's
nebular hypothesis and features of the specific verses of Milton that
Kant cites in 1792 could only have intensified his interest in Milton's
way of tracing, and hypothesizing, constellations *to sublime effect.* In the
Universal Natural History, Kant already sees in the tracing of the end-
lessness of constellations almost all the terms that would go into his
mature theory of the sublime. In 1755, however, he sees these terms,
on the affective side, only as parts of an activity that creates astonish-
ment, wonder, and religious awe—not yet as that which creates the ex-
perience of the sublime and its capacity for disclosing moral law or
moral feeling. Here is Kant in 1755:

27. This theory (confirmed by Edwin Hubble in 1924) is now seen as perhaps
Kant's most enduring contribution to the so-called "nebular hypothesis," which was
proposed in different forms and by different pens throughout the eighteenth and
nineteenth centuries. On the place of this aspect of Kant's theory in the history of
the nebular hypothesis, see Martin Schönfeld, *The Philosophy of the Young Kant: The
Precritical Project* (New York: Oxford University Press, 2000), p. 116.

The theory which we have proposed opens up for us a view of the infinite field of creation and offers an idea of the work of God appropriate to the infinite nature of the Great Masterbuilder. If the size of a planetary system in which the Earth is hardly seen as a grain of sand fills the understanding with astonishment, how delightfully astounded we will be when we examine the infinite crowd of worlds and systems which fill the totality of the Milky Way. But how much greater this wonder when we know that all these immeasurable arrangements of stars once again create a numbered unity, whose end we do not know and which is perhaps, like the previous one, inconceivably large and yet, once again, only a unit in a new numbered system. We see the first links of a progressive relationship of worlds and systems, and the first part of this unending progression already allows us to recognize what we are to assume about the totality. Here there is no end, but an abyss of a true infinity, in which all capacity of human thought sinks, even when it is uplifted [*erhoben*] with the help of mathematics. The wisdom, goodness, and power which has revealed itself is limitless and, to exactly the same extent, fruitful and busy. The plan of its revelation must, therefore, be, just like it, infinite and without borders. (*AA*, 1:256)

In the "Analytic of the Sublime" of the *Critique of Judgment*, where Kant's main point is the connection between experience of the sublime and disclosure of moral feeling, the mind's attempt to trace the stars of "the system of the Milky Way" is explicitly one of his examples of the mathematical sublime (5:256). In 1755 Kant's tracing of "this unending progression" *(dieser unendlichen Progression)* already presents and represents the impossibility of thinking "the infinite" together with "the totality," so that "all capacity of human thought sinks." In the phrase "uplifted [*erhoben*] with the help of mathematics" there is even a hint of what will become (now as a productive force) Kant's exposition of the mathematical sublime *("Vom Mathematisch-Erhabenen")* in the "Analytic of the Sublime" (*CJ*, 5:248–260). So, too, this early "view of the infinite field of creation" *(Aussicht in das unendliche Feld der Schöpfung)* in tracing the constellations continues to echo in the *Critique of Judgment*, not only in his repetition of the example of the Milky Way but in his language there, in §49, for the sublime representations that open a "prospect into a[n immeasurable] field of kindred representations [*die Aussicht in ein unabsehliches Feld verwandter Vorstellungen*]" (5:315).[28]

By the time Kant cited, in his lecture of 1792, Milton's verses giving Raphael's report of the possibility of the constellation of male and female stars, extending into the unknown, he had crystallized his interest in a succession procedure of a Miltonic kind, that is, a succession to an infinite progression such as Milton's poetry of the sublime represents and traces. In the period 1785–90, each time Kant encounters Milton his following of Miltonic light is preceded by his engagement with the constellation of interpretation of Miltonic aesthetic light. Therefore, what could be understood as sources and analogues to or, in some instances, even direct influences upon Kant's following of Milton's poetry partakes of something very like the significance that Henrich attaches to the *Konstellationen* of post-Kantian Idealist philosophy. Yet, as I have said, even if Kant's procedure of succession is continuous with his engagement with constellation, and perhaps even developed from it, Kantian succession is a qualitatively different activity and, we will see more and more, comes to be seen by Kant as an activity that is functionally of central importance in his aesthetic and moral theory.

Fred Rush has pointed out that Henrich's concept of *Konstellation*, like that of Walter Benjamin before him, has its antecedents in Kant's account of aesthetic ideas in §49 of the *Critique of Judgment*.[29] In Chapter 6 I will demonstrate that Kant's Miltonic succession procedure informs his account of aesthetic ideas not only in his Elsner lecture comment but in his account of aesthetic ideas in §49. One implication of this demonstration may well be that Kant's Miltonic procedure

28. In §49 it is possible that for Kant one of the dimensions of his example of "Jupiter's eagle, with the lightning in its claws" and of the neighboring "peacock" of Juno may be that of astronomical constellations proper. In the lore of constellations, Aquila, the eagle, was by Kant's time long established as the royal eagle of Jupiter, whose talons grip Jupiter's mighty thunderbolts; just as Pavo, the peacock (following Ovid and others) was the constellation of Juno. In a footnote of the *Universal Natural History and Theory of the Heavens,* Kant uses the constellation of the eagle to establish the center of the Milky Way (*AA,* 1:328n).

29. See Fred Rush, "Jena Romanticism and Benjamin's Critical Epistemology," in *Walter Benjamin and Romanticism,* ed. Beatrice Hanssen and Andrew Benjamin (New York: Continuum, 2002), pp. 123–136, especially pp. 124–125, 135.

of succession is indeed an early, highly advanced development *from Konstellation* in German Idealist philosophy. The fact that in the *Critique of Pure Reason* Kant already developed his own model of "community or reciprocity" that is distinct from "influence" lends credence to his early preoccupation with constellation in Henrich's sense. In the Third Analogy of the Transcendental Analytic, he exemplified this model of how we are led "from one object to another" as follows: "The light, which plays between our eye and the celestial bodies, produces a mediate community between us and them, and thereby shows us that they coexist" (A211–213/B258–260). In its full emergence Kant's Miltonic procedure of succession takes the phenomenon of constellation (in this case, tracing both interpretive and astronomical constellations) to an entirely different level. For Kant the procedure of succession to aesthetic light is first and foremost an experience of the sublime that produces freedom and moral feeling.[30] The Kantian connection between tracing succession and disclosing moral law amounts almost to an identity. After seeing the full extent of this identity, we may come to feel that a moment of transition from heteronomous constellation to heteronomous and autonomous succession is quite precisely represented in the famous coda to the *Critique of Practical Reason:* "Two things fill the mind with ever new and increasing admiration and reverence, the more often and more steadily one reflects on them: *the starry heavens above me and the moral law within me*" (5:161). ["Zwei Dinge erfüllen das Gemüth mit immer neuer und zunehmender Bewunderung und Ehrfurcht, je öfter und anhaltender sich das Nachdenken damit beschäftigt: *der bestirnte Himmel über mir und das moralische Gesetz in mir.*"]. (I will return to this passage in Chapter 4.)

~

Two aspects of Henrich's constellation model are of special relevance to Kant's engagement with the constellation of German Miltonism and, in turn, to his choice of objects for his procedure of succession.

30. Here, too, however, the correspondences between Kantian and post-Kantian constellations may not be merely coincidental. Paul Franks has suggested that the post-Kantian *Konstellation* and *Konstellationsforschung* that Henrich has pictured are a development from Kant's attempts to approach the infinite in an encounter with the finite. See *"Fragen an die Konstellationsforschung,"* in *Konstellationsforschung,* ed. Muslow and Stamm, pp. 179 and 216–217. Henrich has welcomed this suggestion (p. 217).

A bi-polar "tension," Henrich explains, is structurally central to a "typology of constellations" so that each constellation is actually a *"Di-Kon-Stellation."*[31] I will show in the next chapter that in the case of the constellation of German Miltonism, which Kant and his co-luminaries constitute, the tension between *cognition* and *sensation* (or *feeling*)— *Erkennen* and *Empfinden*—was made prominent in the firmament of German philosophical life by Edward Young's "epoch-making" *Conjectures on Original Composition.*[32] Most especially, this tension becomes the basis of Herder's presentation of his sensation-centered alternative to Kant. Herder's alternative, moreover, emphasizes the role of analogy and literature in philosophy. I will show that Herder is Kant's opposite pole in the constellation of German Miltonism, so much so that Kant and Herder repeatedly take up antithetical orientations within the tension of that constellation.

The elements of this Herderian-Kantian tension vis-à-vis Milton are extremely rich. In fact, they are directly related to the decisive turnabout in Kant's attitude toward the role of analogy and literature in philosophy. This transpired in 1784–85, right at the beginning of the five-year period in which Kant's engagement with Milton's poetry is of greatest philosophical significance. The turnabout to which I refer occurred almost immediately after Kant began to write his severely critical remarks on Herder's employment of analogy and literature in the first volumes of the *Ideen zur Philosophie der Geschichte der Menschheit* (1784, 1785). Indeed, the changes in Kant's views were probably gestating even while he was articulating, and considering more deeply, his criticisms of Herder. (Very much the same thing occurred, in fact in the same year, in the way Kant was sharply critical of, but also profoundly influenced by, Christian Garve's *Philosophical Remarks and Es-*

---

31. *Konstellationsforschung,* ed. Muslow and Stamm, pp. 26–29.

32. Often repeated, the term *epochemachend* was perhaps first applied to Young's book by Otto Schlapp, *Kants Lehre vom Genie und die Entstehung der 'Kritik der Urteilskraft,'* p. 61, who at that point has the terms *genius* versus *imitation* especially in mind. In fact, the binary of genius/imitation is closely related to the tension between *Erkennen* and *Empfinden,* but this remains to be shown hereafter. With regard to Kant's comment on the passage cited from *Paradise Lost,* it may be that for Kant as well as Milton, and perhaps for Herder also, the tension and complementarity between *Erkennen* and *Empfinden* would conventionally be viewed as being implicit in constellating the binaries of Male/Female or Sun/Moon.

says on Cicero's Book on Duties.)[33] Herder's insistence on analogy was part of his reaction against what he regarded to be Kant's and the Enlightenment's narrowly individualistic anthropology and obliviousness to human "plasticity."[34] Beginning in 1785 Kant's response to Herder, in part incorporating Herder's views, was the development of the Miltonic succession procedure of the sublime that, while still maintaining an *a priori* foundation, integrated an anthropology of culture with an individualistic anthropology and provided for a plasticity of the freest kind. Kant had just famously written, in 1784, that we must "use the mind without the guidance of another": "*Sapere aude!* [*Dare to know!*] Have the courage to use your own understanding! This is the motto of Enlightenment" (*AA*, 8:35). Kant's Miltonic succession procedure would mark the emergence of his formula for using one's understanding both without the guidance, yet also within the line of language, of another thinker or writer, indeed of countless others. Thus after 1784 Kant began to adopt, in practice, a carefully circumscribed but also highly positive view of the role of analogy in philosophical discourse. Operating within the constellation of German Miltonism that included Herder and many others, Kant focused his use of analogy and literature in response to Herder's repeated, indeed (as we will see) often wild, invocations of Milton's poetry in order to attack Kant.

Herder's attempts to enlist Milton against Kant may well have stemmed from Herder's early, clear recognition of Kant's deep intellectual affinity with Milton. Be that as it may, especially in the years after Herder's initial Miltonic attacks on him, Kant's systematic understanding of principal features of Milton's poetry went immeasurably deeper than Herder's largely belletristic appreciations.[35] It is notable

33. Later in this chapter I will note Klaus Reich's demonstration of the deep influence of Cicero's *De officiis* on the *Groundwork of the Metaphysics of Morals*. See Manfred Kuehn, *Kant: A Biography* (Cambridge: Cambridge University Press, 2001), pp. 277–282 and 485nn11–12, for an overview of this topic and a listing of scholarship in the wake of Reich's work.

34. On this point see Frederick C. Beiser, *The Fate of Reason: German Philosophy from Kant to Fichte* (Cambridge, Mass.: Harvard University Press, 1987), pp. 140, 143.

35. In coming to realize how central Herder's provocations were to Kant's reflections on Milton, I have been both encouraged and aided by John H. Zammito's extensive demonstrations of the importance of Kant's rivalry with Herder in the composition of the third *Critique*: see *The Genesis of Kant's Critique of Judgment* (Chicago: University of Chicago Press, 1992), p. 9ff. Zammito, however, does not treat either Kant's Miltonism or his response to Herder's anti-Kantian Miltonism.

that virtually all of the Miltonic texts with which, in my view, Kant significantly engaged—including the sonnet "When I consider" and *Samson Agonistes*, as well as specific passages of *Paradise Lost*—were ones upon which Herder's comments impinged. This impingement is significant even if Herder's comments on these texts were for Kant conceptually less important than other commentaries within the German Miltonist constellation. To identify what Herder saw, and feared, in the Miltonic affiliations of Kant's *"Formel"* (formula)—or aesthetic and ethical formalism—we will need to attend to the Kantian-Miltonic formal elements that Herder himself locates and *shows*, rather than to the mass of rhetoric under which he *tells about* and tries to bury them.

Henrich's noting of the phenomenon that he terms keeping "Distance" *from* the constellation is helpful in explaining a perplexing aspect of Kant's Miltonic succession procedure. Henrich points out that the major figures of the post-Kantian Idealist constellations needed to achieve *"Distanz"* from the constellation in which they were nonetheless profoundly located.[36] One of the striking phenomena in Kant's relation to the Miltonic constellation in which he operated is that despite his deep indebtedness to that constellation, we see him, again and again, veiling that indebtedness, as if *distancing* were indispensable to what he was achieving. Henrich describes Hegel's distancing of himself from the constellation in which a poet, Hölderlin, was at the center. Kant had already done something analogous with regard to the constellation in which a poet, Milton, was at the center.[37]

---

36. *Konstellationsforschung,* ed. Muslow and Stamm, p. 29.

37. It should be said that from another point of view Kant's omission of acknowledgment of his debt to Milton could seem perfectly acceptable within the eighteenth-century decorum of such omissions, as, for example, in Lessing's copying from Calepio—without acknowledgment—the entire intellectual underpinning of the *Hamburgische Dramaturgie.* Indeed, we should recall here the observation of Oskar Walzel, who established the astonishing extent of this unattributed debt in his review of Friedrich Braitmaier's *Geschichte der poetischen Theorie und Kritik* in *Anzeigen für deutsches Alterthum und deutsche Litteratur* 17 (1891): 55–74: "No eighteenth-century author perceived himself as a plagiarist in scholarly representation when, in further developing unfamiliar ideas, he did not name his immediate sources [kein schriftsteller des 18 jhs. fühlt sich eines plagiats in wissenschaftlichen darstellungen schuldig, wenn er fremde ideen weiterentwickelnd seine nächste quelle nicht namhaft macht]" (69n). The difference, however, to which I am pointing here is that in Kant's case the act of incurring so large and so systematic a debt—i.e., his procedure of succession to Milton—functions as an integral part of his philosophical system.

A further explanation of why Kant distances himself from what he himself calls "sources" (*Quellen, CJ,* 5:283) may be possible here. Kant's engagement with Milton's poetry and the constellation of German Miltonism is, I am proposing, highly concrete in nature. Yet we must locate Kant's Miltonic succession procedure very much within the realm of what he terms "supposition." This status of supposition does not amount to a diminished force of intellectual encounter but is rather continuous for Kant with the defining suppositional status of the sublime and moral feeling. In the "sublime," he says,

> the judgment refers the imagination to reason, as a faculty of ideas. . . . We do so only under a subjective supposition [*unter einer subjectiven Voraussetzung*], (which, however, we believe we are warranted in making,) namely, that of the moral feeling in man. And, on this assumption, we attribute necessity to the latter aesthetic judgment also.
>
> In this modality of aesthetic judgments, namely, their assumed necessity, lies what is for the Critique of Judgment a moment of capital importance [*ein Hauptmoment*]. For this is exactly what makes an *a priori* principle apparent in their case, and lifts them out of the sphere of empirical psychology, in which otherwise they would remain buried amid the feelings of gratification and pain (only with the senseless epithet of *finer* feeling), so as to place them, and, thanks to them, to place the faculty of judgment itself, in the class of judgments of which the basis of an *a priori* principle is the distinguishing feature, and, thus distinguished, to introduce them into transcendental philosophy. (*CJ,* 5:266)[38]

My claim is that Kant's succession procedure of the experience of the sublime is his formal, objective way of calling forth, in another supposition, the "subjective supposition" that is "the moral feeling in human beings." Even while Kant is deploying these insights, that is, he is actively deriving them from the supposition entailed in the succession procedure itself. This is the succession procedure of the experience of the sublime. For Kant this supposition is an attested, self-consciously tested, and efficacious supposition, in other words, an *als ob* (a think-

38. I have altered Meredith's translation of Kant's word *Menschen* from *man* to *human beings* and of *Voraussetzung* from *presupposition* to *supposition*.

ing of "as if") that is worked through by Kant himself and which he sees, and continues to experience, as a necessity and "main point" of aesthetic judgment and moral reason.[39]

Because the procedure of succession discloses the mind's unconditioned causality of freedom, we cannot ever know, or be certain, that a particular procedure of succession has occurred. We can only demonstrate and propose its potentiality in an array of significant correspondences. It is likely (though also unprovable) that Kant's ways of distancing himself from his "sources" are intended to make certain that we *cannot* say that a particular procedure of succession has occurred. Such safeguarding would be a direct corollary of the special kind of "influence" that Kant says is entailed by a "succession," which suffers none of the limiting of freedom that is incurred in "imitation" (*CJ*, 5:309). In the *Critique of Practical Reason* Kant will call the correlate of this sustaining of independence a thinking of "the *unconditioned* in the series of causal connection" (5:3). (In Chapter 4 I will have more to say about the causality of freedom and the status of the Kantian supposition in the *Critique of Practical Reason*.) Thus a causality of freedom, such as is disclosed to the mind's self-consciousness in its procedure of succession, must not be constrained, or (in a philosopher's rigorous representation) even seem to be constrained, in any way. A caution and a qualification of these kinds similarly apply to every proposal of a concrete procedure of succession that I will make in this book. Even hedged in this way, however, plausible proposals of specific Kantian procedures of succession can suggest how, in practice, Kant must be subjectively disclosing his freedom and moral feeling.

∼

The Kantian sublime has been voluminously discussed for two hundred years, yet the Miltonic formal constituents of Kant's sublime have been totally neglected. This neglect on the part of scholars must seem

39. The classic discussion of Kant's "as if" is that of Hans Vaihinger, *The Philosophy of "As If": A System of the Theoretical, Practical and Religious Fictions of Mankind,* trans. C. K. Ogden (New York: Harcourt, 1925). Wolfgang Iser engages Vaihinger's ways of developing the "as if" in *The Fictive and the Imaginary: Charting Literary Anthropology* (Baltimore: Johns Hopkins University Press, 1993), especially pp. 134–140. Iser's approach to the "as if" is different from, and bears no responsibility for, what I have to say about the Kantian supposition.

astounding if we consider that in Kant's Germany during the thirty years that culminate in the publication of the *Critique of Judgment* (1790) one cannot begin to canvass the term *erhaben* (sublime) without first acquiring a substantive understanding of the centrality of Milton's poetry—whether explicit or implicit—in virtually every significant usage of that term, particularly, indeed, in Kant's own usages. For reasons that will be considered more fully hereafter, Kantian scholarship has completely missed this rudimentary recognition. These reasons are complex, but one of them should be mentioned now, since at the outset it will help neutralize disbelief that anything of importance in Kant's thought could have been entirely passed over.

I refer to the fact that in the specific case of Kant's relation to Milton, a quite conscious exclusion was laid down by the most influential commentator on the *Critique of Judgment* of the early twentieth century, Alfred Baeumler. Ernst Cassirer early identified Baeumler's exclusion as an expression of German nationalist prejudice. Even before Baeumler's commentary appeared, Ernst Bergmann (who, like Baeumler, later became an openly National Socialist philosophizer) had stunted inquiry into the significance of Milton's poetry for German philosophy in his highly regarded *Die Begründung der deutschen Ästhetik durch Alex. Gottlieb Baumgarten und Georg Friedrich Meier,* which includes accounts of Meier's relations to both Milton and Kant. Bergmann flattened "Milton" to a mere accessory role to Klopstock, even though, as we have begun to see, Milton's poetry was of far greater theoretical and practical importance to Meier than Klopstock's and even though Kant regularly and contemptuously compared Klopstock's poetry with Milton's in order to insist on the unbridgeable difference between *"Schwärmerei"* (enthusiasm of a ranting sort) and *"Genie."*

It was intolerable to Baeumler to acknowledge that his magisterial recovery of the Germanism of Kant's eighteenth-century philosophical roots should have to be revised to admit Kant's creative debt to English writings on genius and the sublime as well as, correlatively, to the deep Miltonic preoccupations (manifested, among other ways, in eighteenth-century Christian Hebraism) of many of the same German thinkers whose cultural purity Baeumler certified. For Bergmann, later the author of *Die deutsche Nationalkirche* (1933) and *Die 25 Thesen der Deutschreligion* (1934), two of the leading Nazi calls to a non-Judeo-Christian religion, the full nature of Milton's clearly powerful impact on the heartland of German thought was a subject to be avoided. Thus, by excluding, in particular, investigation of the Miltonic dimensions of Meier's aesthetics and of Kant's relation to those dimensions (in Meier and related others), Bergmann's and Baeumler's suppressions bear heavy responsibility for blocking one necessary line of Kantian inquiry.[40] Especially because the heart of Kant's interest in Milton's poetry is the latter's unique way of disclosing freedom and moral feeling, Baeumler's and Bergmann's apparently minor suppressions at this formative juncture of modern Kantian scholarship gener-

40. See Baeumler, *Kant's Kritik der Urteilskraft: Ihre Geschichte und Systematik* (Halle/ Saale: Niemeyer Verlag, 1923), p. 142 and n. and p. 162. Cassirer's response appears in *The Philosophy of the Enlightenment,* trans. Fritz C. A. Koeln and James P. Pettegrove (Princeton: Princeton University Press, 1951; German edition, Tübingen, 1932), pp. 319–320 and n. Bergmann's chapter is in his *Die Begründung der deutschen Ästhetik durch Alex. Gottlieb Baumgarten und Georg Friedrich Meier* (Leipzig: Röder & Schunke, 1911), pp. 187–199. In more recent scholarship this obliviousness to the unique aesthetic impact of Milton's poetics on eighteenth-century Germany is still in evidence, as, for example, in Georg-Michael Schulz's comment in *Tugend, Gewalt und Tod: Das Trauerspiel der Aufklärung und die Dramaturgie des Pathetischen und des Erhabenen* (Tübingen: Max Niemeyer, 1988), p. 113, "Research has long ago recorded 'that the roots of Bodmer's Milton enthusiasm lie in religiosity, but not in the aesthetic.' [Die Forschung hat längst registriert 'daß die Wurzeln der Miltonbegeisterung Bodmers im Religiösen, nicht aber im Ästhetischen liegen.']" Schulz is citing Wolfgang Bender's *Nachwort* to his facsimile edition of Bodmer's *Critische Abhandlung von dem Wunderbaren in der Poesie* (1740) (Stuttgart: Metzlersche Verlagsbuchhandlung, 1966), p. 6*. To be sure, Bender discusses what he considers to be aesthetic aspects of Milton's poetry, but these aspects are almost all historical and thematic—rather than critical and formal—such as the concept of the poet as creator, epic machinery of *das Wunderbare,* or even sublime affect historically considered. Interestingly enough, Bender approvingly invokes Baeumler's downgrading of Milton's importance, especially of Addison's Milton, for the aesthetics of Bodmer and Breitinger as well as of Kant (pp. 9*–10*). A refreshing perspective, however, is offered by Gerhard Sauder in the *Nachwort* to his facsimile edition of H. E. von Teubern's 1760 translation of Edward Young's *Gedanken über die Original-Werke* (Heidelberg: Lambert Schneider, 1970), p. [36]: "Baeumler's thesis, according to which all essential features of Kant's genius theory are to be understood from [purely] German evolution, is . . . untenable. [Baeumlers These ist, . . . nicht haltbar, wonach alle wesentliche Züge von Kants Genielehre aus der deutschen Entwicklung zu verstehen seien.]" One may add that although in modern times there has been a good deal of excellent German formalist criticism of Milton's poetry, it has not been brought to bear in understanding the aesthetic impact of Milton's poetry and poetics on eighteenth-century German thought after 1732.

ated an ever-enlarging distortion, at very least in the identification of what needs to be investigated.[41] To begin to rectify this distortion, we need to recover not only neglected dimensions of Kant's writings but, no less demanding, direct knowledge of those aspects of Milton's poetic genius that inspired Kant.[42]

No doubt the temptation to ignore Milton's impact on Kant has been particularly attractive because on its deepest levels Milton's poetry requires an expenditure of intellectual energy that is no less daunting than that required by Kant's moral philosophy. At one time or another perhaps most of us have experienced, to our cost, the skirting of difficult matters in the paths or bypaths of our research only because we are not masters of the specific language (or lexicon) in which important texts made their mark. (This can even be the case with native speakers.) As a recidivist of this kind, I suggest that this, too, has been a significant cause of the neglect of Kant's engagement with Milton, that is, on the part of both philosophers and, indeed, Miltonists.

41. By the time of Hitler's rise to power, Bergmann's rejection and exclusion of that which forms the mythos of *Paradise Lost*—in more or less close juxtaposition with Kant—is undisguised. In *Die deutsche Nationalkirche* (Breslau: Ferdinand Hirt, 1933), pp. 184–185, it is axiomatic that "der Kantische, der deutschethische Mensch" can have nothing to do with the ethos and mythos of Genesis that Milton renewed.

42. As I have indicated in detail in my text and notes, I am much indebted to Schlapp's *Kants Lehre vom Genie*. Even a hundred years after the publication of his book, his knowledge of eighteenth-century German aesthetics in its particular relevance to the complexity of Kant's writings is unequaled. To be sure, Schlapp took note of many of Kant's expressions of interest in Milton; and he was familiar with at least the most prominent writings that I have adduced in what I have called the constellation of German Miltonism. Yet Schlapp is one of those who suggested that Kant's manifestations of interest in literature, especially his preferences for English literature, were misguided. (For example, Schlapp says that "a whole series of remarks show his detailed preoccupation with works of literature and his self-reliant albeit partly wrong judgment of those works. He admired the English writers above all others" while, Schlapp notes, showing no appreciation of works such as "*Goethes Werther*" [pp. 298–299].) Correlative to these suggestions, his book neglects the emergence of Kant's mature thinking about the sublime. The three elements that in my view are most lacking in Schlapp's accounts, and which have continued to be absent in Kantian scholarship to the present time, are an attempt to understand (a) the nature of Milton's poetry of the sublime, (b) the nature of Kant's reflection on that poetry in his own struggle to know the sublime, and, finally, (c) the catalytic power of Milton's poetry within Kant's thinking. Once we have these things in our grasp, a great many of the writings that Schlapp had mastered, and quite a few that may not have seemed to him worthy of interest, take on a new significance.

But, it is time to ask, could Kant read English? This question must apparently be crucial for a book such as this one. By many it has been assumed that Kant did not know English, which would mean that he could only read and refer to Milton's language—as well as, say, Hume's and Hutcheson's—in translations.[43] Even if this were true it would not be an argument against the possible profound impact of Milton's works on Kant, since all of Milton's major poetry was available to Kant in multiple German translations. But if it were the case that Kant had no direct access to Milton's language, it would indeed be hard to imagine how, being in all other matters a responsible philologist, Kant could repeatedly insist on the preeminence of Milton's poetry and, most important, how he could have risked linking his specific assertions about Milton's poetry to the key terms of his aesthetic and moral theory. We might also wonder, incidentally, how the University of Königsberg could have acted so irresponsibly as to offer its chair in poetry—as it did to Kant—to someone who couldn't read English, and that, precisely at a time when English poetry and prose had emerged as the dominant foreign literature on the German cultural horizon. Additionally, the allegation of Kant's ignorance of English must seem puzzling in light of the fact that by far the closest and most long-lasting friend that Kant ever had—and the one who, as Manfred Kuehn and others have shown, personally influenced the development of Kant's moral theory—was the Englishman Joseph Green. At the time of Kant's death, his friend and colleague Christian Jacob Kraus recalled that "the relationship with the original and highly righteous Englishman *Green* certainly had no small influence on Kant's way of thinking and especially on his study of English authors [*und besonders auf sein Studium englischer Schriftsteller*]. In *Green's* last years Kant spent a number of afternoon hours with him every day."[44] (Kraus does not say who these "English authors" were, though Kuehn records Green's complaint that the way poems are printed on the page is disorienting

43. See, for example, Zammito, *The Genesis of Kant's Critique of Judgment,* p. 29: "Kant could not read English."

44. This is recorded from Kraus's manuscript by Rudolph Reicke, *Kantiana: Beiträge zu Immanuel Kants Leben und Schriften* (Königsberg, 1860), p. 60: "Der Umgang mit dem originalen höchst rechtschaffenen Engländer *Green* hat gewiß nicht wenig Einfluß auf Kant's Denkart und besonders auf sein Studium englischer Schriftsteller gehabt. Er brachte bey *Green* in dessen letzten Jahren täglich einige Nachmittagsstunden zu."

to him.) Kuehn has calculated that "Kant was a constant and very regular visitor at Green's house" beginning at least as early as 1766 and until Green's death in 1784.[45] That Kant, in public, felt very hesitant about his shortcomings in speaking English is fully understandable. Aside from his tête-à-tête study of English authors with Green, he had to confront, in society, a circle of intellectual acquaintance that included many of Germany's leading translators and disseminators of English texts, including Abbt, Garve, Hamann, Herder, Hippel, Lessing, Lichtenberg, Lindner, Mendelssohn, and Sulzer. Kant learned to hold his English tongue.

One more general word about the materials and perspectives that I have attempted to recover here. Seventy years ago Klaus Reich discovered the direct use that Kant made of Cicero's De officiis in composing the Groundwork of the Metaphysics of Morals. Reich's profound account of Kant's relation to Cicero's essay proposed far more than a previously unappreciated source for Kantian ideas. Rather, he claimed that "there is really a reference here to Cicero," that is, to specific passages of the De officiis. Kant, Reich claimed, requires the inscription of Ciceronian references into the Groundwork in order to fulfill a particular function: "This function consists exclusively in enabling us to intuit and feel the content of the moral law." This, Reich asserted, is "a task which Kant undertakes only in this one work." For this singular undertaking, says Reich, Kant directly invoked a single "image, stirring up the feelings and making intuition possible, a special stimulus"—only, Reich insists, in this one case, only in this one work.[46] Reich's discovery of Kant's intimate engagement with Cicero's De officiis in the Groundwork is without doubt of lasting value, and, indeed, this same Stoic ethics is a deep part of the root system of the Miltonic works that I am proposing Kant followed. Yet Reich was rash in assuming that he could know the full extent of Kant's intimate engagement, in his moral writings, with specific images and special stimuli. Negative hypotheses in philology and the history of ideas are always perilous. Most important, Reich was not moved to hypothesize that Kant must have been equally, or even more, engaged with other images and stimuli which might

45. Kuehn, Kant, p. 155–156.

46. Reich, "Kant and Greek Ethics," Mind 48 (1939): 338–354, 446–463, translated, entire, by W. H. Walsh from Reich's Kant und die Ethik der Griechen (Tübingen: J. C. B. Mohr, 1935). My citations are from "Kant and Greek Ethics," 459, 461, 462.

have given him access, most especially, to "the principle of the auton-
omy of the will," which, Reich himself noted, "the Stoics lacked" but
which was indispensable, even central, to the *Groundwork* and to Kant's
other ethical writings as well.[47] The kind of moral reason that Kant fol-
lowed—in *succession*—in the *exemplarity* of Milton's poetry may usefully
be described as Stoic ethics raised to the power of the experience of
the sublime, thereby providing (I will try to show) exactly that auton-
omy of the will. All of these topics must be traced out in the Miltonic
constellation that Kant followed and, indeed, in which he was em-
bedded. That Kantian-Miltonic constellation, leading to the Kantian-
Miltonic procedure of succession, will, I believe, continue to yield
more insights than any of us have yet dreamed, both into Kant's philos-
ophy and into Milton's poetry.

47. Ibid., 463.

CHAPTER 2

Kant's Journey in the Constellation of German Miltonism

Toward the Procedure of Succession

In the previous chapter I suggested that what is especially significant for Kant in the passage that he calls "Milton's journey of the angel" (i.e., *Paradise Lost*, V.247–287) is its representation of a linear progression, "down thither prone" (266), which is constituted by aesthetic light and shadow. Such "light" (250) is *veiled, shaded, shadowed* (250, 277, 284). Originating at a point that we cannot reach, this effectively infinite line is in Kant's terms simultaneously positive and negative. Aesthetic light and shadow of this kind is a successive oscillation of *energeia* between "reality" that is sensory content and "negation" of that sensory content. "Following" this progression of light and shadow is the precondition of succession in the experience of the sublime and therefore of the disclosure of moral feeling. I now propose to show some of the principal ways in which Kant's Miltonic successions (i.e., with regard to this and other passages of Milton's poetry) are prepared by his encounters with the constellation of German Miltonism. As I have begun to suggest, Kant's engagement with this constellation is especially intense because the defining subject of the constellation is the idea and experience of aesthetic light in Milton's poetry, including what Kant will view as the successions within that poetry. Thus, in the case of Kant's interest in "Milton's journey of the angel," it is not enough to note (as did Otto Schlapp) that Kant's attention was likely drawn to the passage by Meier's use of it.[1] What is important here for

---

1. Otto Schlapp, *Kants Lehre vom Genie und die Enstehung der 'Kritik der Urteilskraft'* (Göttingen: Vandenhoeck & Ruprecht, 1901), p. 177n.

Kant is Meier's citing of these verses as an exemplification of "liveliness of thoughts" that is represented by "aesthetic light," which for Meier means light *with* shadow. Meier emphasizes that this "**aesthetic shadow** *(umbra æsthetica)*" is a "praiseworthy privation, as distinct from the blameable kind."[2] I will try to show something of the wealth of significance that attaches to Meier's and others' comments on Milton's poetry of light and shadow, that is, within the collective constellation of those comments. The deep shadows cast by Herder's pseudo-Miltonic attacks on Kant no doubt lent a special immediacy to Kant's experience of the full range of this constellation. We will see that Herder even identified Kant with Milton's Prince of Darkness.

∼

Kant's chief early conduits for the concept of aesthetic ideas were Baumgarten and Meier, who indeed constituted their own phenomenon of succession and (it was thought by some) even genius.[3] Over many years Kant used a volume each of Baumgarten and Meier as the

2. Meier, *Anfangsgründe aller schönen Wissenschaften*, I.252, 258, 264. I cite the three volumes of the *Anfangsgründe* from the edition published at Halle, 1754–59 (first published at Halle, 1746–48). I return to these phrases of Meier below, where they are given in context and with the German originals. With regard to Meier's distinguishing of the kind of deficited image that he names "**aesthetic shadow** *(umbra æsthetica)*" as a "praiseworthy privation, as distinct from the blameable kind," it is worth recalling (from the last chapter) Kant's incomplete gesture in the same direction (specifically in thinking of Milton's poetry) in his Dohna lecture (probably 1791–92). Aiming toward his exposition of exemplary originality, he, too, almost distinguishes (under the heading "*Of the dimness and clarity of representations* [*Von der Dunkelheit und Klarheit der Vorstellungen*]," p. 11) between shadow that is a praiseworthy privation and shadow, mere obscurity, of a blameable kind: "A poet must be able to substitute shadow for things, since he can create shadow. One sees this in **Milton's** journey of the angel. In the poet is found only the manner, mode, and method of things—the shadow-images of things—not however things themselves [Ein Poet muß an die Stelle der Sachen Schatten setzen können, denn Schatten kann er erschaffen. Man sehe **Miltons** Reise des Engels. Beim Poet kommt nur Manier, Art und Weise der Sachen vor, nicht aber die Sachen selbst(,) es sind nur Schattenbilder derselben]" (p. 110). Given the muddiness of the passage, one may suspect that the transcriber of the lecture missed, and left out, the full point or distinction at which Kant was aiming.

3. Moses Mendelssohn, "Zwei hundert und achter Brief. Ueber die Fortsetzung des Versuchs vom Genie," *Briefe, die Neueste Litteratur betreffend* 13 (1762): 11, applies the term genius to Baumgarten and Meier and tries to measure it within the continuity of their aesthetic thought.

textbooks for his lectures on metaphysics and logic, respectively.[4] Without reference to Meier's Miltonism, Schlapp pointed out that in Kant's lectures on logic, using Meier's *Auszug aus der Vernunftlehre* as the textbook, Kant already invoked (probably in 1771) Meier's term "aesthetic concepts" *(ästhetische Begriffe)* and, following Meier, characterized these "aesthetic concepts" as "lively, rich, pregnant" *(lebhaft, reich, prägnant)*. Schlapp also noted that Kant's fullest source for what was to become his concept of *"aesthetische Ideen"* in the *Critique of Judgment* was Meier's Baumgarten-derived but independently elaborated concept of "energetic ideas" *(nachdrückliche Ideen)*.[5] This appeared in Meier's three-volume *Anfangsgründe aller schönen Wissenschaften* (first printed in Halle, 1746–48; reprinted 1754–59). In those volumes Meier's first and longest example of the "energetic ideas" of "aesthetic light" is his two-and-a-half-page citation of Milton's "splendorous and glittering method" *(prächtige und schimmernde Art)* in describing the earthward journey of the angel as supersensible light.[6] In all its splendor, this is the Miltonic imagination of light and shadow that Meier and Kant contemplated. Meier's aim in bringing this long Miltonic citation is explicitly to exemplify "the liveliness of thoughts" *(die Lebhaftigkeit der Gedanken)* in "aesthetic light" *(aesthetisches Licht)* *(Anfangsgründe*, I.252), which for him very much means the interplay of "light and shadow" *(Licht und Schatten)* *(Anfangsgründe*, I.265–268). In more ways than one Kant followed Meier's prooftext of Miltonic light for the philosophical import located there by Meier.

A parallel, directly supplementary observation should be made about Ernst Bergmann's way of noting that Meier's term *energetic ideas* was built on Johann Jacob Breitinger's exposition of "words of command" *(Machtwörter:* decrees, fiats). Bergmann does not mention that Meier's understanding of *aesthetisches Licht* as *conceptus praegnantes*

---

4. Prussian law required the use of textbooks in lecture courses.

5. See Schlapp, *Kants Lehre vom Genie*, p. 60. Though Meier was Baumgarten's avowed and devoted disciple, his presentation of the concept of *nachdrückliche Ideen*— in the *Anfangsgründe*—preceded the appearance of Baumgarten's by ten years and, as Ernst Bergmann, *Die Begründung der deutschen Ästhetik durch Alex. Gottlieb Baumgarten und Georg Friedrich Meier* (Leipzig: Röder & Schunke, 1911), pp. 158, 162–163, pointed out, is considerably richer than Baumgarten's eventually published remarks on the same subject.

6. Meier, *Anfangsgründe*, I.253–255.

(§126) and his closely related exemplifications from Milton's poetry follow from Breitinger's twenty-four-page literary and philosophical demonstration that even in German translation Milton's words "call forth a complete and energetic concept" *(einen vollständigern und nachdrücklichern Begriff erwecken).* Not accidentally, Breitinger's analysis focuses on (among other examples) Milton's description of *pregnance* in the *fiat lux* of the Holy Spirit, creating (first of all) light against chaos. In this instance the heading of Breitinger's analysis is Milton's famous phrase "And mad'st it pregnant" *(Und machtest ihn trächtig).* Milton's phrase is the center of his invocation of the Holy Spirit's creativity (which is, incidentally, both male and female, impregnating and pregnant) at the inception of *Paradise Lost.* There, setting out on his journey, the blind poet already aspires to a way of following a creativity of light and shadow:

> Thou from the first
> Wast present, and with mighty wings outspread
> Dove-like satst brooding on the vast Abyss
> And mad'st it pregnant: What in me is dark
> Illumine, what is low raise and support. (*Paradise Lost,* I.19–23)

Anticipating Kant as much as (or even more than) Meier, Breitinger attends to the way the Miltonic energetic concept is called forth by a particular kind of representation of light and shadow, namely, an *energeia* of reality and negation. Breitinger terms this Milton's representations of *"non ens oder negatio entis."*[7] This, too, is a vivid pointer to-

---

7. Johann Jacob Breitinger, *Fortsetzung Der Critischen Dichtkunst* (Zürich, 1740), pp. 73–74, 86–87. The analysis of Milton's *Machtwörter* extends over pp. 66–90. Here and elsewhere I am concerned with the most substantive commentators on *aesthetisches Licht* who also, not incidentally, are the ones who rely on what they consider Milton's inimitable capacity to exemplify that *Licht.* This is surely an important part of Meier's claim that "*Milton* is incomparable in his poetic pictures [*Milton* ist in seinen poetischen Bildern unvergleichlich]" (*Anfangsgründe,* I.313). Kant, in *Reflection* 914; *AA,* 15:400, is of the same mind, so much so, in fact, that he warns against Meier's later confusion of Klopstock with Milton: "Klopstock can be imitated very well, but Milton only with difficulty because his pictures are original. [Klopstock kann sehr gut nachgeahmet werden, aber Milton schwer, weil seine Bilder original sind.]" But one may add here that this line of thought is early expounded by Wolff in rudimentary form as the "concept of wit" *(Begriff des Sinnreichen),* as Schlapp notes (p. 60n), and it

ward the Miltonic dimensions of Kant's aesthetic ideas. Yet Meier is still of far greater significance to Kant than Breitinger is, especially because Meier begins to show Kant the outlines of a Miltonic procedure of succession.

Meier, Milton, and the Procedure of Succession

Schlapp suggested that in the *Critique of Judgment* (in §49) Kant took the terms of his low valuation of *Nachahmung* from §415 of Meier's *Anfangsgründe*.[8] That may be correct, though Kant could have gleaned similar views from a host of other authors. What surely did, however, stand out for Kant in these pages of Meier is the beginning of an attempt to differentiate an exceptional "way of imitation" that is "the only kind that can be commended" (an *Art der Nachahmung* that is *die einzige, die angepriesen werden kann*). Making little headway in clarifying what this "way" might be, Meier calls it *"manly imitation" (die männliche Nachahmung)*—imitation that also achieves originality—and tries, fumblingly, to define its relation to "rules of wit" *(Regeln des Witzes)* (*Anfangsgründe*, II.382). In another essay written in the same year in which the *Anfangsgründe* began to appear, entitled "Inquiry into the Question: Whether in a Heroic Poem Made by a Christian the Angels and the Devil Can and Must Replace the Pagan Gods" (1746),[9] Meier identifies in *Paradise Lost* just such a complete antithesis

---

is perhaps also worthy of mention that, just before Kant takes it up (again) in the *Critique of Judgment*, the line is extended by Johann August Eberhard's brief comments in *Theorie der schönen Wissenschaften* (Halle, 1786), pp. 58–60, on the *aesthetisches Licht und Schatten*, which afford "judgment and taste especially in the artist and art critic" (*insonderheit in dem Künstler und Kunstrichter Beurtheilungskraft und Geschmack*). Eberhard's book is dedicated to Mendelssohn (who helped disseminate Burke's comments on aesthetic light) and in these pages invokes the work of Kant's friend Marcus Herz, *Versuch über den Geschmack* (Berlin, 1790, first published 1776), for the closely related concept of *Haltung* (composure), on which Herz remarks, "By this same concept the artists generally understand light, shadow, and colors [Die Künstler verstehen unter demselben gemeiniglich das Licht, den Schatten, und die Farben]" (p. 38), to which he adds a footnote to Sulzer on *Haltung*.

8. Schlapp, *Kants Lehre vom Genie*, p. 248n.

9. "Untersuchung der Frage: Ob in einem Heldengedichte, welches von einem Christen verfertiget wird, die Engel und Teufel die Stelle der heydnischen Götter vertreten können und müssen?" The essay was published in the *Critischer Versuch zur*

to *Nachahmung* and just such "a more manly way of succeeding to the ancients" *(eine männlichere Art den Alten nach[zu]folgen).* Among his chief examples drawn from Homer's and Virgil's representations of pagan gods are those of Jupiter and Juno. In Chapter 6 we will see that in the *Anfangsgründe* he has much to say about Jupiter and Juno; and we will see, as well—what Kant no doubt also saw—that, after Meier, Herder gave a different answer to very much the same question, and in relation to Milton, and even with regard to Jupiter and Juno. (We recall that Kant's major, in fact his sole, substantive exemplification of aesthetic ideas in the *Critique of Judgment* is a representation of Jupiter and Juno. This representation will be at the center of my discussions in Chapter 6.) Here I point to Meier's remarks, in the "Inquiry," on the need to differentiate an act of imaginative "succession" *(nachfolgen)* from imitation:

> My inquiry is a source of many significant effects [*eine Quelle vieler wichtigen Folgen*] which might serve our contemporary poets, so that they may learn a more manly way of succeeding the ancients [*auf eine männlichere Art den Alten nach(zu)folgen*], than the majority of them are accustomed to do. But it will be possible to show this more clearly at the end of this inquiry. ("Untersuchung," 180)

> One need only put oneself in the place of a pagan, and read *Homer,* in order to be able to contemplate *Jupiter, Juno,* etc. with deference. . . . We cannot be struck with wonder by any deed of Jupiter's because we regard him and his deeds as a chimera. . . . A Christian poet proceeds artlessly, and does not achieve his goal, if he brings forward the pagan gods [*"Mars, Bellone, Jupiter, Juno"*] as did *Homer* and *Virgil.* ("Untersuchung," 184, 186, 187) [10]

Aufnahme der Deutschen Sprache 15 (1746): 179–200. I cite the essay from the reprinting in *Georg Friedrich Meier, Frühe Schriften zur ästhetischen Erziehung der Deutschen in 3 Teilen,* ed. Hans-Joachim Kertscher and Günter Schenk (Halle: Hallescher Verlag, 1999–2002), I.126–140. The page numbers given in my notes are those of the 1746 printing.

10. "Meine Untersuchung ist eine Quelle vieler wichtigen Folgen, welche unsern heutigen Dichtern dazu dienen können, daß sie in ihren Erdichtungen auf eine männlichere Art den Alten nachfolgen lernen, als die meisten zu thun gewohnt sind. Doch dieses wird sich am Ende dieser Untersuchung deutlicher zeigen lassen"

At the end of the essay Meier tries to spell out what this activity of "succeeding"—*nachfolgen*—might be. He tells us that the modern Christian poet, who avoids mere imitation, "succeeds [*nachfolgt*] the ancients in a rational and manly way . . . as Milton has sometimes done in an irreproachable way [auf eine vernünftige und männliche Art den Alten nachfolgt . . . wie Milton manchmal auf eine untadelhafte Art gethan hat]" (197–198). Meier's idea of "a source of many significant effects [eine Quelle vieler wichtigen Folgen]" is that of an inherited form into which a new, superior content is poured by framing predecessor pagan images with appropriate skepticism and by replacing pagan epic machinery with Christian equivalents. This is what he means by Milton's "irreproachable way." Meier, however, has little notion of what might make the modern or Christian poet's representations philosophically (not just doctrinally) more true, that is, in their very structure of representation.

Thus, on the one hand, Kant may well take part of the suggestion for the succession procedure within aesthetic ideas from Meier's formulations of a succession procedure specifically with regard to Milton's representations. Yet, on the other hand, Kant had to develop his own philosophical rationale for what it means to say that the poet can, in Kant's words, succeed in "going to the same sources for a creative work as those to which he [the predecessor] went for his creations [*aus denselben Quellen schöpfen, woraus jener selbst schöpfte*]" and, even of "learning from one's predecessor no more than the mode [*die Art*]"—that is, the procedure of succession—"of availing oneself of such sources." Here, once again (but seen in a new light) is the relevant passage in Kant's third *Critique:*

> *Succession* [*Nachfolge*] which has reference to a precedent, and not imitation [*Nachahmung*], is the proper expression for all influence which the products of an exemplary *author* [*originator*] may exert upon oth-

---

("Untersuchung," 180). "Man darf sich nur als einen Heyden anstellen, und den *Homer* lesen, so wird man den *Jupiter,* die *Juno* u.s.w. nicht ohne Ehrerbietigkeit betrachten können. . . . Wir können uns über keine That des *Jupiters* wundern, weil wir ihn mit samt seinen Thaten für ein Hirngespinst halten. . . . Genug . . . daß ein Christlicher Dichter einfältig handelt, und seinen Zweck nicht erreicht, wenn er in einem Heldengedichte die Heydnischen Götter ["Mars, Bellone, Jupiter, Juno"] eben so anführen wolte, als *Homer* und *Virgil* gethan" ("Untersuchung," 184, 186, 187).

ers—and this means no more than going to the same sources for a creative work as those to which he went for his creations, and learning from one's predecessor no more than the mode of availing oneself of such sources. (*CJ*, 5:283)[11]

Kant's heteronomous succession procedure is far more complex than Meier's idea of succession. For one thing, Kant's procedure is formally isomorphic with the autonomous succession procedure in which all individuals "who follow" their "predecessors" not as "mere imitators" can and "must create . . . from the common *a priori* source" (*CJ*, 5:283). But what immeasurably distances his idea of succession from Meier's is his way of focusing on the representation of the infinite "series" or *Progressus*. Kant saw that the kind of succession procedure that might derive, in freedom, from an "exemplary originator" in freedom had to come from the sublime effect of following an effectively infinite series of representations of a deficited kind. (I will return to this kind of representation later in this chapter.) Only such following can produce a new "exemplary originality" (*CJ*, 5:318).

Meier, Milton, and "Aesthetic Light"/"Aesthetic Shadow"

Meier realized that the kind of representation that forms the aesthetic idea represents the mind's own *energeia* or *Nachdruck*. This is the heart of his "energetic idea" *(nachdrückliche Idee)*. He expands on Baumgarten by systematically referring to this energy as aesthetic "light and shadow," and, going beyond Baumgarten, he finds it exemplarily in Milton's representation of light and shadow. Thus even if Meier cannot explain why or how this light and shadow of the mind is represented in Milton's poetry, he makes many connections that Kant internalized by the time he articulated his *aesthetische Ideen*. Kant criticized Meier for being satisfied with a kind of "confused knowledge."[12] Very likely the confusion that Kant saw in Meier was his failure to dis-

---

11. I have here adopted the translation of the term *Nachfolge* as *succession* in accord with Paul Guyer's and Eric Matthews's translation of the same term in Kant's *Critique of the Power of Judgment*. See my Notes on Citations and the Term *Succession* in the front matter.

12. Kant, *Reflection* 2387 (? 1755–56), cited and discussed by John H. Zammito, *The Genesis of Kant's Critique of Judgment* (Chicago: University of Chicago Press, 1992), pp. 19–21, with regard to Kant's criticisms of both Meier and Baumgarten.

tinguish aesthetic heteronomy from aesthetic autonomy. Kant believed that, given an exemplary representation for analysis, this kind of confusion could be sorted out. Mendelssohn observed that Meier's "genius" was manifested in transforming Baumgarten's "abstract truths" into "intuitive concepts" *(anschauende Begriffe)*.[13] In the *Anfangsgründe* Milton's poetry was a special venue for Meier's transformative activity. Here are two excerpts from Meier's exposition of the aesthetic light and the "endlessly various, resplendent concepts" *(unendlich viele glänzende Begriffe)* that he finds in the greatest poets, especially in Milton's "analogous fictions" *(analogische Erdichtungen [fictiones analogicæ])* *(Anfangsgründe,* I.236–237ff.). Kant would follow and further transform the ideas that Meier presented in these passages:

> The vitality of thinking is . . . its *aesthetic clarity,* and *aesthetic light* (perspicuitas & lux æsthetica) and the higher degrees of this light constitute *aesthetic radiance* (nitor & splendor æstheticus). . . . In order to provide my readers with a sensation of aesthetic light and radiance, I wish to cite here a splendid passage from the fifth book of *Paradise Lost* [i.e., V.247–287]. *(Anfangsgründe,* I.252–253)

> Accordingly aesthetic light demands far more than the clarity of all words and concepts. . . . Doesn't one find endlessly various, resplendent concepts in all the great poets. . . ? *(Anfangsgründe,* I.257–259)[14]

Parallel to Meier's attention to Milton's *analogische Erdichtungen* and to the "clarity" *(Klarheit)* that the "aesthetic light" of the greatest poets "requires" *(erfordert)* for "resplendent concepts," we have a passage

13. Mendelssohn, "Zwei hundert und achter Brief. Ueber die Fortsetzung des Versuchs vom Genie," 11.

14. "Die Lebhaftigkeit der Gedanken heißt . . . *die aesthetische Verständlichkeit* derselben, und *das aesthetische Licht* (perspicuitas & lux æsthetica) und die größern Grade dieses Lichts, machen den *aesthetischen Glanz* (nitor & splendor æstheticus) aus. . . . Um meinen Lesern eine Empfindung von dem aesthetischen Lichte und Glanze beyzubringen, wil [*sic*] ich eine vortrefliche Stelle, *aus dem V Buche des verlornen Paradieses* hersetzen" *(Anfangsgründe,* I.252–253). "Folglich erfordert das aesthetische Licht weit mehr, als die Klarheit aller Wörter und Begriffe. . . . Findet man nicht i[n] . . . allen grossen Dichtern unendlich viele glänzende Begriffe. . . ?" *(Anfangsgründe,* I.257–259).

of Kant on what "the greatest talent of the poet requires [*das grösste Talent des Dichters erfordert*]." This requirement is analogy and "clarity" *(Klarheit)* of a certain kind.[15] The passage appears in Brauer's transcription of Kant's anthropology lectures and is quoted by Schlapp, though without suggesting the relation to Meier. Kant's insistence on denying precisely this kind of excellence to Klopstock, specifically as opposed to Milton, expresses far more than his strong disapproval of both Meier's and Herder's speaking of Klopstock in the same category as Milton. Kant's strictures on this apparently incidental matter are, I suggest, another instance of his thinking through the question of what kind of poetic analogy—which he calls "ein **analogon veritatis** [an analogue of the truth]"—philosophy can employ, specifically with regard to the "intuitive lucidity" *(anschauende Klarheit)* of Miltonic light. Kant observes:

> In his writings the poet must always observe an **analogon veritatis;** the conditions of his story must accord with the character assumed, and he therefore does not have the **license** to say whatever he wants. **Milton** is a poet in the true sense. **Klopstock** does not come near him because he moves through sympathy, in speaking sentimentally, in that way agitating the reader, just like seeing someone grow pale—and growing pale with him. Those who have drawn the parallel between **Klopstock** and **Milton** have not realized this. The poet must invent and must know how to place his invention into an intuitive lucidity.[16]

> [Der Dichter muß in seinen Schriften immer ein **analogon veritatis** beobachten; die Bedingungen seiner Erzählung müssen mit dem angenommenen Charakter übereinstimmen, und er hat also nicht die **Licenz** zu sagen, was er will. **Milton** ist ein Dichter im eigentlichen Verstand. **Klopstock** kommt ihm nicht bei, denn er rührt **per Sympathie;** indem er gefühlvoll redet, so bewegt er den Leser mit, gleichwie einen Erblassten sehen und mit ihm erblassen. Die, welche **Klopstock** mit

15. Schlapp, *Kants Lehre vom Genie*, pp. 98–101—and, following him, Bergmann, *Die Begründung der deutschen Ästhetik durch Alex. Gottlieb Baumgarten und Georg Friedrich Meier*, p. 159n—points out Kant's debt on the same score to Meier's *Vernunftlehre*.

16. Schlapp, *Kants Lehre vom Genie*, pp. 169–170. I have filled in part of Schlapp's quotation and restored "Klarheit zu geben wissen" as well as some spellings and emphases, according to the Marburg Kant Archiv transcription of Brauer's text (p. 54).

dem **Milton** verglichen haben, haben dies nicht eingesehen. Der Dichter muss erfinden, und seine Erfindung in eine anschauende Klarheit zu setzen, wißen.]

Here, too, Kant inherits Meier's Miltonic line of inquiry, especially into the special conditions of Miltonic light. We should reap the benefit, as likely Kant did, of Meier's Milton criticism even when it does not function in terms of a direct interknitting of citation and commentary. Milton's poetry in its chiaroscuro brilliance, represented in progressions from the deepest psychological and cultural sources, is unmistakably described in Meier's poetics of light and shadow. Meier has Milton's poetry in mind not just here but (as I will confirm a few pages on) also in a later passage of the *Anfangsgründe* that was to be of special significance for Kant:

> We shall call this praiseworthy privation, as distinct from the blameable kind, **aesthetic shadow** *(umbra æsthetica)*. . . . The aesthetic shadow is so to speak a place of rest where the spirit recuperates and rallies its powers in order to contemplate the subsequent brighter elements all the better. . . . In an aesthetic construction, light and shadow must succeed one another and be distributed in the whole. (I.258, 264–265)

> The universal source of aesthetic light is the richness of thoughts. <u>A thought is vital</u> insofar as it contains very many properties and parts. The multitude of parts of the whole constitutes the richness. . . . At any time a representation has certain <u>effects</u> in the soul, which arise from it, as from its own sources. We now assign an energy to the representation to the extent that *these effects* can be perceived by us. (I.268–269; underlining added)[17]

17. "Wir wollen diesen lobenswürdigen Mangel, zum Unterscheide [*sic*] von dem tadelhaften, den **aesthetischen Schatten** *(umbra æsthetica)* nennen. . . . Der aesthetische Schatten ist gleichsam ein Ort der Ruhe, wo der Geist sich wieder erholt, und seine Kräfte samlet [*sic*], um die folgenden hellern Theile desto besser zu betrachten. . . . Licht und Schatten müssen in einer aesthetischen Ausführung mit einander abwechseln, und in dem Gantzen vertheilt werden" (*Anfangsgründe*, I.258, 264–265). "Die algemeine [*sic*] Quelle des aesthetischen Lichts ist, der Reichthum der Gedanken. <u>Eine Gedanke ist lebhaft,</u> in so fern er sehr viele Merckmale und Theile enthält. . . . Die Menge der Theile eines Gantzen macht den Reichthum aus. . . . Eine Vorstellung hat jederzeit in der Seele gewisse Folgen, welche aus

A closely related version of this poetics and mental life of light and shadow, linked to a concept of how these "effects" and their vitality or "richness of thoughts" are produced, would ultimately emerge in the *Critique of Judgment*, especially in Kant's formulation of aesthetic ideas. But this would not happen before he saw the direct relation of aesthetic light and shadow to the succession procedure in the experience of the sublime.

Following, Aesthetic Light, Negative Poetics, and the Experience of the Sublime: Longinus, Addison, Lowth, Burke, Lessing—Kant

Clearly Meier figures prominently in the constellation of German Miltonism that Kant encountered. I will yet return to Meier's Miltonic examples and Kant's engagement with their exemplary originality. Yet, as I have said, Meier's thought achieved no integral relation to the experience of the sublime. For this ingredient, complementary to Meier's aesthetic light, Kant needed the expositions of other writers specifically on the sublime. Kant found these expositions in works both earlier and later than Meier's *Anfangsgründe*.[18]

For a connection between the experience of the sublime and the procedure of succession that closely resembles Kant's in §49 of the *Critique of Judgment*, I turn, first, to a source that has somehow not been noticed before in relation to Kant, though it appears in a collection of essays that was widely read, even virtually naturalized, in Kant's Germany. I refer to a particular dimension of a well-known passage in Addison's *Spectator* essays on *Paradise Lost* which stands, indeed, at the fountainhead of the entire German Miltonist line, beginning with Bodmer and Breitinger.[19] The passage occurs in Addison's *Spectator*

---

derselben, als aus ihrer Quelle, entstehen. In so ferne nun diese Folgen von uns angemerkt werden können, in so ferne schreiben wir der Vorstellung eine Kraft zu" (*Anfangsgründe*, I.268–269; underlining added).

18. How thickly interwoven, however, was the Miltonism of Kant's intellectual circles can be seen in Johann Gotthelf Lindner's *Kurzer Inbegrif der Aesthetik, Redekunst und Dichtkunst*, 2 vols. (Königsberg, 1771–72), I.226, 249, 255–256, where Lindner not only brings Milton and Lowth together but also, in the course of expounding the sublime, quotes Meier on Milton and cites Meier's extended examples from Books V and VI of *Paradise Lost*.

19. Kant mentions the *Spectator*, though not specifically the essays on *Paradise Lost*, on many occasions, among them in the *Observations* (*Obs*, 83).

338 (29 March 1712), where his subject is Milton's representation of creation (one of those subjects that Kant, in §49, considers the particular province of the poet of the sublime) as an "Instance" of "the Talent of writing in the great and sublime Manner" described by Longinus. If one preferred to read a translation of Addison's essay, it was already available in French in 1729 and was in this form published in Leipzig in 1753:[20]

> Among the Rules which he lays down for succeeding in the sublime way of writing, [Longinus] proposes to the Reader, that he should imitate the most celebrated Authors who have gone before him, and have been engaged in Works of the same Nature. . . . By this Means one great Genius often catches the Flame from another, and writes in his Spirit without copying servilely after him. There are a thousand shining Passages in *Virgil*, which have been lighted up by *Homer.*
>
> *Milton*, tho' his own natural Strength of Genius was capable of furnishing out a perfect Work, has doubtless very much raised and enobled his conceptions, by such an Imitation as that which *Longinus* recommended.

It is clear that Addison's linking of his exemplary modern genius, *Milton*, to his citation of Longinus's idea of the *following, not imitation*, which is to be found among poets who produce the experience of the sublime, stands in the line behind Meier's account of a Miltonic *nachfolgen* that is distinct from "aping" *(nachäffen)*. We saw this in Meier's identification of Milton as the model for the modern poet who "follows the ancients in a rational and manly way . . . as *Milton* has sometimes done in an irreproachable way."

Thus in Addison directly, and/or in his followers, Kant learned the

20. *Œuvres de Milton,* 4 vols., trans. N. F. Dupré de Saint Maur, Pierre de Mareuil, and Bernard Routh (Amsterdam, 1753). Word-for-word translations of the passages I cite from *Spectator* 338 appear in III.324–325. More than 150 pages of Addison's *Spectator* essays on *Paradise Lost* are included in the translation. The earlier edition is *Le Paradis Perdu de Milton . . . Avec les remarques de Mr. Addison,* 3 vols., trans. N. F. Dupré de Saint Maur (Paris, 1729). Schlapp, *Kants Lehre vom Genie,* p. 229n, suggests that to Kant (who usually refers to the "Spectateur" rather than the "Spectator"), and to Königsberg readers in general, the French translation was perhaps better known than the original.

centrality for Milton of the succession procedure that was without doubt already familiar to him in Longinus's text. For Kant this emphasis on the procedure of succession within Milton's poetry, encountered in a line of representations, provides the opening for his own larger theorizing of the sublime and of a sublime succession procedure that creates the condition of exemplary originality. This is to say that Addison's and Meier's succession procedure, followed out by them *in concreto* in Milton's poetry, is the core idea that Kant follows, specifically in relation to the experience of the sublime, and which, in §49 as a whole, he deepens in order to produce his own exemplary originality and his own idea of the role of analogy in philosophy:

> Genius, according to these presuppositions, is the exemplary originality of the natural endowments of an individual in the *free* employment of the cognitive faculties. On this showing, the product of a genius (in respect of so much in this product as is attributable to genius, and not to possible learning or academic instruction,) is an example, not for imitation (for that would mean the loss of the element of genius, and just the very soul of the work), but for succession [*Nachfolge*] by another genius—one whom it arouses to a sense of his own originality in putting freedom from the constraint of rules so into force in his art, that for art itself a new rule is won—which is what shows a talent to be exemplary. (*CJ*, §49, 5:318)[21]

What we must restore here to greater visibility, that Kant set at a distance, is the exemplary originality or archetype of Milton's poetry that forms and informs this sinuous line of following. This Miltonic exemplary originality informs the line of following for Kant (i.e., in the procedure of succession) even a great deal more than it does for Addison and Meier. To render this greater visibility, more information must be provided.

Especially because of its close parallelism to Kant's formulation, Addison's clear statement of the way a genius may catch the flame from another genius without servile imitation may seem to make Meier's comments superfluous for our discussion. Yet, for Kant, Meier was an

---

21. I have emended Meredith's translation of *Nachfolge*, "to be followed," to "for succession."

indispensable access point to Addison's ideas. In offering his own version of Addison's Miltonic succession procedure, even if without a clear realization of the importance of the sublime, Meier created perhaps the nearest equivalent that Kant knew to aesthetic ideas. And this near equivalence had another dimension, also with a unique Miltonic linkage, namely, the aesthetic light that both Meier and Kant saw at the heart of aesthetic ideas. We should note here the special connection with light that is already to be found embryonically in Longinus and in Addison's linkage of following (not imitation) with the experience of the sublime and with poetry, specifically with Milton's poetry. Remarkably enough, Longinus even directly quoted "Let there be light" from Genesis as a prime instance of the sublime. It is in this connection that, a few lines after the passage of *Spectator* 338 cited above, Addison remarks,

> The great Critick I have before mentioned, though an Heathen, has taken Notice of the sublime Manner in which the Law-giver of the *Jews* has described the Creation in the First Chapter of *Genesis;* and there are many other Passages in Scripture, which rise up to the same Majesty, where this subject is touched upon. *Milton* has shewn his Judgment very remarkably, in making use of these as were proper for his Poem.[22]

Addison proceeds to cite passage after passage from Book VII of *Paradise Lost* to show Milton's exemplary representation of these matters in describing creation. In fact, it was largely Addison's doing that Milton's way of following God's sublime light took on a special significance for writers as diverse as Burke, Lessing, Lowth, Meier, Herder, and, as we shall see, Kant himself. Precisely how this intertwining of the sublime and Miltonic light was understood among Kant's predecessors is the next element of aesthetic ideas that needs explaining.

I noted earlier that Kant saw that the kind of succession procedure that might achieve exemplary originality and freedom had to come from the sublime effect of an effectively endless series of representations of a certain kind. We can try to spell out what kind of representation this was, even though Kant leaves the matter veiled. Indeed, he

---

22. Cited from Joseph Addison and others, *The Spectator,* 4 vols., ed. Gregory Smith (London: Dent, Everyman's Library, 1979), 3.57–58.

even contradicts himself, saying—directly after giving examples of the experience of the sublime in the pyramids and St. Peter's—that "we must not point to the sublime in works of art." Between his examples of works of art and this puzzling disclaimer, he writes a reverse disclaimer (briefly seen earlier), which now seems to point *exclusively* to the experience of the sublime in works of art:

> At present I am not disposed to deal with the ground of this delight [of the sublime], connected as it is, with a representation in which we would least of all look for it—a representation, namely, that lets us see its own inadequacy, and consequently its subjective want of finality for our judgment in the estimation of magnitude. (*CJ*, 5:252)

In fact, in a variety of treatises that Kant knew intimately, he would have noted exactly what kind of carefully structured representation of the sublime this was.

In Robert Lowth's and Edmund Burke's famous accounts of the experience of the sublime, early available in German translation and both made parts of the German conversation on aesthetics by Mendelssohn, Kant found suggestive and even precise ideas for understanding the kind of representation that he was after.[23] As far as Kant's interests were concerned, the heart of Lowth's theory was the "continued negation" in the "action and energy of the mind itself" that is definitive of the experience of the sublime. Lowth directly associated this *energeia* with transmission and perception of light. Here is what Lowth means by "understanding" the sublime topos "Let there be light":

> The importance of the circumstance and the greatness of the idea (the human mind cannot well conceive a greater) is no less remarkable than the expressive brevity and simplicity of the language:—"And God said, Let there be light, and there was light." . . . The understanding . . .

---

23. Mendelssohn's review of Lowth's *De sacra poesi Hebraeorum* (1753) appeared in *Bibliothek der schönen Wissenschaften und der freyen Künste,* 1 (1757): 122–155 and 269–297; as mentioned earlier, his review of Burke's *A Philosophical Enquiry into the Origin of Our Ideas of the Sublime and Beautiful* (London, 1757), appeared in *Bibliothek der schönen Wissesnschaften und der freyen Künste* 3 [*sic*] (1758): 290–320. These reviews are detailed summaries with extensive paraphrases and translations.

comprehends the Divine power . . . perhaps most completely, when it is not attempted to be explained; the perception in that case is the more vivid, inasmuch as it seems to proceed from the proper action and energy of the mind itself.

What may appear to be left merely vague here is soon sharpened to a single cogent point with two sides to its coin. This point correlatively concerns, first, the mind's failure to comprehend (its continuance in vagueness with regard to) the object that induces the experience of the sublime. "The human mind," he says, "is absorbed, overwhelmed as it were in a boundless vortex, and studies in vain for an expedient to extricate itself. . . . While the imagination labours to comprehend what is beyond its powers, this very labour itself, and these ineffectual endeavours, sufficiently demonstrate the immensity and sublimity of the object." Yet the obverse of the same point, which is for Lowth the key to representation of the sublime, is that the experience of the sublime is the effect created by *continued negation within representation*. This occurs within the descriptive progression that is "carried on . . . towards infinity." It is this partially negative phenomenon that for Lowth defines "the proper action and energy of the mind itself" in following the progression:

Nothing of this kind is nobler or more majestic, than when a description is carried on by a kind of continued negation; when a number of great and sublime ideas are collected, which, on a comparison with the object, are found infinitely inferior and inadequate. Thus the boundaries [of the mind] are gradually extended on every side, and at length totally removed; the mind is insensibly [Kant will say supersensibly] led on towards infinity, and is struck with inexpressible admiration, with a pleasing awe, when it first finds itself expatiating in that immense expanse.[24]

24. Robert Lowth, *Lectures on the Sacred Poetry of the Hebrews*, 2 vols. (London, 1787; Latin, 1753; German translation 1758), facsimile, intro. Vincent Freimarck (Hildesheim: Olms, 1969), I.350–354. Samuel H. Monk, *The Sublime: A Study of Critical Theories in XVIII-Century England* (Ann Arbor: University of Michigan Press, 1960), p. 82, points to these pages and notes that they influenced Burke and Kant, but in describing Lowth's views Monk slides between "the greatness of the subject" and "the sublimity of the object" in a confusing way that he blames on Lowth's vagueness. Admittedly,

In Lowth's descriptions he comes close to explaining that what Meier and his German predecessors call "the liveliness of thoughts" in "aesthetic light" is the effect of following an infinite, oscillatory "continued negation" within representation. The infinite progression of self-negating representation, of light against darkness, is a powerful representation of the exchange of being and non-being. This produces the sublime "energy of the mind itself"—the light—that for Lowth is called forth, or created, in contemplating a sublime representation such as "And God said, Let there be light, and there was light." The oscillation in this example could not be more radical: all-pervading light after absolute darkness, material being itself created, lit up, by the invisible God who is eternally before and after all material being, all mere light. The reflux of energy or light from this effect is what Kant will call "a discharge all the more powerful" after the "check to the vital forces." In Lowth's terms the latter is the effect of the mind's being "insensibly led on towards infinity." As a result, the mind loses its defining "boundaries" or is "absorbed, overwhelmed as it were in a boundless vortex."

Lowth thus deserves more credit than he has been given for seeing the elements of the experience of the sublime that would be especially important to Kant. What remains confused in Lowth, however, is the process of the mind's following of the infinite progression, that is, of representations of continued negation. For this process Kant would provide sharp clarification in his accounts of aesthetic ideas. Yet after Meier and Lowth other developments in the constellation of German Miltonism—in which, as I say, Lowth was a kind of naturalized citizen—were also of great importance to Kant.

Four years after the publication of Lowth's analysis of the experience of the sublime, Burke (1757) applied the principles of a negative poetics (and its relation to light and darkness) specifically to Miltonic light and darkness and what he called Milton's "idea" that is "strictly and philosophically just":

---

there is vagueness, and some sliding as well, in Lowth, but there are also significant distinctions and rich meanings that Monk passes over, particularly when taken in conjunction with Lowth's chapters on Job and especially vis-à-vis Kant's articulation of principles of a negative poetics in the *Critique of Judgment* as well as his analysis, in the *Critique of Practical Reason*, of the role of a series of negations in attaining moral sublimity. I will discuss the latter in Chapter 5.

Darkness is more productive of sublime ideas than light. Our great
poet [Milton] was convinced of this; and . . . was entirely possessed with
the power of a well managed darkness. . . . And what is no less remark-
able, our author [Milton] had the secret of preserving this idea, even
when he seemed to depart the farthest from it, when he describes the
light and glory which flows from the divine presence; a light which by
its very excess is converted into a species of darkness,

Dark *with excessive* light *thy skirts appear.*

Here is an idea not only poetical in an high degree, but strictly and
philosophically just. Extreme light, by overcoming the organs of sight,
obliterates all objects, so as in its effect exactly to resemble dark-
ness. . . . Thus are two ideas as opposite as can be imagined reconciled
in the extremes of both; and both in spite of their opposite nature
brought to concur in producing the sublime.[25]

We saw in Chapter 1 that Lessing's defense of Milton in the *Laokoon*
(1766) is a harmonious counterpart of Lowth's and Burke's negative
poetics. Lessing is especially indebted to Burke's identification of that
poetics with Milton's sublime of light born of eclipse or darkness. And
we have seen the use that Lessing makes of the following passage from
Paradise Lost, Book III:

> Thus with the Year
> Seasons return, but not to me returns
> Day, or the sweet approach of Ev'n or Morn,
>
> . . . . .
>
> So much the rather thou Celestial Light
> Shine inward, and the mind through all her powers
> Irradiate, there plant eyes, all mist from thence
> Purge and disperse, that I may see and tell
> Of things invisible to mortal sight. (40–55)

25. Edmund Burke, *A Philosophical Enquiry into the Origin of Our Ideas of the Sublime
and Beautiful* (1757), ed. Adam Phillips (Oxford: Oxford University Press, 1990), sec.
XIV, pp. 73–74. The line cited is *Paradise Lost,* III.380, where, Phillips notes, Milton
has "bright" instead of "light."

Kant surely noticed that it was this passage that Herder, in the first volume of his enormously successful *Vom Geist der ebräischen Poesie* (1782), praised highly indeed, but not for its exemplification of a negative poetics.[26] Herder showed off his mastery of English by freshly translating the whole of Milton's invocation to light and his acceptance of blindness (III.1–55, sixty-four lines in the German) and claimed that the poetry of Job (continued in the Prophets and in Psalms) established the characteristic panegyric tone of modern European poetry that is achieved above all by Milton in *Paradise Lost*. While Herder identifies the stylistic element of Job's tone as *schweigende Erhabenheit* ("silent sublimity"), he shows no understanding of how a poetics of negation might be embodied in a characteristic structure of representation, let alone how it might be part of a sublime procedure of succession that is manifested in formal symmetry between the empirical and the *a priori*.[27] Yet, limited as his understanding of the Miltonic sublime

26. See the *Kritische Wälder* (1769), *SW*, III.1–188, for other aspects of Herder's disagreements with Lessing in the *Laokoon*.

27. Herder, *Vom Geist der ebräischen Poesie*, 2 vols. (Dessau, 1782–83), I.85–88; *SW*, XI.277: "To my knowledge there is only one tone of the panegyric in all the presently living European languages; and that is the tone of Job, of the Prophets and of Psalms. Milton has above all woven it into his immortal poem. [Meines Wißens giebts nur Einen Ton des Lobgesanges in allen jetzt lebenden Europäischen Sprachen; und der ist der Ton Hiobs, der Propheten und Psalmen. Milton hat ihn insonderheit in sein unsterblich Gedicht eingewebet.]" Herder's comment on a *schweigende Erhabenheit* (a "silent sublimity") is in *Vom Geist*, I.137; *SW*, XI.312. Kant would have felt that Herder misses the boat here with regard to Job and Milton both. Job for Herder represents "the true theodicy," "an epic representation of [the epic dimensions of] humanity" that is on that account a "theodicy of God" or a moral justification of God's action in creation *(die wahre Theodicee, an Epopee der Menschheit, Theodicee Gottes)* (*Vom Geist*, I.147–148; *SW*, XI.319). Yet Herder's parallelism between Job and Milton's poem, the greatest of all modern poetic theodicies, is thus implicitly further deepened. Kant could not have failed to note these connections when he came to write his "On the Miscarriage of All Philosophical Trials in Theodicy" (1791), in which, among other things, he argues that an authentic theodicy must be built around the representation of something *Seelenerheben*, soul-uplifting or sublime, which God has created as an *eingepflanzte Neigung* (an "implanted inclination") in the character of humanity (*AA*, 8:269, 271). Kant's extensive exemplification of such a theodicy is the book of Job (8:264–267). In his laudatory comments on Kant's essay, "Ueber Hrn. Kants Aufsatz, in Betref [*sic*] der Theodicee," *Berlinische Monatschrift* 2 (1791): 411–421, J. E. Biester called Kant's analysis "sublime . . . of godlike beauty" [*erhaben . . . göttlichschön*] and made explicit the hovering relevance of Milton's theodicy by quoting—in English—

was, Herder was of considerable, even dramatic, importance in Kant's experience of the constellation of German Miltonism.

~

Kant's grasp of Milton's poetry as a procedure of succession in the experience of the sublime was primarily inspired by the extended line or constellation that we have been tracing. Yet it is impossible to grasp the *tension* which gives definitive shape to that constellation without taking in Herder's role here. In fact, one of the striking ways in which Kant engaged in his decades-long sparring with Herder was via their views of Milton. To my knowledge this salient aspect of their relationship has not previously been described.

Kant's interest in Milton, even in specific texts of Milton, was to a great extent occasioned by Herder's writings. More than anyone else, Herder saw the emerging deep affinity between Kant and Milton. Moreover, he provoked its further deepening and then retrospectively

---

Paradise Lost, II.557–567, where Milton consigns "false Philosophie," i.e., the misconceived theologizing that Kant's essay comes to defeat, to the fallen angels in Hell (420–421). We might note incidentally that since Kant was here Biester's principal addressee and since Biester was in frequent contact with Kant at this time, the quotation is one more piece of evidence suggesting that Kant could read Milton in English.

The linkage of the poetry of Milton with that of Job became commonplace around the time of—and no doubt partly because of—the publication of William Smith's widely read translation and edition, *Dionysius Longinus on the Sublime* (2nd ed., London, 1742; first edition 1739), which both continues Addison's identification of the modern sublime with Milton and anticipates Lowth's extensive exposition of the sublime in Job (see pp. 118–119, 126–127, 155, et al.). Smith even gives examples of the sublime of Milton and of Job on facing pages. After Addison's essays on Milton's sublime and after Albert Schulten's great edition of Job, *Liber Jobi . . . Commentario Perpetuo* (Leiden, 1737)—used by Lowth and Herder and every other serious scholar —which frequently emphasized the sublimity of Job's imagery, the connection between Milton and Job became inevitable, that is, even without any awareness of Milton's direct emulations of Job. Barbara Kiefer Lewalski, *Milton's Brief Epic: The Genre, Meaning, and Art of Paradise Regained* (Providence: Brown University Press, 1966), records and explains the pervasive importance of Job for *Paradise Regained,* as does Mary Ann Radzinowicz, *Toward Samson Agonistes: The Growth of Milton's Mind* (Princeton: Princeton University Press, 1978), for *Samson Agonistes.* I have recently discussed some further linkages of this kind in "Milton's Joban Phoenix in *Samson Agonistes,*" *Early Modern Literary Studies* 11.5 (2005): 1–15.

(almost always disapprovingly) identified the principal terms of Kant's Milton-derived conceptions. Chief among these terms, for Herder, are

a. the negative representation that in Kant's view is a representation that represents "its own inadequacy" to represent and is thus built around loss or blindness;
b. the Miltonic sublime;
c. the endless progression;
d. a unique kind of *Nachahmung* (which Kant calls *Nachfolge*) which is not merely of examples but rather of the exemplarity of examples.

I will show how Kant's employments of these terms—employments that Herder highlights, indeed, in their relation to Milton—operate in crucial ways in Kant's sublime succession procedure. These operations can be laid out in the following propositions:

1. Empirically or heteronomously the mind follows an effectively endless progression of representations (*CJ*, 5:318).
2. Each representation in the progression that admits of succession, *Nachfolge* (as opposed to *Nachahmung*, imitation), represents "its own inadequacy" to represent (*CJ*, 5:252–253).
3. The act of following a progression of examples of this kind issues in the sublime effect (*CJ*, 5:255) and in exemplarity (*CJ*, 5:309, 318).
4. This heteronomous succession procedure discloses an isomorphic, autonomous ("self-maintaining") succession procedure that also issues in the sublime effect, hence in freedom and moral feeling (*CJ*, 5:313, 318). (I will later try to show that this disclosure is closely related, perhaps identical, to what Kant calls "the grand disclosure" of freedom and moral feeling in the *Critique of Practical Reason* [5:94].)
5. Parallel to this isomorphism of the heteronomous and the autonomous succession procedures, a transfer takes place, in the experience of the sublime (*CJ*, 5:266–267, 352–353), from the sensible (and the example, the individual) to the supersensible (and exemplarity, the universal). In both succession procedures reason "transfers" (a) that which "can . . . be . . . exhibited by

actions in the sensible world in accordance with the formal rule of a law of nature" into (b) the realm of the "supersensible" (*CPrR*, 5:71).

6. For Kant one principal, recurring succession procedure is to Milton's poetry of the sublime, from which Kant also derives the main principles of the sublime succession procedure.

These propositions require detailed substantiation and systematic unfolding, but even in this telegraphic form they can help us attend to the Miltonic link between Kant and Herder. This link is defined by mutual attention and by sharing in the same constellation of German Miltonism.

An intimate connection of this sort between Kant and Herder may seem surprising. Throughout the decades of Kant's mature writing, he regarded Herder as something very like his nemesis. Kant likely felt that Herder had only a fragmentary and superficial understanding of Kantian critical philosophy.[28] And it was surely obvious to Kant that whatever Herder did or did not understand of Kantian philosophy was frequently distorted by envy veering (as in the *Kalligone*) toward rage. Yet despite all this, Kant also knew that Herder was preternaturally gifted and that his criticisms of Kant's ideas sometimes identified heart-of-the-matter issues that needed to be addressed. Especially with regard to Kant's aesthetic and moral thought, Herder was immensely provocative. John H. Zammito has argued that "the origins of the *Third Critique* lie in Kant's bitter rivalry with Herder" and that "the *Third Critique* was almost a continuous attack on Herder," especially in the "Critique of Teleological Judgment," where Herder is the primary "unnamed antagonist."[29] Zammito's recoveries are undoubtedly of great significance. My concerns in this book center on the "Critique of Aesthetic Judgment," particularly the "Analytic of the Sublime," where Kant discloses the nexus of the experience of the sublime and of moral reason. I propose that Herder's articulation of an anti-Kantian

28. On Herder's misunderstanding of Kant's critical philosophy, see Rudolf Haym, *Herder nach seinem Leben und seinen Werken dargestellt*, 2 vols. (Berlin, 1877–85; reprinted Berlin: Aufbau Verlag, 1958), II.760. Even if later commentators are partially or even substantially correct in disagreeing with Haym on this point, Kant likely saw the matter as did Haym.

29. Zammito, *The Genesis of Kant's Critique of Judgment*, pp. 9–10.

Miltonism together with his anti-Kantian argument for the role of analogy in philosophy (the specific issue on which Kant leveled his most severe public criticism of Herder in 1784–85) had a transformative impact on Kant's moral philosophy. In my view this impact was manifest already in the *Groundwork of the Metaphysics of Morals* (1785) and was deepened in the second and third *Critiques*.[30] The highly specific kind of dynamic analogy that was Kant's slowly evolved response to Herder—namely, the Miltonic sublime succession to Miltonic light and shadow—became the keystone of Kant's theory of aesthetic ideas and a moral sublime. Zammito counsels that "we must assume Kant read almost everything Herder wrote."[31] This is valuable advice for locating the ways in which Herder provoked Kant's development of his own kind of Miltonic analogy, namely, in Kant's Miltonic procedure of succession within the experience of the sublime.

More than anyone else, Herder caught glimpses of Kant's deeply Miltonic affiliations, even if he did not fully understand, or even willfully distorted, their philosophical import. By virtue both of Herder's unsurpassed sensitivity to the historical continuities of culture as well as his picayune aggressiveness toward Kant, he provides brilliant flashes of a mirror image of Kant's Miltonism. It would be reasonable to suppose that Herder was especially vexed by these Kantian developments because they represented a debt to him that Kant had concealed. These developments were, after all, Kant's unacknowledged about-face from his derisive comments on Herderian analogy. Furthermore, Herder's superior knowledge of English and his life-long interest in Milton's poetry no doubt added to this vexation. For Herder, Kant's far more profound illumination of the structures of Milton's poetry—projected in the majestic structure of Kant's aesthetic and moral system—must have been something of a nightmare. Indeed, it must have given Herder a perverse kind of pleasure to describe Kant's Miltonism precisely in terms of the most nightmarish aspects of Mil-

30. On Herder's use of analogy and, among other things, some of his differences from Kant, see Hans Dietrich Irmscher, "Beobachtungen zur Funktion der Analogie im Denken Herders," *Deutsche Vierteljahrsschrift für Literaturwissenschaft und Geistesgeschichte* 55 (1981): 64–97, and "Der Vergleich im Denken Herders," in *Johann Gottfried Herder: Academic Disciplines and the Pursuit of Knowledge*, ed. Wulf Koepk (Columbia, South Carolina: Camden House, 1996), pp. 78–97.

31. Zammito, *The Genesis of Kant's Critique of Judgment*, pp. 36–37.

ton's poetry. Outrageous as it must seem, Herder equated what he considered to be Kant's pseudo-Miltonic philosophical system with the radically perverted mind of Milton's Satan.[32] In late writings Herder spells out his logic for these equations. Once we overcome incredulity by seeing how Herder concretely and extensively applies this logic in his later writings, the structure of the same logic becomes unmistakable—without any forcing of meanings—in his earlier anti-Kantian, pseudo-Miltonism as well.

Herder's Anti-Kantian Miltonism, Late

In the *Kalligone* (*SW,* XXII.245–246) Herder shows his keen awareness of the Miltonic affiliations of the Kantian sublime even while he reveals that he has missed completely (or suppressed) how a poetics of representational inadequacy is the transcendental component of that sublime, for Milton and Kant both. Herder quite faithfully quotes from the *Critique of Judgment,* §23:[33]

> In what we are wont to call sublime in nature there is such an absence of anything leading to particular objective principles and corresponding forms of nature, that it is rather in its chaos, or in its wildest and most irregular disorder and desolation, provided it gives signs of magnitude and power, that nature chiefly excites the ideas of the sublime. [from *CJ,* 5:246]

Herder uses this passage to claim that Kant has taken his idea of a sublime-inducing representation of Chaos from Milton but that Kant has perverted it, just as Satan's imagination does in *Paradise Lost:* "Only a spirit in *Milton's* Hell could . . . lay claim to feelings of the sublime [nur einem Geist in *Miltons* Hölle könnten Gefühle des Erhabenen

---

32. In effect, Herder restricted his vision of Kant's Miltonic sublime to something like Kant's early comments on "Milton's portrayal of the infernal kingdom" (*Obs,* 47) in the *Observations,* though even in that work Herder had to have noticed Kant's much broader appreciation of the Miltonic sublime in a wide variety of examples.

33. Herder uses the same text of the third *Critique* that would be followed in the Akademie Textausgabe of *Kants Werke* and that is the basis of Meredith's translation. In the passage cited here Herder gives "an der Natur" instead of Kant's "an ihr," "dieser" for Kant's "diesen," and here omits "regellosesten" after "wildesten," though he restores it in his response. I give Meredith's translation according to Kant's text.

dabei geziemen]" (*SW*, XXII.246). Milton's true sublime, according to Herder, abides no break in representational mode between negative (or emptied) imagining and positive imagining, between the desolateness of chaos and the beauty of heaven (or earth or sea). Each kind of representation is made possible by the other:

> No one ever saw the Chaos of Nature. Strictly speaking it is inconceivable, since Chaos and Nature cancel each other. Thus the poets describe it only as a transition to Order. We cannot intuit it otherwise. . . . He who would, with sublime feelings, brood endlessly over Chaos, without any creation emerging, must suffer from a fantasy that is itself *Tohu Vabohu:* [a fantasy] for nothing, against nothing, from nothing, sublime without purpose, purposelessly sublime. (*SW*, XXII.246)

> [Das Chaos der Natur sah niemand; absolut genommen ists ein Unbegriff: denn Chaos und Natur heben einander auf. Die Dichter schildern es also nur als einen Uebergang zur Ordnung. Nicht anders denkts unsre Seele. . . . Wer mit erhabnen Gefühlen ewig und immer über dem Chaos brütete, ohne daß je eine Schöpfung würde, dessen Phantasie wäre das *Thohu Vabohu* selbst, für nichts, wider nichts, aus nichts, Zwecklos-erhaben, erhaben-Zwecklos.]

Herder's characterization of Kant's perverse representational sublime as "sublime without purpose, purposelessly sublime" *(Zwecklos-erhaben, erhaben-Zwecklos)* is his caricature of Kant's adding (right after the passage that Herder cites) that "the concept of the sublime . . . gives on the whole no indication of anything final [*Zweckmäßiges*] in nature itself, but only in the possible *employment* of our intuitions of it in inducing a feeling in our own selves of a finality quite independent of nature [der Begriff des Erhabenen . . . überhaupt nichts Zweckmäßiges in der Natur selbst, sondern nur in dem möglichen Gebrauche ihrer Anschauungen, um eine von der Natur ganz unabhängige Zweckmäßigkeit in uns selbst fühlbar zu machen, anzeige]" (*CJ*, 5:246). Here and (as we will see shortly) elsewhere Herder claims that Kant's false sublime, "sublime without purpose, purposelessly sublime" *(Zwecklos-erhaben, erhaben-Zwecklos)*, is an impoverished response to Milton's sublime imagining of a *Paradies* that is *verlohren (lost)*, so that, Herder alleges, in Kant's imagining it becomes merely *los (negated, empty)*.

Herder anchors his claim against Kant's allegedly Satanic half-

Miltonism by paraphrasing Milton's much quoted description of Satan walking in Hell:

> He walkt with . . . uneasy steps
> Over the burning Marl, not like those steps
> On Heaven's Azure. (*Paradise Lost,* I.295–297)

Referring as well to Kant's key description of the experience of the sublime and its aesthetic idea that animate "the mind by opening out for it a prospect into a field of kindred representations stretching beyond its ken [das Gemüth zu beleben, indem sie ihm die Aussicht in ein unabsehliches Feld verwandter Vorstellungen eröffnet]" (*CJ,* 5:315; underlining added), Herder (now quoted more fully) writes:

> Only a spirit in *Milton's* Hell could . . . lay claim to feelings of the sublime by walking over smoking scenes of fire, or by wandering on through endlessly stretching fields [unabsehliche Felder], without one cheering image of the beautiful heavens. (*SW,* XXII.245–246)

> [Gehe man über rauchende Brandstäten [*sic*], oder durch unabseh-liche Felder . . . ohne Ein [*sic*] erfreuliches Bild . . . des schönen Himmels . . . nur einem Geist in *Miltons* Hölle könnten Gefühle des Erhabenen dabei geziemen.]

For Herder, Kant's Milton-derived "formless concepts" *(formlose Begriffe)* are only Kant's distortion, à la Satan, of Milton's poetics of a true sublime: they are "not concepts" *(keine Begriffe);* they are not from Milton but stem from a "poetry that has no being" or that does not exist *(bestandlose Dichtung).* Rather than recognizing Kant's grasp of a Miltonic poetics that discovers the experience of the sublime in representational ascesis, Herder sees in Kant "a desolation of the soul" *(eine Verödung der Seele)* (*SW,* XXII.246).[34]

34. Herder's importing of the phrase *unabsehliche Felder* into the above passage is an echo of the phrase that, we will see in Chapter 6, Kant used in his key definition and exemplification of aesthetic ideas in the Jupiter passage of §49. That usage stands in marked parallelism with the closely similar phrases of his comments on aesthetic ideas in Milton's poetry (that is, in his anthropology lecture and in the letter to Schiller that I will discuss in Chapter 6).

Herder makes clear that he is attacking Kant's basic formula *(Formel)* of the experience of the sublime, which he realizes Kant has rendered with the help of Milton's sublime. Herder quotes Kant's *Formel* as follows:

> Precisely because there is a striving in our imagination towards progress *ad infinitum*, while reason demands absolute totality, as a real idea, that same inability on the part of our faculty for the estimation of the magnitude of things of the world of sense to attain to this idea, is the awakening of a feeling of a supersensible faculty within us; and it is the use to which judgment naturally puts particular objects on behalf of this latter feeling, and not the object of sense, that is absolutely great, and every other contrasted employment small. Consequently it is the disposition of soul evoked by a particular representation engaging the attention of the reflective judgment, and not the Object, that is to be called sublime. (Herder, *SW,* XXII.249; Kant, *CJ,* 5:250)[35]

Herder asserts that Kant's *Formel* of the experience of the sublime is meaningless because it is the product of an impaired reason, one that, specifically, has *negated* human boundaries in a "fantasy without bounds," a *Grenzenlose Phantasie* [*sic*], and *lost* its normative gauge—*ihr Richtmaas verlohren:*

> Whose feeling does not tell him/her that the feeling of the sublime is *not* from supersensible nature, that it is *not* founded upon reason supersensibly accosting absolute totality? Only a fantasy without bounds will proceed towards infinity, only a reason that has lost its normative gauge dreams of an *absolute totality.* (*SW,* XXII.250)

35. "Eben darum, daß in unsrer Einbildungskraft ein Bestreben zum Fortschritt ins Unendliche, in unsrer Vernunft aber ein Aufspruch [Anspruch] auf *absolute Totalität* als [auf] einer reellen Idee liegt, ist selbst jene Unangemessenheit unsres Vermögens der Größenschätzung der Dinge der Sinnenwelt für diese Idee, die Erweckung des Gefühls eines übersinnlichen Vermögens in uns, und der Gebrauch, den die Urtheilskraft von gewissen Gegenständen zum Behuf des letzteren Gefühls natürlicher Weise macht; nicht aber der Gegenstand der Sinne ist schlechthin groß, gegen ihn [aber] jeder andre Gebrauch klein, mithin [ist] (die) Geistesstimmung [durch eine gewisse die reflectirende Urtheilskraft beschäftigende Vorstellung], nicht aber das Objekt ist erhaben zu nennen" (in brackets are the different readings in the *AA* text).

[Daß . . . das Gefühl des Erhabnen von einer übersinnlichen Natur sey; daß es auf einer *absoluten Totalität* [*sic*] übersinnlich-ansprechenden Vernunft beruhe, wem sagt da sein Gefühl nicht etwas Andres? Nur eine Grenzenlose Phantasie [*sic*] schreitet ins Unendliche, nur eine Vernunft, die ihr Richtmaas verlohren hat, träumt von einer *absoluten Totalität.*]

Herder clearly understands that Kant's *Formel* of the experience of the sublime is Miltonic. Herder, however, claims that it is the false sublime of Milton's Satan, which corresponds, he further alleges, to the false sublime that Longinus distinguished from the true sublime:

This sublime mysticism in the abyss of the infinite, this out- and forth-pouring abundance in the absolute Nothing and All, in vacancy and eternal vacancy, is just as un-Greek as it is superhuman. No Greek poet would know anything about immeasurable feelings being tran-scendent; Longinus has given this its proper name, Transcendence (υπερβατον), thus counting it with the false-sublime.

. . . The true sublime properly rests upon the entire progressive work of the poet. He who, in Milton . . . tarries in the foreground of his poem, in Hell, and cannot stop admiring Pandaemonium, the bridge over chaos, the figure of the fallen spirits, their sudden fall, their auda-cious resolutions, without becoming aware of the inferior status that this abyss is meant to take on in the whole artistic structure of the poet, how far is he from the true sublime of *Milton,* for whom this fearful-ness, wretchedness, gruesomeness only serve a cold and emboldened despair. (*SW,* XXII.274–275)

[Dieser erhabne Mysticismus im Abgrunde des Unendlichen, diese aus- und fortströmende Fülle im absoluten Nichts und All, im Lee-ren und immer Leeren, ist eben so ungriechisch als übermenschlich. Von einer Transcendenz unermeßlicher Gefühle weiß kein griechis-cher Dichter; *Longin* hat sie mit ihrem eigentlichen Namen *Transcen-denz,* (υπερβατον) zum falsch-Erhabnen gezählet.

. . . Ruht das wahre Erhabne eigentlich im ganzen progressiven Werk des Dichters. Wer sich, bei Milton . . . im Vorgrunde seines Gedichts, in der Hölle verweilt, und in ihr das Pandämonium, die Brücke über das Chaos, die Gestalt der gefallnen Geister, ihren Sturz, ihre kühnen

Entschlüße nicht gnug [*sic*] bewundern kann, ohne die untergeord-
nete Stelle zu bemerken, die dieser Abgrund im ganzen Kunstbau des
Dichters einnehmen soll, wie fern ist er vom wahren Erhabnen *Miltons,*
dem dies Fürchterliche, Traurige, Grausende einer kalten und kühnen
Verzweiflung nur dienet.]

Aside from Herder's significant distortion of Longinus, which he uses
to make Kantian *Transcendenz* sound like an abortion in nature, his te-
nacious work of obscuring Kant's *Formel* of the experience of the sub-
lime is here, too, focused on its Miltonic concepts. Herder senses that
Kant has penetrated exactly to the negativity of the Miltonic sublime,
in other words, to the momentarily world-emptying effect of following
an effectively endless progression of representations, each of which
shows its inadequacy to represent.[36] Indeed, Herder's detours at this
point even suggest that on some level he realizes that the true Miltonic
sublime (the *wahre Erhabne Miltons*) is really and authentically at the
heart of Kant's "moral sublime" *(Sittlich-Erhabne).* Herder knows and
indicates (*SW,* XXII.276–279) that Kant had delineated this moral sub-
limity both in the categorical imperative of the *Groundwork* and in the
coda of the *Critique of Practical Reason.* Before the philosophical power
of Kant's Miltonic sublime, Herder's response is principally, as I have
said, a kind of rage.

Yet this rage, I say again, is of very great interest, because it high-
lights the Miltonism of Kant's key concepts and fixes most particularly
on the connection—the Echo-effect, as Herder phrases it—between
the Miltonic imagination of negativity, the *los* (the *lost,* the *verlohren*),
and the moral imperative, the *sol(l),* which generate each other, back-
wards *(rückwärts).* This word game is Herder's would-be revenge on
what, in a different word game, he calls the "objectless, empty reason"
(objektlosen leeren Vernunft) of Kant's Miltonic sublime. With this and
similar phrases Herder implies that he has extended his unmasking
to the whole of Kant's critical philosophy, from the *Kritik der reinen*

36. My presentation of Herder's failure to acknowledge, or even understand,
Kant's sublime is at variance with the recent high estimate of Herder's "holistic," "cul-
tural" aesthetics and "optimistic" ethics, especially in comparison with Kant. See Ra-
chel Zuckert, "Awe or Envy: Herder contra Kant on the Sublime," *Journal of Aesthetics
and Art Criticism* 61 (2003): 217–232, for generally pro-Herderian comments on the
Kalligone, but including some "Objections" (224–227).

Vernunft onwards. These allegations reach their climax in Herder's explicit, pseudo-Miltonic, anti-Kantian allegory, which he sardonically titles *Das Erhabne im Wissen*—"the sublime in knowing"—and which is the "grave" *(Grab)* of "the true sublime" *(der wahren Erhabenheit)*:

> This [the true sublime] is not the "Transcendence" whose sublime bestows on us the Plenty of Nothing—clamorously powerless—empty schematisms and forms. As we approach its Pandaemonium we reach two "blind intuitions" [*blinde Anschauungen*] who themselves acknowledge that they see nothing and offer nothing, like the gatekeepers of a forecourt where suspended "phantasms" themselves acknowledge that they are "object-less shadows" and do not know how words are abstracted from objects conglomerated in them. Thereupon a sharp draft of "Paralogisms" carries us through windy cloisters of "Antinomies" into the empty hall of "empty reason," where after long anticipation the empty peal, "thou shalt," rings out from the absolute Nothing. The echo rings distinctly back the absolute Shall/Soll, backwards, in the word Emptied/Los, because that which was unconditionally bound by supersensible-absolute duty, may, through supersensible-absolute freedom be cut free unconditionally. Thus we leave the temple empty-handed, yet, by supersensible lawgivers and originators of nature, we are esteemed in the absolute Nothing from the fullness of power of objectless, empty reason. Arrogant game! Illusion of illusions! (*SW*, XXII.280–281)

> [Dieses ist nicht die "Transcendenz," deren Erhabnes uns mit Vielem Nichts giebt, geräuschvoll-ohnmächtig, leere Schemate [*sic*] und Formen. Nahen wir uns ihrem Pandämonium, so gelangen wir durch zwei "blinde Anschauungen," die selbst bekennen, daß sie nichts sehen und nichts geben, als durch Hüterinnen der Pforte in einem Vorhof, wo aufgehangene "Schattentafeln" selbst bekennen, daß sie "Objektlose Schemen" sind und nicht wissen, wie von Objekten abgezogne Worte auf sie zusammenflogen. Ein scharfer Zugwind von "Paralogismen" führt uns sodann durch windige Kreuzgänge von "Antinomieen" in die leere Halle der "leeren Vernunft," wo nach langer Erwartung der leere Schall, "du sollst," aus dem absoluten Nichts ertönet. Die Echo tönt das absolute "Soll" rückwärts sehr vernehmlich im Worte "Los" wieder; denn was durch übersinnlich-absolute Pflicht Bedingungslos gebun-

den ward, kann durch übersinnlich-absolute Freiheit Bedingungslos gelöset werden. Also gehen wir leer aus dem Tempel, aber zu übersinnlichen Gesetzgebern und Naturschöpfern im absoluten Nichts aus Vollmacht der objektlosen leeren Vernunft gewürdet [*sic*]. Stolzes Spiel! Traum der Träume!]

Herder's phantasmagoric allegory is his anti-Kantian version of Milton's allegory of Satan's offspring, Hell's gatekeepers, Sin and Death (*Paradise Lost,* II). Herder plays wittily on a Satanic emptiness, blankness, blindness—"blind intuitions," "phantasms," "object-less shadows" *(blinde Anschauungen, Schattentafeln, Objektlose Schemen)*—that he claims is the heart of Kant's critical philosophy. The "sharp draft of 'Paralogisms'" *(scharfer Zugwind von "Paralogismen")* that Herder says carries Kant aloft "into the empty hall of 'empty reason'" *(in die leere Halle der "leeren Vernunft")* is a clever citation of Milton's brilliant invention of a "strong rebuff of some tumultuous cloud" that by "ill chance" raises Satan "miles aloft" when he is falling helplessly in his journey through Chaos (*Paradise Lost,* II.935–938). Because Herder understood Kant either only partially or all too well, he works in these ways to deflect the reader from the creative poetics of blindness that Kant—following Burke, Lessing, and others—realized is for Milton the heart of a redeemed or creative imagination. (In his antagonism to Kant, Herder even disregards his own strong views of the limitations of visualism in poetry, which is one of his themes in the climactic, last pages of the fourth of the *Kritische Wälder.*)[37] In these ways Herder equates Kant with Satan.

Yet from Kant's own Miltonic point of view, it is Herder's reason and imagination that closely resemble those of Milton's Satan. Kant likely felt that, at similar crucial moments, Satan and Herder both miss, or refuse, the extra turns of the screw that can change a special kind of blindness into moral vision. Milton's fully realized poetics of blindness became the key to Kant's moral sublime. As in Kant's Miltonic concept of aesthetic ideas, Kant's Miltonic moral sublime is a function of the unconditioned negativity produced in the succession procedure. This

---

37. In these same pages Herder proposes his own ideas on the importance of "succession," and even of "dissolutions," in poetry. See *Selected Writings on Aesthetics: Johann Gottfried Herder,* trans. and ed. Gregory Moore (Princeton: Princeton University Press, 2006), pp. 286–287.

is a succession to an endless progression of representational negativity that is sustained in each representation within the progression. In this Miltonic picture Kant discloses the mind's experience of the sublime that is the unconditioned, free source of moral feeling and the categorical imperative. Herder acknowledges in his own distorted way that the world of Miltonic *"Los"* is indeed the profound source of the Kantian "absolute '*Soll*' ['shall']," that is, in Herder's paraphrase, of that which in Kant's thought is "unconditionally bound by supersensible-absolute duty . . . through supersensible-absolute freedom" *(übersinnlich-absolute Pflicht Bedingungslos gebunden . . . durch übersinnlich-absolute Freiheit)*. Despite himself, Herder thus brilliantly highlights the firm connection for Milton and Kant between *los* and *soll*.

Kant gave Herder, Miltonically, as good as he got, so much so that Kant no doubt even egged Herder on to some of his excesses. Even in Kant's 1785 reviews of Herder's *Ideen zur Philosophie der Geschichte der Menschheit*, there is, I suggest, evidence that Miltonism and counter-Miltonism were a battlefield on which Kant and Herder frequently conducted their skirmishes. Kant's barbs are more subtle than Herder's, so that we need to summon up the passage in *Paradise Lost* that Kant was using to see what Herder no doubt saw and long remembered from Kant. This is the very same Miltonic scene of "the gate-keepers [i.e., Sin and Death] of a forecourt [i.e., Chaos]" that, as we have seen, Herder turned against Kant in the *Kalligone*. In Book II Milton represents the monstrousness of Satan's self-replicating mind in the allegory of Satan's and Death's incest with the primordial womb of Sin—a figure from whom all the Host of Heaven "recoil'd." Kant invokes this image, in its monstrousness, to criticize Herder. Here is Milton's unforgettable allegory:

> till on the left side op'ning wide,
> Likest to thee in shape and count'nance bright,
> Then shining heav'nly fair, a Goddess arm'd
> Out of thy head I sprung; amazement seiz'd
> All th' Host of Heav'n; back they recoil'd afraid
> At first, and call'd me *Sin*, and for a Sign
> Portentous held me; but familiar grown,
> I pleas'd, and with attractive graces won
> The most averse, thee chiefly, who full oft
> Thyself in me thy perfect image viewing

Becam'st enamor'd, and such joy thou took'st
With me in secret, that my <u>womb</u> conceiv'd
A growing burden. Meanwhile War arose,
And fields were fought in Heav'n; wherein remain'd
(For what could else) to our Almighty Foe
Clear Victory, to our part loss and rout
Through all the Empyrean: down they fell
Driv'n headlong from the Pitch of Heaven, down
Into this Deep, and in the general fall
I also; at which time this powerful Key
Into my hand was giv'n, with charge to keep
These Gates for ever shut, which none can pass
Without my op'ning. Pensive here I sat
Alone, but long I sat not, till my <u>womb</u>
Pregnant by thee, and now excessive grown
Prodigious motion felt and rueful throes.
At last this odious offspring whom thou seest
Thine own begotten, breaking violent way
Tore through my entrails, that with fear and pain
Distorted, all my nether shape thus grew
Transform'd: but he my inbred enemy
Forth issu'd, brandishing his fatal Dart
Made to destroy: I fled, and cri'd out *Death;*
Hell trembl'd at the hideous Name, and sigh'd
From all her Caves, and back resounded *Death.*
I fled, but he pursu'd (though more, it seems,
Inflam'd with lust than rage) and swifter far,
Mee overtook his mother all dismay'd,
And in embraces forcible and foul
Ingend'ring with me, of that rape begot
These yelling <u>Monsters</u> that with ceasless cry
Surround me, as thou saw'st, hourly conceiv'd
And hourly born, with sorrow infinite
To me, for when they list, into the <u>womb</u>
That bred them they return, and howl and gnaw
My Bowels, thir repast; then bursting forth
Afresh with conscious terrors vex me round,
That rest or intermission none I find. (*Paradise Lost,* II.755–
802; underlining added)

I suggest that this allegory stands subtly but directly behind the following passage of Kant's first 1785 review of Herder's *Ideen:*

> If the species are established in succession according to their likeness . . . there is only one relationship among them, but this would lead to ideas which are so <u>monstrous</u> that reason <u>recoils</u> from them: either one species would have emerged out of the other and all out of one single original species, or perhaps all would have emerged out of a single primordial <u>womb.</u> (p. 38; underlining added)

This is the passage that Kant repeats in his reply to Reinhold's attack on his review, just after saying "nor can analogy fill this immense void between the contingent and the necessary" (p. 41).[38] To make his subtle assault on Herder even more unmistakable, Kant, in addition, may be summoning the following apparently innocuous image of "an uncharted waste"— "*unbefahrene Wüste*"—that is vividly reminiscent of Milton's Satan to describe (with apparent and/or real generosity) Herder's journey as a thinker:

> In an uncharted waste a thinker, like a traveler, must be free to choose his route at discretion. We should attend to how he succeeds; and if, after he has reached his goal, he returns home again to the domicile of reason, safe and sound, at the correct hour, he can even anticipate having successors. (*AA,* 8:64)[39]

38. Because Kant's language here may also seem to allude to Satan's journey across chaos, it is worth pointing out that Kant's saying "nor can analogy fill this immense void between the contingent and the necessary [auch kann keine Analogie diese unermeßliche Kluft zwischen dem Zufälligen und Nothwendigen ausfüllen]" (*AA,* 8:57) is only in immediate response to K. L. Reinhold's attack on Kant's review ("Schreiben des Pfarrers . . . Ueber eine Recension von Herders Ideen zur Philosophie der Geschichte der Menschheit," *Der Teutsche Merkur* 19 [1785]: 148–174), in which Reinhold writes that Herder "had probably long perceived the immense chasm that separates our metaphysics from history, our speculation from our experiences [Er hatte wohl schon lange die ungeheure Kluft wahrgenommen, die unsre Metaphysik von der Geschichte, unsre Spekulation von unsern Erfahrungen trennt]" (159).

39. Kant, "Reviews of Herder's *Ideas for a Philosophy of the History of Mankind,*" trans. Robert E. Anchor in Immanuel Kant, *On History,* ed. Lewis White Beck (Indianapolis: Bobbs-Merrill, 1963), p. 49. I have given *waste* for *Wüste,* where Anchor gives *desert.*

[In einer unbefahrenen Wüste muß einem Denker gleich Reisenden frei stehen, seinen Weg nach Gutdünken zu wählen; man muß abwarten, wie es ihm gelingt, und ob er, nachdem er sein Ziel erreicht hat, wohlbehalten wieder zu Hause, d. i. im Sitze der Vernunft, zur rechten Zeit eintreffe und sich also auch Nachfolger versprechen könne.]

Having been accused by Herder of being himself the Satan of philosophy, Kant may be repaying Herder in kind by recalling (albeit gently, almost hopefully), and applying to Herder, the close of Book II of *Paradise Lost,* where Satan, having departed from Sin and Death, crosses Chaos—"in the emptier waste" (1045)—to reach his goal, Eden, so that he can then return to Hell and lead his followers, the legions of fallen angels. Herder may well have keenly felt, and later remembered, this Miltonic barb when he returned to these same Miltonic passages in order to revenge himself on Kant.[40]

Herder's Anti-Kantian Miltonism, Early

In the *Kalligone* Herder is responding to Kant's Miltonism well after the publication of the *Groundwork* and the second and third *Critiques.* To understand Kant's Miltonism in these works, it is important to realize that even before they were published Herder was attacking what he saw as Kant's undercurrent use of an unearned Miltonism. Presumably this usage was known to Herder from reports of Kant's lectures or perhaps from remarks that are now lost to us. What is certain, however, is that, at the latest, by the end of the 1770s Kant was fully aware of the attack on his Miltonism that Herder openly mounted in all three versions of *Vom Erkennen und Empfinden,* that is, of 1774, 1775, and 1778.

40. Marshall Grossman has suggested to me that Kant is here alluding to Jesus (who has overcome Satan) in the closing verses of *Paradise Regained:* "hee unobserv'd / Home to his Mother's house private return'd." Following Grossman's suggestion we can see that by putting into play the allusion to *Paradise Regained* in this passage Kant may be opening two equal possibilities in the complexity of his feelings of both disdain and admiration for Herder. Either, as Grossman suggests, Kant thinks of himself as "the Jesus whom Herder has confused with Satan" or Kant is proposing that a somewhat confused "Herder-Jesus [is] unaware of his own identity." The latter possibility implies Herder's inevitable acknowledgment of the truth of Kant's views, when, as Kant says, "He [Herder] returns home to the domicile of reason."

Thus even if the sequence of give-and-take between Herder and Kant on these matters may never be fully known, we need to correct our perspective on the principal chronology as far as is now possible. In his introduction to Herder's "Metakritik zur Kritik der reinen Vernunft" (1799) and *Kalligone* (1800), Suphan noted Herder's April 1799 letter to Johann Wilhelm Ludwig Gleim, in which he mentions that his metacritique of Kant had been "contemplated" *(gedacht)* twenty years earlier (*SW,* XXI.v).[41] In fact, it had been more than just contemplated. Herder's *Vom Erkennen und Empfinden* already offers a prototype of his anti-Kantian, pseudo-Miltonic allegory in the *Kalligone.* As part of an unmistakable attack on Kantian abstraction and even on the Kantian sublime, all three versions contain Herder's invocation of Milton's representation of Satan building Pandaemonium and a bridge over Chaos (*SW,* VIII.219, 259, 311). In the 1775 version the attack is most explicit and most aggressive, though the 1778 version is not far behind. In 1775 Herder uses his analogy of Milton's Satan, building Pandaemonium and/or a bridge over Chaos, to describe the speculative philosopher who is either a Kantian disciple or Kant himself, probably including derisive allusions to Kant's well-known weak physical constitution and hypochondria.[42] One can assume that Kant responded to this passage with some degree of emotional upset, but I suggest that what was ultimately of far greater interest to him, as an intellectual provocation or occasion, was Herder's use of an alleged Miltonic concept to describe Kantian speculative philosophy. Here it is difficult to say whether Herder based his Miltonic attack only on the interest in Milton that Kant had shown in his *Observations on the Feeling of the Beautiful and Sublime* (1764). But what seems to be beyond doubt is that, at very least in part, Kant was moved to deepen the Miltonic dimensions of his thought in response to Herder's pseudo-Miltonic provocations in *Vom Erkennen und Empfinden.*

We see a sample of these provocations in the following extended parallelism between the *sublime Narrheit* (the "sublime folly" or madness) of the constructions of *Miltons Teufel* ("*Milton's Devil,*" Satan) and

41. Gleim's alignment with tendencies antipathetic to Kant is specified by Kant in the *Blomberg Logik, AA,* 24.1:192.

42. On Kant's well known early and late hypochondria, even described in mocking detail by Hamann to Herder in at least one letter of 1783, see Manfred Kuehn, *Kant: A Biography* (Cambridge: Cambridge University Press, 2001), pp. 151, 238–239.

the Kant-like philosopher whose endless abstractions (as Herder views them) evoke only a false or mad sublime:

> Every power of passion or strength, without understanding or good-ness of heart, is adventurism or depravity, sublime folly in both cases. Milton's devil built Pandaemonium and even a bridge over Chaos; with the building of both he became neither happier nor greater. The more the human condition becomes purer and more perfect the more is it inclined to deride or despise that adventurism.
>
> Must it not be an almost similar case with the speculators whose sen-sations are feeble? They are weaklings either by nature or by practice. If they received (from nature) weak organs, weak stimuli—so it was their end to serve holy Abstraction. . . . Or they maimed themselves, continu-ously weakening their sensations through abstraction; dividing whole objects until they finally remain incapable of any whole sensations: the powers of feeling which have lain dormant so long would actually become extinct. In either case one sees that we are speaking here of sick people, by whom there is no way to draw conclusions concerning whole minds of healthy humanity. A weak brain that is no longer capa-ble of contemplating because of speculation, or to believe and act be-cause of Abstraction, spins cobwebs instead of the silk of truth.
>
> Every genuine sensation provides the mind with nourishment, en-ergy, drive. It penetrates intimately into the object and becomes object, that is, it has become sensible of the object. The speculator whose sen-sation is empty and weak is an objectless and deedless head, a scientist, a word-counter; but is he any longer a whole, healthy human being?
>
> Let us assume for a moment that wretched speculation goes by the name philosophy; poor philosophy! mournful wisdom! It is debarred, says Shaftesbury, from sensation and enjoyment of nature; it sits in prison and famishes. Cut off from sensation, what is knowledge? With-out matter what does knowledge know? . . .
>
> Thus abstraction of this sort is an accursed idol! Enemy of God and of humankind! It puts asunder what God has joined, takes from hu-manity the strength and joy of its noblest activity, destroys all objects of healthful nature and turns them into shadow and delusions. (*SW,* VIII.311–312)[43]

43. "Alle Stärke von Leidenschaft und Kraft, ohne Verstand und Güte, ist Eben-theuer [*sic*] oder Laster, in beidem Falle sublime Narrheit. Miltons Teufel baute das

Later, in the *Kalligone,* we see Herder's open, no-holds-barred, anti-Kantian, pseudo-Miltonism after (as we shall see) Kant has made powerful use of his Miltonic succession procedure in the *Groundwork of the Metaphysics of Morals,* the *Critique of Practical Reason,* and the *Critique of Judgment.* But it is in many ways far more interesting to see Herder's suggestions of Kant's Miltonism already in *Vom Erkennen und Empfinden,* that is, in the period when Kant was gestating his major ethical writings and was, I have suggested, perhaps even agitated by Herder to deepen the Miltonism that would become indispensable to Kantian moral reason.

Already at the end of the 1770s Kant responded to *Vom Erkennen und Empfinden* in ways that make clear both that he understood himself to be Herder's principal target and that Herder was attacking him—in

---

Pandämonium und gar eine Brücke übers Chaos; er ward mit beidem weder glücklicher noch größer. Je reiner und vollkommener auch die Menschliche Verfaßung würde, desto lieber würde sie jene Abentheuerer entbehren, sie verlachen oder verachten—

Sollte es mit den Spekulanten von schwacher Empfindung nicht beinahe ein ähnlicher Fall seyn? Sie sind Schwächlinge entweder durch Natur oder durch Uebung. Bekamen sie von jener schwache Organe, schwache Reize. . . . So waren sie eben damit bestimmt, der heiligen Abstraktion zu dienen. . . . Oder sie verstümmelten sich selbst, indem sie durch Abstraktion unaufhörlich Empfindungen schwächten, ganze Gegenstände zertheilten, bis sie zuletzt keiner ganzen Empfindungen mehr fähig blieben: die so lange schlummernden Kräfte gingen würklich unter. In beiden Fällen, sieht man, daß von Kranken die Rede sei, von denen auf den ganzen Verstand der gesunden Menschheit nicht geschloßen werde. Ein schwaches Hirn, das für lauter Spekulation nicht mehr anzuschauen, für lauter Abstraktion nicht mehr zu glauben und zu thun vermag, webt Spinnwebe statt Seide der Wahrheit.

Jede richtige Empfindung gibt dem Verstande Nahrung, Energie, Thatkraft. Innig dringt er in die Sache hinein und wird Sache, das ist, er hat die Sache empfunden. Der Spekulator mit leerer schwacher Empfindung ist Sachen- und Thatloser Kopf, Wißenschaftler, Wortzähler; ist er aber ganzer gesunder Mensch mehr?

Laßet uns einen Augenblick setzen, daß die traurige Spekulation Philosophie heiße; arme Philosophie! traurige Weisheit! Sie ist, sagt Shaftesburi, von Empfindung und Genuße der Natur ausgeschloßen, sitzt in [*sic*] Gefängniß und darbet. Von der Empfindung getrennt, was ist Erkenntniß? Ohne Materie was erkennet sie? . . .

Unseliges Idol also, Abstraktion dieser Art! Feindin Gottes und der Menschen! Sie trennt, was Gott verband, nimmt der Menschheit am edelsten Geschäft Kraft und Freude, zerstöret alle Gegenstände der gesunden Natur und macht sie zu Schatten und Schemen." (*SW,* VIII.311–312)

what Herder considered to be Miltonic ways—for Kant's alleged betrayal of a true Miltonism. Considering how pointed Kant's responses to Herder are, we may guess that he already had grounds for anticipating the barrages that Herder would level at him in the *Kalligone*. But the verbal similarities, on these matters, between *Vom Erkennen und Empfinden* and the *Kalligone* not only indicate a strong continuity in Herder's views of these matters but also suggest that Kant was steeped in these Miltonic issues (that is, those raised by Herder) as early as the 1770s.[44]

Herder's Anti-Kantian Miltonism and the Issue of Analogy

In *Vom Erkennen und Empfinden* the philosophical issue between Herder and Kant was, to be sure, the possible role of *sensation (Empfinden)* in *cognition (Erkennen)*. With regard to the *a priori* knowing that Kant was trying to isolate, Herder was well aware that he and Kant were directly at loggerheads. Of all the arguments that Herder offers for the indispensability of sensation for cognition, the one that most gripped Kant's attention was Herder's contention that it was impossible to think about what we know, to do philosophy, without recourse to analogy. For Herder, analogy is the bridge between sensation and cogni-

---

44. With an eye to parallelisms in details and ideas, I cite, fragmentarily, Herder from *Vom Erkennen und Empfinden* (VIII.311–312) and then (/), in italics, Herder from the *Kalligone* (XXII.245–246, 274–281): "sublime Narrheit. Miltons Teufel baute das Pandämonium und gar eine Brücke übers Chaos" / "*nur einem Geist in* Miltons *Hölle könnten Gefühle des Erhabenen dabei geziemen . . . Wer sich, bei Milton . . . im Vorgrunde seines Gedichts, in der Hölle verweilt, und in ihr das Pandämonium, die Brücke über das Chaos . . . Wer mit erhabnen Gefühlen ewig und immer über dem Chaos brütete, ohne daß je eine Schöpfung würde, dessen Phantasie wäre das* Thohu Vabohu *selbst, für nichts, wider nichts, aus nichts, Zwecklos-erhaben, erhaben-Zwecklos . . . wie fern ist er vom wahren Erhabnen* Miltons"; "die Menschliche Verfaßung . . . von Kranken die Rede sei . . ." / "*eine Grenzenlose Phantasie schreitet ins Unendliche, . . . eine Vernunft, die ihr Richtmaas verlohren hat*"; "leerer schwacher Empfindung" / "*Leeren und immer Leeren . . . die leere Halle der 'leeren Vernunft' . . . der leere Schall, 'du sollst,' aus dem absoluten Nichts ertönet . . . leer aus dem Tempel*"; "Sachen- und Thatloser Kopf" / "*aus Vollmacht der objektlosen leeren Vernunft*"; "die traurige Spekulation Philosophie heiße; arme Philosophie! traurige Weisheit" / "*dies Fürchterliche, Traurige, Grausende einer kalten und kühnen Verzweiflung . . . dienet*"; "nimmt der Menschheit am edelsten Geschäft Kraft und Freude" / "*übermenschlich . . . eine Verödung der Seele*"; "Schatten und Schemen" / "*Schattentaffeln . . . Objektlose Schemen.*"

tion, between our "inner and outer worlds." Directly referring to both the *Critique of Practical Reason* and the *Critique of Judgment*, a late letter in Herder's *Briefe zu* [*sic*] *Beförderung der Humanität* reflects (in benign mood) on what the role of analogy actually could be according to Kant's critical philosophy:

> *How are the inner and outer world connected?* Can we penetrate no further into the latter than that we presuppose an unknown *x* as a substratum? Or are there in outward appearances themselves various *degrees and orders of relations and analogies to us,* which, more and more alike, offer higher equations and rules until finally the *x* is left that is as dispensable as it is inaccessible to our knowing [?] (*SW,* XVIII.328)

> [*Wie hängt die äußere und innere Welt zusammen?* können wir in jener nicht weiter dringen, als daß wir ein unbekanntes x als ein Substratum voraussetzen? oder gibt es in den Erscheinungen selbst mancherlei *Grade und Ordnungen der Verhältniße und Analogieen zu uns,* die immer und immer einerlei, nur höhere Gleichungen und Regeln geben, bis endlich das unserm Wißen so entbehrliche, als unzugängliche x zurückbleibt (?)]

In *Vom Erkennen und Empfinden* Herder (in a malign mood) was sure that Kant had denied himself all significant access to analogy and therefore to the bridging of his inner and outer worlds. Throughout large portions of *Vom Erkennen und Empfinden,* Kant is one of Herder's silent, unnamed opponents:

> For the most part it was a *single* new image, a *single* analogy, a *single* striking metaphor that gave birth to the greatest and boldest theories. The philosophers who declaim against figurative language and themselves serve nothing but old, often uncomprehended figurative idols are at least in great contradiction with themselves. . . . What we know we know only through analogy. . . .
>
> I cannot imagine at all how my soul should spin something out of itself and dream a world out of itself, indeed I cannot even imagine how it should sense something outside itself of which there exists no analogon in it and its body. If there were in this body no light, no sound, then we would have no sensation in the whole wide world of

anything that was sound and light; and if there were nothing analogous to sound, to light, in the soul itself, or around it, then any concept of this would still be impossible. . . . The philosophy-of-preprinted-forms [*Formular-Philosophie*] which unwinds everything out of itself, from out of the monad's inner force of representation, admittedly has no need of all this, since it has everything in itself; but I do not know how it got there, and this philosophy itself does not know. . . .

Our cognition is therefore, although admittedly it *is* the deepest self *in us,* not as autonomous, voluntarily choosing, and unbound as is believed. . . . [Those are] liars or enervated people who boast of having nothing but pure fundamental principles and curse inclinations, from which alone true fundamental principles arise![45]

Herder's suggestions concerning the shape of Kant's Miltonism, which, as we have seen, he contends is a distortion of "Milton's true sublime" (*SW,* XXII.274–276), take on Kantian significance because they suggest that Kant is himself (poorly) using analogy as part of his philosophical method. Whether or not Kant directly acknowledged the justice of this suggestion, soon after criticizing Herder on the issue of analogy in the 1785 reviews, he found a way of concurring with Herder about the need for philosophy to use something like analogy, even if not what Herder meant by analogy. Moreover, far from denying Herder's allegations that he had recourse to a kind of Miltonism in his philosophizing, Kant clarified and deepened his Miltonism and assigned it—in the form of the Miltonic sublime succession procedure—a central place in his moral philosophy.

Herder, Klopstock, and Analogy

In *Vom Erkennen und Empfinden* Herder does not evaluate Milton's poetry on its own terms but merely invokes it against Kant for hostile purposes. Herder here makes a substantive claim for the significance of "the sublime Klopstock" and his use of "analogy" as a way of fusing *Erkennen* with *Empfinden,* cognition with sensation. Klopstock's poetry, he says, represents "the basic straits from which a human being grows

45. Herder, *Philosophical Writings,* trans. and ed. Michael N. Forster (Cambridge: Cambridge University Press, 2002), pp. 188, 208, 212–213.

. . . the most secret waves and oscillations of a pure, heavenly soul."[46]
As is well known, Herder heaped extravagant praise on Klopstock
over many decades. Herder's letter 102 of his *Briefe zu Beförderung der
Humanität* (published in 1796 but no doubt written much earlier; *SW,*
XVIII.118–119) is particularly helpful for understanding Kant's deep-
ening of his Miltonism in response to Herder.[47] Very likely as part of an
effort to stave off Kant's criticism of Herder's reductive conflation of
Klopstock's poetry with Milton's, Herder directly contrasts Milton's
law- or reason-centered muse with Klopstock's muse of the heart and
sentiments. Yet even and especially here, Herder's comparison of Mil-
ton and Klopstock, as well as his implicit preference for the alleg-
edly superior stage of spiritual development represented by Klopstock,
points to the vast differences between Herder's and Kant's Miltonisms.
Herder writes: "They stand opposite each other like Moses and Christ,
like the Old and New Testament [Wie Moses und Christus, wie das alte
und neue Testament stehen sie gegenüber]." Milton's *Paradise Lost* is
a "carefully thought out edifice" *(durchdachtes Gebäude).* Klopstock's
Messias is a "magical painting that floats in the most delicate human
sensations and scenes of humanity, from Gethsemane out over earth
and heavens. Milton's muse is masculine, like his iamb; the more deli-
cate muse of Klopstock streams through the midpoint of her world,
our complete soul, in stories, elegies, and hymns [ein Zauberge-
mählde, das in den zartesten Menschenempfindungen und Men-
schenscenen von Gethsemane aus über Erd' und Himmel schwebet.
Die Muse Miltons ist eine männliche Muse, wie sein Jambus; die Muse
Klopstocks eine zärtere Muse, die in Erzählungen, Elegieen und
Hymnen unsre ganze Seele, den Mittelpunkt ihrer Welt durch-
strömet]" (*SW,* XVIII.118).[48] Herder is generous to Milton, but he de-

46. Ibid., pp. 119, 189, 200.

47. See Frederick Henry Adler, *Herder and Klopstock: A Comparative Study* (New
York: Stechert, 1914), for the numerous ways in which Herder championed Klop-
stock's muse.

48. Among other things that indicate the pointedly anti-Kantian nature of
Herder's comparison of Milton's muse with Klopstock's is Herder's sideswipe, in
league with his remarks both in *Vom Erkennen und Empfinden* (VIII.190, 233) and the
Kalligone (XXII.278), at Kant's third chapter of *Observations on the Feeling of the Beauti-
ful and Sublime* (1764), entitled "On the Beautiful and the Sublime in the Inter-
relations of the Sexes." In his chapter Kant does indeed associate the sublime pre-
dominantly, even if not exclusively, with the masculine and the beautiful with the
feminine. That this battle over the sublime in Milton and Klopstock was a matter of

clares his greater enthusiasm for Klopstock. Kant's preference for Milton is far more decisive—and far less generous to Klopstock. With regard to the Miltonic pretentions of Herder's charges and with regard to the issue of analogy in *Vom Erkennen und Empfinden,* Kant is, in fact, already responding forcefully at the end of the 1770s. Kant's own Miltonic way of addressing Herder's anti-Kantian Miltonism is, we can now see, to expose the shallowness of Herder's understanding of Milton by pointing most specifically to the absurdity of Herder's ranking of Klopstock with Milton. This is what Brauer records in his transcription of Kant's 1779 anthropology lecture: "Milton is a poet in the true sense. Klopstock does not come near him." Milton, not Klopstock, observes *"an analogon veritatis."*

After Bodmer and Meier, Herder not only became the leading exponent of the vaunted genius of Klopstock but was more than anyone else responsible for the ardor with which the poets of the *Sturm und Drang* took him up. Thus when Kant expresses his contempt for Klopstock in comparison with Milton, he is attacking not only Herder's shallow understanding in speaking of Klopstock in the same breath as of Milton but the *Schwärmerei* that, in Kant's view, underlies Klopstock, Herder, and the *Sturm und Drang.* This is the nature of the counterattack that I cite again from Kant's *Reflection* 914:

> The characteristic of the genius is that what he performs cannot be performed [copied] by many others, but could only have come from him; the contrary phenomenon is called *vulgare* [common, usual]. Idiosyncrasies are assumed manners through which one sets oneself apart, and which others could imitate should they wish to. The fanatical way of writing is that of the eccentric but has no originality, because many can imitate it. The originality of the genius comes from a special disposition of talents which can very seldom be met in another per-

---

some wide concern at this time can be seen (a year after Herder published the *Briefe zu Beförderung der Humanität*) in Carl Friedrich Benkowitz's *Der Messias von Klopstock, aesthetisch beurteilt und verglichen mit der Iliade, der Aeneide und dem Verlohrnen Paradiese* (Breslau, 1797), where Benkowitz, commenting on Addison's claim that a particular passage of *Paradise Lost* is the most sublime in the poem, writes: "If this is really the most sublime passage [of Milton], then on every page of [Klopstock's] *Messias* we have passages that are more sublime than Milton's most sublime passage [Ist dies würklich die erhabenste Stelle, so haben wir auf jeder Seite im Messias Stellen, die erhabner sind, als die erhabenste Stelle Miltons]" (p. 152).

son yet is [in itself] harmonious. Klopstock can be imitated very well, but Milton only with difficulty because his images are original. (*AA,* 15:399–400)

Herder's Klopstockian-Miltonic Imitation and Kant's Miltonic Succession

We have begun to see that Kant's idea of a Miltonic succession procedure was formed as a differentiation from Herder's championing of a Klopstockian-Miltonic imitation. To understand what Kant understood by Herder's idea of imitation, we need to recall Herder's highly visible response to Edward Young's *Conjectures on Original Composition* (1759; German translation 1760). Herder played an important part in giving Young's book the epoch-making *(epochemachend)* status that it acquired in Germany, setting the issue of imitation versus *Originalität* and *Genie* at the top of the agenda of German aesthetics.[49] After I have presented Herder's response to Young, I will adduce the evidence that Kant was vividly aware of it. Schlapp repeatedly notes what he considers to be the influence of Young's idea of "emulation" on Kant's idea of a *Nachfolge.*[50] I will show, however, that Young's influence here, as well as the influence of Herder following Young, functioned for Kant as a complex clarification of what he needed to supersede with a far more cogent philosophical explanation of "emulation."

Here, at the center of the *Conjectures,* is the passage that especially sets out Young's distinction between emulation and imitation:

Imitation is inferiority confessed; emulation is superiority contested, or denied; imitation is servile, emulation generous; that fetters, this fires; that may give a name; this, a name immortal: This made *Athens* to succeeding ages the rule of taste, and the standard of perfection. Her men

49. As mentioned earlier, *epochemachend* is Schlapp's frequently quoted description of Young's *Conjectures* in *Kants Lehre vom Genie,* p. 61. Here it is worth recalling Herman Wolf's remark in "Die Genielehre des jungen Herder," *Deutsche Vierteljahrsschrift für Literaturwissenschaft und Geistesgeschichte* 3 (1925), 412, also with regard to Young's *Conjectures,* that "Dr. Johnsons Ausspruch [pronouncement]: 'The highest Praise of Genius is original invention' umschreibt das Ideal einer ganzen Epoche [circumscribes the ideal of an entire epoch."Johnson's statement is, of course, about Milton.

50. Schlapp, *Kants Lehre vom Genie,* pp. 52n, 61n, 305–306, 344n and 417.

of Genius struck fire against each other; and kindled, by conflict, into glories, which no time shall extinguish. We thank *Eschylus* for *Sophocles;* and *Parrhasius* for *Zeuxis; emulation,* for both. That bids us fly the general fault of *imitators;* bids us not be struck with the loud report of former fame, as with a knell, which damps the spirits; but, as with a trumpet, which inspires ardour to rival the renown'd. Emulation exhorts us, instead of learning our discipline for ever, like raw troops, under antient leaders in composition, to put those laurel'd veterans in some hazard of losing their superior posts in glory.[51]

This passage closely follows Addison's similar remarks, cited earlier. In fact, Young's book was inspired by Addison to such an extent that fully its final third is an uninterrupted paean to Addison. Yet for Young emulation is chiefly distinguished from imitation by the energy of competition—of *contest, conflict, rivalry*—or what Harold Bloom would term an Oedipal agon. Although Young's figure of "fires" closely follows Addison's figure of "flames," he does not acknowledge the centrality for Addison of the Longinian sublime with its own figure of "fire." This is the figure, with its very different idea, that Addison especially applies to Milton's sublime. Elsewhere in the *Conjectures,* Young adopts Addison's immensely high valuation of Milton's poetry. Yet Young does not take on Addison's focus on the means "for succeeding in the sublime way of writing." For Addison the means to this success are a procedure of succession, a way in which "one great Genius"—Milton in particular—"often catches the Flame from another, and writes in his Spirit without copying servilely after him. . . . *Milton,* tho' his own natural Strength of Genius was capable of furnishing out a perfect Work, has doubtless very much raised and enobled his conceptions, by such an Imitation as that which *Longinus* recommended." As I have indicated, this procedure is identified with the Longinian-Addisonian-Miltonic phenomenon of progression, in the experience of the sublime, that Kant emulates and that he explains *in concreto* in his theory of the sublime in the *Critique of Judgment.*[52]

51. Cited from Edward Young, *Conjectures on Original Composition,* ed. Edith J. Morley (Manchester: University of Manchester Press, 1918), pp. 29–30.

52. We will see in the next chapter that as part of Young's attempt to distinguish emulation from imitation, he did register an important Miltonic connection that Addison did not mention and that Kant took in via the constellation of German Miltonism.

Already in 1767 Herder analyzed Young's characteristic "fire" *(Feuer):* "The Youngian spirit rules within, which speaks from his own heart as if into another heart, out of the genius into another genius, imparting itself like the electric spark. . . . It is the model of an imitation which remains original."[53] And Herder even gestured toward a qualitatively different "emulation" *(nacheifern).*[54] Yet, like Young, he did not comprehend the conceptual potentialities of a sublime succession procedure that stands waiting in Addison and Longinus, behind Young. We have seen to some extent, and will soon see in greater detail, how these potentialities had already been heralded by Meier, that is, even earlier than the appearance of the *Conjectures.*

To begin to understand how the controversy surrounding Young's *Conjectures,* and Herder's part in that controversy, might have fitted into Kant's sharpening of his idea of succession, I turn now to the fascinating relation between a passage in Johann Gotthelf Lindner's *Lehrbuch der schönen Wissenschaften, insonderheit der Prose [sic] und Poesie,* 2 volumes (Königsberg, 1767, 1768), and a passage in the *Critique of Judgment.*

Schlapp pointed out that Kant's comments on originality and genius in the *Logik-Philippi* (1772), which are clearly forerunners of his fully developed ideas in the *Critique of Judgment,* correspond so closely to the passage in question in Lindner's *Lehrbuch der schönen Wissenschaften* that it is impossible to doubt that one was copying from the other. Perhaps Lindner was copying from Kant's even earlier oral pronouncements, though, even if that had been the case, Kant would surely have taken note of the additional references provided by Lindner's sentences. After Kant had declined the chair in poetry at Königsberg, he nominated Lindner for the same position, to which Lindner was appointed in 1765. The *Lehrbuch* was Lindner's first major publication as incumbent. Here are Kant's comments on originality in the *Logik-*

53. "der Youngische Geist drinn herrscht, der aus seinem Herzen gleichsam ins Herz; aus dem Genie in das Genie spricht; der wie der Elektrische Funke sich mittheilt. . . . Sie ist ein Muster einer Nachahmung, die Original bleibt": Herder, *Über die neuere Deutsche Litteratur. Eine Beilage zu den Briefen, die neueste Litteratur betreffend. 1767. Zwote Sammlung von Fragmenten,* cited here from Gerhard Sauder's collection of documents (including large excerpts from Johann Jacob Rambach's 1771 version— but not the original 1765 version—of *"Schreiben über die Frage"* in his facsimile edition of H. E. von Teubern's 1760 translation of Edward Young's *Conjectures, Gedanken über die Original-Werke* (Heidelberg: Lambert Schneider, 1970), pp. [134]–[135].

54. Ibid., [136].

Philippi, including, as does Lindner's passage, disapproval of English originality when it makes "false leaps":

> Genius is a spirit of originality that creates consummate products without imitation. The original distinguishes himself before others, is distinctive. An original spirit is 1. one who has no near competitors, 2. one who has his skill from himself, not from imitation. N.B. to be original is not always to be a prototype; it means only that it does not imitate; the English, original spirits who wrote without imitation, from themselves, have frequently produced inimical and false statements, just to be original.[55]

It is clear that this passage was the forerunner of the distinction between imitation and succession in the *Critique of Judgment,* which I cite here again:

> Genius, according to these presuppositions, is the exemplary originality of the natural endowments of an individual in the *free* employment of his cognitive faculties. On this showing, the product of a genius (in respect of so much in this product as is attributable to genius, and not to possible learning or academic instruction,) is an example, not for imitation (for that would mean the loss of the element of genius, and just the very soul of the work), but for succession by another genius—one whom it arouses to a sense of his own originality in putting freedom from the constraint of rules so into force in his art, that for art itself a new rule is won—which is what shows a talent to be exemplary. (§49, 5:318)

I now cite the passage in Lindner that Schlapp quotes but from which he omits elements that illuminate and place the discussion of originality, and of emulation versus imitation, within the constellation

---

55. "Genie ist ein Originalgeist, der ohne Nachahmung vollkommene Producte hervorbringt. Das Originale zeichnet sich vor andern aus, ist kharacteristisch; und ein Originalgeist ist 1. der keinen neben sich hat 2. der seine Geschicklichkeit nicht durch Nachahmung, sondern durch sich selbst hat. NB. Original ist nicht allemal ein Urbild, es heißt nur der nicht nachahmt. die Engelländer, Originalgeister, die ohne Nachahmung aus sich selbst geschrieben, haben öffters wiedrige und falsche Sätze vorgetragen nur um Original zu sein" (*AA*, 24:1:321). Schlapp quotes from the passage (and modernizes spellings) in *Kants Lehre vom Genie,* pp. 61–62.

of German Miltonism. I have underlined the material that Schlapp omits:

> Not every genius is an original, that is, an extraordinary genius, a spirit who has his own characteristics, full of <u>fire, inborn wit,</u> primary powers and endowments, or talents in the higher sense of having their archetype and model in themselves. An original is no copy, and just as the original also signifies the archetype, so to be an original means self-inventively drawing one's treasures out of oneself, <u>like a sun, and displaying certain characteristic traits that distinguish oneself from other geniuses, as sometimes special features cause one face to stand out from others.</u> So *Homer* was more of an Original, *Virgil* more an *artistic* genius. . . . So <u>*Milton* seems more of an Original than *Klopstock* who nevertheless remains a great sublime genius.</u> . . . *Shakespeare* is one of the greatest singular *originals,* but, unfortunately, again and again at the expense of taste. <u>A Pleiades of German original authors might very soon rise on the beautiful bright sky of *Fragmente über die neueste Litteratur,* now in press, a work full of acute observations.</u> See moreover Young's *Conjectures on Original Composition.*[56]

Kant did not learn any profound distinction between originality and imitation from these well-worn, merely circular assertions about the independence and superiority of originality and the contemptibility of imitation. Nevertheless, what is of significance here are the polemical

56. Lindner, *Lehrbuch der schönen Wissenschaften,* I.26–27: "Nicht jedes Genie ist ein Original, d.i. ein ausserordentliches Genie, ein Geist, der seine Eigenthümlichkeiten hat, voll <u>Feuer, eigenem Witz,</u> ursprünglichen Kräften und Gaben, oder Talenten im höhern Verstande, die ihr Urbild und Muster in sich selbst haben. Ein Original ist keine Kopie, und so wie Original auch das Urbild bedeutet, so heißt selbst Original seyn, so viel als selbst erfinderisch seine Schätze aus sich ziehen, <u>wie eine Sonne, und gewisse eigenthümliche Striche zum Unterschiede von andern Genies an sich tragen, wie zuweilen besondre Züge ein Gesicht vor dem andern hervorstechen machen. So war Homer mehr Original, Virgil mehr ein künstlerisches Genie. . . . So scheint Milton mehr Original als Klopstock, der deswegen doch ein großes erhabnes Genie bleibt.</u> . . . Eines der grösten [*sic*] seltsamsten Originale ist Shakespear, nur Schade! hin und her auf Unkosten des Geschmacks. <u>Ein Siebengestirn [Pleiades] deutscher Originalschriftsteller möchte ehestens in *Fragmenten über die neueste Litteratur,* einem Werke voll feiner Bemerkungen, das unter der Preße ist, bey schönem klaren Himmel aufgehen.</u> Siehe sonst *Young* von *Originalwerken.*"

coordinates of discussion that Lindner lays out. Here are those coordinates, which, taken together, help locate the constellation in which Kant's mature concept of original genius would continue to develop:

1. Lindner focuses on the distinction between originality and imitation that is exemplified by the difference between Milton and Klopstock (while the celebration of Shakespeare's inexplicable singularity or the lamenting of his lapses in taste explains nothing).

2. Without specifying (or perhaps understanding) their significance for this distinction, Lindner invokes Herder's views from his not yet published *Ueber die neueste Litteratur. Fragmente . . . Zwote Sammlung* (1768).

3. With regard to Herder's *Fragmente,* Lindner directs the reader to Young's *Conjectures on Original Composition* (1759; German translation 1760).

Whether Kant was learning from Lindner or Lindner from Kant, the setting of Lindner's reference, in 1767, contextualizes the studied severity of Kant's May 1768 letter to Herder about that work. In his letter Kant gently but very firmly ranges himself against what he considers to be Herder's empty effusions on genius, which do not substantively locate originality. For Kant the topics of genius and originality inevitably have profound implications for the human capacity for moral feeling and moral conduct. This is perhaps the chief reason for Kant's mention, in the letter, of his project of a "Metaphysics of Ethics." Beginning with the *Groundwork of the Metaphysics of Morals* and continuous with the second and third *Critiques,* this project will, in fact, be linked to a substantive explanation of the possibility of the freedom to *follow* or *succeed* others in order to become original and exemplary. Kant tells Herder that he hopes the completed work, presenting "the evident and fruitful principles of conduct and the method that must be employed," will be ready within the year (*AA,* 10:73–74). In the event, even the first installment of that undertaking—the *Groundwork of the Metaphysics of Morals* (1785)—appeared seventeen years later. Yet already in 1768 Herder's response to Kant's letter confirms their antithetical orientations by speaking of his "misgivings about several of your [Kant's] philosophical hypotheses and proofs, especially when you touch on the science of the human" (*AA,* 10.78). Long afterwards, an embittered Herder still remembered Kant's early reproach about his views of originality and genius as well as Kant's claims for his prospective "Metaphysics of Ethics." In the *Kalligone* (1800) Herder tried to pay Kant back by directly linking the question of originality with a metaphysics of morals and with Milton's genius for the sublime as well. Herder's tirade there is an inverted testimonial to what, I have proposed, Kant had in the interim achieved in his own way of linking these matters, specifically with Milton's poetry, and making them part of a theory of succession.

In fact, Herder's remarks about the *Conjectures* in the *Fragmente* related to another highly visible controversy which, from Kant's perspective, foregrounded a valuable philosophical resource, namely, the Longinian concept of a *line* of succession. This was the concept that Addison specifically linked with Milton's poetry. The connection between *Milton und Addison* is an explicit point of reference in Johann Jacob Rambach's repeated paraphrases of the Longinian idea of succession in his 1765 treatise, *Epistle on the Question: Whether Reading the Ancients is to Blame for the Lack of Original Compositions.*[57] Herder's hostile review of this work sparked a clash with Rambach in which Herder fared more badly than he was willing to admit. In Kant's letter to Herder he condescendingly uses the specific terms of Herder's quite humiliating clash with Rambach over the significance of Young's *Conjectures.*

What was worth learning about genius and originality in this clash was provided by Rambach not Herder. From Kant's point of view what was especially interesting is Rambach's observation that Herder has himself acknowledged the indispensability of the earlier genius in the process of achieving originality—"out of the genius into another genius, imparting itself like the electric spark"—and that Herder and Young have, in fact, derived this recognition from the same Longinian line as has Rambach. But Herder has failed to comprehend what this

57. Johann Jacob Rambach, *Schreiben über die Frage: Ob das Lesen der Alten an dem Mangel der Original-Scribenten Schuld sey* (Quedlinburg, 1765), p. 13. The reference to "Milton und Addison" does not appear in the 1771 version of Rambach's essay, from which (as mentioned above) Sauder cites long portions in his edition of Young's *Gedanken über die Original-Werke.*

recognition entails for understanding the genius of the sublime. Here is Rambach on Herder vis-à-vis Longinus:

> Thus it seems to me that what Herr Herder says without further proof is quite dictatorial: "The art of imitating the ancients develops the genius, but because it also *very often* oppresses it, Young, in his writing, *Conjectures on Original Composition,* is correct that for most people the reading of the ancients is harmful." [Here Rambach footnotes Herder's "*Fragmente über die neuere deutsche Litteratur. Th. 3. S. 45.*"] I wish to allow Longinus to speak, for though he is not infallible he yet thinks quite otherwise and more correctly about the matter at hand: "There is yet another way that leads to the sublime. And which one is it? The imitation and emulation of great authors and poets who lived before us.—In this way emanate from the spirit of those they emulate, as from holy springs, certain effluences by which even those who do not easily take fire by themselves are inspired and become established in [sublime] enthusiasm through the greatness of others." [Rambach here footnotes the passage in Longinus, *On the Sublime,* xiii, quoting much of it in Greek.][58]

---

58. Rambach, *Vermischte Abhandlungen aus der Geschichte und Litteratur* (Halle, 1771), pp. 69–70: "So kömmt mir das, was Herr Herder ohne weitern Beweis sagt, sehr diktatorisch vor. 'Die Kunst, die Alten nachzuahmen, ist bildend für das Genie; weil sie es aber auch sehr oft unterdrückt, so hat Young in seiner Schrift von Originalwerken Recht, daß meistens das Lesen der Alten schädlich wird.' Ich will den Longin reden lassen, der, ob er gleich nicht infallibel ist, doch von dieser Sache ganz anders und richtiger denkt. 'Es ist noch ein andrer Weg, der zum Erhabnen führt. Und welcher ist es? Die Nachahmung und Nacheiferung grosser Schriftsteller und Dichter, die vor uns gelebt haben. —Auf die Art gehen aus den grossen Genies der Alten auf den [sic] Geist derer, die ihnen nacheifern, wie aus heiligen Quellen gewisse Ausflüsse über, von welchen auch die, die von sich selbst nicht leicht erhitzt werden, begeistert, und durch die Grösse andrer in Enthusiasmus gesetzt werden.'" Here is W. Rhys-Roberts's translation of the passage of Longinus cited by Rambach: "Another way (beyond anything we have mentioned) leads to the sublime. And what, and what manner of way, may that be? It is the imitation and emulation of previous great poets and writers. . . . Similarly from the great natures of the men of old there are borne in upon the souls of those who emulate them (as from sacred caves) what we may describe as *effluences,* so that even those who seem little likely to be possessed are thereby inspired and succumb to the spell of the others' greatness": *Longinus on the Sublime* (Cambridge, 1899), chap. xiii.

Rambach's points to Herder are (a) that Herder's assertions are only an uncomprehending paraphrase of the key passage in Longinus and (b) that while Herder merely trumpets the emergent originality (which Rambach also describes and values) and revels in the mystery of the paradox that originality has somehow emerged from an act of imitation, Rambach—thinking of *Milton und Addison*—tries to understand the formal procedures of Longinus's sublime "emulation" *(nacheifern)*. These formal procedures became the focus of Kant's linked Miltonic reflections on originality and exemplarity, for which he would use the term "exemplary originality" *(musterhafte Originalität)* (*CJ,* 5:318).

Kantian Exemplarity

The key term in Kant's formulation of the role of analogy in philosophy is *exemplarity*.[59] Seeing Herder's resistance to this term sharpens our understanding of how Kant developed the term and how it fits into his Miltonic procedure of succession. In his critique of Kant's aesthetics in the *Kalligone,* Herder quotes from §46 of the *Critique of Judgment* and comments as follows:

> "Genius is 1) a *talent* for producing that for which no definite rule can be given; *originality* must be its primary property." Not to mention that this determination is merely negative, in addition to leading astray! Yet genius does work according to rules, did arise according to rules, and is a rule unto itself, granted that not every third person could point it out. The "originality" (a much abused word) of genius can only mean that the genius produces a work of his own powers, not imitated, nowhere borrowed; else there can be, as the *Kritik* itself says, "original nonsense." 2) "The products of the genius must at the same time be models, that is, be *exemplary;* and serve others for imitation, that is, as a standard or rule of *estimating.*" The work of genius exists, even if it is never imitated; it stands unique of its kind. For imitation, or much

59. A stimulating discussion of the issue of exemplarity in literature is Karlheinz Stierle's "Three Moments in the Crisis of Exemplarity: Bocaccio-Petrarch, Montaigne, and Cervantes," *Journal of the History of Ideas* 59 (1998): 581–595.

more, for *estimation,* the work was never created, and is desecrated by imitation without genius. (*SW,* XXII.197–198)[60]

John Louis Kind remarks on this passage that Herder "is wasting time quibbling over words, not thoughts. . . . His views are identical with Kant's."[61] This, however, is not the case. Herder does not acknowledge, and perhaps did not understand, the kind of non-imitative relation in which talent, genius, and exemplarity have their meanings for Kant. Here is what Kant had actually written in §46 of the *Critique of Judgment,* from which Herder is distortively quoting:

> From this it may be seen that genius (1) is a *talent* for producing that for which no definite rule can be given, and not an aptitude in the way of cleverness for what can be learned according to some rule; and that consequently *originality* must be its primary property. (2) Since there may also be original nonsense, its products must at the same time be models, i.e., be exemplary; and, consequently, though not themselves derived from imitation, they must serve that purpose for others, i.e., as a standard or rule of estimating. (3) It cannot indicate scientifically how it brings about its product, but rather gives the rule as *nature.* Hence, where an author owes a product to his genius, he does not him- self know how the *ideas* for it have entered into his head, nor has he it

60. "'Genie ist 1) Ein *Talent,* dasjenige, wozu sich keine bestimmte Regel geben läßt, hervorzubringen; *Originalität* muß seine erste Eigenschaft seyn.' Zu geschweigen, daß diese Bestimmung blos verneinend ist, ist sie auch verführend. Allerdings arbeitet das Genie nach Regeln, erstand nach Regeln, und ist sich selbst Regel, gesetzt, daß jeder Dritte ihm diese auch nicht vorzählen könnte. Seine 'Originalität,' (ein sehr mißbrauchtes Wort,) kann blos bedeuten, daß der Genius ein Werk seiner Kräfte darstellt, nicht nachgeahmt, nirgend erborget; sonst kann es, wie die Kritik selbst sagt, 'auch originalen Unsinn geben.' 2) 'Die Produkte des Ge- nies müssen zugleich Muster, d.i. *exemplarisch* seyn, und andern zur Nachahmung, d. i. zum Richtmaas oder Regel der *Beurtheilung* dienen.' Das Werk des Genies bestehet, auch wenn es nie nachgeahmt würde; es stehet sodann einzig in seiner Art da. Zur Nachahmung oder gar zur *Beurtheilung* ward das Werk nicht geschaffen, und wird durch Nachahmung ohne Genie geschändet."

61. John Louis Kind, *Edward Young in Germany* (New York: AMS, 1966), p. 54. In my translation of the passage of Herder (*SW,* XXII.197–198), I have incorporated parts of Kind's rendering.

110 · KANT AND MILTON

in his power to invent the like at pleasure, or methodically, and communicate the same to others in such precepts as would put them in a position to produce similar products. (5:307–308)[62]

In Chapter 6 we will see how in §49 Kant integrates these propositions into the "succession" to a progression of representations made by a line of talents or geniuses. The succession procedure that can achieve exemplary originality is of a series of representations of a certain kind, each represented by a genius who possesses the requisite talent. Each such "representation . . . lets us see its own inadequacy, and consequently its subjective want of finality for judgment in the estimation of magnitude" (*CJ*, 5:252). Kant derives his idea of the line of geniuses and talents (in a succession of the experience of the sublime) from the passage in Longinus that Addison had exemplified with Milton's poetry. For the Kant of §49 it is this succession procedure that, in the realm of art—especially of poetry—issues in the transformative energy of the experience of the sublime. The product of this procedure of succession is "not imitation" *(nicht . . . Nachahmung)* of the merely empirical but an "exemplary originality" *(musterhafte Originalität)* (*CJ*, 5:318) which bridges the individual material example and the archetypical or universal.

In the *Kalligone* and even to some considerable extent in *Vom Erkennen und Empfinden*, Herder shows his awareness of the importance for Kant, as separate items, of exemplarity, succession, the endless progression, talent, genius, and even the connection between the constraint of *soll* and a kind of reason that capitalizes on the imagina-

---

62. "Man sieht hieraus, daß Genie 1) ein Talent sei, dasjenige, wozu sich keine bestimmte Regel geben läßt, hervorzubringen: nicht Geschicklichkeitsanlage zu dem, was nach irgend einer Regel gelernt werden kann; folglich daß *Originalität* seine erste Eigenschaft sein müsse. 2) Daß, da es auch originalen Unsinn geben kann, seine Producte zugleich Muster, d. i. *exemplarisch,* sein müssen; mithin, selbst nicht durch Nachahmung entsprungen, anderen doch dazu, d. i. zum Richtmaße oder Regel der Beurtheilung, dienen müssen. 3) Daß es, wie es sein Product zu Stande bringe, selbst nicht beschreiben, oder wissenschaftlich anzeigen könne, sondern daß es als Natur die Regel gebe; und daher der Urheber eines Products, welches er seinem Genie verdankt, selbst nicht weiß, wie sich in ihm die Ideen dazu herbei finden, auch es nicht in seiner Gewalt hat, dergleichen nach Belieben oder planmäßig auszudenken und anderen in solchen Vorschriften mitzutheilen, die sie in Stand setzen, gleichmäßige Producte hervorzubringen" (*CJ*, 5:307–308).

tion of *los*, which is to say on "representation . . . that lets us see its own inadequacy." Herder unswervingly resists seeing the Kantian relations among these terms, in other words, the relations that Kant had made the crown of his aesthetic and moral theory. Yet Herder's very resistance throws these relations into bold relief and even shows how they are central in Kant's thinking about Milton's poetry.

On the same page of the *Kalligone* in which Herder obfuscates Kant's concept of the genius's talent to be exemplary, he distorts what Kant has said about the antithesis of this talent, shown by the *"Pinsel"* or "shallow-pate," the mechanical imitator. Here is Kant at the opening of §47:

> Every one is agreed on the point of the complete opposition between genius and the *spirit of imitation*. Now since learning is nothing but imitation, the greatest ability, or aptness as a pupil (capacity), is still, as such, not equivalent to genius. Even though a man weaves his own thoughts or fancies, instead of merely taking in what others have thought, and even though he go so far as to bring fresh gains to art and science, this does not afford a valid reason for calling such a man of *brains,* and often great brains, a *genius,* in contradistinction to one who goes by the name of *shallow-pate* [Pinsel/pencil], because he can never do more than merely learn and follow a lead. For what is accomplished in this way is something that *could* have been learned. Hence it all lies in the natural path of investigation and reflection according to rules, and so is not specifically distinguishable from what may be acquired as the result of industry backed up by imitation. (*CJ*, 5:308)[63]

63. "Darin ist jedermann einig, daß Genie dem Nachahmungsgeiste gänzlich entgegen zu setzen sei. Da nun Lernen nichts als Nachahmen ist, so kann die größte Fähigkeit, Gelehrigkeit (Capacität) als Gelehrigkeit, doch nicht für Genie gelten. Wenn man aber auch selbst denkt oder dichtet und nicht bloß, was andere gedacht haben, auffaßt, ja sogar für Kunst und Wissenschaft manches erfindet: so ist doch dieses auch noch nicht der rechte Grund, um einen solchen (oftmals großen) *Kopf* (im Gegensatze mit dem, welcher, weil er niemals etwas mehr als bloß lernen und nachahmen kann, ein *Pinsel* heißt) ein *Genie* zu nennen: weil eben das auch hätte können gelernt werden, also doch auf dem natürlichen Wege des Forschens und Nachdenkens nach Regeln liegt und von dem, was durch Fleiß vermittelst der Nachahmung erworben werden kann, nicht specifisch unterschieden ist" (*CJ*, 5:308).

Herder quotes Kant as follows: "He goes by the name of *shallow-pate*, who can never do more than [Kant wrote "merely," only, *bloß*] learn and follow a lead. [*Wer niemals was mehr als lernen und nachahmen kann, heißt ein Pinsel.*]" Herder then comments: "This is not what he is called, if he learns faithfully and imitates exactly, with his acquired knowledge, with his faithful imitation of the most beautiful and best, he can be a wise, skilfull, useful man; else whole faculties and schools would be *shallow-pates* by profession" (*SW*, XXII.198).[64] Herder refuses to understand the specific kind of imitation that Kant is here, and in §49, making the center of his theory and which, as Herder probably knew, Kant was in part echoing from Winckelmann's analysis of Milton's inimitable, supersensory talent in the single most famous work of art criticism of eighteenth-century Germany, the *Geschichte der Kunst des Altertums* (1764):

> The Greek's exquisite talent for art still shows itself at present in the great, almost general talents of people in the warmest regions of Italy; and in this exquisite capacity for art imagination reigns, as among the British reason rules over imagination. Not without good grounds, someone has said that the poets on the other side of the Alps speak through images but they give few images; one must acknowledge that the astounding, partly dreadful, images, of which *Milton's* greatness consists, are in no way the theme of a noble pencil [*Pinsel*/shallow-pate], but are completely inept if attempted in painting. Excepting the unique *love* in Paradise, the *Miltonic* descriptions are like beautifully delineated *Gorgons*, which are alike as they are frightful. The images of many other poets are great to the *ear*, but small to the *mind*.[65]

---

64. "Das heißt er nicht, wenn er treu lernte und genau nachahmet; er kann mit seinem Gelernten, mit seiner treuen Nachahmung der Schönsten und Besten ein vielwissender, geschickter, nützlicher Mann seyn, oder ganze Facultäten und Schulen wären Berufs-mäßig *Pinsel*." My translation here closely follows that of Kind, *Edward Young in Germany*, p. 55.

65. Johann Joachim Winckelmann, *Geschichte der Kunst des Altertums* (1764–68), in *Sämtliche Werke*, 13 vols., ed. Joseph Eiselein (Nachdruck der Ausgabe 1825, Osnabrück: Otto Zeller, 1965), III.137: "Das vorzügliche Talent der Griechen zur Kunst zeiget sich noch izo in dem großen fast allgemeinen Talente der Menschen in den wärmsten Ländern von Italien; und in dieser vorzüglichen Fähigkeit zur Kunst herschet die Einbildung, so wie bei den denkenden Briten die Vernunft über die

Not only had Herder himself specifically praised this analysis of Milton already in 1769, in his *Kritische Wälder* (*SW,* III.234–235), but, as Herder (who was one of Lessing's closest readers) had surely seen, Winckelmann's comments had been monumentally reinforced by Lessing's comment in the *Laokoon* (1766) on Milton's special kind of nonpainterly talent. Following not only Winckelmann but also Burke's expositions (1757) of Milton's negative poetics, Lessing, I recall once more, wrote,

> Count Caylus . . . would make the test of a poem its usefulness to the painter. . . . The contemptuous judgment which Caylus passes on [Milton] was the result as much of national taste as of his would-be rule. The loss of sight, he says, may well be the strongest point of similarity between Milton and Homer. Milton cannot fill picture galleries, it is true. But if the range of my physical sight must be the measure of my inner vision, I should value the loss of the former in order to gain freedom from the limitations on the latter. . . . *Paradise Lost* is . . . the finest epic after Homer.[66]

The importance of noting the resemblances among Kant's, Winckelmann's, and Lessing's ways of distinguishing representation of poetic genius is that they are all focused on representation that shows its inadequacy to represent—at least in a painterly way—and on what Winckelmann calls "reason" and "understanding" *(Vernunft, Verstande),* which Kant will locate in aesthetic ideas or ideas of reason *(Vernunft).* Winckelmann, together with Lessing, indicates how inevitable it was for German writers to think of Milton's sublime precisely in this con-

---

Einbildung. Es hat jemand, nicht ohne Grund gesaget, daß die Dichter jenseit der Gebirge durch Bilder reden, aber wenig Bilder geben; man muß auch gestehen, daß die erstaunenden, theils schrecklichen Bilder, in welchen *Miltons* Größe mitbestehet, kein Vorwurf eines edlen Pinsels sein könne, sondern ganz und gar ungeschickt zur Malerei sind. Die *miltonischen* Beschreibungen sind, die einzige *Liebe* im *Paradiese* ausgenommen, wie schön gemalete *Gorgonen,* die sich ähnlich und gleich fürchterlich sind. Bilder vieler andern Dichter sind dem *Gehöre* groß, und klein dem *Verstande.*"

66. Gotthold Ephraim Lessing, *Laocoön: An Essay on the Limits of Painting and Poetry* (1766), trans. Edward Allen McCormick (Indianapolis: Bobbs-Merrill, 1962), chap. 14, p. 74. This translation is based on *Lessings Laokoon,* ed. Hugo Blümner, 2nd ed. (Berlin, 1880).

nection, just as, we will see in a moment, Kant would think of it in unfolding his theory of the sublime succession procedure, of exemplarity, and of aesthetic ideas.

Kant's quantum leap came from applying the Addisonian-Miltonic version of Longinus's concept of the sublime succession to Burke's, Winckelmann's, and Lessing's Miltonic concept of deficited or negativity-centered representation.[67] Despite and even because of his resistance to Kant, here as elsewhere Herder is an important part of the constellation of German Miltonism with which Kant engaged. Kant, I have proposed, deepened an idea of *energeia* from Breitinger's and Meier's emphasis on "energetic ideas" in the oscillations of "aesthetic light and darkness"; and Kant took his inspiration for a procedure of succession in the experience of the sublime from the Addisonian-Longinian tradition. Yet Kant could not have been oblivious to the way in which Lessing and Herder had also made striking use of the terms *energeia* and *succession* in their efforts to distinguish poetry from the plastic arts. Herder, following James Harris in his *Three Treatises (Drei Abhandlungen),* had in some ways even gone beyond Lessing.[68] In these ways and more, even if Kant differentiated an entirely different meaning for a procedure of succession, here, too, Herder helped vitalize the constellation of ideas within which Kant could be creative.

In addition, and correlatively, Herder highlights for us exactly that which he tried to block out in Kant: namely, the whole series of strong

67. By the time we reach the third *Critique,* Kant is explicitly acknowledging his close reading of Burke on the sublime (see *CJ,* 5:277).

68. Lessing's ideas of progression and succession in poetry are set out in Chapters 15 to 18 of the *Laokoon.* Herder's following of Lessing's usages of these terms and his elaboration of the Aristotelian idea of energy appears, among other places, in his comments on Abbt's *Vom Verdienste* (*SW,* I.80), where he explicitly follows James Harris's *Three Treatises* (London, 1744; German translations, Danzig, 1756 and Halle, 1780), as much as, or more than, Lessing. On Herder's relation to Harris's writings, see Haym, *Herder,* I.262–263, and Pierre Pennison, "Trieb et energie chez Herder," *Revue Germanique Internationale* 18 (2002): 45–52. Herder's comments on Harris's terms are now available in English in the translation of the "Critical Forests, or Reflections on the Art and Science of the Beautiful: First Grove, Dedicated to Mr. Lessing's *Laocoön,*" in *Selected Writings on Aesthetics: Johann Gottfried Herder,* trans. Moore, pp. 155–157. In the next chapter I will briefly turn directly to Harris's writings.

and clear connections that constitute what Herder accurately termed Kant's "moral sublime" *(Sittlich-Erhabne)*. This was Kant's representation of "Milton's true sublime." And, as we have seen, Kant's discovery of a kind of analogy that was distinctly Miltonic owes much to Herder's provocations, however different Kant's and Herder's two kinds of analogy are.

Finally, we can take in at one glance just how dramatic and central Kant's shift was away from his blanket rejection of Herderian analogy or example. In his reviews of Herder's *Ideen* (1785), where Kant had excluded analogy from philosophical discourse on the grounds that analogy cannot fill or bridge the "immense void between the contingent and the necessary," he had singled out the following passage for particular derision:

"Around the throne of Jupiter the hours (those of the earth) perform a round dance, and whatever is formed under their feet only represents indeed an imperfect perfection because everything is founded on the fusion of heterogeneous elements; but through an inner love and communion with one another is the child of nature—physical regularity and beauty—everywhere born."

In 1785 Kant wrote that "critics of discriminating philosophic style" must agree that such "excursions out of the area of the philosophic into the sphere of poetic language . . . conceal the corpus of thought as under a farthingale."[69] The reference to a farthingale (a hooped petticoat) no doubt suggests the titillation of eros-driven "commu-

69. Kant, "Reviews of Herder's *Ideas for a Philosophy of the History of Mankind*," trans. Anchor, in Kant, *On History*, ed. Beck, pp. 41, 45–46. *AA*, 8:57, 60–61: "Übergänge aus dem Gebiete des philosophischen in den Bezirk der poetischen Sprache . . . den Körper der Gedanken wie unter einer Vertugade . . . verstecken . . . . Wir überlassen es Kritikern der schönen philosophischen Schreibart . . . . [Kant then quotes Herder:] 'Um den Thron Jupiters tanzen ihre (der Erde) Horen einen Reihentanz, und was sich unter ihren Füßen bildet, ist zwar nur eine unvollkommne Vollkommenheit, weil alles auf die Vereinigung verschiedenartiger Dinge gebauet ist, aber durch eine innere Liebe und Vermählung mit einander wird allenthalben das Kind der Natur geboren, sinnliche Regelmäßigkeit und Schönheit.'" Herder employs a highly similar figure in his poem "Die Horen" and cites, in the *Kritische Wälder*, an analogous figure from *Paradise Lost*, IV.266–268 (*SW*, III.236–237). In Chapter 6 I will have a word to say about Herder's Milton quotations in the *Kritische Wälder*.

nion" that is allegedly inherent in such poetic language. It is difficult, if not impossible, to imagine that Kant had forgotten this extended, deep mocking of Herder's image of Jupiter's throne when, just six years later in the *Critique of Judgment,* he chose the image of "Jupiter's eagle, with the lightning in its claws, . . . and the peacock of [heaven's] stately queen [Juno]" as his capital example of aesthetic ideas.[70] The fact, as I will explain in Chapter 6, that Kant's representation of Jupiter and Juno is also a following of Meier's following of Milton's Jupiter-and-Juno representations only underlines the resolute cogency of the turn that Kant had made. Kant makes his representation of Jupiter and Juno the pivot of his account of aesthetic ideas in the *Critique of Judgment.* With his richer Miltonic resources, he quietly meets Herder head on not only with regard to the analogical use of an image of Jupiter but with regard to Herder's anti-Kantian Miltonism. A very large change, indeed, has taken place in Kant's way of conceiving the relation of poetic to philosophic language. In Chapter 6 I will describe what amounts to the Kantian systematization of this change in the *Critique of Judgment* (1790). In the next chapter I propose that within a year of writing the reviews of the *Ideen,* Kant was already following multiple elements of a Miltonic analogy and a Miltonic succession in representing primary concepts of the *Groundwork of the Metaphysics of Morals* (1785). To a great extent Kant's embeddedness in the constellation of German Miltonism and its ways of treating specific works of Milton prepare him for this analogy and succession. In fact, the idea of the succession procedure comes to define Kant's relation to that constellation. By the end of this book it will be clear, I believe, that the procedure of succession gave him his place to stand, in freedom, within that constellation, even in relation to Herder.

70. In Phidias's lost but vividly remembered sculpture of Zeus on his throne—one of the Seven Wonders of the ancient world—the eagle, perched on Zeus's scepter, was located as part of the throne. See, for example, Pausanias, *Description of Greece,* trans. W. H. S. Jones and H. A. Omerod (Cambridge, Mass.: Harvard University Press, 1918), 5.11.1.

CHAPTER 3

Kant's Miltonic Transfer to Exemplarity

The Succession to Milton's "On His Blindness" in the *Groundwork of the Metaphysics of Morals*

"Two standpoints" *(zwei Standpunkte),* and the human capacity to "transfer" between them, are the deepest subjects of the *Groundwork of the Metaphysics of Morals.* The transfer between these standpoints is itself the groundwork of Kant's claim that he has located the "one resource" of autonomous moral reason, the categorical imperative. In the first standpoint "we represent ourselves in terms of our actions as effects that we see before our eyes." We transfer ourselves into the second "different standpoint [*anderen Standpunkt*] when by means of freedom we think ourselves as causes efficient a priori" (*GMM,* 4:450–453). From this standpoint we do not *see* the objects of thinking. Earlier in the *Groundwork* Kant had written, "When moral worth is at issue, what counts is not actions, which one sees, but those inner principles of actions that one does not see. . . . The insightful . . . avert their eyes" (4:407, 409). Kant repeatedly elaborates the standpoints between which this transfer takes place. The individual "has two standpoints," he explains, "*first,* insofar as he belongs to the world of sense . . . (heteronomy); *second,* as belonging to the intelligible world. . . . When we think of ourselves as free we transfer ourselves into the world of understanding as members of it and cognize autonomy of the will along with its consequence, morality." Again and again Kant asserts that the person who performs this process of thinking "transfers himself in thought into an order of things altogether different from that of his desires in the field of sensibility. . . . He can expect only a greater inner worth of his person . . . when he transfers himself to the standpoint of a member of the world of understanding" (4:452–453, 454–455).

Commentators who refuse to credit the reality of this Kantian transfer argue, like Bernard Williams, that it requires the achievement of an impersonal standpoint that Kant either cannot achieve or, even if he could achieve it, would be destructive of morality because of its detachment or alienation from the self of the thinker.[1] I believe we can begin to answer at least a significant part of these criticisms in terms of the Kantian procedure of succession. In this procedure Kant transfers viewpoints from the heteronomous to the autonomous yet remains anchored in his experience of the sublime in his own life and his own world. Impersonality of a special kind results from this transfer. To substantiate these assertions I now wish to show how Kant's second standpoint is disclosed, and to a great extent defined, by his Miltonic succession procedure in the experience of the sublime. Specifically, I propose in this chapter that Kant's transfer between standpoints in the *Groundwork* is achieved in a procedure of succession to Milton's astonishingly compressed paradigm of sublime succession, and of transfer between heteronomous and autonomous standpoints, in his great sonnet "On His Blindness," also known as "When I consider" from its opening phrase.[2] Here we find a dramatic exemplification of Kant's

1. Williams's critique, expounded principally in *Moral Luck* (Cambridge: Cambridge University Press, 1981) and *Ethics and the Limits of Philosophy* (Cambridge, Mass.: Harvard University Press, 1985), is treated in some detail by Henry E. Allison, *Kant's Theory of Freedom* (Cambridge: Cambridge University Press, 1990), pp. 191–198. What I have to say largely bypasses Williams's objections by trying to demonstrate that Kant's way of achieving the second standpoint, and therefore also his conception of the second standpoint itself, is substantially different from what Williams, or even Allison, imagines.

2. No early German translation of the sonnet has yet been identified, though it was widely available in Germany in English, including the two-volume complete poetry of Milton published in 1784 in Göttingen, that is, the year before Kant published the *Groundwork*. This German publication of Milton's poetry was undertaken under the inspiration of Kant's friend and philosophical correspondent Georg Christoph Lichtenberg. I repeat here, from my note in Chapter 1, that Enrico Pizzo, *Miltons Verlornes Paradies im deutschen Urteile des 18.Jahrhunderts* (Berlin: Felber, 1914), p. 104, is mistaken in saying of volume two of this edition of Milton's poetry that it was pub-

explanations of the meaning of "succession" as "the proper expression for all influence which the products of an exemplary *author* [originator] may exert upon others." Kant's succession—"not imitation"—is to Milton's sonnet, which he encounters within the constellation of German Miltonism. For Kant this procedure of succession finally "means no more than going to the same sources" that become available in the experience of the sublime provided by "one's predecessor" (*CJ*, 5:283), that is, by the immediate predecessor working in a series of precedents. In Kant's other words, "The artist's ideas arouse like ideas on the part of his pupil" *(Lehrling)* (*CJ*, 5:309). In the case before us the pupil or successor to the artist Milton is the philosopher Kant. It cannot be emphasized enough, however, that for Kant what defines and enables this procedure is the freedom, generated in a true sublime truly grasped, in which these "sources" or "ideas" are spontaneously redeployed. In the light shone from this originality in personal freedom, any erstwhile anxiety of influence shrinks to insignificance. A *Lehrling* of this order, whether poet or philosopher, is sovereign and self-possessed in individually earned exemplarity.

I pointed out earlier that, in Kant's world, poetry and philosophy had not yet experienced the virtual divorce that characterizes our own age. Yet if it nevertheless seems absurd to suggest that a poet's procedure for disclosing the autonomy of the will could take on exemplary significance for a philosopher, I suggest that we take note at the outset of a somewhat earlier instance of this kind, in the aesthetic and moral writings of James Harris. In Harris's case the object of succession is Milton's other sonnet on his loss of sight, "To Mr. Cyriack Skinner upon His Blindness." With regard to the terms that especially concern us here, Harris's writings enjoyed currency in Germany from the mid-1750s to the early 1780s. I mentioned in the previous chapter that, going beyond Lessing, Herder found his authority for his versions of the terms *energeia* and *succession* or *progression* in Harris's *Three Treatises*, published in London in 1744. A German translation of this volume was published in Danzig in 1756. An enlarged German translation, fol-

lished in 1785. The title page indicates 1784 quite clearly. To date the only extensive listing of German translations of Milton's works is that of Hermann Ullrich, "Bibliographie der deutschen Übersetzungen von Miltons Werken," in *John Miltons Poetische Werke* (Leipzig: Max Hesses Verlag, 1909), pp. 138–152.

lowing the 1772 English edition of the work, was published in Halle in 1780.[3] Side by side with his philosophical work, Harris was well known for his veneration of Milton's poetry.[4] In his philosophical writings, which were mostly argued from within the traditions of eighteenth-century Stoic philosophy, he instanced Milton's poems (as did Hutcheson and Hume) for an equivalent depth of moral insight.[5] My interest here is in one such instance.

In the third treatise, "Concerning Happiness," which is by far the longest part of the *Three Treatises*, Harris argues that we must "place the **Sovereign Good** in . . . a *Rectitude of Conduct*—in the **Conduct** *merely, and not in the* **Event**."[6] His idea is that a "*Law Universal*" of "*Rectitude of Conduct*" "alone" is possible "if we make our Natural State [where Kant would locate the *a priori*] *the Standard only to determine our Conduct;* and place this Happiness in *the Rectitude of this Conduct alone*. . . . We should [then] not want a *Good* perhaps, *to correspond to our Pre-conceptions*." Harris's idea of such a standard is worked out in what Kant would call differentiating *autonomy* from *heteronomy;* and it is located "in *Mind*," or the *a priori*, where Harris grounds an idea of maxims that he terms "just [i.e., morally right] *Selecting* and *Rejecting*": "Now *a steady, durable Good,* cannot be derived from an *external* Cause, by reason all derived from *Externals* must *fluctuate*, as they *fluctuate*. . . . What then remains but the *Cause internal;* the very Cause we have supposed, when we place the *Sovereign Good* in *Mind;* in *Rectitude of Conduct;* in just *Selecting*

3. Jakob Harris, *Abhandlungen über Kunst, Musik, Dichtkunst und Glückseligkeit ; aus dem Englischen, nach der dritten sehr vermehrten und verbesserten Londner Ausgabe übersetzt* (Halle, 1780). The translation is in almost all instances scrupulously faithful to the original.

4. Harris had the same veneration for Handel's music. Combining his deep admiration for the composer and the poet, Harris provided Handel with a draft of a libretto based on Milton's "L'Allegro" and "Il Penseroso." Charles Jennens then completed the libretto for what became the oratorio *L'Allegro, Il Penseroso, ed Il Moderato*, but it was Harris who had hit on the crucial idea of interweaving verses from the two poems. Harris also influenced Handel to undertake his *Samson*, the libretto which was extensively derived from Milton's *Samson Agonistes*. I will have another word to say about Handel's *Samson* in Chapter 5.

5. For Hume's citation of Milton's verse see Chapter 6; for Hutcheson's see below.

6. Harris, *Abhandlungen*, pp. 177–178: "Wir wollten das **höchste Gut** in eine solche Richtigkeit des Betragens setzen—blos in das **Betragen,** und nicht in den **Ausgang**."

and *Rejecting?*"[7] To these things we should add Harris's formulation of a "transfer" that takes place simultaneously in aesthetic and moral experience: a *"transfer*," he says, of *"subordinate* Beauty, to Beauty of a *higher Order* [such as the sublime, perhaps, which Harris invokes in other passages]; it is but to pass from the *External,* to the *Moral* and *Internal.*"[8] These things might easily have caught Kant's attention. But for Kant, I propose, the real interest of Harris's analysis would lie elsewhere, in fact in his notes, which are often far more analytical and extensive than his text and were frequently a principal source of interest in themselves (as, for example, to Herder).

Harris concludes his five-page endnote (which appears as page after page of footnote in the 1780 German translation) to his "new and strange" Hypothesis of how "TO PLACE THE SOVEREIGN GOOD IN RECTITUDE OF CONDUCT" by trying to find the mind's capacity for reaching *"Law Universal"* in the *"Progression"* of *"Energies"* in "the *Reasoning Faculty.*" He ends the note and exemplifies the *"Progression"* this way:

> I cannot conclude this Note, without remarking on an elegant Allusion of *Antoninus* to the *primary* Signification of the Word Κάτορθωσις, that is to say . . . *right onwards, straight and directly forwards.* Speaking of the *Reasoning Faculty,* how, without *looking farther, it rests contented in its own Energies,* he adds—. . . *For which Reason Actions of this sort are called* **Rectitudes,** *as denoting the Directness of their Progression* **Right Onwards.** . . .
>
> One would imagine that our Countryman *Milton,* had this Rea-

7. Ibid., p. 224: "Nun aber kann ein beständiges, dauerhaftes Gut nicht von einer äusserlichen Ursache hergeleitet werden, weil alles, was von äusserlichen Dingen hergeleitet wird, eben so vorüberrauschend seyn muß, wie sie es selbst sind. . . . Was bleibt demnach anders übrig, als die innere Ursache; eben die Ursache, die wir angenommen haben, wenn wir das höchste Gut in Verstand, in Rechtschaffenheit des Betragens, in richtiges Wählen und Verwerfen setzen?"

8. James Harris, *Three Treatises* (London, 1744). I quote here from the 1792 edition, which is the first volume in Harris's *Miscellanies,* 5 vols. (1775–92), I.185, 213, 218–219. *Abhandlungen,* p. 229: "so ist es blos darum geschehen, um dasjenige, was wir von dieser niedrigen Schönheit gesagt haben, auf Schönheit von höherm Grade anzuwenden; es ist blos der Uebergang vom Aeussern zum Moralischen und Innern."

soning in view, when in his 19th Sonnet, speaking of his own Blindness, he says with a becoming Magnanimity,

> —Yet I argue not
> Against Heav'n's Hand or Will; nor bate one jot
> Of Heart or Hope; but still bear up, and steer
> **Right onwards.—**

The whole Sonnet is not unworthy of Perusal, being both sublime and simple.[9]

As I have said, Harris is citing "To Mr. Cyriack Skinner upon His Blindness." This is one of two famous sonnets that Milton wrote on his blindness. Harris proposes that there is a significant relation between the kind of direct progression described by Milton in the sonnet, in its movements of "Rectitude," and the Stoic attainment of the Sovereign Good. Harris's claim for this progression corresponds to the idea of succession that he has made central to his aesthetics. But he does not make clear what that significant relation might be.

In fact, the Miltonic paradigm of sublime experience underlies and explains that relation. Thus it would be almost equally easy to spell out Milton's paradigm in this sonnet on his blindness as in "When I consider." But the abundance of correspondences between Kant's *Groundwork* and "When I consider" makes the latter route of inquiry far more relevant and profitable for us. It is possible that another writer, before Kant, noted Harris's exposition and was prompted to apply it to Milton's second, far greater sonnet on his blindness. In any case, I propose to demonstrate that Kant, very much in the spirit of Harris, extensively used this other sonnet, where Milton is also "speaking of his

9. Harris, *Miscellanies,* I.305–306. The sentence after the citation is not translated in the German, which appears as follows (including the citation itself in English): "Man sollte fast denken, **Milton** habe dieß Raisonnement vor Augen gehabt, wenn er in seinem neunzehnten Gedichte, wo er von seiner Bindheit spricht, mit einer anständigen Großmuth sagt
> —yet I argue not
> Against heav'n's Hand or Will; nor bate one jot
> Of Heart or Hope; but still bear up; and steer
> *Right onwards—*" (*Abhandlungen,* p. 180n)

own Blindness . . . with a becoming Magnanimity." Kant even *succeeds to* the sonnet in order to explain and exemplify the relation between succession and moral law in the progression of aesthetic light and shadow. For Kant this is the experience of the sublime in the procedure of succession.

~

Karl Viëtor called A. W. Schlegel the first *Sonetten-Philosoph* because, in his *Vorlesung über das Sonett* (1803–04), he was the first to describe rigorously the philosophical shifts of inner and outer standpoints that are quintessentially achieved in the sonnet form. Viëtor added that Schlegel "without doubt only gave voice to an old conviction when he recognized in this artform a special and definite dynamic, a generic inherent tension."[10] We have repeatedly seen that this or a highly similar tension gives shape to the entire constellation of German Miltonism. The Miltonic sonnet was at the heart of the reemergence of the sonnet in England and Germany after 1775, especially of the sudden, new attention to the sonnet form in the 1780s, that is, when Kant composed the *Groundwork*.[11] My argument concerning Kant's engagement with Milton's sonnet is centered on the "tension" between inner and outer standpoints. Kant's understanding of the Miltonic sublime and of the Miltonic representation of aesthetic ideas put him in a unique position to understand Milton's colossal transfer between heteronomous and autonomous standpoints in the sonnet. Kant's transfer between standpoints in the *Groundwork* is, among other things, the effect of tracing and following the *energeia* of Milton's poem, that is, primarily in the

10. Schlegel's essay is reprinted by Jörg-Ulrich Fechner, *Das deutsche Sonett: Dichtungen, Gattungspoetik, Dokumente* (Munich: Fink, 1969), pp. 342–352. Viëtor's observation is in his *Deutsche Sonette: Aus vier Jahrhunderten* (Berlin: Euphorion, 1926), p. 157: "Schlegel, der einzige 'Sonetten-Philosoph', hat aber darin sicherlich nur eine alte Überzeugung ausgesprochen, wenn er dieser Kunstform eine besondere, bestimmte Dynamik, eine gattungsmäßig innewohnende Spannung zuerkannt."

11. See Raymond Dexter Havens, "Milton and the Sonnet," in *The Influence of Milton on English Poetry* (Cambridge. Mass.: Harvard University Press, 1922), pp. 478–548, especially pp. 499, 526–528, and Walter Mönch, *Das Sonett: Gestalt und Geschichte* (Heidelberg: Kerle, 1955), p. 139, where Mönch's particular example is "When I consider. . . ." The revised entry for the "Sonett" in Sulzer's *Allgemeine Theorie der Schönen Künste* (Frankfurt, 1798), 4:480, marks the place of the Miltonic sonnet in the reemergence of the sonnet in Germany.

poem itself but also (here perhaps to an unusual degree, even for Kant) in the forms in which the poem was reflected in the constellation of German Miltonism. The compressed, powerful transfer to the condition and maxim of exemplarity in Milton's poem is followed by Kant, I propose, to the standpoint of the categorical imperative and its maxim in the *Groundwork*. This transfer is the effect of a sublime succession procedure of aesthetic light and shadow.

I will next set out an analysis of the sonnet itself and then some of the ways in which Milton's sonnet and Milton's way of interpreting the New Testament parable of the talents were integrated into the German discussion of exemplarity. After that I will demonstrate how Kant's procedure of succession to this sonnet in the *Groundwork* transfers him into the condition of exemplarity that is required by the categorical imperative.

～

Here is Milton's sonnet on his talent, in which he follows, partly resisting, Matthew's (and Luke's) telling of Christ's parable of the talents and the tested servants (Matthew 25:14–30):[12]

> When I consider how my light is spent,
> Ere half my days, in this dark world and wide,
> And that one Talent which is death to hide,
> Lodg'd with me useless, though my Soul more bent
> To serve therewith my Maker, and present
> My true account, lest he returning chide;
> "Doth God exact day-labor, light denied,"
> I fondly ask; But patience to prevent
> That murmur, soon replies, "God doth not need
> Either man's work or his own gifts; who best
> Bear his mild yoke, they serve him best; his State
> Is Kingly. Thousands at his bidding speed
> And post o'er Land and Ocean without rest:
> They also serve who only stand and wait."[13]

12. A slightly different version of the parable appears in Luke 19:12–27.

13. So far no persuasive precedent has been found for Milton's handling of Matthew's parable, nor, therefore, for what I have called Milton's rewriting of the parable. Suggestions for partial sources are listed by John Carey, ed., *John Milton: Complete Shorter Poems*, 2nd ed. (London: Longman, 1997), p. 332.

In Christ's parable the third servant, to whom a lord has loaned just one talent and who has hidden that talent rather than putting it to use (or usury) as do the servants who have been loaned more talents, is by that lord "cast . . . into outer darkness" (Matthew 25:30)—apparently just as Milton has been made blind by God. In the sonnet Milton denies far more than the justness of a possible application of the parable to his own affliction. He denies that the parable can possibly mean that God expects any returns from his gifts of talents to human beings. This denial, and, indeed, the thrust of the entire sonnet, depends on a radical shift in standpoints, which Milton discloses in the parable itself.

Even and especially in Milton's condition of being unable to see or render visible things, he employs his capacity to see invisible things. The deepest disclosure of this sonnet is that Milton's light is spent (and exhausted or emptied) to great profit. In Kant's terms, derived not least from Milton's poetics, this is to say that his poetry of aesthetic light and shadow is identical with the *energy* of the succession procedure (to a progression or typology) that produces the experience of the sublime and exemplarity. In this succession Milton succeeds in representing, personally, as the *Imitatio* of a Christian, both God's moral perfection which has no need of human gifts and the human moral perfection that is analogously independent of material incentives or rewards. The maxim that issues from this representation is that human moral perfection is manifested in merely sustaining the disposition that is an independent goodwill: "They also serve who only stand and wait." For Milton doubtless this same verse locates a principal idea of the godhead of Christ who archetypically also just stands and waits (as Milton emphasizes at the climax of *Paradise Regained*). Milton, however, does not merely imply or assert these things. His poem produces them in work or service that effects a transfer from mere material work.

Milton's concept of God's "mild yoke" that is given to human beings is cited from Matthew's phrase "My yoke is easy" (11:30) and is defined by contrast with a harness for profit-making "work." But the sonnet's concept of immaterial value, or the real good, is informed by Matthew 19:17, where Christ affirms that the good is not in the things we can see but in what we cannot see, namely God: "Why do you call me good? none is good but God only." This is the one biblical verse that Kant directly invokes in the *Groundwork*. "Even the Holy One of the Gospel," he writes, "must first be compared with our ideal of moral perfection before he is cognized as such; even he says of himself: why do you call me (whom you see) good? none is good (the archetype of the good) but God only (whom you do not see). But whence have we the concept of God as the highest good? Solely from the *idea* of moral perfection that reason frames a priori and connects inseparably with the concept of a free will" (*GMM*, 4:408–409).

In this complex of connections, which are as much Miltonic as they are Kantian, we find the beginnings of an explanation for that quality in the conclusion of Milton's sonnet that Paul Goodman called no ordinary humility.[14] What is most insightful and audacious in Milton's way of following Matthew's parable is that he finds the meaning and free employment of his talent in an inseparable connection between his will and moral reason. His will is independent of all material incentives. His rational capacity—even in his immobilized condition—is to frame an archetype or exemplarity of moral perfection, both divine and human. Kant will provide an explanation of how this will and moral reason are connected, but their effects are dramatically clear in Milton's verses. In the sonnet the sharp break or transfer between the octave and the sestet marks this breaking away from the material world and material demands, such as are levied on the servants who have been given talents to invest for material profit. The blind poet breaks away to freedom and exemplarity. In Kant's terms this is the breaking away from the world of "actions as effects that we see before our eyes" to the "greater inner worth of his person . . . when he transfers himself to the standpoint of a member of the world of understanding" that we do not see. I will return to the inner workings of Milton's sonnet later in this chapter.

∽

In a variety of ways Milton's sonnet was introduced into Kant's world specifically to exemplify the distinction between slavish imitation and the originality of a free selfhood. The parable of the talents, not infrequently in its Miltonic form, assumed a prominent place in these exemplifications.

14. Paul Goodman, *The Structure of Literature* (Chicago: University of Chicago Press, 1968), pp. 205–215. Douglas Bush comments on Goodman's insight in *A Variorum Commentary on the Poems of John Milton*, ed. A. S. P. Woodhouse and Douglas Bush (London: Routledge and Kegan Paul, 1972), vol. 2, pt. 2, pp. 454–455, 457.

Young's *Conjectures* (German translation 1760) deserves credit for being among the first works to insert Milton's interpretation of the parable at the crucial juncture of the German debate about originality versus imitation:

> We have great *Originals* already: *Bacon, Newton, Shakespeare, Milton.* . . .
> What foreign genius strikes not [i.e., does not hoist its colors or ship's flag, as a mark of respect] as they pass? Why should not their posterity embark in the same bold bottom of new enterprize, and hope the same success? Hope it they may; or you must assert, that either those *Originals,* which we already enjoy, were written by Angels, or deny that we are Men. . . . For man not to grasp at all which is laudable within his reach, is a dishonour to human nature, and a disobedience to the divine; for as heaven does nothing in vain, its gift of talents implies an injunction of their use.[15]

Milton is the poet who famously addressed the "disobedience to the divine," the *Ungehorsam gegen die göttliche (Natur),* in the opening phrase of *Paradise Lost,* "Of Man's First Disobedience." After naming Milton as an inspiring original, Young's reference to the parable of the talents even seems to summon up the originality of Milton's use of that parable in his sonnet, that is, in affirming that he has, after all, indeed heeded the divine injunction to employ his talent even in just standing

15. "Haben wir schon große **Originale. Bacon, Boyle, Newton, Shakespeare, Milton.** . . . welches fremde Genie streichet nicht vor ihnen der Seegel [*sic*]? Warum können nicht ihre Nachkommen sich in eben das verwegene Schiff einer neuen Untersuchung einschiffen, und auf eben den glücklichen Erfolg hoffen? Sie können darauf hoffen; oder sie müssen behaupten, daß jene **Originale,** die wir schon besitzen, von Engeln geschrieben worden, oder leugnen, daß wir Menschen sind. . . . Es ist ein Schimpf für die menschliche Natur, und ein Ungehorsam gegen die göttliche, wenn der Mensch nicht alles das zu erreichen strebt, was lobenswürdig ist, und in seinem Gesichtskreise liegt. Denn wie der Himmel nichts vergebens thut, so befiehlt er auch, wenn er uns Talente giebt, zugleich ausdrücklich, daß wir die gebrauchen sollten." The English text is cited from Edward Young, *Conjectures on Original Composition,* ed. Edith J. Morley (Manchester: University of Manchester Press, 1918), pp. 33–34. The German is cited from the facsimile reprint of Young's *Gedanken über die Original-Werke,* trans. H. E. von Teubern (Leipzig, 1760), pp. 65–66, that is included in Gerhard Sauder's edition of Young's work (Heidelberg: Verlag Lambert Schneider, 1977).

and waiting. Milton's self-reliant way of following his Lord's instruction—so runs Young's logic—is what first and foremost (in his soul) made him an original rather than a slavish imitator, such as were the conventional first and second servants of the parable. This logic, here exemplified by Milton, is central to Young's argument.

In fact, the paradox at the heart of Milton's deployment of the parable of the talents is even the ruling paradox of the entirety of Young's *Conjectures*. The elaboration of just this paradox won for the *Conjectures* its status as the *epochemachend* work of Kant's Germany. Proceeding in his own way, this is the paradox that Kant unfolds in his theory of the succession procedure. As we have seen, according to Kant's theory, the mind may exercise a talent for originality—in specific, for exemplary originality—that discloses its autonomous genius through its special way of following great examples. In the *Groundwork* Kant's interest in the talent that can use the procedure of succession is exactly the transfer from the standpoint of examples that we see to the standpoint of a categorical imperative which is neither more nor less than this exemplarity. I am proposing that Kant performs his procedure of succession to Milton's sonnet as well as to the interpretive way stations in the German Miltonic constellation that interpret the sonnet. Each of the representational items in this succession procedure, stretching from the immediate transfer of standpoints exemplified in Milton's sonnet—back through endless intermediate representations, reaching to the archetype of Christ's transfer recorded in the parable—is a shift in standpoints that meets the Kantian conditions of the succession procedure. Before describing Kant's handling of these matters, I wish to present a range of relevant German writings that made special use of the parable of the talents and/or Milton's version of it.

～

We see the impact, or a collateral line, of Young's invocation of Milton's sonnet in Kant's Germany of the 1760s in a passage that has special relevance to our discussion for a number of reasons. It occurs in the principal work of an author, Thomas Abbt, whom Kant mentions and who was virtually idolized by Herder; it is a passage that was specifically praised by Herder and Mendelssohn; it shares with Kant (and Herder) the revolutionizing of the idea of talent of the common man and woman toward a status of equality with the capacity of genius; and it presents this revolutionary idea of talent in the particular form of a Miltonic rewriting of Christ's parable of the test of talents in Matthew 25. If Kant required any further prompting to pore over this work by Abbt, it was provided by Kant's friend Johann Gotthelf Lindner, who in the first volume of his *Kurzer Inbegrif* (1771) directly linked Kant's early thoughts on "the great and the sublime" with Abbt's in *Vom Verdienste* (1765), where the relevant passage occurs.[16]

Abbt's *Vom Verdienste—On Merit*—achieved fame in its day because of its richly imagined, everyday way of presenting philosophical, especially ethical, ideas. Herder's appreciation of these qualities, in *Ueber Thomas Abbts Schriften* (1768), was among the most impassioned accounts of a contemporary author that Herder ever wrote.[17] Among the treatises of the *Genieliteratur, Vom Verdienste* was almost alone in being itself considered a work of both talent and genius. In his elaborations of *Verdienst* Abbt tries to identify especially those dimensions of goodness that cannot be defined by rules. In the course of his book he proudly exhibits his extensive and deeply contemplated intimacy with Milton's poetry. At one point, for instance, he quotes at length from *Paradise Regained* (a text that was not particularly familiar to most German readers) in order to articulate a complex idea of moral power (pp. 301–302). At other points he weaves rich allusions to Milton's shorter poems.[18] Abbt's description of a Miltonic imaginative power that is born of blindness begins to bring us close to my core concerns in this chapter. Published a year before Lessing's *Laokoon*, Abbt's ideas about Milton's exercise of his poetic talent, specifically in blindness, already include equivalents of Lessing's ideas and are, in addition, more precise and more far-reaching:

16. *Kurzer Inbegrif der Aesthetik, Redekunst und Dichtkunst,* 2 vols. (Königsberg, 1771–72), I.152.

17. It is relevant to our concerns that Herder, *Ueber Thomas Abbts Schriften* (n.p., 1768), remarked that Abbt had learned his "picture composition and humour . . . from British writers" *(Bildercomposition und Laune . . . von den Britten)* (p. 36). For an account of the friendship and sharing of intellectual interests between Abbt and Mendelssohn, see Alexander Altmann, *Moses Mendelssohn: A Biographical Study* (London: Routledge, 1973), pp. 100–112.

18. Interestingly enough, Abbt stresses that the genius of both *der göttliche Homer* and *der göttliche Milton* is of less interest to him—as exemplifications of the quality of genius, at least—than the genius of moral statesmen like William Penn (p. 38).

Let us then consider the poet whose vivacious fantasy is nature's dowry. Even on that account isn't he also called especially the man rich in sentiments? Did the Homers and Miltons need to see the dawn, need to see the sun stepping forth from its chamber like a bridegroom, in order to melt in sentiments of joy, and to salute the awakening world with a hail to the fresh day? [referring to Milton, "L'Allegro," 44–46][19] O surely not: their fantasy replaced the senses: and as long as these are busy the poet is not yet master of his thoughts. Sentiments come to him, so to speak, when he shuts his eyes and ears and just lets his imagination do its painting. The room must be darkened if those paintings are to become visible. [referring to "Il Penseroso," 13–14, 78–80, 147–150, 159–166, and a voluntary kind of blindness to external things][20] (pp. 159–160)

The passage to which I wish to draw special attention in *Vom Verdienste* was, as I have said, singled out by both Mendelssohn and Herder immediately upon publication.[21] Kant's note mentioning Abbt

19. "Till the dappled dawn doth rise; / Then to come in spite of sorrow, / And at my window bid good-morrow."

20. Abbt, *Vom Verdienste* (Berlin, 1765), pp. 159–160: "Man nehme also den Dichter, den Mann, bey dem eine lebhafte Fantasey die Mitgift der Natur ist. Heisst er nicht eben deswegen auch besonders der Mann reich an Empfindnissen? Hatten die Homere die Miltone noch nöthig, die Morgenröthe zu Sehen, nöthig die Sonne, wie einen Bräutigam aus seiner Kammer, hervortreten zu sehen, um in Empfindnissen der Wonne zu zerfließen, und der erwachenden Welt Heil zu dem jungen Tage zuzurufen? O gewiß nicht: ihre Fantasey vertrat die Stelle der Sinne: und eben so lange diese noch beschäftigt sind: wird der Dichter noch nicht Herr über seine Gedanken. Die Empfindnisse kommen bey ihm, wenn er gleichsam Augen und Ohren verschließt, und nur noch die Einbildungskraft mahlen zu lassen. Das Zimmer muss verfinstert seyn, wenn jene Gemählde sollen gesehen werden." The relevant verses in Milton are these: "Whose Saintly visage is too bright / To hit the Sense of human sight; / . . . Some still removed place will fit, / Where glowing Embers through the room, / Teach light to counterfeit a gloom / . . . And let some strange mysterious dream / Wave at his Wings in Airy stream, / Of lively portraiture display'd, / Softly on my eyelids laid. / . . . And storied Windows richly dight, / Casting a dim religious light."

21. For Mendelssohn's comment on the passage, see the volume of *Freundschaftliche Correspondenz* (letter to Abbt dated 14 June 1765), printed in Abbt's *Vermischte Werke*, ed. Friedrich Nicolai (Berlin, 1771), 3:353–354; for Herder's singling out, *insonderheit*, of this passage, see *Ueber Thomas Abbts Schriften*, p. 26. As shown below, two years after the publication of *Vom Verdienste* Herder himself used the talent image, very much in the way that Abbt, like Milton, uses it. Interestingly enough, a

probably refers to a passage just a few pages earlier.[22] Here is Abbt on the "only one talent" *(nur ein Talent)* of "useful people" *(brauchbarer Leute),* the common man and the common woman, who are "faithful *servants" (treue Knechte):*

> In order to hear of their merits one needs to live in the town, in the house, if possible drink at the well with them, or have been part of a coffee-party with them. Common sense instead of Genius; patience that has been learned through long experience instead of Courage; a good heart instead of Benevolence—these suffice to acquire that which without further codicil one simply names merit.
>
> Do I think or speak contemptuously of this common merit? That's far from my intention! O my brothers, with whom I by chance have the honor to stand in the same class, this merit is perhaps the highest that we can achieve. And let us not be downcast [*or* cast down] because of this. Merit of this kind is sufficient to make every one of us a faithful *servant.* Providence needs only few individuals as instruments of its reign on earth, even fewer for the realization of the great changes that form the periods of a nation, and only one or another for a total revolution in human affairs. Hence most people receive just one *talent:* if they don't bury it a certain wealth of merit emerges for the world. Opulence is divided among a small number: for the larger number it is always "great enough never to have been other than what one should be!" (pp. 277–278; the emphases are Abbt's)[23]

---

significant part of Abbt's use of the parable—namely, "Die meisten bekommen also nur **ein Talent:** wenn sie dieses nicht vergraben: so kömmt schon eine gewisse Wohlhabenheit der Welt an Verdiensten heraus. Der Reichthum bleibt unter die geringe Anzahl vertheilt"—was omitted (seven years after Abbt's death) in the 1772 edition of *Vom Verdienste.* This omission may be related to Mendelssohn's extended comment, in his letter of 14 June 1765, on Abbt's use of the word *Wohlhabenheit.*

22. Kant wrote, "The beautiful must always be unusual. See Thomas Abbt. [Das Schöne soll immer ungebräuchlich sein. vid. Thomas Abbt.]" The sentence appears in Kant's preparatory notes for the *Critique of Judgment* and is quoted by Schlapp, *Kants Lehre vom Genie und die Enstehung der 'Kritik der Urteilskraft'* (Göttingen: Vandenhoeck & Ruprecht, 1901), p. 65. Schlapp adds that he has not been able to identify Kant's reference. I suggest that Kant may have been referring to Abbt's discussion on pp. 269–271.

23. Abbt, *Vom Verdienste,* pp. 277–278: "Man muß in der Stadt, in dem Hause wohnen, allenfalls den Brunnen mit ihnen getrunken, ein Kränzchen mit ihnen gehalten haben, um von ihren Verdiensten was zu hören. Der gesunde Menschen-

Instead of being an exceptional quality called genius, for Abbt the one talent, *Verdienst,* which defines the test of the faithful servant, is only commonplace rationality. Instead of being the hero's courage, this common rationality, experienced in a line of commonplace recurrence, is the same as the patience that is learned only through long experience. Instead of the benevolence that prides itself on bestowing material goods, this talent is purely that of the good heart, which is to say (as Francis Hutcheson or Kant would say), a benevolence that is disinterested.[24] Closely following the Miltonic version of Matthew's

---

verstand an Statt des Genies; eine durch lange Erfahrung erlernte Gedult [*sic*] an Statt [*sic*] des Muthes; ein gutes Herz an Statt des Wohlwollens reichen zum Erwerbe dessen hin, was man schlecht hin ohne weitern Zusatz **Verdienst** nennet.

Denken, sprechen wir denn verächtlich davon? Das sey ferne. O meine Mitbrüder, mit denen ich ohngefähr die Ehre habe in einer Klasse zu stehen, dieses Verdienst ist vielleicht das höchste, wozu wir gelangen können. Und laßt uns deswegen nicht niedergeschlagen werden. Ein solches Verdienst ist hinreichend, um jeden von uns zum treuen **Knechte** zu machen. Die Vorsicht braucht nur wenige zu Werkzeugen ihrer Regierung auf Erden; noch wenigere zur Ausführung der großen Veränderungen, welche die Perioden einer Nation ausmachen, und nur einen oder den andern zu einer gänzlichen Umwälzung menschlicher Dinge. Die meisten bekommen also nur **ein Talent:** wenn sie dieses nicht vergraben: so kömmt schon eine gewisse Wohlhabenheit der Welt an Verdiensten heraus. Der Reichthum bleibt unter die geringe Anzahl vertheilt: für die mehrere Zahl ist es immer 'gross genug, nie was anders gewesen zu seyn, als was sie seyn sollte!'"

24. The specifically Miltonic field of reference that Kant encountered with regard to a redefined, higher "Benevolence" is very rich. This can be seen in the writings of Hutcheson, the one modern philosopher whom Kant cites approvingly in the *Groundwork* (4:442n). It is widely acknowledged that in Kant's thinking about the "benevolence from basic principles" that alone has "inner worth" (*GMM,* 4:435) he drew, to a great extent, the centrality of "disinterested" moral conduct (*GMM,* 4:439) from Hutcheson. (See Dieter Henrich, "Hutcheson und Kant," *Kant-Studien,* 49 [1957–58]: 49–69, and "Über Kants früheste Ethik: Versuch einer Rekonstruktion," *Kant-Studien* 54 [1963]: 404–431.) In the context of our present discussion we should note that in Hutcheson's *Inquiry into the Original of Our Ideas of Beauty and Virtue* (1725; *Untersuchung unsrer Begriffe von Schönheit und Tugend,* trans. Johann Heinrich Merck, 1762: I give the page references to the translation in italics) his guiding principle is that "wherever then *Benevolence* is suppos'd, there it is imagin'd *disinterested,* and design'd for the *Good* of others" (p. 129, *144*). He extends this principle to saying, "Without acknowledging some other Principle of Action in rational Agents than *Self-Love,* I see no Foundation to expect *Beneficence,* or *Rewards* from *God*" (p. 139, *165*). It is noteworthy that, among the arts, Hutcheson saw a unique connection between the "*moral Sense*" and the "Foundation . . . of **Poetry**" (p. 240, *275*) and that he frequently quotes Milton's poetry, far more often, indeed, than any other modern

parable in this way, Abbt attaches supreme value to the private, even merely passive and internal, exercise of this talent, which was precisely the talent of the previously contemned and "cast down" *(niedergeschlagen)* individual. Though this individual talent does not, or cannot, serve providence in earthly matters or determine the character of an era or bring about revolutions in human affairs, it is "sufficient" *(hinreichend)* in merely being itself: "Merit of this kind is sufficient to make every one of us a faithful *servant*." This sufficiency in mere moral being is the same as expressing this being in a maxim for all of humankind: "Great enough never to have been other than what one should be!"

Considering Herder's intense scrutiny of both Young's *Conjectures* and Abbt's *Vom Verdienste,* it is not surprising that one of Herder's best known essays, published in the 1767 collection of the *Fragmente,* uses similar terms. In this case Herder is in protest against the stifling of youthful talent and genius through oppressive Latin education. Here, too, Herder (like the author of the *Verlornes Paradies*) reverses the apparent logic of Matthew's telling of the parable by identifying with the person whose talent is buried—and by identifying, most of all, with the intrinsic value of that one talent, which Herder, however, views as irretrievably lost:

> Thus everything is <u>lost:</u> <u>lost</u> is the first, mysterious sagacity . . . <u>lost</u> the great, introspective, intuitive grasp . . . <u>lost</u> landlord- and proprietary

---

poet. A striking feature of Hutcheson's moral philosophy is his repeated invocation of the example of the "abject" or helpless individual who nevertheless serves goodness merely by the rational activity of his will to goodness. In the *Inquiry,* besides other citations from *Paradise Lost* (pp. 81, 133, *92, 160*), Hutcheson quotes the following verses from Satan's acknowledgment of this moral activity, which, even Satan must admit, is absolute for all rational beings in their relation to goodness: "A grateful mind / By owing [i.e., meaning both *continuing to owe a debt which is unpaid* and *owning* or *acknowledging*] owes not, and still pays, at once / Indebted and discharg'd" (*Paradise Lost,* IV.55–57; quoted in English in Merck's translation). Hutcheson's point in citing these verses is that this maxim is true, and shows the purity of disinterestedness, even in "the *most abject Beneficiary,*" that is, "when he is utterly incapable of any other Return [*Erwiederung, sic*], and when we expect none from him" (p. 152, *176*). The language of "Return" here is clearly that of return on an investment (such as, we might add, talents of gold or silver). Further on he says, "No external Circumstances of Fortune, no involuntary Disadvantages, can exclude any Mortal from the *most heroick Virtue*" (p. 178, *209*).

right. . . ; in short, <u>lost</u> is that which signifies genius. . . . <u>The talent is buried in the dust,</u> genius arrested . . . until it loses its power. (underlining added)[25]

[So ist alles <u>verloren:</u> <u>verloren</u> der erste unerklärliche Scharfsinn . . . <u>verloren</u> das große innerliche Gefühl . . . <u>verloren</u> das Hausherren- und Eigenthumsrecht. . . ; kurz verloren, das was man Genie nennt. . . . <u>das Talent in Staub vergraben,</u> das Genie aufgehalten wird, bis es . . . seine Kraft verliert.] (underlining added)

There are collateral reasons for believing that Kant paid close atten- tion to what Herder had to say here about educating the young. We will see in the next chapter that Herder's views on this subject even provided Kant with a uniquely irritating stimulation to the composi- tion of the second *Critique*.

In verses that survive in manuscript in the *Herder Nachlass*, Herder, in fact, directly contemplated the figure of the blind Milton who is yet "right rewarded" *(recht belohnt)* and "suffers no need" *(hat ke[ine] Noth)*. We do not know if Kant saw any version of these lines, though Johann Georg Hamann and others were continually provoking Kant and Herder by ferrying, back and forth, accounts of each other's do- ings. Herder here pointedly reworks verses by Christian Wernicke enti- tled "Milton punished by blindness." Herder titles his verses "Blind are you! Lost"— *"Blind bist du! Verl[ohren]* ":

> Blinded! Right rewarded—he who against the king
> Wrote so boldly—suffers no need.
> Those who for Charles
> Wrote so indulgently—are dead.
>
> [*Erblindet! Recht belohnt- der widern König*
> *So frech schrieb—hat ke[ine] Noth.*
> *die für den Karl*
> *So milde schrieben—sind todt.*][26]

25. From *Ueber die neuere Deutsche Litteratur. Fragmente. Dritte Sammlung* (Riga, 1767), pp. 39–40; *SW,* I.380–381.

26. From ms. p. XVIII.356 in the *Herder Nachlass* of the Preußischer Kulturbesitz, Staatsbibliothek zu Berlin. On the recto of the same page Herder refers to *Wernikens*

Herder sharpens and substantially reverses the meaning of Wernicke's lines by levying on Milton's interpretation, in the sonnet, of the parable of the talents, that is, of his own condition of being cast into darkness and yet neither expecting nor needing any (further) reward. With an ear to Luther's translation of the parable, Herder's use of the word *recht, right,* plays against the "Lord"'s (or "King"'s, in Luke's version of the parable) twice saying *Recht so* in rewarding the servants of ten and five talents. In Herder's allusion to the parable, the use of the word *frech, audacious,* reverberates with the one-talent servant's back talking to the Lord: "Lord, I knew thee that thou art an hard man, reaping where thou hast not sown, and gathering where thou hast not strawed [Herr, ich wußte, daß du ein harter Mann bist: du erntest, wo du nicht gesät hast, und sammelst ein, wo du nicht ausgestreut hast]" (Matthew 25:24). Charles and the first-level Lord/King of the parable fit seamlessly together as Milton's would-be victimizers who cannot touch his inner being. Strongly implicit in Herder's allusion to the parable and the sonnet is the second-level, higher king who is now well

---

Poetische Versuche in Überschriften (Zürich, 1763), where the following verses appear (with footnotes) on p. 253:

> Milton mit Blindheit gestraft.
> Der blinde Milton ward von wenigen beklagt:
> Und als hierauf ein Freund von seinem König sagt,
> Daß diese Straf ihm sey vom Himmel zugeschickt,
> Weil seinen frechen Kiel er wider Karl gezückt.
> Daß widern König ich geschrieben viele Jahr,
> Und daß ich nunmehr blind geworden bin, ist wahr;
> Sprach Milton, der es hört. Doch hab ich keine Noth:
> Denn die sind, die für ihn geschrieben haben, todt.

> [Milton punished by blindness
> Blind Milton was by few lamented:
> And as was said of him by a friend of his king,
> "This punishment is visited on him from heaven.
> Because he drew his impudent quill against Charles."
> "That I wrote against the king for many years,
> And that I have at present become blind, is true,"
> Said Milton when he heard this. "Yet I suffer no need:
> Since they, who wrote for the king, are dead."]

For aid in establishing an accurate transcription of Herder's handwriting in his verses, as well as for securing the text of Wernicke's verses, I am grateful to Dorothea Barfknecht, Bibliotheksamtsrätin in the Handschriftenabteilung of the Staatsbibliothek zu Berlin.

satisfied with the mere standing and waiting of the Milton who "suffers no need" *(hat keine Noth)*.

In the same vein, in the last sentences of the 1778 published version of *Vom Erkennen und Empfinden,* Herder counsels "the *standing and waiting* for judgment of our inner human being" *(das Bleiben und Warten unsres innern Menschen aufs Gericht)* (*SW,* VIII.234). Considering Herder's explicit references to Milton in *Vom Erkennen* fifteen pages earlier, it seems plausible to assume that (among other things) Herder is invoking the last line of Milton's sonnet: "They also serve who only stand and wait."[27] In the 1774 version of *Vom Erkennen,* Herder similarly describes the strong soul "in its endless continuance. . . . It aspires upwards towards divinity . . . each one at its post [in seine ewige Dauer. . . . Er strebt hinauf zur Gottheit . . . jede auf ihrer Stelle]" (*SW,* VIII.262); and indeed this occurs three pages after the following juxtaposition of positive and negative Miltonic alternatives, and even the digging up of buried talent, which I cited only partially in the previous chapter:

> The strongest soul also has the talent for the strongest virtue when it suitably uses and sifts the sensations. It has much to evolve out of every sensation, but it also has extensive evolutionary power and intensive composure. What it unearths is the purest gold. Only souls of this kind should be called great, because they alone are great indeed. *Milton's* Satan built Pandaemonium and threw a bridge over Chaos, yet he became neither happier nor greater with both (of these actions). All strength without reason and goodness is adventurism, sublime folly, or repulsiveness. (*SW,* VIII.259)

27. No doubt Herder was also alluding, in some measure, to Lamentations 3:26–28, which is likely part of Milton's own allusion, though the Lamentations passage is focused on salvation, rather than on judgment of the inner human being, as are Matthew 25, Milton's sonnet, and Herder's "das Bleiben und Warten unsres innern Menschen aufs Gericht." Here is Lamentations 3:26–28: "It is good that a man should both hope and quietly wait for the salvation of the LORD. It is good for a man that he bear the yoke of his youth. He sitteth alone and keepeth silence, because he hath borne it upon him." In Luther's words: "Es ist ein köstlich Ding, geduldig sein und auf die Hilfe der HERRN hoffen. Es ist ein köstlich Ding für einen Mann, daß er das Joch in seiner Jugend trage. Er sitze einsam und schweige, wenn Gott es ihm auferlegt."

[Die stärkste Seele hat auch zur stärksten Tugend Anlage, wenn sie die Empfindungen gehörig erschöpft und ordnet. Sie hat in jeder Empfindung viel zu entwickeln, sie hat aber auch viel Entwicke-lungskraft und intensive Ruhe. Was sie hervorgräbt, ist Gold an Werth und Schwere. Seelen von der Art sollte man allein groß nennen, weil sies auch allein sind. *Miltons* Teufel baute das Pandämonium und schlug eine Brücke übers Chaos; er ward aber mit beidem weder glücklicher noch größer. Alle Stärke ohne Vernunft und Güte ist ent-weder Abentheuer, sublime Narrheit oder Abscheulichkeit.]

We have seen that Kant was Herder's ultimate target in the pseudo-Miltonic passages that recur in *Vom Erkennen und Empfinden*. Reflecting (among other things) on Herder's attack on him, Kant cultivated his own "extensive evolutionary power and intensive composure." He achieved this by giving philosophical depth to exactly the Miltonic al-ternative of a true sublime, such as we find in Milton's following and reworking of the parable of the talents. Compared to Kant's carefully derived formalism for standing and waiting, Herder's passionate and flowery assertion of sensation can indeed seem like the *Schwärmerei* of which Kant accused him.

If Kant might have hesitated to philosophize upon a place of scrip-ture, he had Meier's warrant for allowing an exception in the case of just this one text. In Meier's "Thoughts on Philosophical Preaching" *(Gedancken vom philosophischen Predigen)* (1753), he had issued a whole-sale condemnation of philosophizing—"philosophical preaching"—upon scriptural texts: "He who thoroughly understands what philoso-phy is, is at the same time convinced that philosophical preaching is a piece of silliness and an abuse of philosophy which deserves no jus-tification. . . . In most cases philosophical preaching is set in motion by philosophic pedantry or charlatanism."[28] But in 1774, in his *Philoso-phische Betrachtung* [Philosophical Reflection] *über Matthäi c. 25. v. 31–46*, he had changed his mind for the sake of this one chapter of scrip-ture. Contemplating this chapter, especially the description of the Last Judgment which immediately follows (in the same chapter) from the

---

28. "Wer die Philosophie gründlich versteht, der ist zu gleicher Zeit überzeugt, daß das philosophische Predigen eine Thorheit, und ein Mißbrauch der Weltweisheit sey, die keine Rechtfertigung verdienet. . . . Bey den meisten rührt das philoso-phische Predigen aus einer philosophischen Pedanterey und Charlatanarei her."

judgment issued in the parable of the talents, Meier focused on the "sublime" *(erhabene)* representation of the innermost category of the moral life. Upon this representation, he says, "mere, self-reliant, but disinterested, reason can manage a profound philosophical reflection [worüber die blosse ihr selbst überlassene, aber unpartheyische, Vernunft eine sehr wichtige philosophische Betrachtung anstellen kan]." Meier's emphasis here on the "duty," *Pflicht,* to oneself that is a *Pflicht* to all and on a progressive lifting of the soul or mind toward *a sublimated disposition of the will* could only have seemed deeply congenial to Kant. Meier even gives his own version of the leap that Kant would describe in the categorical imperative:

> The whole of benevolent piety is a portion of the highest perfection of the human soul. He who makes efforts to raise his mind gradually, through the employment of those means which reason and the holy scriptures commend, up to that godly disposition, fulfills one of the greatest duties toward himself. Thus Christian piety especially consists in the eager striving to attain, through a well-disciplined self-love, that degree of perfection whereby an individual becomes adept at being a universal and benevolent humanitarian, and at producing continuously in himself, as well as in as many other people as possible, as much good as he is capable of producing [*als er zu würken im Stande ist*].
> . . . For the sake of this cognition he must fittingly guide his inborn self-love, to turn himself into a gracious benefactor of all of humanity.[29]

29. "Die ganze gütige Frömmigkeit ist ein Stück der höchsten Vollkommenheit einer menschlichen Seele, und derjenige beobachtet eine der grösten [*sic*] Pflichten gegen sich selbst, welcher sich bemühet, sein Gemüth nach und nach, durch den Gebrauch der Mittel, welche die Vernunft und die heilige Schrift anpreisen, bis zu dieser göttlichen Gesinnung zu erheben. Die christliche Frömmigkeit besteht also vornemlich in dem eifrigen Bestreben, durch eine wohlgeordnete Eigenliebe denjenigen Grad der Vollkommenheit zu erreichen, wodurch ein Mensch geschickt wird, ein allgemeiner und gütiger Menschenfreund zu seyn, und unausgesetzt in sich selbst, und ausser sich in so vielen andern Menschen als ihm möglich ist, so viel Guts zu wirken, als er zu würken [*sic*] im Stande ist.
. . . Um dieser Erkenntniß willen muß er seine ihm angebohrne Eigenliebe gehörig lenken, um sich zu einem gütigen Wohlthäter des ganzen menschlichen Geschlechts zu machen."
These essays of Meier appeared in the *Wöchentliche Hallische Anzeigen* 12 (1753): 193–202, and 50 (1774): 801–823, respectively. My citations from the first are from pp. 196 and 202; from the second, from pp. 801–802, 805–806. Many of Meier's

But what of the individual who is not capable *(im Stande)* of doing so, that is, the individual who *stands incapable* of producing good in himself and in other people?

In the same year (1774) that Meier made Matthew 25:31–46 an exception for philosophy, he also explicated verses 14–30 of the same chapter, that is, the parable of the talents itself, in his *Reflections on the Authentic Religion of Humankind (Betrachtungen über die würkliche Religion des menschlichen Geschlechts).* In this explication we find the following interpretation of the parable, precisely in Milton's spirit in his sonnet:

> No one can be obliged beyond his own capacity. So there is no true divine law, whether natural or arbitrary, whereby anyone can be held responsible for not doing that which, without his being in any way to blame, exceeds the total measure of his strength. God knows this measure most perfectly. He is the free distributor of human talents, and he would proceed cruelly if he required something of a person which exceeded these talents. When therefore an individual does not achieve something, or fails to undertake it, he does not thus sin, and God cannot and will not punish him on that account, neither in time nor in eternity.[30]

> [Niemand kan über sein Vermögen verbunden werden. Folglich giebt es auch kein wahres göttliches Gesetz, es mag natürlich oder willkührlich sey, wodurch irgends, ein Mensch wozu verbunden werden könnte, welches ohne alles sein Verschulden das ganze Maaß seiner Kräfte übersteigt. GOtt kennt dieses Maaß aufs vollkommenste. Er ist der freye Austheiler der menschlichen Talente, und er würde grausam handeln, wenn er etwas von einem Menschen fodern [*sic*] wolte, welches diese Talente übersteigt. Wenn nun ein Mensch so etwas nicht erlangt, oder unterläßt: so sündiget er nicht, und GOtt kan ihn deswegen, und wird ihn auch deswegen, weder in der Zeit noch in der Ewigkeit, strafen.]

---

terms resemble Kant's language in numerous passages of the *Groundwork,* the second and third *Critiques,* and the *Religion.* In purely philosophical contexts Kant, to be sure, usually speaks of *moralische Gesinnung,* though in the *Critique of Judgment* he also uses the term *gottgefällige Gesinnung* (5:263).

30. Meier, *Betrachtungen über die würkliche Religion des menschlichen Geschlechts* (Halle, 1774), pp. 46–47.

Considering Meier's veneration of Milton's poetry, it is difficult to imagine that Meier was not thinking of Milton's sonnet on his buried talent, as well as his triumph in the face of adversity, not only here but also when Meier wrote, two years later, in *Reflections on the Natural Predispositions to Virtue and Vice (Betrachtung über die natürliche Anlage zur Tugend und zum Laster)*, "Hence an inborn divine genius can remain [no more than] a talent which is buried in a sweat rag. . . . a superb inborn poetic genius can remain incapacitated for life from producing a superb poem."[31] Abbt was wont to follow in Meier's footsteps; the above may be evidence that on occasion the master followed the disciple.[32]

In *Religion within the Boundaries of Mere Reason*, Kant, in fact, twice invokes the parable of the unused talent. Although in both of these instances he condemns the servant for not making active use of his talent, he still (inconsistently, it would seem) defines that talent as an "original predisposition to the good" and "the natural predisposition to goodness that lies in human nature" (*Rel*, 6:52, 161). I propose that he had been far bolder in the *Groundwork of the Metaphysics of Morals* and that his boldness is very much in the line of Milton's and Meier's—and Young's, Abbt's, and Herder's—invocation of the parable of the talents.

∿

In the opening of the *Groundwork* Kant suggests that "a special talent" *(ein besonderes Talent)* of the philosopher is required for the "teaching" *(Belehrung)* of pure reason that he is about to present (4:388–389). This teaching is the categorical imperative. Although few other teachings in modern Western culture have been as voluminously discussed, as far as I am aware the meaning of this "special talent" for Kant re-

31. Meier, *Betrachtung über die natürliche Anlage zur Tugend und zum Laster* (Halle, 1776), p. 27; cf. pp. 61, 63–66: "Daher kan ein angebohrnes göttliches Genie ein Talent bleiben, welches in einem Schweißtuche vergraben bleibt. . . . Ein vortrefliches angebohrnes poetisches Genie kan zeitlebens unvermögend bleiben, ein vortrefliches Gedicht zu machen."

32. Otto Gruber, *Herder und Abbt, Ein Beitrag zur Geistesgeschichte des 18. Jahrhunderts* (Marburg: Nolte, 1934), p. 14, remarks: "Abbt's aesthetic conceptions rely essentially on Baumgarten and his successor and continuator G. F. Meier [Abbts ästhetische Anschauungen fußen im wesentlichen auf Baumgarten und dessen Nachfolger und Fortsetzer G. F. Meier]."

mains largely unexplained. It may be plausible to assume that the meaning or functioning of the special talent is covered by Kant's elucidation, in the categorical imperative, of the not-special, vastly general, even universal capacity of rational beings to think and will that which is universally generalizable to all rational beings. Yet if this is the case some further explanation is still necessary of how "special" and "universal" can here describe one thing. How, in particular, does Kant resolve the apparently glaring contradictions between meanings of special and universal in his use of examples?

Even beyond the differences with Herder that climaxed in Kant's reviews of the *Ideen,* Kant's contempt for examples, up to 1784–85, is unmistakable. In the *Critique of Pure Reason* he famously remarked that "examples are the go-cart" or "walker" *(der Gängelwagen)* of "those who are lacking in the natural talent" of judgment (A134/B173–174). The strictly limited reach of teaching and learning that are bound down by examples is clearly also what he has in mind in the *Critique of Judgment* when he pronounces that "learning is nothing but imitation [Lernen nichts als Nachahmen ist]" (5:308). Just so, in the *Groundwork* he declares that "the imperative of *morality* . . . cannot be made out *by means of any example*" (4:419). Yet in the *Groundwork,* Kant presents, seriatim, four examples to help teach the categorical imperative (4:421–423).[33] To be consistent he must be speaking here of an exemplarity in these four examples that is somehow without the limiting force of example. This is to say that these examples must engender something other than imitation. Indeed, Kant says that these examples are being taught and learned in a "metaphysics carefully cleansed of everything empirical" (*GMM,* 4:438). But how is this cleansing achieved?

The problem of these empirical or even just empirically experienced examples is an instance of the larger problem that is encoun-

33. Some earlier views of Kant's use of these and other examples are those of Jonathan Harrison, "Kant's Examples of the First Formulation of the Categorical Imperative," and J. Kemp, "Kant's Examples of the Categorical Imperative," in *Kant: A Collection of Critical Essays,* ed. Robert Paul Wolff (Notre Dame: University of Notre Dame Press, 1968), pp. 228–245 and 246–258, respectively; Günther Buck, "Kants Theorie des Beispiels," in *Lernen und Erfahrung: Zum Begriff der didaktischen Induktion,* 2nd ed. (Stuttgart: Kohlhammer, 1969), pp. 97–114, David Lloyd, "Kant's Examples" and Cathy Caruth, "The Force of Example: Kant's Symbols," in *Unruly Examples: On the Rhetoric of Exemplarity,* ed. Alexander Gelley (Stanford: Stanford University Press, 1995), pp. 256–276 and 277–302, respectively.

tered in Kant's offering, and our reading, the book, published on a day in 1785, called *Groundwork of the Metaphysics of Morals*. How can we think of a represented groundwork (with all its adventitious ticks of individual choices of form and expression) as anything but an example? What, again, is the cleansing procedure that can render any individual's teaching "a priori" or "cleansed of everything . . . empirical" (*GMM*, 4:389), either in the teacher's act of teaching or in the student's act of receiving the empirical experience of this text? Thus Kant's putting his *Groundwork* before a reader, another mind, raises his own most troubling questions about a teaching and a learning of that teaching that do their work, even partly, through example.

The contradictions implicit in Kant's use of examples in the *Groundwork* seem only to be exacerbated by his famous corollary to the categorical imperative, the "kingdom of ends," in which each member has a "*share . . . in the giving of universal laws,*" apparently by providing categorical imperatives (or their effects or "maxims") to each other (4:435). He defines a kingdom as "a systematic union of various rational beings through common laws." The concept of being members of the same "kingdom of ends" *(Reich der Zwecke)* seems to require at least a reciprocal service of individually instanced groundworks, each of which would necessarily have the character, at least in part, of an example (4:433). Kant surely saw this. Here, too, we can assume that he already has in mind some distinction between kinds of examples, or between kinds of relation to examples, which is effected by the special talent that is at work in the *Groundwork*. My hypothesis is that this distinction is at least embryonically related to the concepts, in the *Critique of Judgment*, of exemplary originality, of the talent to be exemplary, and of putting that talent to the test of another such talent.

In the *Critique of Judgment* the context in which the concept of testing talent is broached is indeed one in which Kant is just as contemptuous of the use of examples for imitation as he is in his comments about examples in the *Groundwork*. In the *Critique of Judgment* just ten pages after he has said that what is called "learning is nothing but imitation" (5:308), he leaves no doubt that "academic instruction" is no different from this mere learning by imitation (5:318). Yet within these same pages, while clearly not being distracted from his views of the liabilities of using examples for imitation, he holds out the possibility of what is in effect a higher kind of teaching and learning, in which example has an indispensable role. This occurs, in fact, when he speaks of the effect of putting one's "talent to the test" by receiving an example—and its line of examples—"as a model, not for *imitation,* but for *succession*"(*CJ,* 5:309).[34] The procedure of succession somehow discloses the "talent to be exemplary" (*CJ,* 5:318).[35] We need to understand the form that the disclosure of this talent takes.

~

34. In the notes to the first edition of his translation, *Kant's Critique of Aesthetic Judgement* (Oxford: Clarendon Press, 1911), p. 282, Meredith explains that Kant actually wrote "nicht der Nachahmung, sondern der Nachahmung," while Kiesewetter emended the first *Nachahmung* to *Nachmachung* and informed Kant of the change. There is no record of Kant's response to Kiesewetter on this point; and, in fact, Kiesewetter's emendation, as Meredith explains, involves Kant in confusions or contradictions with regard to the contexts of his statement. Meredith therefore emends the second *Nachahmung* to "following" / *Nachfolge,* which accords with Kant's choice of the term at 5:318, "ein Beispiel nicht der Nachahmung . . . sondern der Nachfolge." Kant uses the term *Nachfolge* precisely in this way in many other passages in which no emendation is necessary. (This usage is acknowledged, or even regarded as normative, in modern scholarship, where the connection between genius and its talent also figures. Thus Eva Schaper, "Taste, Sublimity, and Genius: The Aesthetics of Nature and Art," in *The Cambridge Companion to Kant,* ed. Paul Guyer [Cambridge: Cambridge University Press, 1994], pp. 390–391, writes of "Genius" defined as "talent" in sections 46 to 49 of the *Critique of Judgment:* "The products of genius are original exemplars, and that means that they can be followed either by another genius, 'one whom it arouses to a sense of his own originality,' or imitated by a lesser mortal." Schaper, too, leaves this *following,* for Kant, in the realm of the inexplicable.) As I have suggested earlier, the special usefulness of this particular passage is that here Kant comments directly on the undetermined condition of the talent to be exemplary that is experienced in this *Nachfolge*—and says, "The possibility of this is difficult to explain [Wie dieses möglich sei, ist schwer zu erklären]," thus in fact opening the door to explanation, difficult as it may be. (On *CJ,* 5:309 he uses the term *unbestimmbar;* later, speaking of *genius* and the *talent to be exemplary* together [5:318], he uses the terms "im *freien* Gebrauche" and in "Zwangsfreiheit.") It may be that one of the reasons for the failure of commentators to focus on and follow out the significance of this *Nachfolge* was the fog created, in this richly interconnected passage, by Kant's error and its editorial aftermath. Meredith's note in the 1911 edition lists some of the passages (*CJ,* 5:283, 318, 355) that make it difficult or impossible to believe that Kant could have meant to write anything but "nicht der Nachahmung, sondern der Nachfolge" (not for imitation, but for succession).

35. Kant uses the term *talent to be exemplary* twice in the *Critique of Judgment,* §49, 5:318: "wodurch das Talent sich als musterhaft zeigt," which Meredith translates

This higher function of *testing* and *succession* is not everyone's lot—or choice. For the unspecified other "others" (*anderen*), who do not engage in the test of the talent to be exemplary, these "models . . . though not themselves derived from imitation . . . must serve [the] purpose," Kant says, of mere imitation (*CJ*, 5:308).[36] As we have seen, he then seems to close off inquiry about "succession" by saying, "the possibility of this is difficult to explain." Fortunately, as we have also seen, the hints that he gives before this discouraging statement point toward an explanation of just this possibility.

Kant's comments on the talent to be exemplary in the *Critique of*

"Which is what shows a talent to be exemplary"; "das Talent zu besitzen, dabei zugleich musterhaft zu sein," which Meredith translates "The talent requisite to enable one to be at the same time *exemplary*."

36. That the *andere* described at *CJ*, 5:309 are employing (*aufgeweckt* to) a kind of talent that amounts to genius is seen from the following passage, which paraphrases the chief elements of the earlier passage, but using the term *Genie* in most of the cases where the earlier passage used *Talent*. This later passage follows Kant's statement in the previous paragraph that "genius . . . is a talent for art [Genie . . . ein Talent zur Kunst sei]." Kant's term for the activity of this talent of genius is "nicht der Nachahmung . . . sondern der Nachfolge": "Nach diesen Voraussetzungen ist Genie: die musterhafte Originalität der Naturgabe eines Subjects im freien Gebrauche seiner Erkenntnissvermögen. Auf solche Weise ist das Product eines Genies (nach demjenigen, was in demselben dem Genie, nicht der möglichen Erlernung oder der Schule zuzuschreiben ist) ein Beispiel nicht der Nachahmung (denn da würde das, was daran Genie ist und den Geist des Werks ausmacht, verloren gehen), sondern der Nachfolge für ein anderes Genie . . ." (*CJ*, 5:318; underlining added). This describes the same class of *andere* (*CJ*, 5:309) who follow the products of talent in this special testing way, in sharp contrast to the other *anderen* who can only imitate, not follow, the exemplary products provided by such talent: "seine Producte zugleich Muster, d. i. *exemplarisch*, sein müssen; mithin, selbst nicht durch Nachahmung entsprungen, anderen doch dazu, d. i. zum Richtmaße oder Regel der Beurtheilung, dienen müssen" (*CJ*, 5:308). After "sondern der Nachfolge für ein anderes Genie," the passage continues, "welches dadurch zum Gefühl seiner eigenen Originalität aufgeweckt wird, Zwangsfreiheit von Regeln so in der Kunst auszuüben, daß diese dadurch selbst eine neue Regel bekommt, wodurch das Talent sich als musterhaft zeigt. . . . das Talent zu besitzen, dabei zugleich musterhaft zu sein" (*CJ*, 5:318). The logical and rhetorical correspondences between these passages do not blur the distinction between genius and any kind of technical talent but rather obliterate the distinction between genius and the higher talent to be exemplary or the talent of genius to be exemplary. As a result, I am proposing, the otherwise inscrutable achievement of genius can be scrutinized and even unfolded—though with difficulty—in the workings of such talent.

Judgment are remarkable in their own right. These comments elevate one kind of talent to an equality with genius. A hundred years ago Rudolf Hildebrand observed that this equation has almost no parallel in the whole of the German *Genieliteratur*. Kant and Herder virtually alone, Hildebrand notes, "saw both [Talent and Genius] under one concept, entirely without distinction [ganz ohne Unterscheidung, beide unter einem Begriff gesehen]."[37] (To Hildebrand's duo we should perhaps add Abbt, whom Herder was openly emulating on this specific issue.) My interest here is in the specific way in which Kant shifts his focus from the impenetrable term *genius* to the rationally explicable term *talent,* specifically the talent to be exemplary. Since for him reason can only be universal reason, this accessibility of the talent to be exemplary to rational specification means that the talent to be exemplary must be universally accessible to rational beings.

The mere fact that, in the *Critique of Judgment,* Kant can directly contemplate a way in which the talent to be exemplary achieves exemplary originality and freedom (5:318) is itself of considerable interest in studying shifts from the *Groundwork.* In the *Groundwork* Kant says that "freedom is no concept of experience, and moreover cannot be one" (4:455); "we shall never be able to comprehend how freedom is possible" (4:456); "freedom . . . cannot be presented in any possible experience; . . . it can never be comprehended or even only seen" (4:459); "how a categorical imperative is possible, can indeed be answered to the extent that one can furnish the sole presupposition on which alone it is possible, namely the idea of freedom, . . . but how this presupposition itself is possible can never be seen by any human reason" (4:461). In the *Critique of Judgment* he still says that the possibility of "following" an example in "freedom" is "difficult to explain." But

---

37. I quote from his monograph-length article on "Genie" in Jacob and Wilhelm Grimm, *Deutsches Wörterbuch,* ed. Rudolf Hildebrand and Hermann Wunderlich (Leipzig, 1897), p. 3449. (I have not reproduced Hildebrand's italics or his use of lower case letters even for nouns.) Schlapp, *Kants Lehre vom Genie,* p. 7, calls attention to Hildebrand's *phänomenalen Artikel,* though it rarely gets its due in later scholarship on the *Genieliteratur.* Particularly useful for finding one's way to the major and minor works of the *Genieliteratur* are, besides Hildebrand's and Schlapp's work, Herman Wolf, *Versuch einer Geschichte des Geniebegriffs in der deutschen Ästhetik des 18. Jahrhunderts: I. Band Von Gottsched bis auf Lessing* (Heidelberg: Carl Winter, 1923), and Klaus Gerth, *Studien zu Gerstenbergs Poetik: ein Beitrag zur Umschichtung der ästhetischen und poetischen Grundbegriffe im 18. Jahrhundert* (Göttingen: Vandenhoeck & Ruprecht, 1960).

now he says "difficult," not impossible. A world of potential difference has emerged in his thinking—or, more precisely, in what he is able to acknowledge about this thinking—of the representation of freedom. Now he says explicitly that though "*the inscrutability of the idea of freedom* precludes all positive representation," he can now describe, in sublime experience, an access to "the purely negative . . . presentation [*Darstellung*]" of freedom itself (*CJ,* 5:275). This "presentation" becomes available in sublime experience when the "imagination by its own act of depriving itself of its freedom . . . gains an . . . inner freedom" (*CJ,* 5:269–271). I propose that in practice—though not yet in theory—Kant was already presenting freedom in this way in the *Groundwork.*

In the *Critique of Judgment* the primary or "capital importance" that Kant attaches to the capacity to experience the sublime as "a faculty of mind transcending every standard of sense" and as "the basis of an *a priori* principle" (5:254, 266) suggests that his ensuing comments on talent and genius have a continuous relevance to his thinking about how we think freedom. It may seem, indeed, that these comments describe only the "talent in the line of art," the *Kunsttalent,* which is conventionally called "genius" and which can make an artistic "representation . . . universally communicable" (*CJ,* 5:317). I suggest, however, that, to the contrary, his idea of the talent to be exemplary, and of how it is tested, applies far more broadly to what he means by the highest powers of this talent and, especially, to what he means, in the *Groundwork,* by the "special talent" of the philosopher (and all rational beings) to express the teaching of exemplarity in the categorical imperative.[38]

In Kant's view we can represent exemplarity with the "talent to be exemplary [das Talent . . . musterhaft zu sein]." Those who achieve this exemplarity do so in *succession* to a performance of exemplarity in its progression. They can do this by putting "their own talent to the test, so as to let it serve as a model, not for *imitation,* but for *succession* [ihr eigenes Talent prüfen mögen, um sich jenes zum Muster nicht der *Nachmachung,* sondern der *Nachfolge* dienen zu lassen]." This must

38. There are moments in the "Analytic of the Sublime" when the experience of the sublime seems to be expressed as the categorical imperative. For example: "The feeling of the sublime in nature is respect for our own vocation . . . the idea of humanity in our own self" (*CJ,* 5:257).

mean that they test their talent to be exemplary in a succession of the experience of the sublime in order to produce their own exemplarity of the experience of the sublime to which someone else may then succeed (*CJ,* 5:309, 318). This heady formula describes the way of the Kantian moral world that is called the "kingdom of ends." I propose that this testing of talent is Kant's implementation of what Henry Allison has called "the universalizability test . . . expressed in the categorical imperative."[39] This means that the universalizability test is neither after the fact nor a seal of approval of the categorical imperative but is rather itself the means for achieving the condition "expressed in the categorical imperative." Moreover, in each case that produces exemplarity, the succession and its test begin with a particular, chosen, heteronomous example of sublime succession, such as we find preeminently in poetry of the sublime. Allison argues that for Kant "even heteronomous or nonmorally based actions are free . . . since they are conceived . . . as products of the practical spontaneity of the agent."[40] I am suggesting that the practical spontaneity of the agent—in fact, its freedom as well as its basis in moral feeling—is disclosed to reason only in the procedure of succession in the sublime. Fearful or hesitant about his own revolutionary claims for the moral sublime, Kant does indeed, at one point, call his "theory of the sublime" an "appendage" (*CJ,* 5:246.) Yet already in the *Critique of Practical Reason,* and even in the *Groundwork,* he shows that the procedure of succession in the sublime implements what he has the courage to call "a determinate formula" of "the most sublime practical principles" (*CPrR,* 5:7–8). The upshot of this exercise of the procedure of succession (in which each individual can only succeed in an individual way) is that poetry or art of the sublime is indispensable to the workings of moral reason.

Some of Kant's comments on poetic talent in the *Critique of Judgment* can indeed give the impression that he identifies "poetic art" restrictively as "a talent . . . of the imagination" (5:314), a talent that is therefore different from, and of a lower order than, the "special talent" of reason in the philosopher. Yet we must consider that he notes in the same place that "the poet essays the task of interpreting to sense the ra-

39. Allison, *Kant's Theory of Freedom,* p. 205. Allison largely discounts the ethical importance of Kant's theory of the sublime per se.
40. Ibid., p. 6.

tional ideas of invisible beings, the kingdom of the blessed, . . . etc." as opposed to "examples" that "occur in experience" (5:314). Even if only parenthetically, he emphasizes the relation of poetry to a special kind of exemplarity: "*Poetry* (which owes its origin almost entirely to genius and is least willing to be led by precepts or example) holds the first rank among all the arts" (*CJ*, 5:326). We can therefore view in yet another kind of Kantian light his claim (previously examined in relation to aesthetic ideas) that poetry "puts the faculty of intellectual ideas (reason) into motion—a motion, at the instance of a representation, towards an extension of thought, that, while germane, no doubt, to the concept of the object, exceeds what can be laid hold of in that representation" (*CJ*, 5:315). In other words, poetry uses examples to disengage the mind from what is empirical in examples. As I have proposed before, according to Kant the reader's experience, in representation, of "an extension of thought" which exceeds his or her capacity for thought and representation, is thus highly suggestive of Kant's description, in the experience of the sublime, of encountering "the impossibility of [grasping] the absolute totality of an endless progression." As a result of that experience of exceeded capacity, the mind suffers something very like the "momentary check to the vital forces" that Kant understands to be, or to make possible, the sublime condition of freedom—and of originality in a new beginning.

Kant says that poetry's exemplary "talent" ("which is termed soul"— *Geist*) is the talent to make "a particular representation . . . universally communicable" (*CJ*, 5:317). His notion of universal communicability is also rooted in the experience of the sublime. We see this, for instance, in his account of how an individual achieves, in the first place, a "sensus communis" that can be universally communicated. This process is reminiscent of the categorical imperative in many ways, including the use of "maxims." One achieves "a *universal standpoint*" of a sensus communis, he says, by "following maxims of common human understanding . . . : (1) to think for oneself; (2) to think from the standpoint of every one else; (3) always to think consistently" (*CJ*, 5:294–295). Here, too, he implies the role of sublime experience in making possible an exemplarity that can be disengaged from example: the "*sensus communis* . . . the idea of a *public* sense, i.e. a critical faculty which in its reflective act takes account (*a priori*) of the mode of representation of every one else" depends, he says, upon our ability to achieve "a mere abstraction from the limitations which contingently affect our own estimate. This, in turn, is effected by so far as possible letting go the element of matter, i.e. sensation, in our general state of representative activity" (*CJ*, 5:293–294). The decisive step here, too, is the "letting go," which for him means, I propose, the liberation effected in the experience of the sublime by encountering an effectively endless series of examples of a deficited kind.

I am suggesting that in the *Groundwork* the performance or production of both the transfer to the universal standpoint and the categorical imperative already very much depends upon the sublime experience of the succession procedure that Kant clarified and made explicit only a few years later in the *Critique of Judgment*. This sublime experience already makes it possible for him to represent an exemplarity, which is a "letting go" of examples, very much while achieving the freedom of exemplary originality. The term *sublimity (Erhabenheit)* already occurs a number of times in the moral lexicon of the *Groundwork*. In each case it denotes an effect of being independent—autonomous or free—from incentives, as in the following statements: "It is just in this independence of maxims from all . . . incentives that their sublimity consists" (*GMM*, 4:339); "The principle of *one's own happiness* . . . bases morality on incentives that undermine it and destroy all its sublimity" (4:442).[41] Yet in the *Groundwork* he gives no explicit idea of the cause, in the universal case, of this sublimity, which is defined as freedom from all incentives. In the specific case of his own special talent for his present teaching of the categorical imperative, he also gives us no explicit idea about how he himself is gaining access, right now, to thinking this freedom of sublimity.

Assuming, then, that the cause of transfer and freedom in the categorical imperative is sublime experience, what, according to Kant, is the cause, in its turn, of this sublime experience? Although Kant says in the *Groundwork* that this question must remain unanswerable, he ex-

---

41. Other instances are: "The sublimity and inner dignity of the command in a duty is all the more manifest the fewer are the subjective causes in favor of it and the more there are against it" (*GMM*, 4:425); "We . . . represent a certain sublimity and *dignity* in the person who fulfills all his duties. For there is indeed no sublimity in him insofar as he is *subject* to the moral law, but there certainly is insofar as he is at the same time *lawgiving* with respect to it and only for that reason subordinated to it" (*GMM*, 4:439–440).

pressed himself otherwise in the *Critique of Judgment* and even came to subscribe to a theory of putting the talent to be exemplary to the test of other such talents, as in reading sublime poetry. I repeat the elements of that theory:

1. Empirically or heteronomously the mind's talent to be exemplary follows an effectively endless progression of representations (*CJ*, 5:318). In each case the succession and its test begin with a particular, chosen example of sublime succession.
2. Each representation in the progression that admits of succession (as opposed to imitation) represents "its own inadequacy" to represent (*CJ*, 5:252–253).
3. The test of the talent to be exemplary in the succession issues in the sublime effect (*CJ*, 5:255) and in exemplarity (*CJ*, 5:309, 318).
4. This heteronomous succession discloses an isomorphic, autonomous ("self-maintaining") succession that also issues in the sublime effect, hence in freedom and moral feeling (*CJ*, 5:313, 318).
5. Parallel to (or identical with) this isomorphism of the heteronomous and the autonomous, a *transfer* takes place, in the experience of the sublime, (*CJ*, 5:266–267, 352–353), from the sensible (and the example, the individual) to the supersensible (and exemplarity, the universal).
6. For Kant himself, one principal, recurring succession is to Milton's poetry of the sublime, from which Kant also derives the main principles of the sublime succession.

Kant is silent about the instances of the examples, the performances (as he calls them), which he has followed in being (in his terms in the *Critique of Judgment*, §49) "aroused" to his own "exemplary originality" in the categorical imperative in the *Groundwork*. His reasons for this silence or distancing are quite likely related to other such distancings that we have discussed. Be that as it may, I now propose that his test of the talent to be exemplary in the *Groundwork* is a succession to Milton's—and German Miltonism's—prior performances of the test of the talent to be exemplary. In its paradigmatic sonnet form, this succession produces the transfer to freedom and exemplarity. Here I return briefly to Milton's sonnet itself.

For Milton, as for Kant, the possibilities of freedom and the talent to be exemplary are ultimately God-created, yet for each individual they can only be disclosed by putting the talent to be exemplary to the test of another such talent in a line of such tests. Even in his immobilized condition, Milton's freestanding reason tests his talent to be exemplary in a following of Christ's parable of the test of talents. Indeed, looming vast, even if invisible, behind Christ's authority for speaking the parable is a climactic event of Christian history. Christ's own exemplarity is to be the fulfillment of all prophetic types—to be the example that serves as exemplary "prototype" *(Urbild)*, Kant will say in the *Religion*.[42] This exemplarity is achieved by putting himself to the test of the virtually endless line of tests beginning with the test of a son (of Abraham) and including all the other Old Testament prefigurations of the testing of Christ. For Milton this Christian typology—this *Typik*, in Kant's terms (*CPrR*, 5:67–71)—of tests of the talent to be exemplary locates the specific sublimity of Christian experience in its typology and *imitatio Christi* (traditionally translated in German as the *Nachfolge Christi*).

To appreciate how intensely Milton already works these effects, we need to see the prominent ways in which he locates the testing of another servant—"my servant Job" [Job, 1:8], as God calls him—within this typology. John Carey has noted that in verses 9–10 of the sonnet, Milton refers, as he does more explicitly in *De doctrina Christiana*, to Job 22:2–3: "Can a man be profitable unto God, as he that is wise may be profitable unto himself? Is it any pleasure to the Almighty, that thou art righteous? or is it gain to him, that thou makest thy ways perfect?"[43] We might even say, therefore, that the reply of patience in the sonnet, "God doth not need / Either man's work or his own gifts," is spoken specifically by the patience of Job. (The commonplace phrase "the patience of Job" is from James 5:11.)

As far as I am aware it has not been noted that another citation from Job is also centrally placed—joined to the citation noted by Carey—

---

42. See especially *Rel*, 6:119, 128–129.
43. Carey, ed., *John Milton*, p. 333.

at the turning point in the sonnet. In Kant's time it was perhaps eas-
ier than now to recognize that the sonnet's "murmur" or complaint,
"Doth God exact day-labor, light denied," echoes the complaint and
plea on behalf of the sufferer in Job 14:6: "Turn from him, that he may
rest, till he shall accomplish, as an hireling [day-laborer, Luther: *ein
Tagelöhner*] his day [i.e., day's pay]." In his lectures on the sublime in
Job, Lowth had called this passage "a most perfect specimen of the Ele-
giac" mode that produces the experience of the sublime. Mendels-
sohn, reviewing Lowth, called the same passage an example of the
way "the passions in Job are sublime" (*die Leidenschaften im Hiob sind
erhaben*) and gave the following beautiful translation, different from
Luther's but also naming the afflicted *Tagelöhner*: "Laß ab von ihm, daß
er ruhe, / Daß er seine Zeit wie ein Tagelöhner abwarte."[44] (In Chap-
ter 5 we will encounter Kant's special interest in the sublimity of the
book of Job as well as its Miltonic afterlife.) Job thus provides an un-
mistakable station in the typology or progression of sublime accep-
tance of worldly loss that, I am suggesting, is the condition for the
transfer in this sonnet. This is preeminently the Job who finally can ac-
knowledge the transfer of standpoint that is disclosed to him and con-
firmed by God in the whirlwind. We are now almost at that nexus of
transfer in the sonnet itself.

It is noteworthy that though Milton developed the experience of the

44. Robert Lowth, *Lectures on the Sacred Poetry of the Hebrews*, 2 vols. (London, 1787;
Latin, 1753; German trans. 1758), facsimile, intro. Vincent Freimarck (Hildesheim:
Olms, 1969), II.424–425; Moses Mendelssohn, review of Lowth's *De sacra poesi
Hebraeorum*, in *Bibliothek der schönen Wissenschaften und der freyen Künste* 1 (1757): 295–
296. It must have been noticed before, and indeed Milton may well have noticed it,
that the powerful ambiguities of Job 14:6 in the Hebrew (and its Arabic etymologies
or affiliations), may be a source for the New Testament parable of the talents. The
ambiguities in this Joban verse are clearly laid out in the 1787 edition of Lowth's *Lec-
tures on the Sacred Poetry of the Hebrews*, where the verse is translated "Turn from him,
that he may have some respite, / Till he shall, like a hireling, have completed his
day." In a footnote added by "H.," the Hebrew *ad yirtseh kisachir yomo*, which is the sec-
ond half of the verse, is glossed as follows: "Or until he *shall acquiesce*: or *shall make sat-
isfaction* (the original will bear either interpretation); for the word [*yirtseh*] in the
Arabic dialect sometimes signifies, He *did or afforded to another, what he held to be agree-
able to himself.*" Thus from the tensions of ambiguity in this one word *yirtseh*, the entire
parable of the day laborers and their rendering satisfaction to another, or not, or one
of them satisfying himself, not to speak of Milton's probing of these ambiguities,
might plausibly have been generated or at least enriched.

sublime to the greatest extent of any modern Western poet, he hardly ever refers to Longinus. This may well be because Milton felt that the sublime of Christian experience leaves Longinus far behind. Milton sees in Christian typology a uniquely great impact of the sublime. This impact is the effect of the Christian's encounter of an endless line of deficited representations that yields Christian liberty. Proportionate to this impact, a deathliness in life emerges in the chilling last line of Milton's sonnet. Here the poet achieves, indeed, suspension within life (a holding of the breath, a withholding even of thought) at exactly the instant in which he achieves the freedom of the talent to be exemplary.

By the end of the sonnet Milton has left behind the visible objects and examples of his plight, just as the one-talent servant has refused the demands for imitation and even replication to which the other servants submit. Now the poet knows and exemplifies, and articulates in an unforgettable maxim, service to God that is purely an end in itself. Milton's performance in the sonnet thus already responds systematically yet with extraordinary economy to the problem of how to teach and learn an exemplarity that is disengaged from the limitations and coercions entailed by examples. This disengagement occurs in the momentary letting go of the sensory and visible. In propounding his law of exemplarity in this instant, Milton asserts that even the supreme being must view a mere goodwill that is free of all incentive—even, and perhaps especially, in a blind, immobilized human being—as a fulfillment of the talent to serve in a pure service. A human being of this sort offers only the exemplarity—achieved in the sublime succession—of a moral disposition that is free of all material, visible incentives.

For Kant, Milton's performance opens the experience of an effectively infinite series of similar performances of the transfer. This series includes the transfer in standpoints that are to be found in Job and the parable of the talents as well as in writers in the constellation of German Miltonism such as Abbt and Meier. Here the continuity between constellation and succession seems to be especially strong. In the series of performances that Kant encounters, each talent to be exemplary is plunged into momentary sublime loss of all external incentive yet gains freedom in the same instant. In Kant's succession, his talent to be exemplary achieves the freedom, transfer, and exemplarity of the categorical imperative in the moment of the sublime disengagement of exemplarity from imitation and examples. He achieves this disengagement and becomes an equivalent of the true servant in Milton's telling of the parable, the servant who succeeds in transcending the demands of imitation and replication while disclosing his one true talent to be exemplary.

~

We are now poised to observe Kant's succession to Milton's performance and to Milton's "ideas" or "sources" of the talent to be exemplary. For Kant as well as Milton this succession depends upon being embedded in a line of performances of such talent. This line certainly includes, in my view, Matthew's telling of the parable of the talents itself. At this point we should again briefly recall Kant's invocations of the parable of the talents in *Religion within the Limits of Reason Alone*. Written soon after the *Critique of Judgment*, Kant there uses this parable to derive nothing less than a Christian formulation of the categorical imperative from the verses of Matthew. This is hard evidence of the contiguity of the categorical imperative and the parable of the talents in Kant's later thinking. Yet it is ossified evidence, since here the formulation of the categorical imperative, as well as the interpretation of the parable, does not achieve the valuation of the goodwill that is manifested even and especially in inactive disposition.[45] This inactive way of

45. In the *Religion,* here cited from *Religion within the Limits of Reason Alone,* trans. T. H. Greene and Hoyt H. Hudson (New York: Harper and Row, 1960), Kant, in fact, interprets Matthew 5:20–48 to mean that "the pure moral disposition of the heart alone can make man well-pleasing to God" (6:159). Yet he does not integrate the idea into either this formulation of the categorical imperative, which he derives from Christ's words in Matthew (Chapters 5, 6, 7, and 13), or his interpretation of Christ's parable of the talents. Kant writes: "He combines all duties (1) in one *universal* rule (which includes within itself both the inner and the outer moral relations of men), namely: Perform your duty for no motive other than unconditioned esteem for duty itself, *i.e.,* love God (the Legislator of all duties) above all else; and (2) in a *particular* rule, that, namely, which concerns man's external relation to other men as universal duty: Love every one as yourself, *i.e.,* further his welfare from good-will that is immediate and not derived from motives of self-advantage. These commands are not mere laws of virtue but precepts of *holiness* which we ought to pursue, and the very pursuit of them is called *virtue.* [There is no paragraph break here in the German, as there is in the English translation.] Accordingly he destroys the hope of all who intend to wait upon this moral goodness quite passively, with their hands in their laps, as though it were a heavenly gift which descends from on high. He who leaves unused

valuing the good is indispensable to the pure rationality of the categorical imperative in the *Groundwork* and, equally (I am claiming), to the disposition isolated in Milton's reworking of the parable of the talents in the sonnet. In fact, the correspondences between Kant's presentation of the categorical imperative in the *Groundwork* and Milton's ways of rewriting Matthew's parable are incomparably more detailed and more significant than the linkage of parable with categorical imperative in the *Religion*.

In the space of Milton's fourteen-line reworking of the parable, we encounter a performance of the talent to be exemplary, and its transfer, that is a model of all of the following elements or "ideas" in Kant's teaching of the talent to be exemplary in the categorical imperative in the *Groundwork:*[46]

1. All four examples of duties that Kant derives from the categorical imperative, namely, (a) the man who has come to "the point of despair," (b) the man who has "borrow[ed] money" which he cannot repay, (c) the man who "finds in himself a talent that by means of some cultivation could make him a human being useful for all sorts of purposes," (d) the man who contemplates service to "others . . . whom he could very well help." (This fourth example at first seems to have no counterpart in Milton's verses, though Milton's maxim, shared with others in God's kingly state, ultimately encompasses this example, too, in a redefined concept of service.)
2. Kant's principle that the thinking of the categorical imperative must divest itself of all incentives that are referred to the self.

the natural predisposition to goodness which lies in human nature (like a talent entrusted to him) in lazy confidence that a higher moral influence will no doubt supply the moral character and completeness which he lacks, is confronted with the threat that even the good which, by virtue of his natural predisposition, he may have done, will not be allowed to stand him in stead because of this neglect ([Matthew] XXV, 29)" (6:160–161). It would be interesting but difficult to speculate on why Kant now allows—what he rejected with contempt in the *Groundwork* (4:430n)—the identification of a secondary, groundless Golden Rule with the categorical imperative or why, in this interpretation of the parable of the talents, he now accepts the literal demand for outward, active fulfillments.

46. Page references for all the elements and "ideas" in the list are given, and contextualized, in the succeeding pages.

3. Kant's idea that the possibility of the categorical imperative depends on a "transfer" between two "standpoints," the first (visible to some) in the world of sense, the second (invisible to all) in the world of pure intelligences.

4. Kant's idea that what is exemplary in the exemplarity of the categorical imperative is only a "disposition" to action rather than an action itself.

5. Kant's apparently strange insistence that the categorical imperative is achieved in the exemplarity not only of human beings but of all "rational beings" (which is to say, from humanity on up) though not of "the sovereign." We recall that Milton's "thousands" who "speed And post" are angels.

6. Kant's assertion that "even [the] sole absolute lawgiver would . . . have to be represented as appraising the worth of rational beings only by their disinterested conduct. . . . That which . . . alone constitutes the worth of a human being is that in terms of which he must also be appraised by whoever does it, even by the supreme being."

7. Kant's concept of a kingdom of ends (i.e., "ends" which are not referred to the self).

8. Kant's idea that the categorical imperative must issue in a "maxim" that is derived in freedom, even though he says he can provide no explanation of how maxims come to us in freedom.[47]

In Kant's testing of his talent to be exemplary, his third (usually contemned) example assumes central importance. This is the example of the individual ("a third"—*ein dritter,* Kant says) who "finds in himself a

47. T. C. Williams, *The Concept of the Categorical Imperative: A Study of the Place of the Categorical Imperative in Kant's Ethical Theory* (Oxford: Clarendon Press, 1968), p. 19, comments: "In the *Groundwork* Kant renounces any aim of showing *how* maxims arise." For recent interesting comments on Kant's maxims, see Onora O'Neill, "Consistency in Action," in *Kant's Groundwork of the Metaphysics of Morals,* ed. Paul Guyer (Lanham, Maryland: Rowan & Littlefield, 1998), pp. 112–119. For my argument it is useful to recall Julius Ebbinghaus's emphasis on Kant's preposition "through" with regard to the operation of the maxim: see "Interpretation and Misinterpretation of the Categorical Imperative" (German version, 1948), in *Kant: A Collection of Critical Essays,* ed. Wolff, p. 223, though Ebbinghaus does not suggest the kind of *Nachfolge* that I am tracing.

talent [*findet in sich ein Talent*] that by means of some cultivation could make him a human being useful for all sorts of purposes" (*GMM*, 4:422–423). Robert Paul Wolff said of this example: "Nothing much need be said about this argument for cultivating one's talents. Considering the oppressive odor of relentless moralism which clings to the passage, it is just as well that the argument is so obviously bad."[48] Yet I believe that this example in fact organizes Kant's choice of all four examples and is closely related to the exercise of his special talent to be exemplary in teaching the categorical imperative.

∼

I will now offer a gathering of quotations from the *Groundwork of the Metaphysics of Morals* which, I am saying, are a cento of the "ideas" to which Kant succeeds from Milton's own proceeding to a categorical imperative in his sonnet. Let me emphasize, however, that it is for me a working assumption that Kant's encounter with Milton's sonnet took place, and acquired its full significance for him, within the constellation of German Miltonism. Indeed, for my purposes it would mean the same thing if it turned out that Kant was actually following the performance (within that constellation) of someone else's talent that closely followed Milton's or, indeed, if he were following the performance of someone else altogether. It would mean the same thing, that is, as long as the given performance performed the identical followings in this line of followings and under the Miltonic or Kantian conditions of Miltonic typology or Kantian Typic and procedure of succession. If these conditions are met—as they are, I believe, here—we have found a good deal more than the "special stimulus" to the *Groundwork* that Klaus Reich discovered in Cicero's *De officiis*. This was, Reich thought, Kant's totally exceptional invocation of a single "image, stirring up the feelings and making intuition possible."[49] Instead, or in addition, we find an integrated representational complex that is even replete with the crucial element that Reich acknowledged was entirely lacking in the Ciceronian source, the principle of the autonomy of the will.

48. Robert Paul Wolff, *The Autonomy of Reason: A Commentary on Kant's Groundwork of the Metaphysic of Morals* (New York: Harper & Row, 1973), p. 169.
49. I cited Reich's claim at the end of Chapter 1.

What I will now present, then, in Kant's own language in the *Ground-work,* is his closely correspondent succession (always, no doubt, in the constellation of German Miltonism) to the ideas of Milton's performance in his own succession to Matthew's retelling of Christ's parable of the test of talents. For the purposes of my overview, I will first set out in compact form a close paraphrase of Kant's terms for these ideas in their collective cogency:

a goodwill that has been incapacitated from acting

a condition of being unable to repay a sum of borrowed money

the (third) man with a talent that could be useful, even exemplary

the gift of patience as purely rational sustainer of laws, not as tutelary spirit whispering apodictic solutions

the transfer between the standpoint of the world of sense (and heteronomy) and the purely intelligible world (and autonomy)—as well as between the world that (some)one sees and the world that no one sees

the (disinterested) perfection of God and His valuing of disinterested conduct

the maxim

the maxim and its freedom

the maxim and the categorical imperative

the maxim and a world of rational beings as a kingdom of ends

Not only do these Kantian elements follow every significant element of Milton's sonnet, but Kant's way of explaining their integration constitutes a full and profound interpretation of that sonnet, especially of its transfer between standpoints, that is, between Milton's octave and sestet.[50]

Herewith, I reproduce, piece by piece, verses from Milton's sonnet in brackets. The rubrics in italics are from the list of elements above. All other passages are from the *Groundwork:*

50. The pregnancy, or spontaneity, of the moment for Milton is indicated by the fact that the transfer between standpoints takes place in a break from the conventional Petrarchan clean division between octave and sestet.

[When I consider how my light is spent,
Ere half my days, in this dark world and wide,
And that one Talent which is death to hide,
Lodg'd with me useless, though my Soul more bent
To serve therewith my Maker, and present
My true account]

a goodwill that has been incapacitated from acting

Even if, by a special disfavor of fortune . . ., this will should wholly lack the capacity to carry out its purpose . . . and only the good will were left . . . it would still shine by itself, as something that has its full worth in itself. . . . We shall put this idea to the test from this point of view. (4:394–395)

If adversity and hopeless grief have quite taken away the taste for life; if an unfortunate man, strong of soul and more indignant about his fate than despondent or dejected, wishes for death and yet preserves his life without loving it, not from inclination or fear but from duty, then his maxim has moral content. (4:397–398)

a condition of being unable to repay a sum of borrowed money

Another finds himself urged by need to borrow money. He well knows that he will not be able to repay. (4:422)

the (third) man with a talent that could be useful, even exemplary

A third [*ein dritter*] finds in himself a talent [*ein Talent*] that by means of some cultivation could make him a human being useful for all sorts of purposes . . . [4:422–423]. There are in humanity talents [aptitudes: *Anlagen;* Gregor gives "predispositions"] for greater perfection, which belong to the end of nature with respect to humanity in our subject. (4:430)

Because we also regard enlarging our talents [*unsere Talente*] as a duty, we represent a person of talents [*eine Person von Talenten*] also as, so to speak, an *example of the law* (to become like him . . . in practice). (4:401n)

> ["Doth God exact day-labor, light denied,"
> I fondly ask; But patience to prevent
> That murmur, soon replies, "God doth not need
> Either man's work or his own gifts; who best
> Bear his mild yoke, they serve him best; his State
> Is Kingly. Thousands at his bidding speed
> And post o'er Land and Ocean without rest]

the gift of patience as purely rational sustainer of laws, not as tutelary spirit whispering apodictic solutions

. . . he himself is provided with the special gift of patience . . . [4:398]. . . . Here philosophy is to manifest its purity as sustainer of its own laws, not as herald of laws that . . . who knows what tutelary nature whispers to it. (4:426)

> ["Doth God exact day-labor, light denied,"
> I fondly ask]

the transfer between the standpoints of the world of sense (and heteronomy) and the purely intelligible world (and autonomy)—as well as between the world that (some)one sees and the world that no one sees

One resource . . . still remains to us, namely to inquire whether we do not take a different standpoint when by means of freedom we think ourselves as causes efficient a priori than when we represent ourselves in terms of our actions as effects that we see before our eyes. (4:450)

He has two standpoints . . . *first,* insofar as he belongs to the world of sense . . . (heteronomy); *second,* as belonging to the intelligible world. . . .

When we think of ourselves as free we transfer ourselves into the world of understanding as members of it and cognize autonomy of the will along with its consequence, morality. . . .

He transfers himself in thought into an order of things altogether different from that of his desires in the field of sensibility. . . ; he can expect only a greater inner worth of his person . . . when he transfers himself to the standpoint of a member of the world of understanding. (4:452, 454–455)

The proper worth of an absolutely good will—a worth raised above all price—consists just in the principle of action being free from all influences of contingent grounds. (4:426)

When moral worth is at issue, what counts is not actions, which one sees, but those inner principles of actions that one does not see. [4:407] . . . The insightful . . . avert their eyes [*Einsehende . . . ihre Augen wegwenden*]. (4:409)

[God doth not need
Either man's work or his own gifts]

the (disinterested) perfection of God and his valuing of disinterested conduct

Even the Holy One of the Gospel must first be compared with our ideal of moral perfection before he is cognized as such; even he says of himself [Matthew 19:17]: why do you call me (whom you see) good? none is good (the archetype of the good) but God only (whom you do not see). But whence have we the concept of God as the highest good? Solely from the *idea* of moral perfection that reason frames a priori and connects inseparably with the concept of a free will. (4:408–409)

. . . Even this sole absolute lawgiver would . . . have to be represented as appraising the worth of rational beings only by their disinterested conduct. . . . That which . . . alone constitutes the worth of a human being is that in terms of which he must also be appraised by whoever does it, even by the supreme being. (4:439)

[They also serve who only stand and wait.]

the maxim

An action from duty has its moral worth *not in the purpose* to be attained by it but in the maxim in accordance with which it is decided upon . . . when every material principle has been withdrawn. (4:399–400)

the maxim and its freedom

> Freedom as a negative determination is combined with a (positive) capacity as well, and indeed with a causality of reason that we call a will, a capacity so to act that the principle of actions conforms with the essential constitution of a rational cause, that is, with the condition of universal validity of a maxim as a law. (4:458)

the maxim and the categorical imperative

> The categorical imperative can also be expressed thus: *act in accordance with maxims that can at the same time have as their object themselves as universal laws of nature.* In this way, then, the formula of an absolutely good will is provided. (4:437)

> > [his State / Is Kingly. Thousands at his bidding speed
> > And post o'er Land and Ocean without rest:
> > They also serve who only stand and wait.]

the maxim and a world of rational beings as a kingdom of ends

> The concept of every rational being as one who must regard himself as giving universal law through all the maxims of his will, so as to appraise himself and his actions from this point of view, leads to a very fruitful concept dependent upon it, namely that *of a kingdom of ends. . . .* A rational being belongs as a *member* to the kingdom of ends when he gives universal laws in it but is also himself subject to these laws. . . . A rational being must always regard himself as lawgiving in a kingdom of ends possible through freedom of the will, whether as a member or as sovereign. (4:433–434)

> The practical imperative will therefore be the following: *So act that you use humanity, whether in your own person or in the person of any other, always at the same time as an end, never merely as a means.* (4:429)

> . . . if there is a categorical imperative (i.e., a law for every will of a rational being) it can only command that everything be done from the maxim of one's will as a will that could at the same time have as its object itself as giving universal law. (4:432)

For when we think a will of this kind, then although a will that *stands under law* [*der unter Gesetzen steht*] may be bound to this law by means of some interest, a will that is itself the supreme lawgiver cannot possibly, as such, depend upon some interest. (4:432)

I say that the human being and in general every rational being *exists* as an end in itself, *not merely as a means*. . . . From the representation of what is necessarily an end for everyone . . . it is an *end in itself*, it constitutes an *objective* principle of the will and thus can <u>serve</u> as a universal practical law [*zum allgemeinen praktischen Gesetz <u>dienen</u> kann*]. (4:428; underlining added)

He must always take his maxims from the point of view of himself, and likewise every other rational being, as lawgiving beings (who for this reason are also called persons). Now in this way a world of rational beings *(mundus intelligibilis)* as a kingdom of ends is possible, through the giving of their own laws by all persons as members. (4:438)

It is just in this independence of maxims from all such incentives that their sublimity consists [*die Erhabenheit derselben bestehe*]. (4:439)

～

For the laying down of the categorical imperative, these passages (among others) in the *Groundwork* constitute the internal act that is described explicitly by Kant in the *Critique of Judgment.* This is the act of putting the talent to be exemplary to the test of the performance of another such talent in its line of performance. In the case of the *Groundwork* the performance of another such talent is the procedure of succession in Milton's sonnet, set within the constellation in which Kant encounters it. In Kant's terms for the sublime experience that provides freedom and the transfer (the conditions for the categorical imperative), the test of talent in the *Groundwork* must be experienced by him in an effectively endless line of such tests of talent. Kant remarks in the *Critique of Judgment* that he speaks of freedom in fine art "in a sense opposed to contract work," *Lohngeschäft* (5:321) or, in Milton's terms, "day-labour." Each individual test of talent on the line that Kant experiences, flowing through Milton (in the sonnet as well as in the major poems of Milton, of which the sonnet is a paradigm or

Formel), is itself a free performance of moral disposition in the form of the categorical imperative. Kant's concept of the kingdom of ends in a "world of rational beings," following Milton's concept of the kingly state in the world of pure intelligences, is a synchronic description of the diachronic endless line of maxim-givers whom Kant experiences. We have seen that we can name some specific names for Kant in his contemporary and inherited kingdom of ends, that is, in the line or constellation of those who put themselves to the test of Milton's talent and those to whom Milton also puts his talent to the test: Young and Abbt, Herder and Meier, Milton most immediately, and, standing behind Milton, Matthew and Job.

As I noted earlier, this kingdom of ends doubtless includes, for Milton and for Kant, Christ the archetype who defines Christian typology and who puts his talent to be exemplary (to be the type of types, the exemplarity of examples) to the test of the effectively endless Old Testament line of performances of the Christ-like test. Experienced in something like this virtually endless lineal way, Kant's putting of his talent to be exemplary to the test of this line of talents to be exemplary plunges him into momentary sublime loss of all external incentive. Although it may never become fully or merely impersonal, this experience of letting go is indispensable for his teaching as well as learning of the categorical imperative. In this moment of freedom, the test of the talent to be exemplary, as well as the exemplarity of the categorical imperative, are disengaged from examples. This disengagement from examples enables Kant to exercise his special talent and to achieve a learning and teaching in freedom that—momentarily—escape imitation and its demands. In this instant his individual goodwill stands only, purely, in the autonomy of reason, having been transferred by its own test of talent to this exemplary, waiting *Standpunkt,* standpoint.

CHAPTER 4

Kantian Tragic Form and Kantian "Storytelling"

The goal of this chapter and the next is to demonstrate that the activity of representing sublime tragic form is central to the *Critique of Practical Reason*.[1] For Kant this activity emerged as an *a priori* "moving force" (*CPrR*, 5:88, 152)—an inner force of inner *change*—in moral reason.[2]

1. Suggestive recent comments on the need to grapple with Kant's interest in tragedy are those of Miguel de Beistegui and Simon Sparks, eds., *Philosophy and Tragedy* (London: Routledge, 2000), pp. 1–8, and Dennis J. Schmidt, *On Germans and Other Greeks: Tragedy and Ethical Life* (Bloomington: Indiana University Press, 2001), pp. 73–83. For a complexity, or complicaton, of tragic attitudes and undertones in Kant, see Theodor Haering, "Der tragische Kant: Versuch einer Ergänzung des herrschenden Kantbildes," *Zeitschrift für deutsche Kulturphilosophie* 3 (1937): 113–140.

2. I had best offer two observations to avoid, or at least anticipate, later perplexity: (a) It would be unwarranted to assume that, in principle, representation of tragic form cannot be *a priori* for Kant, at least not on the grounds that the tragic is defined by change, which, we might presume, cannot be known *a priori* in Kantian terms. We should recall that in the *Critique of Pure Reason* he is unmistakably inconsistent on this point. On the one hand he says that "alteration is a concept which can be derived only from experience" while "*a priori* modes of knowledge are entitled pure when there is no admixture of anything empirical" (B3) and that the "*a priori* knowledge . . . that pure understanding yields" is not "derivative," so that "pure understanding distinguishes itself not merely from all that is empirical but completely also from all sensibility" (B89). Yet, on the other hand, he also says that "change" is one of the "pure but derivative concepts of the understanding" that is "*a priori.*" The other such concepts that Kant mentions here are "force, action, passion, . . . presence, resistance . . . coming to be, ceasing to be" (B108). Together with "change" this enumeration furnishes, indeed, a cast of concepts that suggests how it might be possible to have an

Although the idea that such an activity can be *a priori* may at first seem unintelligible, I will try to show how, for Kant, the representation of sublime tragic form constitutes the pure self-determination that is the ground of personality.[3] In the *Critique of Pure Reason* he spoke of how "the mind is affected through its own activity (namely, through . . . positing . . . its representation), and so is affected by itself" (B67–68).[4]

---

a priori representation of tragic form in moral reason. For the moment, however, I wish only to apply the same reminder to the idea of an *a priori* force that moves, or brings about change, within moral reason. Used in this sense perhaps the clearest occurrence of the phrase "moving force" in the *Critique of Practical Reason* is at 5:152: "die bewegende Kraft der reinen Vorstellung der Tugend" (5:152). To the same effect, in fact, are "die eigentliche bewegende Kraft" (*CPrR*, 5:88), "die Wirkung einer bewegenden Kraft" (*CPrR*, 5:156), and "subjectiv bewegende Kraft einer Triebfeder" (*CPrR*, 5:158). It is worth noting here, as well, that in the *Critique of Judgment* Kant instances "change" as a law that transcendental judgment can cognize *a priori* (5:183). (b) In the *Critique of Practical Reason* there is, to say the least, significant overlap among the roles of reason, understanding, and judgment (e.g., at 5:91–92). Although I do not address in any systematic way the question of how Kant conceives the relation of these roles in the second *Critique,* my discussion of the *Typik* of judgment will sketch a picture of such relation. In offering this picture I have felt liberated— likely more than he would feel warranted—by Henry E. Allison's argument that "Kant's claim that the understanding is spontaneous (A51/B75) can best be understood in terms of his identification of its fundamental activity with judgment (A73/B94)," namely "the activity of 'taking as' [that] is constitutive of judgment": see *Kant's Theory of Freedom* (Cambridge: Cambridge University Press, 1990), pp. 36–37.

3. To avoid monotony I will not repeat the point every time it applies, but it should be clear that what I am attempting to demonstrate in Kant's account of practical judgment is what he shows us *logically ought to happen, not what happens,* in *a priori* judgment. Kant makes this distinction forcefully, for example, in the caveat that precedes his instancing of an *a priori* judgment of change (cited in the previous note) in the third *Critique:* "If we propose to assign the origin of . . . elementary rules, and attempt to do so on psychological lines, we go straight in the teeth of their sense. For they tell us, not what happens, i.e., according to what rule our powers of judgement actually discharge their functions, and how we judge, but how we ought to judge; and we cannot get this logical objective necessity where the principles are merely empirical. Hence the finality of nature for our cognitive faculties and their employment, which manifestly radiates from them, is a transcendental principle of judgements, and so needs also a transcendental Deduction, by means of which the ground for this mode of judging must be traced to the *a priori* sources of knowledge" (*CJ,* 5:182).

4. The fuller context of the citation is as follows: "That which, as representation, can be antecedent to any and every act of thinking anything, is intuition; and if it contains nothing but relations, it is the form of intuition. Since this form does not

Lewis White Beck stated that the problem treated in the *Critique of Practical Reason* is "the subjective determination of the will."⁵ I suggest that the more specific problem that it treats is the will's subjective determination of its own freedom. In Kant's language this is the problem of how we can succeed in thinking "the *unconditioned* in the series of causal connection" (*CPrR*, 5:3). I am proposing that, expanding upon and deepening the concept of the transfer in the *Groundwork of the Metaphysics of Morals,* Kant in the second *Critique* shows how the mind "transfers" itself (*CPrR*, 5:71) into freedom and moral feeling through the representation of sublime tragic form.⁶ He deepens our "amazement" (*CPrR*, 5:156) at what he calls this "grand disclosure" (*CPrR*, 5:94) by finding it in the mind's "inward" "storytelling" (*Erzählen*) (*CPrR*, 5:88, 153). This ultimate Kantian storytelling is distinctly *a priori* and autonomous, though it also has an empirical and heteronomous counterpart, notably in certain kinds of tragedy and philosophy.

In this chapter the heart of my argument concerning Kantian moral reason consists of two propositions, which I will lay out here and then adduce below step-by-step. First, the inner succession to an effectively endless series of sublime tragic representations reveals to each person, in a flash that creates personality, that person's moral motive. In Kant's terms in the *Critique of Practical Reason,* this can be expressed as follows: in pure practical reason the *a priori* succession (*Nachfolge*) (5:85)—in a serial *Typik* (5:67–71) or "endless progress" (5:83) of tragic representations—is that which discloses within the mind (5:94) the "*archetypal*" forms (5:43, 5:83) of "sublimity" (5:71, 86, 87, 88) and of the "feeling

---

represent anything save in so far as something is posited in the mind, it can be nothing but the mode in which the mind is affected through its own activity (namely, through this positing of its representation), and so is affected by itself."

5. Lewis White Beck, *A Commentary on Kant's* Critique of Practical Reason (Chicago: University of Chicago Press, 1960), p. 67.

6. As we have seen, Kant wrote in the *Groundwork of the Metaphysics of Morals* that "freedom . . . cannot be presented in any possible experience" (4:459). By the time of the *Critique of Judgment,* he was affirming that "the purely negative . . . presentation" of freedom was distinctly available in the sublime, the "faculty of mind transcending every standard of sense" in which "the basis of an *a priori* principle is the distinguishing feature" (5:275, 254, 266). I am suggesting that in the *Critique of Practical Reason* he had already worked out, and put in practice, his concept of negative presentation of freedom in the sublime.

of respect" (5:80).[7] Kant calls the "inward" form of these tragic representations "storytelling" (*CPrR*, 5:88, 153). In *Religion within the Boundaries of Mere Reason*, we are given to understand that this process is a moment of "revolution" or "rebirth" or rational "conversion," which constitutes "personality" (6:47–48, 73; cf. 5:87). Second, individual moral reason is made free to choose and follow this autonomous succession of the tragic sublime by an isomorphic, heteronomous succession, also of the tragic sublime. In the next chapter I will propose that in the case of the *Critique of Practical Reason*, Kant applied this heteronomous procedure of succession to Milton's tragedy, *Samson Agonistes*—and its procedure of succession.

In following out Kant's succession procedure in the *Critique of Practical Reason*, I will be attending, in particular, to the impetus of discovery that drives this work as a whole. More than is usual in his other writings, he here leaves open the possibility that the person exercising moral reason will come upon the "strange" and the "singular" or that which is "unexpected even by himself" (*CPrR*, 5:31, 79, 152).[8] We may

7. To be sure, a demonstration of this proposition must succeed in overcoming serious objections or problems that have been raised with regard to particular features of Kant's moral thought, such as Paul Crowther's denial of Kant's claim for the *a priori* status of the sublime, Lewis White Beck's puzzlement about Kant's virtually identical accounts of the sublime and the feeling of respect, and Dieter Henrich's doubts about Kant's claim for *a priori* existence of the feeling of respect. I have spelled out these objections or doubts, and tried to face them, below.

8. Here, more fully, is the evidence of this impetus of discovery, that is, in Kant's exploration of a single, unique kind of representation: "The thing is strange enough, and has nothing like it in all the rest of our practical cognition"; "It is not an empirical fact but the sole fact of pure reason" (*CPrR*, 5:31); It is "something different and quite paradoxical" (*CPrR*, 5:47); "It seems absurd to want to find in the sensible world a case which, though as such it stands only under the law of nature, yet admits of the application to it of a law of freedom and to which there could be applied the supersensible idea of the morally good, which is to be exhibited [represented] in it *in concreto* [*das darin* in concreto *dargestellt werden soll*] . . . But here again [*Allein hier*] a favorable prospect opens for pure practical judgment" (*CPrR*, 5:68); "Here we have the first and perhaps the only case in which we can determine a priori from concepts the relation of a cognition (here the cognition of a pure practical reason) to the feeling of pleasure or displeasure" (*CPrR*, 5:73); "Respect for the moral law . . . is the only one [feeling] that we can cognize completely a priori" (*CPrR*, 5:73); "This is the only case in which my interest, because I *may* not give up anything of it, unavoidably determines my judgment" (*CPrR*, 5:143). The following longer passage is especially noteworthy in this connection: "There is something so singular in the boundless esteem for the pure moral law, stripped [*entblößten*] of all advantage—as practical reason . . .

feel, indeed, that Kant's own exercise in "grand disclosure" produces results that take even him by surprise. The explanation of this strangeness may well be the extent—greater than Kant himself expected—to which he was here engaged with the constellation of German Miltonism. This rich dimension of the second *Critique* especially leaves open the door to identifying elements in it which Kant may have articulated only partially. I will suggest that these possibilities particularly are activated and realized in the largely ignored final section of the second *Critique*, the "Doctrine of the Method of Pure Practical Reason" (*CPrR*, 5:148–161). In a *Critique* that from its opening paragraph is assigned the strictly defined goal of locating moral reason's "pure" autonomy, we need to explain why the "Doctrine of the Method of Pure Practical Reason" or *Methodenlehre*—a discussion that is apparently about only heteronomy—should be assigned this climactic position, that is, just before the lyrical *Beschluß* or conclusion. As I have begun to suggest, this placement is determined by the crowning autonomous function of an *a priori* "storytelling" and its heteronomous counterpart.

Focusing mainly on elements of the second *Critique*, but levying upon clarifications from other works of Kant, I will reconstruct his integral representation of *a priori* sublime tragic form. By attempting to acknowledge and reconstruct the place of the experience of the sublime in the second *Critique*, I necessarily set out on a very different route from either Henry Allison or John Rawls, who has each brilliantly described, in that *Critique*, Kant's conception of the person and his account of the procedures for the categorical imperative. Allison and Rawls have both left the experience of the sublime out of Kant's picture.[9] The work of reconstruction that I propose is a matter of put-

---

[re]presents it to us for obedience [*wie es praktische Vernunft uns zur Befolgung vorstellt*]—that one cannot wonder at finding this influence of a mere intellectual idea on feeling quite impenetrable for speculative reason and at having to be satisfied that one can yet see a priori this much: that such a feeling is inseparably connected with the representation of the moral law in every finite rational being. . . . This feeling of respect . . . is directed only to the practical and . . . depends on the representation of a law only as to its form and not on account of any object of the law" (*CPrR*, 5:79–80).

9. Here I refer to Allison, *Kant's Theory of Freedom*, and to Rawls, "Themes in Kant's Moral Philosophy," in *Kant's Transcendental Deductions: The Three Critiques and the Opus postumum*, ed. Eckart Förster (Stanford: Stanford University Press, 1989), pp. 81–113. Rawls's essay primarily discusses the second *Critique*. See especially p. 99 where he dis-

ting together pieces of a complex puzzle. Yet the pervasive relevance
(even to Rawls's and Allison's descriptions) and the ultimate simplicity
of the whole will, I hope, confirm that the reconstruction retrieves
something significant in Kant's representation. The newly supplied el-
ement, I believe, is a vital part of what he was saying about the emer-
gence of moral personality and its capacity to achieve a categorical
imperative. One step beyond reconstructing this representation, I ex-
plore his paradoxical assertion that though the form of moral reason
is always independently available to the most common human under-
standing, the clearly presented *Formel* or "formula" for representing
this form cannot "be dispensed with." Kant announces that his *Ground
work of the Metaphysics of Morals* and second *Critique* both provide a
Formel of this kind (*CPrR*, 5:8 and n). I will propose that a detailed for-
mula for the representation of the tragic sublime, in all its elements,
was in turn readily accessible to Kant—in the procedure of succession
within *Samson Agonistes*—when he worked out his *Formel*. Ultimately I
will argue that Kant's grand disclosure, to himself, of the elements of
his *Formel* in the *Critique of Practical Reason* required his heteronomous
procedure of succession to *Samson Agonistes* or to its virtual equivalent.

～

At the outset I cite a passage from the second *Critique,* which in my
view brings together virtually all the elements of Kant's representation
of tragic form. The passage appears near the close of his exposition of
his claim for the existence of *a priori* respect, a claim which many com-
mentators have resisted.[10] Kant writes, "This is how the genuine moral
incentive of pure practical reason is constituted," immediately after
presenting the following outward and "inward" scene:

> When an upright man is in the greatest distress, which he could have
> avoided if he could only have disregarded duty, is he not sustained
> by the consciousness that he has maintained humanity in its proper

---

cusses the relation of Kant's procedures of the categorical imperative to his concep-
tion of persons.

10. See, for example, Dieter Henrich, "Das Problem der Grundlegung der Ethik
bei Kant und im spekulativen Idealismus," in *Sein und Ethos,* ed. Paulus Engelhardt
(Mainz: Matthias-Grünewald, 1963), pp. 372–375, and Bernard Williams, *Ethics and
the Limits of Philosophy* (Cambridge, Mass.: Harvard University Press, 1985), pp. 68–69.

dignity in his own person and honored it, that he has no cause to shame himself in his own eyes and to dread the inward view of self-examination? This consolation is not happiness, not even the smallest part of it. For, no one would wish the occasion for it on himself, or perhaps even a life in such circumstances. But he lives and cannot bear to be unworthy of life in his own eyes. This inner tranquility is therefore merely negative with respect to everything that can make life pleasant; it is, namely, only warding off the danger of sinking in personal worth, after he has given up completely the worth of his condition. It is the effect of a respect for something quite different from life, something in comparison and contrast with which life with all its agreeableness has no worth at all. He still lives only from duty, not because he has the least taste for living. (*CPrR*, 5:88)[11]

On first view it must seem strange that Kant assumes not only that we have the wherewithal to respond to his question about his protagonist (". . . is he not sustained. . . ?") but that we will surely answer in the affirmative. He presupposes, that is, that we are inwardly well familiar with "such circumstances" and with "this inner tranquility," which the protagonist in Kant's implicit story gains "after he has given up completely the worth of his condition" and "still lives only from duty, not because he has the least taste for living." Not many of us, and perhaps very few, have empirically experienced this condition, or even wit-

11. "Hält nicht einen rechtschaffenen Mann im größten Unglücke des Lebens, das er vermeiden konnte, wenn er sich nur hätte über die Pflicht wegsetzen können, noch das Bewußtsein aufrecht, daß er die Menschheit in seiner Person doch in ihrer Würde erhalten und geehrt habe, daß er sich nicht vor sich selbst zu schämen und den inneren Anblick der Selbstprüfung zu scheuen Ursache habe? Dieser Trost ist nicht Glückseligkeit, auch nicht der mindeste Theil derselben. Denn niemand wird sich die Gelegenheit dazu, auch vielleicht nicht einmal ein Leben in solchen Umständen wünschen. Aber er lebt und kann es nicht erdulden, in seinen eigenen Augen des Lebens unwürdig zu sein. Diese innere Beruhigung ist also blos negativ in Ansehung alles dessen, was das Leben angenehm machen mag; nämlich sie ist die Abhaltung der Gefahr, im persönlichen Werthe zu sinken, nachdem der seines Zustandes von ihm schon gänzlich aufgegeben worden. Sie ist die Wirkung von einer Achtung für etwas ganz anderes als das Leben, womit in Vergleichung und Entgegensetzung das Leben vielmehr mit aller seiner Annehmlichkeit gar keinen Werth hat. Er lebt nur noch aus Pflicht, nicht weil er am Leben den mindesten Geschmack findet" (*CPrR*, 5:88).

nessed it at close range. The outward and inward response—the latter somehow known or intuited by us, in others' experience, as what it is *for them*—must seem equally hard to come by. Indeed, I suggest that the hypothetical case of Kant's representing and of our knowing this scene would make no sense were it not for the presupposition that the capacity to suppose or represent the form of life's greatest distress or tragedy, or at least "receptivity" to representation of that form, is given to us *a priori* as a *"property"* of our minds" (*CPrR*, 5:152).

This can begin to suggest that for Kant the *a priori* representation of <u>the honest person *in extremis*</u> (in the last agonies, at the point of death—this phrase will be my shorthand term for his or her condition) is available as a universal access to the achievement of personality. In Kant's view this is moral personality defined by the feeling of respect. In other words, Kant thinks that the potential for such representation is given to every person *a priori*, though only the exercise of this potential, in the willing of this representation, creates the freedom and moral feeling that define personality. *"Personality,"* he says, is "freedom and independence from the mechanism of the whole of nature, regarded . . . as . . . a capacity of a being subject to . . . pure practical laws given by his own reason" (*CPrR*, 5:87). The idea that begins to emerge here is that the capacity to generate moral maxims in response to reason's representation of the honest person *in extremis* has nothing to do with empirical experience. By itself this *a priori* representation creates and sustains personality. Yet, if this is true for Kant, how—by what process, in what form, and to what end—does Kant himself *represent* the elements of this *a priori* representation?

To obtain answers to these questions, we will need to inquire into Kant's concepts of representation and form as he uses them in these contexts. For this inquiry it will be helpful to record first the specific representations of form that we encounter in our cited passage. Here the most obvious elements of Kant's storytelling representation of the person who achieves personality—by means of this act of representation—form a symmetry and mark a border-crossing or transfer in the following way:

1. In the greatest distress or tragedy of life, the honest person *in extremis,* stripped of every possible sensible incentive to go on living, stands on the verge of death or suicide.

2. Though he or she goes on living, this person "has given up completely the worth" of his or her "condition" and has lost the taste for living.

3. This person maintains humanity in its proper dignity, rejecting suicide by regarding duty alone.

4. This person achieves an inner tranquility that is the effect of a *transfer* of consciousness across the verge of sensible existence or life, which is to say beyond the limit of any sensible incentive or reason to go on living. This respect for the purely intelligible moral obligation that gives meaning to life is thus for something quite different from, and more valuable than, life itself.

Kant may seem to announce the occurrence of this transfer without proof or argument. Yet he carefully adduces it as part of the formal representation of the honest person *in extremis*. As a part of this representation, he says, reason "transfers into the supersensible" that which "can . . . be . . . exhibited by actions in the sensible world in accordance with the formal rule of a law of nature" (*CPrR*, 5:71). In the passage cited above Kant represents this process with the help of references to elucidations of other, complementary elements of the same manifold representation.

Still as part of my listing of the elements of the cited passage, I will next briefly inventory these other elements before discussing a number of them in greater detail. Thereafter I will turn to Kant's concepts of representation and form—in the *Critique of Practical Reason*, at least—in themselves. Among other things, this inventory and discussion will indicate that Kant's representation of tragic form is simultaneously a representation of the *a priori* form of respect and of the *a priori* form of the experience of the sublime. To continue:

5. The person acknowledges reason's cumulative "humiliation" of "self-conceit" (*CPrR*, 5:73–77). This leads toward total negation, or despair, of self-worth.

Two sentences before the cited passage Kant says that he is describing the "striking down" of "self-conceit." In the passage the aggregate effect of this process is indicated by the phrases "only warding off the danger of sinking in personal worth, after he has given up completely the worth of his condition."[12]

6. Intertwined with the cumulative humiliation of self-conceit, the person's tragic representation shows and effects the progressive "rejection" of all of life's "sensible" "incentives" or "inclinations" (*CPrR*, 5:71–73). This process has the "merely *negative*" effect of removing "the hindrance to pure practical reason"; and it has the "*positive*" effect "called respect for the law" (*CPrR*, 5:74–75). In the latter, reason "stripped" of all sensible incentives issues in "the representation of a law only as to its form" (*CPrR*, 5:79–80), which is to say that it "actually produces" the form of this respect which "also contains something *elevating*" (*enthält es auch Erhebung*) (*CPrR*, 5:80–81).

In the passage this is indicated by the "inner tranquility [that] is merely negative with [regard] to everything that can make life pleasant" but has positive existence as "respect for something quite different from life."

7. The person engages in an "endless progress" (*CPrR*, 5:83, 123n) or sequential "succession" *(Nachfolge)* (*CPrR*, 5:85) of representations, a typology that Kant calls a *Typik* (*CPrR*, 5:67–71) and which gives the person access to the "archetype" (*CPrR*, 5:83) and to the "sublime" or "sublimity" *(Erhabenheit)* (*CPrR*, 5:71, 86, 87, 88). Thus the representation of moral form is the *a priori* representation of a virtual repetition in a line of representations that, according to Kant's theory of the sublime (set out in detail a few years later in the third *Critique*), issues in sublime feeling. Representation of the Typic or the succession procedure can also be heteronomous; and, as we will see, Kant goes

---

12. It is clear that this element of Kant's representation in particular has a significant relation to the first case or example of the emergence of the categorical imperative in the *Groundwork of the Metaphysics of Morals*: "Someone feels sick of life because of a series of troubles that has grown to the point of despair . . ." (4:421–422). But now Kant makes clear that the external manifestation of this scenario and condition corresponds to an *a priori* scenario and condition.

through various stages of thinking about the empirical and/or *a priori* status of sublime feeling.

In the passage the *Typik* is reflected in "he has maintained humanity in its proper dignity in his own person and honored it," where "humanity" stands for the person's *a priori* line of representation of tragic form, which is to say of the condition of the honest person *in extremis*. With regard to sublimity: immediately after representing this scene and saying, "This is how the genuine moral incentive of pure practical reason is constituted," he adds, "It is nothing other than the pure moral law itself insofar as it lets us discover the sublimity of our own supersensible existence."

8. The person's tragic representation is the "singular" representation of "respect" (*CPrR*, 5:79) which is indistinguishable from moral feeling or the "feeling" of respect, "the only [feeling] that we can cognize completely a priori" (*CPrR*, 5:73). "This feeling of respect . . . depends on the representation of a law only as to its form" (*CPrR*, 5:80). Kant says that this is "a feeling that can be called pain," yet he seems in doubt in the second *Critique* as to whether it is "the feeling of pleasure or displeasure" (*CPrR*, 5:73). In the third *Critique* he will say that "the sublime" involves "respect, i.e. merits the name of a negative pleasure" (*CJ*, 5:245). (Of course, this is at least reminiscent of Aristotle's term *tragic pleasure*.)

In the passage the possibility of a taste for "something quite different from life"—in other words, a taste for what is represented as the experience of the sublime (and the "momentary check to the vital forces")—is held open by the phrase "not because he has the least taste for living." The entire passage is built around, or represents, the term *respect*, which yet, being a term merely of attention or relation to something, otherwise has no independent meaning.

9. Tragic representations of "disinterested respect" show the person, at least in part, how "not to behold them," so that "a view into the realm of the supersensible" is as much an experience

of what has been "denied" as what has been "granted" in such representation (*CPrR*, 5:147–148). Affirming the effect of this occlusion, the person freely chooses to reject the "incentives" of sensible "inclinations" (*CPrR*, 5:72–76) that are themselves sensibly "blind and servile" (*blind und knechtisch*) (*CPrR*, 5:118). Representation of this kind anticipates Kant's saying in the third *Critique* that a sublime representation "lets us see its own inadequacy" to represent "and consequently its subjective want of finality for our judgment" even if it is "itself a presentation of the subjective finality of our mind" (*CJ*, 5:252, 268). This intelligible seeing is achieved by representing the sensible inadequacy of sensible representation or, in other words, by representing sensible blindness.

In the passage this process is suggested by the phrases "in his own eyes" (twice) and "inward view of self-examination," hinting, at least, at the efficacy of inner sight alone.

10. In this way the person achieves personality, which for Kant can be only sublime, therefore free, personality. In other words, such personality defines the person who has the feeling of respect. We see this intertwining of meanings in the way Kant speaks of "this idea of personality, awakening respect by setting before our eyes the sublimity of our nature (in its vocation)" (*CPrR*, 5:87). (This is the opening of the paragraph in which our cited passage appears.) Responding to the sublime vocation of personality means willing or representing sublime maxims and sublime deeds, such as the person's "magnanimous sacrifice of his life for the preservation of his country" (*CPrR*, 5:158).

In the passage these concepts of personality are suggested by saying that "he has maintained humanity in its proper dignity in his own person. . . . It is the effect of a respect for something quite different from life."

11. By employing the foregoing *a priori* resources, the person achieves the pure freedom that is an "unexpected" (*CPrR*, 5:47,

152) "grand disclosure" (*CPrR*, 5:94) of moral form. This disclosed form is unaccountable in our usual terms for choosing life. It is the one moral incentive.

In the passage the disclosure is of the "something quite different from life," the feeling of "duty" which has nothing to do with the "taste for living."

12. This *a priori* representation of the form of the tragic sublime constitutes the maxim of moral form and the test of its universalizability, its "test as to the form of a law of nature in general" (*CPrR*, 5:69–70).

In the passage the maxim is the duty that he wills. The test of this, in the form of the categorical imperative, is "the inward view of self-examination," which can show the person that he or she has "maintained humanity in its proper dignity in his own person."

Representation and Form

In the *Critique of Practical Reason* Kant's most challenging claim is that moral will is a "representation" of the "mere form" of a law (5:24, 57).[13] For Kant this would seem to be the equivalent of the equally challenging assertion that "to think the *unconditioned* in the series of causal connection" can by itself motivate moral reason in freedom (*CPrR*, 5:3). He says that this *a priori* thinking is possible because "a will for which the mere lawgiving form of a maxim" serves as a law "is a free will" and because "the representation of this form as the determining ground of

13. For what is meant, and what problems are raised, by Kant's use of the term representation in the first *Critique,* one may refer to Wilfrid Sellars, "Some Remarks on Kant's Theory of Experience," *Journal of Philosophy* 64 (1967): 633–647. With regard to the term *form,* Robert B. Pippin, *Kant's Theory of Form: An Essay on the* Critique of Pure Reason (New Haven: Yale University Press, 1982), p. 220 (and n. 9), emphasizes how "obscure" Kant's use of that term is as a "bridge from his theoretical to his practical philosophy." Especially suggestive for my purposes are Henry E. Allison's comments on the relation of representation, apperception, and spontaneity in *Idealism and Freedom: Essays on Kant's Theoretical and Practical Philosophy* (Cambridge: Cambridge University Press, 1996), pp. 94–95. I will turn to one aspect of Allison's views below.

the will is distinct from all determining grounds of events in nature in accordance with the law of causality" (*CPrR*, 5:28–29). Kant's moral thinking thus depends on the idea that unconditioned causality is a unitary and inherent, or synthetic *a priori*, feature of ethical consciousness that is manifested merely in representation of form (*CPrR*, 5:31). Many modern critics have felt that this element is unavailable in Kant's thought, so that Hegel was more or less correct in charging that Kantian ethics, most especially the Kantian theory of respect, is an empty formalism. It is true that the meanings of representation and form, rarely self-evident in Kant's writings, seem to be particularly obscure here, precisely where the concept of moral reason and even the very possibility of moral life are said to depend on them. In statements such as the following it is certainly not self-evident how representation and form can have the impact claimed for them:

> *Pure reason* . . . must be able to determine the will by the mere form of a practical rule. (*CPrR*, 5:24)

> A rational being is to think of his maxims as practical universal laws . . . only by their form. (*CPrR*, 5:27)

> A will for which the mere lawgiving form of a maxim can alone serve as a law is a free will. (*CPrR*, 5:29)

> By a concept of an object of practical reason I understand the representation of an object as an effect possible through freedom. (*CPrR*, 5:57)

> The will is to be determinable . . . merely through the representation of a law in general and its form. (*CPrR*, 5:68)

> This feeling of respect . . . is directed only to the practical and . . . depends on the representation of a law only as to its form. (*CPrR*, 5:80)[14]

14. Other notable usages of these terms in the second *Critique* are "Will [is] a faculty either of producing objects corresponding to representations or of determining itself to effect such objects" (*CPrR*, 5:15); "Since the mere form of a law can be represented only by reason . . . the representation of this form as the determining ground of the will is distinct from all determining grounds of events in nature in accordance with the law of causality" (*CPrR*, 5:28–29).

Kantian "Storytelling"

I propose that we can locate and at least partially explain the meaning of representation and form in these statements by turning to an improbable resource, namely, the representation of form that Kant calls "storytelling" (*CPrR*, 5:153). I take Kant's own storytelling in the *Critique of Practical Reason* to be a realization of his suggestion that, "absurd" as the idea initially seems, representation of moral form can indeed be grasped, as he suggests, *"in concreto"* (5:68). By specifying the interconnections within his considerable storytelling in the second *Critique*, we can begin to describe the design and force of the representation of respect that he makes central to the argument of this *Critique* as a whole. I propose that his representation of this design or particular form together with its inherent "moving force" (*CPrR*, 5:152) are the grounds for his claim that mere representation of form can produce the feeling of respect that is the one incentive to moral will. His claim is grounded, in short, in the form of his storytelling.

My next orders of business will be, first, to lay out Kant's account of the heteronomous or empirical function of storytelling in moral education and, second, to show that for Kant one mode of telling the story of the honest person *in extremis* is itself an *a priori* activity of moral reason. Not least because Kant is extremely guarded about the place of storytelling in his moral thought, its philosophical significance in the second *Critique* has been routinely ignored. Yet his exposition of the "method of founding and cultivating moral dispositions" (*CPrR*, 5:153) is entirely built around "storytelling." His term *founding (Gründung)*—of "moral dispositions"—should give us pause before shelving this *Methode* (of the *Methodenlehre*) merely with the heteronomous.

In the "Doctrine of the Method of Pure Practical Reason" (*CPrR*, 5:151–161), he details and exemplifies the importance of "storytelling" coupled, he says, with the "arguing" that gives "novelty" to storytelling (*CPrR*, 5:153). He may seem to be emphasizing novel arguing rather than commonplace storytelling.[15] Yet if we attend to what his ex-

15. Thus Beck, *A Commentary on Kant's* Critique of Practical Reason, p. 236, sees Kant's "method" in these pages as "the Socratic method," a "moral catechism, in the manner of Rousseau's *Émile*," and as advice to "collect historical examples for such analysis." I do not see how, in practice, Kant's method here is significantly Socratic, though it may well be that exploration of the "manner of Rousseau" in the use of his-

position shows, rather than what he says it shows, we see that the opposite is the case. What reflexively forms or self-educates moral reason is the commonplace tragic story and not at all the novelty of arguing, of which we are given hardly any instances or even suggestions. In fact, in all the chief exempla presented in the second *Critique*, late and early, the telling is continuously of the somehow universally familiar story of a man "at a moment when he wishes that he had never lived to see the day that exposed him to such unutterable pain and yet remains firm in his resolution to be truthful, without wavering or even doubting" (*CPrR*, 5:156). What is central here is the impact, producing freedom and moral feeling, of the individual tragic example in its incremental "step by step" form (*CPrR*, 5:156). This form is constituted, on the one hand, by representing the cumulative humiliations of self-conceit and the progressive rejections of sensible incentives told in the story and, on the other hand, by the commonplaceness or inherent repeatability—as in a law of nature—of the story itself. This repeatability, I propose, has autonomous *a priori* status for Kant.

In its heteronomous form, he says, the effect of the incremental form of storytelling, not of arguing, is that the "spectator" (*Zuschauer*) (*CPrR*, 5:157) is "raised step by step from mere approval to admiration, from that to amazement, and finally to the greatest veneration and a lively wish that he himself could be such a man" (*CPrR*, 5:156). At this point we see a definite slippage in Kant's terminology, so that though he is speaking of the heteronomous he seems to be making a claim for something purely autonomous. The "pure representation of virtue" (*CPrR*, 5:152) or "pure representation of duty" (*CPrR*, 5:153), he says, is itself a morally decisive "moving force" (*CPrR*, 5:152). It provides the incentive to action from duty and it forms moral personality. In Kant's description of storytelling in the *Methodenlehre*, we hear repeatedly that the purity of the incentive (or moral principle) is identical with the purity of the representation: "All the admiration, and even the endeavor to resemble this character, here rests wholly on the purity of the moral principle, which can be clearly represented only if one removes from the incentive to action everything that people may reckon only to happiness" (*CPrR*, 5:156).

---

torical and other kinds of examples, both in *Émile* and in *La nouvelle Héloise*, would yield illuminating parallels to Kant's procedures.

Despite this slippage it is necessary, of course, to be ever mindful of Kant's fundamental distinction between autonomy and heteronomy. In the "Doctrine of the Method" he says that he is describing only the "preparatory guidance" or propaedeutics required "to bring either a mind that is still uncultivated or one that is degraded onto the track of the morally good in the first place" (*CPrR*, 5:152). This propaedeutics is clearly heteronomous. In a moment I will set out the elements of this preparatory guidance, but I want to note beforehand that Kant has already embedded all of these elements in the main body of his argument for pure practical reason. In other words, what seems to be a mere propaedeutics of the form of tragic exempla, which indeed may seem to be required only by the philosophically uninitiated or the degenerate, is for Kant also a continually indispensable part, or counterpart, of the autonomous or *a priori* representation of moral reason and of moral reason's representations. This is the case, that is, in the primary argument of the second *Critique*. Kant, in fact, shows that every rational being can represent the form of the tragic sublime autonomously and *a priori*, with or without the clarifications of philosophers. Description of this representation of form teaches how "respect for the moral law [which] can be called a *moral feeling* . . . must be . . . *practically effected* [*praktisch gewirkt*], and is effected as follows . . ." (*CPrR*, 5:75).

Kant obscures the way in which this effect is worked by storytelling, as if it is beneath serious consideration by philosophers of moral reason. It is true that Kant was intensely interested in the progressive scheme of elementary education of the Philanthropinum in Dessau; and he took a personal interest in the education of Robert Motherby's young son.[16] Yet consciously or unconsciously he throws us off the scent of the *a priori* dimensions of his *Methode* by seeming to say that it describes no more than a kind of advanced child's play, of "say, a ten-year-old boy" (*CPrR*, 5:155) or a pastime "of business people or women" (*CPrR*, 5:154). The latter phrase is both confusing and shocking, considering Kant's repeated claim that nothing but common human understanding is required for even the most difficult operations of moral reason. So, too, the strange example, to be presented to the ten-year-old boy, of the hypothetical Englishman who resists bearing

16. See Manfred Kuehn, *Kant: A Biography* (Cambridge: Cambridge University Press, 2001), pp. 227–229.

false witness to the alleged fornications of Anne Boleyn, seems to be another red herring of this kind (*CPrR,* 5:155), as is the quotation from Juvenal, which contains not even the smallest hint of how the "force of the incentive" to duty—which is Kant's focus at this moment—comes into being (*CPrR,* 5:158–159). It seems likely that he is distancing himself from something specific here. Perhaps he feared that, carefully circumscribed as his storytelling is, his critics would misrepresent it as an endangerment of the purity of philosophy. Yet whatever the full explanation of this missing acknowledgment, or this avoidance, may be, the significant fact here is that the second *Critique* gives us concrete and indispensable instances of Kant's own storytelling, specifically of tragic, sublime exempla.

A Biographical Aside

Even as a detour we should note that Kant's emphasis on storytelling was something that he thought about, and probably lived, over many decades. In his lectures on anthropology he had commented,

> Every conversation in company usually begins with telling a story, is pursued with arguments and debates, and ends with joking.

> Telling a story, arguing, joking are to be found at table, and indeed joking marks the conclusion.

> Conversations at table are: 1. telling a story, 2. arguing, 3. joking. . . . Among all arguments none seems to be more interesting than that over the actions and passions of individuals. The arguing comes when the first appetite is satisfied, and after all comes the joking.[17]

17. *Matuszewski* (Marburg Kant Archiv), 219, 328–329, 344: "Eine jede Unterredung in Gesellschaft fängt gemeiniglich mit Erzählen an, wird mit Raisonnements und Disputen fortgesetzt und endigt mit Scherz." "Erzählen, raisonieren, scherzen kommt bei der Tafel vor, und zwar macht der Scherz den Beschluß." "Die Unterhaltungen bei der Tafel sind: 1. das Erzählen, 2. das Raisonieren, 3. das Scherzen. . . . Unter allen Raisonnements scheint keines interessanter zu sein, als das über die Handlungen und Leidenschaften der Menschen. Das Raisonieren kommt dann, wenn der erste Appetit gestillt ist, und zuletzt kommt der Scherz."

In discussing Kant's relation to his friend Joseph Green, Manfred Kuehn has noted that these comments on storytelling inform us of what was likely Kant's and Green's actual practice over many years.[18] As I mentioned in Chapter 1, Kuehn has calculated that "Kant was a constant and very regular visitor at Green's house" beginning at least as early as 1766 and until Green's death in 1784. We know that "the study of English authors" *(Studium englischer Schriftsteller)* was central to these afternoons. (Green, notes Kuehn, complained that he found disorienting the way poems were printed on the page.)[19] Considering that Green, an Englishman, was the closest friend that Kant ever had and that Green single-handedly precipitated nothing less than a moral revolution in Kant's character and his adoption of a philosophy of maxims, we cannot help wishing that we knew what the subjects of these conversations, especially these storytellings, were, particularly where "the study of English authors" was concerned. During the 1760s, '70s, and '80s Milton's popularity continued to run strong, both in England and in Germany. It is plausible to speculate that Milton's poetic storytelling was at least part of Green's and Kant's storytelling, even of what Jachman called "the story [that] might take an inordinately long time,"[20] even of the preferred kind of story that Kant characterized as "the actions and passions of individuals."

Finding the Autonomous with the Heteronomous

I will soon come to Kant's tragic, sublime exempla in the *Critique of Practical Reason*. At the risk of another brief delay, however, it is first necessary to clarify the fact that in the second *Critique* we often find autonomous functions where we would think that we are in the region of the merely heteronomous. In the following paired passages we find

18. Kuehn, *Kant,* p. 157, writes, "In practicing the art of conversation, Green and Kant . . . probably followed more often than not the schema Kant describes in his lectures on anthropology. A conversation, according to this view, has three parts: a narrative or story, a discussion, and jest. The conversation begins with someone telling a story, which is then discussed. . . . The story might take an inordinately long time." Kuehn refers specifically to *AA,* 25:2:966–967.

19. Kuehn, *Kant,* p. 156.

20. Ibid., p. 157.

striking echoes of terminology and conceptualization, presented at parallel junctures of argumentation, which strongly suggest the close, even strict, analogy between the heteronomous and autonomous activities that are being described. Here, first, is a passage from the climax of Kant's description of the course that his seemingly lesser method of storytelling takes, that is, in the heteronomous educating of the ten-year-old pupil:

> Now, however, the *second* exercise begins its work, namely to draw attention, in the lively presentation of the moral disposition in examples, to the purity of will, first only as a negative perfection of the will insofar as in an action from duty no incentives of inclination have any influence on it as determining grounds; by this, however, the pupil's attention is fixed on the consciousness of his *freedom* and, although this renunciation excites an initial feeling of pain, nevertheless, by its withdrawing the pupil from the constraint of even true needs, there is made known to him at the same time a deliverance from the manifold dissatisfaction in which all those needs entangle him and his mind is made receptive to the feeling of satisfaction from other sources. The heart is freed and relieved of a burden that always secretly presses upon it, when in pure moral resolutions, examples of which are set before him, there is revealed to the human being an inner capacity not otherwise correctly known by himself, the *inner freedom* to release himself from the impetuous importunity of inclinations. (*CPrR*, 5:160–161; underlining added)[21]

21. "Nun tritt aber die *zweite* Übung ihr Geschäft an, nämlich in der lebendigen Darstellung der moralischen Gesinnung an Beispielen die Reinigkeit des Willens bemerklich zu machen, vorerst nur als negativer Vollkommenheit desselben, so fern in einer Handlung aus Pflicht gar keine Triebfedern der Neigungen als Bestimmungsgründe auf ihn einfließen; wodurch der Lehrling doch auf das Bewußtsein seiner *Freiheit* aufmerksam erhalten wird, und, obgleich diese Entsagung eine anfängliche Empfindung von Schmerz erregt, dennoch dadurch, daß sie jenen Lehrling dem Zwange selbst wahrer Bedürfnisse entzieht, ihm zugleich eine Befreiung von der mannigfaltigen Unzufriedenheit, darin ihn alle diese Bedürfnisse verflechten, angekündigt und das Gemüth für die Empfindung der Zufriedenheit aus anderen Quellen empfänglich gemacht wird. Das Herz wird doch von einer Last, die es jederzeit ingeheim drückt, befreit und erleichtert, wenn an reinen moralischen Entschließungen, davon Beispiele vorgelegt werden, dem Menschen ein inneres, ihm selbst sonst nicht einmal recht bekanntes Vermögen, die *innere Freiheit*,

The fault lines in this passage are surprising. Kant's principal terms here do not fully fit either each other or the person they are said to describe. We struggle to understand what kind of ten- year-old Kant has in mind and what "this *second* exercise," supposedly of no more than "preparatory guidance," must be in order to create "a negative perfection of the will," so that "the pupil's attention is fixed on the consciousness of his *freedom*," so that "there is made known to him at the same time a deliverance from the manifold dissatisfaction in which all those needs entangle him" and his "heart is freed and relieved of a burden that always secretly presses upon it," so that, finally, and very much as a positive perfection of the will, "there is revealed" to this "human being an inner capacity not otherwise correctly known by himself, the *inner freedom* to release himself from the impetuous importunity of inclinations." Kant, usually the painstaking anthropologist, has here telescoped very different stages in the unfolding of human potentialities, at very least in his own terms for such unfolding of potentialities. About the consummate moral achievement described here, he was the one to say, "Perhaps there are but few who have attempted this revolution before the age of thirty, and fewer still who have consolidated it firmly before they are forty.—Wanting to become a better man in a fragmentary way is a futile endeavor" (*Anth*, 7:294). As we will soon see in some detail, Kant expressed very similar views about this "revolution" in *Religion within the Boundaries of Mere Reason*.

In the citation above Kant is clearly levying upon the *a priori* successes of a mature practical reason in order to express his enthusiasm for his empirical, pedagogical method centered in "storytelling." Yet he hesitates to reveal the extent of his real claim for the moral, self-reliant power of this storytelling. It is highly significant for Kant's moral theorizing that his "*second* exercise" in the *Methode*, which may seem to be mere heteronomy, is in fact indistinguishable from the implementation of the autonomous "second and highest vocation" of moral reason that he has earlier described in the heartland of the *a priori*. Here is the earlier passage:

---

aufgedeckt wird, sich von der ungestümen Zudringlichkeit der Neigungen dermaßen loszumachen, daß gar keine, selbst die beliebteste nicht, auf eine Entschließung, zu der wir uns jetzt unserer Vernunft bedienen sollen, Einfluß habe" (*CPrR*, 5:160–161; underlining added).

A person as belonging to the sensible world is subject to his own personality insofar as he also belongs to the intelligible world; for, it is then not to be wondered at that a human being, as belonging to both worlds, must regard his own nature in reference to <u>his second and highest vocation</u> only with reverence, and its laws with the highest respect. . . .

This idea of personality, awakening respect by setting before our eyes the sublimity of our nature (in its vocation) while at the same time showing us the lack of accord of our conduct with respect to it and thus striking down self-conceit, is natural even to the most common human reason and is easily observed. (*CPrR,* 5:87; underlining added)[22]

[Die Person also, als zur Sinnenwelt gehörig, ihrer eigenen Persönlichkeit unterworfen ist, so fern sie zugleich zur intelligibelen Welt gehört; da es denn nicht zu verwundern ist, wenn der Mensch, als zu beiden Welten gehörig, sein eigenes Wesen in Beziehung auf <u>seine zweite und höchste Bestimmung</u> nicht anders als mit Verehrung und die Gesetze derselben mit der höchsten Achtung betrachten muß. . . .

Diese Achtung erweckende Idee der Persönlichkeit, welche uns die Erhabenheit unserer Natur (ihrer Bestimmung nach) vor Augen stellt, indem sie uns zugleich den Mangel der Angemessenheit unseres Verhaltens in Ansehung derselben bemerken läßt und dadurch den Eigendünkel niederschlägt, ist selbst der gemeinsten Menschenvernunft natürlich und leicht bemerklich.] (underlining added)

The "second exercise" and the "second and highest vocation" are, I propose, of a piece. They are the way of exerting a seemingly impossible "influence" on autonomy. This process is highly suggestive of Kant's complex of ideas surrounding heteronomous and autonomous

---

22. Another instance of this specific usage of the "second," also in the apparently purer vein of effecting an autonomous unconditioned causality, is this: "A practical rule of pure reason *first,* as *practical,* concerns the existence of an object, and *second,* as a *practical rule* of pure reason, brings with it necessity with respect to the existence of an action and is thus a practical law, not a natural law through empirical grounds of determination but a law of freedom in accordance with which the will is to be determinable independently of anything empirical (merely through the representation of a law in general and its form)" (*CPrR,* 5:67–68).

succession procedures in the *Critique of Judgment.* In the third *Critique,* precisely in the passage in which he elaborates the procedure of succession *(Nachfolge)* and the test of talent *(Talent prüfen)* in which artistic or aesthetic *Ideen* become accessible, we have seen that Kant uses the term *pupil (Lehrling)* for the individual who is fully capable of this procedure. As we have repeatedly noted, this individual creates a

> product, which others may use to put their own talent to the test, so as to let it serve as a model, not for *imitation,* but for *succession.* The possibility of this is difficult to explain. The artist's ideas arouse like ideas on the part of his pupil. (*CJ,* 5:309)

> [. . . Product . . . an welchem andere ihr eigenes Talent prüfen mögen, um sich jenes zum Muster nicht der *Nachmachung,* sondern der *Nachfolge* dienen zu lassen. Wie dieses möglich sei, ist schwer zu erklären. Die Ideen des Künstlers erregen ähnliche Ideen seines Lehrlings.]

Given this association of the pupil with the isomorphism of heteronomous and autonomous procedures of succession, it may well be that he was already thinking of something similar in his comments on the "pupil" in the *Critique of Practical Reason.*

Indeed, as I began to observe in Chapter 1, even the famous opening sentence of Kant's conclusion to the second *Critique* actually conforms to this two-stage movement from the heteronomous to the autonomous:

> Two things fill the mind with ever new and increasing admiration and reverence, the more often and more steadily [*anhaltender*] one reflects on them: *the starry heavens above me and the moral law within me.* (5:161)

Like the reflection on the moral law, reflection on the stars is not a matter of unfocused, blurred seeing, but rather, I propose, is pursued in persistent [*anhaltend*] tracing of a line or constellation. In the procedure of succession this becomes an act of succeeding to an effectively infinite progression through the heavens, each discrete representation of which is highlighted by darkness or intermittent radiance. The act of following this series of representations thus fulfills the requirements of Kant's idea of what creates sublimity, that is, of the heteronomous sublime that arouses awareness of the autonomous sublime:

> The first begins from the place I occupy in the external world of sense and extends the connection in which I stand into an unbounded magnitude. . . . The second begins from my invisible self, my personality, and presents me in a world which has true infinity but which can be discovered only by the understanding, and I cognize that my connection with that world (and thereby with all those visible worlds as well) is not merely <u>contingent,</u> as in the first case, but universal and <u>necessary.</u> (*CPrR,* 5:162; underlining added)

If, as we saw in Chapter 2, in 1784–85 Kant was still ridiculing Herder for expecting that analogy could fill the "immense void between the contingent and the necessary," now, four years later, Kant has found—and implemented in more than one way—exactly a kind of analogical form that can bridge the infinite void between them. In Kant's opening of the conclusion his crucial moral point is therefore that his heteronomous succession procedure in the experience of the sublime is isomorphic with, and discloses his freedom for, his second exercise. This second exercise is the unseen autonomous succession procedure (the inward following of the *series of representations* of rejections of the sensible as well as the inward following of the series of humiliations of self-conceit) which issues in the categorical imperative, "the moral law within me." Kant is on the track of "sublimity" *(Erhabenheit)* when he says that "the first view of a countless multitude of worlds annihilates, as it were, my importance as an *animal creature* . . . provided with vital force." This is the track of "the momentary check to the vital forces" that in the *Critique of Judgment* will be shown to be the sublime effect of such a first (heteronomous) reflection. Kant's famous "two things" are, then, *necessarily and personally* intertwined in the "influence" on autonomy of an appropriate magnitude of chosen heteronomous succession.

In the *Methodenlehre*—which immediately precedes the conclusion—Kant affirms the requirement of just such an "influence" (*CPrR,* 5:151), though only, or so it would seem, for heteronomous purposes. Earlier, apparently in a purer vein, he speaks of an autonomous unconditioned "causality" that is an "influence" under "conditions quite other than those which constitute natural connection." There he says that we can *a priori* know the unconditioned causality of such an influence because "subsumption of an action possible to me in the sensible world under a *pure practical law* does not concern the possibility of the *action* as an event in the sensible world" (*CPrR*, 5:68–69).[23] In other words, everything that matters morally, as influence, is a function of the fact that we can think the unconditioned causality of freedom. Whether or not the thought of unconditioned causality can then somehow be realized or implemented in an act or event does not change the achieved thought or its inner influence in forming moral personality.

This influence is our second and highest vocation or calling. Our heeding of this calling is exercised in the intelligible world and manifested in pure practical reason and moral feeling. Here the wrong kind of influence on autonomy is eliminated while the right kind is left holding the field:

> *Moral feeling* . . . is effected as follows: the representation of the moral law deprives self-love of its influence and self-conceit of its illusion. . . . The representation of the superiority of its objective law . . . is produced in the judgment of reason through the removal of the counterweight. And so respect for the law is not the incentive to morality; instead it is morality itself subjectively considered as an incentive inasmuch as pure practical reason, by rejecting all the claims of self-love in opposition with its own, supplies authority to the law, which now alone has influence. . . . This feeling . . . is therefore produced solely by reason. (*CPrR*, 5:75–76)

Very much the same *a priori* humiliation of self-conceit and "removal of the counterweight" can be seen in the influence *on* and *of* pure

---

23. The concept of a transfer is here an important bridging activity within moral reason: "Only *rationalism* of judgment is suitable for the use of moral concepts, since it takes from sensible nature nothing more than what pure reason can also think for itself, that is, conformity with law, and transfers into the supersensible nothing but what can, conversely, be really exhibited by actions in the sensible world in accordance with the formal rule of a law of nature in general" (*CPrR*, 5:71). I will return to the transfer later.

practical reason—explicitly, that is, by the storytelling that is described as follows in the *Methodenlehre:*

> Here the doctrine of method is understood . . . as the way in which one can provide the laws of pure practical reason with *access* to the human mind and *influence* on its maxims, that is, the way in which one can make objectively practical reason *subjectively* practical as well. (*CPrR,* 5:151)

~

In fact, the problem of how there can be an "influence" on autonomy that does not violate that autonomy and, implicitly, I am suggesting, the problem of how there can be *a priori* "storytelling" are closely related to a problem that remains with regard to the *Formel.* This is the problem that Kant knows he has carried over from the *Groundwork of the Metaphysics of Morals.* This is, once again, the problem of the apparently disabling use of examples that nevertheless enables us to achieve the condition of freedom and exemplarity in moral reason. We may feel that a solution to this problem is at least implicit in Kant's claim, in the *Groundwork,* for the first formulation of the categorical imperative. This is the claim that the individual can leap from the thinking and willing of the case (or example) of the individual to the thinking and willing of the condition of the universal: "*Act only in accordance with that maxim through which you can at the same time will that it should become a universal law*" (*GMM,* 4:421).[24] Yet Kant's awareness that he has not yet made his solution sufficiently clear is, I suggest, that which principally makes him so querulous in the famous footnote to the second *Critique,* where he reacts to G. A. Tittel's criticism of his "formula" for autonomous moral reason in the *Groundwork:*

---

24. Following other translations of this passage (e.g., *The Moral Law, or Kant's Groundwork of the Metaphysics of Morals,* trans. H. J. Paton [London: Hutchinson's Universal Library, 1953]), I have inserted the word *should,* which is no doubt implicit in *that it become* but can be missed. Kant writes, "*daß sie ein allgemeines Gesetz werde,*" translated by Gregor as "*that it become a universal law.*" He is not saying or implying that a given individual's maxim of the categorical imperative has any power to produce universals for all other individuals.

A reviewer who wanted to say something censuring this work hit the mark better than he himself may have intended when he said that no new principle of morality is set forth in it but only a *new formula*. But who would even want to introduce a new principle of all morality and, as it were, first invent it? Just as if, before him, the world had been ignorant of what duty is or in thorough-going error about it. But whoever knows what a *formula* means to a mathematician, which determines quite precisely what is to be done to solve a problem and does not let him miss it, will not take a formula that does this with respect to all duty in general as something that is insignificant and can be dispensed with. (*CPrR*, 5:8n)

The use of formula in mathematics is here invoked as a bridge to the universal mostly on the strength of Kant's personal picture of moral duty. When he set aside his pique at Tittel's criticism, he must have sensed that the truth value that can be claimed for a mathematical formula is in fact not self-evidently relevant here. In the third *Critique* he will painstakingly develop the idea of a "mathematical sublime" that is both heteronomous and autonomous. He will describe this as "a striving in our imagination towards progress *ad infinitum*, . . . the awakening of a feeling of a supersensible faculty within us . . . by a particular representation engaging the attention" (*CJ*, 5:250). This suggests that he came to realize that his invocation of mathematics in his dismissive rejoinder to Tittel was unripe and indeed not yet justified. Already in the second *Critique* the new efforts that he makes in clarifying the status of his formula are his acknowledgment that Tittel's criticism was in part deserved. His clarifications very much move, I am arguing, in the direction of a heteronomous and autonomous mathematical sublime.

Since I have earlier discussed, at some length, the issue of examples and exemplarity in Kant's moral thought, I will now focus on those elements of this topic that are especially relevant to his exposition of his formula in the *Critique of Practical Reason*. In the *Groundwork* Kant argues that in the categorical imperative an individual can leap to the formulation of a maxim of the universal merely, as he will phrase it in the second *Critique*, "by being subject to . . . pure practical laws given by his own reason" (*CPrR*, 5:87). But the maxim of the universal has the force of the universal only for her or him; it can only be tested for such

universality by each individual for herself or himself. It is not self-
evident why the moment that one individual's maxim either *in* or
of the categorical imperative is proposed to any other individual it
can be anything more than an example of what such a maxim might
be for a given individual and why it is therefore any more than a
heteronomous "object of the will" (*GMM*, 4:444) for any other individ-
ual. In the *Groundwork*, we recall, Kant explained why an example as an
object of the will can only incapacitate morality or the categorical im-
perative:

> Wherever an object of the will has to be laid down as the basis for pre-
> scribing the rule that determines the will, there the rule is none other
> than heteronomy; the imperative is conditional, namely: *if* or *because*
> one wills this object, one ought to act in such or such a way; hence it
> can never command morally, that is, categorically. (4:444)

Following this logic, it is not obvious why any one of the formulations
of the categorical imperative, by the individual Immanuel Kant, is not
an example or object of the will of this kind, which must at this instant,
insofar as it exerts any influence whatsoever, disable the free proce-
dures of the categorical imperative in any reader of the *Groundwork*. In
other words, it is not self-evident how Kant achieves a transmissible
condition of the universal.[25] Here serious doubt seems to be cast on
the very possibility of a philosophical language that can, in Kant's
terms, represent moral reason.

Already in the *Groundwork* Kant clearly thinks that he has overcome
these difficulties and that he employs such a language. We have seen
that he there has no hesitation in asserting that, on the one hand, "the
imperative of *morality* . . . cannot be made out *by means of any example*"
(4:419), while with his other hand he presents, seriatim, four examples
to help teach the categorical imperative (4:421–423). Similarly in the
second *Critique* he says, on the one hand, that "the moral law is given,
as it were, as a fact of pure reason of which we are a priori conscious

---

25. Kant's idea of "a kingdom of ends (admittedly only . . . an ideal)," where indi-
viduals enter into "a systematic union . . . through common objective laws" (*GMM*,
4:433), somehow without restricting the condition of absolute freedom of each
other's pure reason, may be meant, among other things, to address this problem. If
so, the solution here is left at least as vague as the idea of the kingdom of ends itself.

and which is apodictically certain, though it be granted that no example of exact observance of it can be found in experience" (*CPrR*, 5:47). Yet he also says—and even illustrates this saying—that "the concept of respect for persons" (which he argues is accessible in pure moral reason) "always rests on consciousness of a duty which an example holds before us" (*CPrR*, 5:81n).

I propose that in the *Critique of Practical Reason* Kant clarifies and significantly deepens his solution to the problem inherent in his thinking of discrete representations or examples. He achieves this by representing in storytelling the generating of exemplarity from an endless progression of representations. Already here, that is, we encounter elements of the thinking of the experience of the sublime that he would specify only in the *Critique of Judgment*. In the *Critique of Practical Reason* this is seen to occur *a priori*, as it will in the *Critique of Judgment*, in the procedure of succession that is distinct from mere imitation. I propose that a succession of this kind occurs in Kantian storytelling of the form of the tragic sublime. The difference made by the impact of the experience of the sublime, as a result of the succession procedure, is the difference that Kant needs to distinguish enabling uses of examples from those that are disenabling or even disabling. This difference emerges (from the succession to a progression of examples) as the condition of exemplarity and freedom in moral reason. I will now try to explain, therefore, how, for Kant in the *Critique of Practical Reason*, the *a priori* "succession" *(Nachfolge)* (5:85) of a serial *Typik* (5:67–71) or "endless progress" (5:83) of tragic representations discloses, within the mind, the *"archetypal"* forms (5:43, 83) of the experience of the sublime and the feeling of respect.

∼

It is striking that Kant's first published use of his distinction between *Nachfolge* and *Nachahmung* occurs in the second *Critique*. Very much anticipating the ideas of the *Critique of Judgment*, the distinction offered here directly introduces his claim for the emergence of a true "sublimity" in *a priori* respect. This claim both opens and concludes (*CPrR*, 5:87.31; 88.23) the representation of the honest person *in extremis*. Kant makes his distinction by saying that, on the one hand, there is a false appearance of the sublime created by the kind of imitation called *Nachahmung;* on the other hand, there is the true sublimity autonomously created in the wake of a wholly different kind of imitation, called "succession" or *Nachfolge:*

> By exhortations to actions as noble, sublime, and magnanimous, minds are attuned to nothing but moral enthusiasm and exaggerated self-conceit; by such exhortations they are led into the delusion that it is not duty—that is respect for the law whose yoke (though it is a mild one [alluding to Matthew 11:29–30] because reason itself imposes it on us) they must bear . . . —which constitutes the determining ground of their actions . . . but that it is as if those actions are expected from them, not from duty but as bare merit. For when they imitate such deeds [durch Nachahmung solcher Thaten]—namely from such a principle—. . . they locate the incentive *pathologically* [i.e., "produced by a feeling of the senses" (*CPrR*, 5:80)] (in sympathy or self-love), not *morally* (in the law) . . . thereby forgetting their obligation, which they ought to think of rather than merit.

> Actions of others that are done with great sacrifice and for the sake of duty alone may indeed be praised by calling them *noble* and *sublime* deeds, but only insofar as there are traces [*Spuren*] suggesting that they were done wholly from respect for duty and not from ebullitions of feeling. But if one wants to represent these to someone as examples to be followed in succession [*als Beispiele der* Nachfolge *vorstellen*], respect for duty (which is the only genuine moral feeling) must be used as the incentive—this earnest, holy precept that does not leave it to our vain self-love to dally with pathological impulses (as far as they are analogous to morality) and to credit ourselves with *meritorious* worth. (*CPrR*, 5:84–85) [26]

The decisive difference between *Nachahmung* and *Nachfolge* is that the latter is made possible by the representation of the "traces" of "respect for duty" from which given deeds, whatever their outcome, were done. In other words, what matters for the succession procedure is only the disposition ("respect for duty") to acting, not at all the external act. I

26. I have broken the passage into two halves to highlight Kant's juxtapositions of *Nachahmung* and *Nachfolge*; and in accord with Meredith's usage in translating the distinction between these terms in the third *Critique*, I have given *followed in succession* where Gregor gives *imitated* in the phrase *als Beispiele der Nachfolge vorstellen*.

propose that the "traces" of which Kant speaks here are themselves produced by the tracing of the succession. He is thus describing a line of representation that includes that which is to be succeeded and the way or procedure of such succession (in or of representation). This is the inner procedure of representation of the honest person *in extremis*, in other words, of succeeding to the endless progress of rejections and humiliations that leave the person with no sensible ("pathological") incentives to life, only with the one supersensible incentive that is called respect for duty. We disclose the traces of this *a priori* incentive by following the track or *Typik* of the endless progress to the point where the transfer from the sensible to the supersensible takes place. This is to say that we finally generate it *a priori* in the tragic sublime of the autonomous succession. My proposal here is that Kant's concept of the succession procedure not only is inseparable from an *a priori* sublime but is the ground of *a priori* respect. I now proceed, therefore, to a description of the relation of Kant's *a priori* sublime procedure of succession to the *Typik* and to *a priori* respect.[27]

27. A number of commentators have observed elements of the picture that I am sketching, but they have dismissed these elements as insignificant or implausible. Thus Beck, *A Commentary on Kant's* Critique of Practical Reason, pp. 220–221, records detailed correspondences between Kant's presentations of the sublime and of the feeling of respect: "The sublimity of the moral law is more than a metaphor for Kant. Not only does he use the language of the aesthetics of the sublime in describing the moral law, but he gives an analogous interpretation of the origins of the feelings of sublimity and respect. In both there is humiliation or thwarting of our sensuous nature (our perceptual faculty and imagination in the sublime, our feeling of worth in respect) which occasions a pain which, in turn, is transmuted into a kind of elation by the discovery in ourselves of a power superior to that which has humiliated us (in the sublime) and superior also to that power in us which has been humiliated (in feelings of both respect and of the sublime)." Yet Beck sees no ground for a causal connection between the sublime and respect because he assumes that the sublime is always partially empirical. And indeed, Paul Crowther, in *The Kantian Sublime: From Morality to Art* (Oxford: Clarendon Press, 1989), denies Kant's claims in the *Critique of Practical Reason* for a sublime that is *a priori* and that operates in moral reason: "It is clear that Kant's attitude to the sublime in his Critical ethics is one that serves to locate it wholly beyond the artistic and aesthetic sphere" (p. 36), in other words, beyond an empirical sublime. Further commenting on the second *Critique*, Crowther remarks, "One must . . . express considerable unease over the very fact that Kant's deduction takes this exclusively moral form. . . . For him it is our supersensible aspect which is sublime" (p. 127). I very much agree with Crowther's emphasis on an "incomprehensible number of possible instantiations" (p. 160) in works of art (Crow-

In the *Religion* we find the apparently special case of the *Nachfolge* of the divine archetype that is in fact strikingly parallel to the apparently special case of the genius's *Nachfolge* in the third *Critique*. Parallel, that is, to the production of exemplarity by the succession procedure of the genius in the *Critique of Judgment*, we find in the *Religion* the disclosure of the *a priori* archetype in an endless progress of *Nachfolge* (6:62). Yet here, too, we have only bare hints, mostly relegated to footnotes, of what the *a priori* moving force, that does the disclosing, might be. Kant affirms that there is a "prototype lying in our reason" that is "not . . . cognized through experience," which is to say, through externally derived religious experience (e.g., of scripture or a historical revelation) or any other kind (*Rel*, 6:119). The web of connections in which, he believes, the procedure of succession is constituted can be seen in the following assertions of the independence of *a priori* reason from religion:

> Only a human being conscious of such a moral disposition in himself . . . would steadfastly cling to the prototype of humanity and follow this prototype's example [*dem Urbilde der Menschheit . . . in treuer Nachfolge ähnlich bleiben*]. . . . There is no need, therefore, of any example from experience to make the idea of a human being morally pleasing to God a model to us; the idea is present as model [*Vorbild*] already in our reason. (*Rel*, 6:62)

> The disposition, which takes the place of the totality of the series of approximations carried on *in infinitum*, makes up only for the deficiency which is in principle inseparable from the existence of a temporal being, [namely] never to be able to become quite fully what he has in mind. (*Rel*, 6:67n)

> This disposition can indeed be . . . conformable to the archetype's disposition. . . . As an intellectual unity of the whole, the disposition takes *the place of* perfected *action*. (*Rel*, 6:74n)

---

ther cites the example of *King Lear*) that could evoke the Kantian sublime. I differ from him in understanding how this incomprehensible number of instantiations is represented—and what its moral effects might be—both in the poetry that interests Kant and in his theory of the sublime.

Earlier in the *Religion* Kant seemed to restrict to God the capacity for integrating the "endless progress" into a unity (6:48). But in the above statements we see that he was at that earlier point speaking only of the capacity to understand and value the intellectual unity of the whole. Albeit without full understanding, this whole is in fact independently achieved in the person's moral reason, specifically in the succession to the infinite series of representations. This procedure of succession can produce the disposition that is the equivalent of the archetype because the disposition and the archetype are both forms of the will's representation. In the *Groundwork* Kant made clear that the "disposition," not the action, is all important in morality, "Let the result [of the chosen action] be what it may" (4:416). As we have seen, in the *Religion* Kant twice invokes (from Luke's and Matthew's versions) the parable of the unused talent. Although in both of these instances he condemns the servant for not making active use of his talent, Kant still (now inconsistently, it would seem) defines that talent as an "original predisposition to the good" and "the natural disposition to goodness that lies in human nature" (*Rel,* 6:52, 161).[28] What is of interest to us here is that though Kant may seem to stipulate an ongoing dependence of moral

---

28. As we have seen, this definition accords with Milton's interpretation of the parable and with Kant's idea of a good will in the *Groundwork,* while the insistence on action, rather than on the good will to action, is inconsistent with both Milton's representation of the parable and with Kant's view in the *Groundwork:* "When moral worth is at issue, what counts is not actions, which one sees, but those inner principles of actions that one does not see" (*GMM,* 4:407). This inconsistency between the *Groundwork* and the *Critique of Practical Reason* on the one side and the *Religion* on the other would seem to be the effect of Kant's loosening his grip on the definitive case of the good will *in extremis*—the case, in the *Critique of Practical Reason,* of the "upright man . . . in the greatest distress" (5:88)—which was also kept sharply at the center of the *Groundwork:* "Even, if by a special disfavor of fortune . . ., this will should wholly lack the capacity to carry out its purpose . . . and only the good will were left (not, of course, as a mere wish but as the summoning of all means insofar as they are in our control) . . . it would still shine by itself, as something that has its full worth in itself" (4:394). It could be argued that the slippage toward the insistence on action in the *Religion* already begins to be seen in the second passage, just quoted, from the *Groundwork.* There may be a hint of hesitation in Kant's qualification in the parenthesis, which is purely redundant after having said, "If by a special disfavor of fortune . . . this will should wholly lack the capacity to carry out its purpose." At least in the *Religion,* Kant's insistence on the servant's action requires an explanation of how a good will (a will to goodness)—which has by definition excluded sensory and personal in-

reason on divine agency when he says that the prototype lying in our reason is "the supreme condition of grace" (*Rel*, 6:118–119), what he is saying is no more than that since God created moral reason in all its independence—even from God—we should be especially appreciative of this best of all possible gifts. This gift is the access to the prototype or archetype of humanity now standing independently in our reason. This much is clear. Yet this still does not answer the question of how that access to the archetype functions, or is called upon, in moral reason. I come now to one possible answer.

~

I have proposed that Kant's reference to succession *(Nachfolge)* in the second *Critique* (*CPrR*, 5:85) indicates, first, empirical and, second, *a priori* activities. His accounts of the succession procedure in the *Critique of Judgment* greatly increase the plausibility of this proposal. They also clarify the way the succession procedure can function in the minds of all individuals, that is, not only in the special cases of the genius or the following of a divine archetype. As we have seen repeatedly, in those later accounts, too, the ostensible subject is a succession of an empirical kind, yet even within the realm of the empirical what concerns him is distinguishing how *the successors (die Nachfolgenden)* remain free while following "an exemplary *author* [originator]." And, in fact, he makes clear that what primarily concerns him is the "*a priori*" succession procedure that can be pursued without "blundering attempts" if the individual only learns from the exemplary precursor nothing more than the clarification of "the mode" for *a priori* "going to the same sources for a creative work." The successor creates, that is, from the common capacity to create from his or her *a priori* agency using the same given materials. Thus, merely made less blundering by the empirical example of the exemplary precursor, this succession becomes that of "free . . . reason itself" (*CJ*, 5:283).

The crossovers between heteronomy and autonomy that are implied in these accounts—that is, in both the second and the third *Critiques*—may seem confusing. Further to earlier proposals that I have made about Kant's use of the term *succession,* a scheme such as the following can clarify these crossovers:

---

centives (certainly, mere creature comfort or laziness)—could not be a good will to action or a will to action that promotes the good.

1. The transfer that ultimately interests Kant is the mind's inward, autonomous transfer between sensible and supersensible standpoints that takes place in an inward autonomous succession (in the second *Critique* Kant details this in the mind's representation to itself of the incremental humiliations of self-conceit).

2. The autonomous transfer is prepared, he will say (also in the second *Critique*), in "preparatory guidance" by an isomorphic, heteronomous succession to representations of a certain kind.

This preparation is "the mode of availing oneself of such sources" learned from the precursor. The preparation is the negative or obstacle-removing way of getting to the inner, *a priori* succession of the endless progress in the *a priori* sublime. Proceeding in the track of this latter way of representing is in itself the *a priori* following and *generating* of the form or archetype of humanity (in each of us subjectively), that is, in the categorical imperative. In other words, this ultimate activity of moral reason is the production of the form of inner life that we can distinguish most clearly in the honest person *in extremis*. In sum, the empirical succession "procedure" *(Verfahren)* of the predecessors puts "those who follow" *(die Nachfolgenden)* onto the "track" of a precedent or series[29] of precedents *(auf einen Vorgang)* of the predecessors and in that way causes them to seek "in themselves" nothing less than "autonomy" and the *"a priori."* Thus even if both in 5:85 of the second *Critique* and in 5:283 of the third *Critique* Kant somewhat confusingly interweaves (a) an empirical succession in a series of such followings with (b) the *a priori* succession in the *a priori* endless progress, he has provided enough clues to disentangle the strands and describe each in its integrity.

To recapitulate what is for me the point of chief significance so far: that which reveals Kantian moral reason as a unified field of the tragic sublime is the *a priori* succession of an endless progress of representations. This endless progress of representations is the storytelling series of tragic sublime representations that is thought within the extensible, archetypal representation of the honest person *in extremis*. In each such representation the person manages purely with the devices of moral reason, namely, the endless rejections of sensible incentives and

---

29. In this instance Meredith translates *Verfahren* as "methods," but as "procedure" at *CPrR,* 5:253.

the endless humiliations of self-conceit that are the person's following of this archetype. In its double manifestation, the succession, then, discloses the *a priori* sublime. It discloses exemplarity, also called the archetype or moral feeling or feeling of respect. Kant's *Urbild*—his archetype or prototype—is neither more nor less than this exemplarity. This is not a materialized concept but rather the representation of a form. Both the activity of representing and the form represented are of the succession procedure. Another name for the grand disclosure that is achieved in this sublime succession is the maxim of the categorical imperative, which in Kant's moral thought expresses the good disposition to action. By itself the good disposition represents the form of this exemplarity. The maxim of the categorical imperative centers in the disposition, not in the act: "*Act only in accordance with that maxim through which you can at the same time will that it should become a universal law*" (*GMM,* 4:421).

The Transfer

To try to complete this account we need to ask how the transfer to exemplarity occurs within the tragic sublime. Kant says that moral reason discloses the good will not piecemeal but in a pinpointed "rebirth" or "*revolution* in the disposition of the human being." No matter how far behind may lag the "gradual reformation in the mode of sense" and action, the "revolution [that] is necessary in the mode of thought" (underlining added) is effected in a "single and unalterable" change in moral disposition (*Rel,* 6:47–48). For Kant this capacity for inward revolution is, then, purely rational and totally autonomous. What interests him is the "conversion" in moral reason alone, not in belief, however important belief may be from other points of view (*Rel,* 6:73). Kant sees this moment of revolution as a transfer of the formal rule of the sensible into the supersensible, that is, for moral feeling, moral disposition or will, and (at least in the *Religion*) moral action. The key role of the experience of the sublime in this transfer from the sensible to the supersensible is strongly suggested by the correspondences between the following passages, one from the second *Critique,* the other from the third:

Only *rationalism* of judgment is suitable for the use of moral concepts, since it takes from sensible nature nothing more than what pure reason can also think for itself, that is, conformity with law, and transfers into the supersensible nothing but what can, conversely, be really exhibited by actions in the sensible world in accordance with the formal rule of a law of nature in general. (*CPrR*, 5:71)

The *sublime* consists merely in the *relation* exhibited by the estimate of the serviceability of the sensible in the representation of nature for a possible supersensible employment. (*CJ*, 5:266–267)

Kant thinks of the moving force behind this transfer into supersensible exemplarity as the succession to sublime representation that suspends all sensible incentives. The experience of the sublime supplies a foretaste of oblivion—even the loss of "the least taste for living" (*CPrR*, 5:88)—in its drive to self-extinction or "momentary check to the vital forces," that is, just before the experience of the sublime renews the mind's vitality in "a discharge all the more powerful" (*CJ*, 5:245). In the face of the choice of suicide that is logically indicated by having no further sensible incentives (not even fear of death) to continue living, the person who nevertheless persists in life does so only from duty. This is the one supersensible incentive to go on living. This transfer from the sensible to the supersensible corresponds to, or perhaps even itself is, the vital "discharge all the more powerful" of the experience of the sublime. It constitutes rebirth, revolution, conversion to a life that is now (most elementally but also most fully) duty itself.

The Endless Progression or *Progressus*

In the second *Critique* the *a priori* endless progression and the succession are closely related to "the typic of judgment" (*CPrR*, 5:70). As Beck noted, Kant presents the Typic as an analogy of the concept of the Schematism that he formulated in the first *Critique*.[30] Just as the schema can be an *a priori* representation because it is "not . . . the schema of a case . . . but . . . the schema of a law itself" (*CPrR*, 5:68), the Typic can represent the schema-like form of a law or, in other words, an archetype. We need to ask what the relation of the Typic might be

---

30. Beck, *A Commentary on Kant's* Critique of Practical Reason, pp. 154–155. Beck does not consider how the *a priori* Typik might be related to the archetype, the endless progress, the *Nachfolge*, and the sublime.

to what Kant calls "the *archetypal*" forms "*die urbildliche* [natura archetypa]" (*CPrR*, 5:43) or the "archetype" (*CPrR*, 5:83). Since the Typic operates in the realm of the *a priori*, we need to ask how the Typic might give us access to the archetype *a priori*. Beck agreed with H. J. Paton in identifying this "archetype" with a "regulative conception of nature, believed by almost all eighteenth-century scientists and philosophers to describe the actual cosmos" and which served as "the model for our thought of the moral realm."[31] Though Kant surely avails himself of this meaning of the archetype, this cannot be the principal force of the term in a work in which the representation of form, as well as of the type (Gk. "figure" or "model"), is said to be identical with pure moral reason. The archetype emerges directly, which is to say formally and constitutively, from the form of the Typic. I suggest that in the second *Critique* the emergence of this form, too, can be understood *in concreto* with regard to the "endless progress" (*CPrR*, 5:83), the succession (*Nachfolge*) (*CPrR*, 5:85), and the "sublime" (*CPrR*, 5:85–86). As we have seen, in this typology of an *a priori* storytelling and an *a priori* sublime, an endless *Progressus* or series of representations allows moral reason to exceed the limitations of examples and to achieve the condition of exemplarity. It achieves this in double procedures of succession, the first heteronomous, the second autonomous.

In the second *Critique* Kant says both that we know "the *archetypal*" world "only in reason" (*CPrR*, 5:43) and that the "archetype" (*CPrR*, 5:83) is approached in an "endless progress," though he does not make clear here how this *a priori* endless progress, of reason alone, brings us closer to the archetype. "Holiness of will," he says here, is "a practical *idea,* which must necessarily serve as a *model* [*archetype, zum Urbilde*] to which all finite rational beings can only approximate without end. . . . The utmost that finite practical reason can effect is to make sure of this unending progress [*ins Unendliche gehenden Progressus*] of one's maxims toward this model [archetype] and of their constancy in continual progress [*zum beständigen Fortschreiten*], that is, virtue" (*CPrR*, 5:32–33). Kant reaffirms this *a priori Progressus* in his theory of respect: the "ideal of holiness [perfect virtue] is not attainable by any creature but is yet the archetype [*das Urbild*] which we should strive to approach and resemble in an uninterrupted but endless prog-

31. Ibid., p. 161.

ress [*unendlichen Progressus*]" (*CPrR*, 5:83).[32] Curiously enough—or perhaps not so curiously if we feel that Kant was concerned about what might be thought to be insuperable heteronomous implications of the storytelling in his moral theory—in the second *Critique* it is only in a footnote that he points explicitly to the underlying relation of the "endless progress and its totality" to the emergence of the archetype:

> Complete *well-being* independent of all contingent causes in the world, . . . like *holiness*, is an idea that can be contained only in an endless progress and its totality [*in einem unendlichen Progressus und dessen Totalität*], and hence is never fully attained by a creature. (*CPrR*, 5:123n)

The similarity or identity between key phrases in this passage and Kant's specification of the conditions for the experience of the sublime in the third *Critique* is striking. The experience of the sublime, located in the mind, not in the object, is "owing to the impossibility of the absolute totality of an endless progression" (*CJ*, 5:255). The unique benefit of encountering this totality of an endless progression is that it discloses to the individual mind, momentarily at least, the archetype toward which the Typic points or which it approaches in infinity.

In the second *Critique* the endless progression of "the *type* of the moral law" is represented, Kant says, independently by "pure practical reason, although reason is entitled and even required to use nature (in the understanding's pure form of nature) as the *type* of judgment" (*CPrR*, 5:69–70). This suggests that the endless progression of commonplace examples of the honest person *in extremis*, which constitutes the form of the tragic sublime and leads to freedom and moral feeling, is an *a priori* representation. This representation does not reside within objects of nature. Though it can be represented by sublime works of art that represent the *Formel* of the tragic sublime and of respect, it exists *a priori* in moral reason.

32. To the same effect: "Since it [holiness] is . . . required as practically necessary, it can only be found in an *endless progress* [*ins* Unendliche *gehenden* Progressus] . . . and . . . it is necessary to assume such a practical progress [*praktische Fortschreitung*] as the real object of our will" (*CPrR*, 5:122). In the passage at *CPrR*, 5:32–33, Gregor translates *Urbild* as *model*.

Kantian storytelling tells a commonplace story in its commonplace-ness. This story is an everyday "experiment with every practical rea-son," only "in thought." Conversely, this "experiment" is the storytell-ing that continually occurs within every person's moral reason. Both in the manner of telling and in the form that is represented, this story-telling is concerned with the realm of "as if" (*CPrR*, 5:92). The supposi-tion of "als ob," "as if," is a counterfactual "pure representation" that, Kant shows (and Kleist famously, pathetically, missed), is yet no "empty fantasy" (*CPrR*, 5:153).[33] There is a given-ness or factuality in this *a pri-ori* storytelling that yields the reality of the archetype or the form of law and its maxims. This is reflected in Kant's saying that "the moral law is given [*gegeben*] . . . as a fact [*ein Factum*] of pure reason" and that the "universal lawful form" of reason's "maxims" gives "practical reality to reason" (*CPrR*, 5:47–48). A connection can be made out between this statement in the second *Critique* and the following statement in the first *Critique:* "The schema of cause, and of the causality of a thing in general, is the real upon which, whenever posited [*gesetzt*, sup-posed], something else always follows [*nach . . . folgt*]. It consists, there-fore, in the succession [*Succession*] of the manifold, in so far as that suc-cession is subject to a rule" (A144/B183). Here we can draw upon F. H. Bradley's account of the logic of a supposition, or counterfactual, for an insight into Kant's presupposed representation of a common-place and how it yields the real. Bradley remarks that though a suppo-sition affirms "the mere ground of . . . connection . . . not the actual existing behavior of the real" and though the supposition or common-place is "known to be ideal," still "it is not the mere *idea* of existence that is used. What we use is the real that is always in immediate contact with our minds." In other words (as I understand Bradley), in the sup-position it is not empirical reality that comes to the mind, mediated by the senses, but the real in "the mere ground"—or form—of "connec-

---

33. Here the "als ob" cuts two ways. It relates both to the charge of emptiness that Kant is rejecting and to the procedure of fictive "pure representation," or pure simu-lation, that he is defending. Kleist, in despair at the apparently all-devastating effect of Kant's subjectivistic emphases, failed to heed his warning that "it would be my own fault, if out of that which I ought to reckon as appearance, I made mere illusion" (B69). For Kleist's response to the first *Critique*, see his letter of 22 March 1801, in Heinrich von Kleist, *Sämtliche Werke und Briefe*, ed. Helmut Sembdner, 4 vols. (Mu-nich: Hanser, 1984), 2:634.

tion," which, Bradley says, "has appeared in the experiment."[34] To be sure, the value of a story for a given auditor is determined by vast numbers of factors that millennia of literary criticism and theory have tried to describe. Yet the factor that is of special importance in Kant's storytelling of moral form has rarely been noticed. This is the degree of the story's embeddedness in what is for the teller or auditor an infinitely extended repetition, or endless progression, of presupposed, commonplace experience, in other words, in the *a priori* representation of the continuity that we individually think or cognize as the shared consciousness of the shared conditions of being human.

In Kant's representation of the honest person *in extremis,* we must attend to the suppositional form of the syntax: "When an upright man is in the greatest distress, which he could have avoided if he could only have disregarded duty, is he not sustained by the consciousness that he has maintained humanity in its proper dignity in his own person and honored it, that he has no cause to shame himself in his own eyes and to dread the inward view of self-examination? [Hält nicht einen rechtschaffenen Mann im größten Unglücke des Lebens, das er vermeiden konnte, wenn er sich nur hätte über die Pflicht wegsetzen können, noch das Bewußtsein aufrecht, daß er die Menschheit in seiner Person doch in ihrer Würde erhalten und geehrt habe, daß er sich nicht vor sich selbst zu schämen und den inneren Anblick der Selbstprüfung zu scheuen Ursache habe?]" With the benefit of Bradley's comments on the supposition, we can see that this syntax has direct implications, especially in the framework of Kant's succession procedure, for the freedom of moral reason. In the condition of having been transferred by the procedure of succession in heteronomous storytelling, the autonomous storytelling thought-experiment (that which Kant calls the "experiment with every human practical reason" [*CPrR*, 5:92]) of representing tragic form then generates freedom, moral feeling, and personality in the *a priori* series and *a priori* sublime. Part and parcel of the same *a priori* capacity, this storytelling also con-

34. Bradley, *The Principles of Logic,* 2nd ed., 2 vols. (London: Oxford University Press, 1922), 1:85–87. I have commented on the sameness of the supposition and the represented commonplace in "Descartes's Cogito, Kant's Sublime, and Rembrandt's Philosophers: Cultural Transmission as Occasion for Freedom," *Modern Language Quarterly* 58 (1997): 27–61, especially 45–47, 51–52, 59–61.

stitutes the feeling of respect and provides the form of exemplarity in the transfer from the individual to the archetypal or universal.[35]

Kantian storytelling dispenses with names, places, or dates, in other words, with all the details that can equally be fictional or historical and which, if supplied, can only be otiose, hanging onto story and blurring its form, as it were, like rags on the marble sleekness of a Discus Thrower (poised to let go). Kantian storytelling is the representation of the mere, pure form of the law in nature. It depends on what Kant calls the "*immanent* use" of moral reason, "in which reason is by means of ideas itself an efficient cause in the field of experience" (*CPrR*, 5:48). In other words, in such storytelling the mind's abstract and *a priori* perception of causality depends on "conditions quite other than those which constitute natural connection" in learned, empirical experience (*CPrR*, 5:69).

At a moment of high expectation in the second *Critique*, Kant says that he is locating "the only way of representing . . . that educates the soul morally" (*CPrR*, 5:85). These phrases may seem to be left merely vague, but I am proposing that they refer quite precisely to a way of representing the form of the tragic sublime. The appearance of vagueness is the result of the two-tiered reference of the

---

35. Intertwined with the features of Kant's representation of tragic form, other features of Kantian storytelling will emerge in the next chapter. They can be anticipated briefly here as follows:

1. This storytelling is personal in that it tells of the achievement of "personality" in the experience of "sublimity" (*CPrR*, 5:87).
2. It tells the story of the person's repeated "humiliation" of "self-conceit," of stripping away or "rejection" of all "sensible" incentives for living, and of losing "the least taste for living" or verging on suicide (*CPrR*, 5:71–77).
3. It is a story of a person's "endless progress" of "succession" *(Nachfolge)* toward an "archetype" and the achievement of exemplarity (*CPrR*, 5:83, 85).
4. It is the story of how a person "transfers" consciousness from the "sensible" realm to the intelligible or "supersensible" (*CPrR*, 5:71).
5. It issues in (and is tested by) the leap from individual will to universal will.
6. It climaxes in the person's "disclosure" of the "feeling" of "respect" which is itself "always directed only to persons" (*CPrR*, 5:94, 76).

Indeed, the production of the form of exemplarity in the sublime seems very close to the representation and the "test" of the "form" of the categorical imperative (*CPrR*, 5:69). It therefore seems possible that, at least in the second *Critique*, Kant thinks of the storytelling thought-experiment that represents tragic form as being closely related to the "as if" form of the categorical imperative (*CPrR*, 5:44.20).

phrase "way of representing." It refers simultaneously to two analogous, though different, activities of representing sublime tragic form: one that is heteronomous and empirical, the other that is autonomous and *a priori* and is therefore a way of self-education.[36] The empirical, heteronomous activity is "to represent" "*sublime* deeds" "to someone as examples to be imitated" (*CPrR*, 5:85), that is, sublime deeds done according to the law of duty. The *a priori* and autonomous activity of representing sublime tragic form is the same as the mind's internal representing, to itself, of the "respect for duty" or "law of duty" that Kant calls the only free "incentive" to moral reason. Both of these activities are thus ways of representing sublime tragic form, though some of the elements of these ways of representing, and therefore their full effects, are by no means identical. The *a priori* and autonomous way of representing corresponds to the description in the Transcendental Aesthetic of an *a priori* "form of intuition," grounded in representation, that is "the mode in which the mind is affected by its own activity (namely, through this positing of its representation)" (*CPR*, B67–68). Moral education of this kind, very much as in the *Religion,* is, in Robert Merrihew Adams's phrase, "purely self-education."[37]

Thus, underlying the entire argument of the second *Critique* is a storytelling that Kant follows from the succession of our humanity within *a priori* reason. This is the story of "an upright man" in the condition of "the greatest distress" or, in one everyday resonance of *Unglück,* tragedy—a *rechtschaffener Mann im größten Unglücke.* Even though Kant does not use the term *Tragödie* in the second *Critique,* the form or manner of this storytelling corresponds extensively and profoundly to what we think of as tragedy, at first sight even to Aristotle's Oedipus exemplar. Yet Kant's tragic concept represents the very opposite of what he calls "flattering" us with notions of personal "merit" or "spontaneous goodness of heart" (*CPrR*, 5:85). He isolates and highlights the stark antithesis of those philosophies of tragedy that Karl Jaspers characterizes as giving "comfort by pandering to our self-esteem." "Tragedy Is Not

36. Here we should recall Allison's explanations (mentioned in the previous chapter) of Kant's view of "direct moral significance" and spontaneity even in heteronomous actions: see *Kant's Theory of Freedom,* pp. 5–6, 39.

37. Robert Merrihew Adams, introduction to *Religion within the Boundaries of Mere Reason and Other Writings,* trans. and ed. Allen Wood and George Di Giovanni (Cambridge: Cambridge University Press, 1998), p. xxviii.

Enough," insists Jaspers; and Kant would have strongly agreed, at least if what is meant by tragedy is a Greek tragedy of recuperation of one kind or another.[38] When Kant dismisses the moral value of depending on "machinery in the hands of a higher power" that "does away with the freedom of . . . will" (*CPrR*, 5:38), he may well be thinking of a Greek variety of deus ex machina tragedy. In the tragic plot that Kant values, the protagonist is self-conducted to the verge of self-annihilation by a progressive "rejection" of all "sensible" (i.e., sensory or sensuous) "incentives" for living (*CPrR*, 5:71–73)—including hope for external deliverance—and by unrelenting "humiliation" of "self-conceit" (*CPrR*, 5:73–77). In Kantian storytelling the protagonist, the teller, and the auditor-"spectator" (*CPrR*, 5:157), severally confronted with what may seem to be the inevitable response to "such circumstances"—the response, that is, of suicide or of giving up on life—each *discloses*, to himself or herself, both freedom and "a respect for something quite different from life." This "something quite different" is moral feeling and the self-reliance of hard won moral reason (*CPrR*, 5:88). Kant does not merely declare suicide out of the bounds of moral reason. He sees that the moment of facing suicide, which is inevitable once we have let go of all sensible incentives for continuing with life, is also the singular, inward transfer-point to the one supersensible incentive. This incentive is not disclosed to us in any other way. Among literary representations of the tragic sublime readily available to Kant in the constellation of German Miltonism, I propose that only Milton's *Samson Agonistes* corresponds to the full range of Kant's Miltonic ideas and that this tragedy even exemplifies, in the play's internal succession procedure, Kant's adopted mode of integrating those ideas. This proposal is the work of the next chapter.

38. See Karl Jaspers, *Tragedy Is Not Enough*, trans. Harald A. T. Reiche et al. (London: Gollancz, 1953), p. 99. For critique of Hegel's tendency to offer "premature contentment" in tragedy, see p. 79. In the chapters of this book, which are extracted from *Von der Wahrheit* (Munich: Piper, 1947), Jaspers does not offer an account of Kant's view of tragedy.

CHAPTER 5

The *Critique of Practical Reason* and *Samson Agonistes*

The aim of this chapter is to describe Kant's heteronomous "preparation" *(Vorübung)* for his autonomous "grand disclosure" *(herrliche Eröffnung)* of moral reason in the second *Critique* (*CPrR*, 5:161, 94). The form of this preparation is the procedure of "succession" *(Nachfolge)* (*CPrR*, 5:85) that Kant now names for the first time. I propose that Kant made his way to his particular procedure of succession in the second *Critique* through his engagement with the constellation of German Miltonism and that this procedure of succession is to Milton's *Samson Agonistes*. In its own right *Samson Agonistes* is constructed as a procedure of succession and is also, explicitly, even overwhelmingly, the equivalent of a Kantian preparation. We will see that the relation between the second *Critique* and *Samson Agonistes* provides another exemplification of the one kind of freedom-granting "influence"—namely, "succession"—that in Kant's view can enable originality and moral feeling. The Milton of *Samson Agonistes* is Kant's "artist" and "predecessor" in representing, concretely and in detail, many of the problems and solutions—the "ideas"—that are at the core of the second *Critique*'s contribution to moral theory. Milton represents these ideas in a powerful procedure of succession that does indeed "arouse like ideas" in his successor.[1]

---

1. Once again I cite Kant's terms for succession from *CJ*, 5:283, 309.

Herder, Samson, Kant

I suggest, first, that the potentialities for Kant's storytelling response to *Samson Agonistes* in the *Critique of Practical Reason* likely came into his ken through Herder's provocation in "On the Influence of the Belles-Lettres on the Higher Sciences" ("Über den Einfluß der Schönen Literatur in den höheren Wissenschaften"), first written in 1779 and first published in 1781, the same year as the publication of the Mannheim translation of *Samson Agonistes*.[2] Zammito observes that, like *On Cognition and Sensation,* "On the Influence of the Belles-Lettres" "argued against dividing human experience into abstract faculties and insisted upon the wholeness which art and poetry above all evoked. In these essays Kant could not help but read an attack on his concept of philosophy and hence on himself. In his *Reflections,* Kant defended himself."[3] Herder's integration of poetry into his kind of philosophical argument in this essay was fully logical, even necessary, he believed, especially where an attack on Kantian philosophy was concerned. In reading "On the Influence of the Belles-Lettres," Kant could not have missed that Herder was once again resorting to his tactic—well familiar from *On Cognition and Sensation*—of positioning a Satan-like Kant against the higher, whole truths of Milton's poetry. Herder twice names Milton explicitly in the essay (*SW,* IX.293, 306), but it is his

---

2. Herder's essay was entered in the prize competition of the Bayerschen Akademie in 1779 and was first published in the *Abhandlungen der Baierischen Akademie über Gegenstände der schönen Wissenschaften* (Munich, 1781), pp. 139–168. The scrupulous, anonymous translation of *Samson Agonistes* to which I will refer is *Simson: Ein dramatisches Gedicht,* published with a translation of *Paradise Regained* and other poems of Milton in *Das wiedereroberte Paradies des Johann Milton, nebst seiner Lebensbeschreibung, einigen dramatischen und verschiednen kleinern Gedichten* (Mannheim, 1781). My references to *Samson Agonistes* in German are to this translation. In Kant's time an alternative translation had already been made available by the German-Swiss Miltonists, who were a vital part of the constellation of German Miltonism. This was Simon Grynaeus's translation of *Samson Agonistes* in his *Johann Miltons wieder-erobertes Paradies, nebst desselben Samson, und einigen andern Gedichten, wie auch einer Lebens-Beschreibung des Verfassers. Aus dem Englischen übersetzt* (Basel, 1752), which is, however, much less faithful to Milton's language than the Mannheim translation is.

3. John H. Zammito, *The Genesis of Kant's Critique of Judgment* (Chicago: University of Chicago Press, 1992), p. 42.

nameless yet unmistakable invocations of Milton that must have struck Kant, especially his way of characterizing certain contemporary philosophical critics of art. Herder compares their empty writing, which is both deluded and deluding, to the smoke- and ashes-filled Sodom apples on which the fallen angels feed in Milton's Hell. Herder's qualified reader, versed in great poetry as well as true philosophy, would have easily recognized the direct allusion to this memorable passage in *Paradise Lost:*

> There stood
> A Grove hard by, sprung up with this thir change,
> His will who reigns above, to aggravate
> Thir penance, laden with Fruit, like that
> Which grew in Paradise, the bait of *Eve*
> Us'd by the Tempter: on that prospect strange
> Thir earnest eyes they fix'd, imagining
> For one forbidden Tree a multitude
> Now ris'n, to work them furder woe or shame;
> Yet parcht with scalding thirst and hunger fierce,
> Though to delude them sent, could not abstain,
> But on they roll'd in heaps, and up the Trees
> Climbing, sat thicker then the snaky locks
> That curld *Megæra:* greedily they pluck'd
> The Fruitage fair to sight, like that which grew
> Near that bituminous Lake where *Sodom* flam'd;
> This more delusive, not the touch, but taste
> Deceiv'd; they fondly thinking to allay
> Thir appetite with gust, instead of Fruit
> Chew'd bitter Ashes, which th' offended taste
> With spattering noise rejected: oft they assay'd,
> Hunger and thirst constraining, drugg'd as oft,
> With hatefullest disrelish writh'd thir jaws
> With soot and cinders fill'd. (X.547–570)

The sophistic critic of art described by Herder, who has learned to "pass judgment on everything," has been "nourished" on the deceiving "taste" shared by Satan's followers:

The fashionable literature of our age is often a garden filled with apples of Sodom: outwardly beautiful, but inwardly full of dust and ashes. A youth who greedily devours the so-called beautiful, with no regard for what it is and how it appears in print, surely does not eat healthily. . . . Taste is corrupted, the soul left uncertain or spoiled. The realm of his knowledge, as narrow as his times, cannot enjoy better fruits than those which the age yields, and he cannot prepare more wholesome sauces. If, moreover, the youth nourished in this manner becomes a judge in the belles lettres before he has become a student, a master before he has become an apprentice, then God forgive him for the havoc he shall wreak! What the Sophists were in the time of Socrates, such critics of art are in our age: they know everything, they pass judgment on everything. (*SW*, IX.292–293)[4]

[Die Modelektür der Zeit ist oft ein Garte [*sic*] voll Sodomsäpfel, auswendig schön, inwendig voll Staub und Asche. Ein Jüngling, der, was und wie etwas sogenanntes Schöne im Drucke herauskömmt, es begierig verschlingt, hält gewiß ungesunde Mahlzeit: . . . Der Geschmack wird verdorben, die Seele unsicher oder verwöhnt. Das Reich seiner Wissenschaft so enge wie seine Zeit, kann nicht bessere Früchte geniessen, als diese giebt, und er nicht gesündere Säfte kochen. Kömmts nun noch dazu, daß der also genährte Jüngling selbst Richter in den schönen Wissenschaften wird, ehe er Schüler; Meister, ehe er Lehrling geworden; gnade Gott, für den Einfluß! Was je die Sophisten zu Sokrates Zeit waren, sind solche Kunstrichter in unsern Zeiten: sie wissen Alles, sie entscheiden über Alles.]

The provocation to Kant was clear. Instead of newfangled "formulas" *(Formeln)*, Herder recommends the use of that which Kant had repeatedly excluded from philosophical discourse: "*beautiful examples . . . beautifully presented*" (*schöne Beispiele, schön vorgestellt*) (*SW*, IX.302).

4. My citations in English from this essay are from *Selected Writings on Aesthetics: Johann Gottfried Herder*, trans. and ed. Gregory Moore (Princeton: Princeton University Press, 2006), pp. 335–346. The passage quoted here is from page 336, the ones below from pages 343 (for *SW*, IX.302), 338–339 (for *SW*, IX.295–296), and 342 (for *SW*, IX.301), of Moore's translation. (I have altered one phrase, giving "critics of art" for *Kunstrichter*, where Moore gives "critics.")

Herder's announced purpose in this essay on education is to "discuss the *order* and *method* that in my opinion and experience might best be employed from childhood [von der *Ordnung* und *Methode* reden, die nach meiner Meinung und Erfahrung von Jugend auf am besten zu nehmen seyn möchte]" (*SW,* IX.301). I suggest that Herder's presentation of the following beautiful example of biblical Samson became a focal point for Kant, moving him, in fact, to find his own counter-*Methode* for thinking of this same example. Herder's presentation of Samson is thickly barbed with aggressions against the "erroneous idea and folly" of Kantian abstract philosophizing:

> *All the powers of our soul are only one power,* just as our soul is only one soul. What we call superior and inferior, high and low is only comparatively and relatively so. On the whole, however, a sound understanding is impossible without sound and well ordered senses, a decisive judgment is impossible without an imagination tamed and heedful of its duty, a good will and character are impossible without passions and inclinations in good order. Hence it is both wrong and foolish *to cultivate the higher sciences without the belles lettres,* to plow the air when the soil lies fallow.
>
> Who has ever known a man of sound understanding to be constantly misled by his sensuous judgment? Who has ever seen aright with his understanding who did not see aright with his eyes and fancy? <u>Who was ever master of his will whose passions did not obey him, who was in thrall to his fancy, who in every one of his secret inclinations felt seven ropes, a thousand ropes binding him, this Samson , without another faculty [*Kraft*=power] freeing him?</u> . . . With the young, therefore, we must begin at an early age to treat and cultivate their sensuous powers sensuously, through simple rules and—even better—through good examples. (*SW,* IX.295–296; underlining added)

> [*Alle Kräfte unsrer Seele sind nur Eine Kraft,* wie unsre Seele nur Eine Seele. Wir nennen oben und unten, hoch und niedrig, was nur vergleichungs- und beziehungsweise so ist; im Ganzen aber ist ein richtiger Verstand ohne richtige, wohlgeordnete Sinne, ein bündiges Urtheil ohne gezähmte und zu ihrem Dienst erweckte Einbildungskraft, ein guter Wille und Charakter ohne gutgeordnete Leidenschaften und

Neigungen nicht möglich. Also ists Irrthum und Thorheit, *die höhern ohne die schönen Wissenschaften anzubauen,* in der Luft zu ackern, wenn der Boden brach liegt.

Wer hat je einen Mann von richtigem Verstande gekannt, den sein sinnliches Urtheil immer irre führte? Wer sah je mit dem Verstande recht, wer mit seinen Augen und der Phantasie nicht recht sah? <u>Wer war Herr über seinen Willen, dem seine Leidenschaft nicht gehorchte, dem die Phantasie befahl, der in jeder seiner geheimen Neigungen Stricke fühlte, die ihn, den Simson, sieben- und tausendfach fesselten, ohne daß ihn eine andre Kraft befreite?</u> . . . Also ist mit der Jugend jugendlich anzufangen, unsre sinnliche Kräfte sinnlich zu behandeln und zu bilden, durch leichte Regeln, und, noch besser, durch gute Exempel.] (underlining added)

Considering how rapidly information and innuendo were transmitted on the Herder-Hamann-Kant network, Kant may well have been aware that Herder's intense interest in the example of Samson had even led him to produce a trial run of a work entirely devoted to Samson.[5] In any case, a year following the publication of "On the Influence of the Belles-Lettres," Kant surely saw in *On the Spirit of Hebrew Poetry*—the great popularity of which Kant sorely envied—Herder's high opinion of *Samson Agonistes* (*SW*, XII.181).[6]

But, even without such additional proddings, Herder's Samson example of his *Methode* in "On the Influence of the Belles-Lettres on the Higher Sciences" had to leap out at Kant since it is simultaneously used both to attack Kantian abstractionism and to encapsulate Herder's vitalist theory. Revolving around the axiom of an all-engendering "power," this was the theory that Herder was offering as a superior alternative to what he considered Kant's abstract moralizing of human existence. "Herder's theory," Frederick Beiser explains, "postulates a single principle, a single concept to unite our notions of mind and body: the concept of power *(Kraft)*. The essence of power is de-

5. The manuscript was mentioned (*SW*, XII.420) but not printed by Suphan. It is printed in *Johann Gottfried von Herder's sämmtliche Werke*, 17 vols., ed. Johann Georg Müller (Tübingen, 1806), III.253–261.

6. Herder's praise of *Samson Agonistes* occurs in the first volume of *Vom Geist der Ebräischen Poesie*, published in 1782 in Dessau.

fined as self-generating, self-organizing activity."[7] It was this theory and this concept that, in addition to Herder's reliance on analogies and literary figures, Kant raked over the coals in his 1785 reviews of the *Ideen*. To Kant this was a case of trying to "explain that which one does not comprehend by that which one comprehends even less," the latter furnished by "the fertile field of the poetic imagination."[8] As I have repeatedly suggested, despite Kant's strong objection to Herder's use of analogy or literary figures, no doubt including this one of the indefinable "power" that liberates Samson, he soon found his own way—within the constellation of German Miltonism and within his own moral theory—to make use of analogy and literary figures of a certain kind. In the second *Critique* this especially took the form of an analogy that was traced in succession to Milton's Samson. Kant, moreover, had a way to define and explain the force by which the Miltonic Samson gains his freedom, namely, in this Samson's own procedure of succession in the experience of the sublime.

This is to say that Herder's specific provocation regarding Samson and his "power" was immensely fruitful for Kant when he came to frame his own *Methode* for educating the young in the second *Critique*. Rudolf Haym showed the centrality of "On the Influence of the Belles-Lettres" in Herder's pedagogical theory.[9] Central to Herder's own *Methode*, exemplified by his example of Samson liberated by his mysterious inner power, is eschewing Kant's kind of philosophical writing. Central to Kant's *Methode* in the second *Critique*, exemplified by his own way of following the example of Samson's liberation, is his way of incorporating what he finally accepted from Herder, namely, not his

7. Frederick C. Beiser, *The Fate of Reason: German Philosophy from Kant to Fichte* (Cambridge, Mass.: Harvard University Press, 1987), p. 146.

8. Kant, "Reviews of Herder's *Ideas for a Philosophy of the History of Mankind*," trans. Robert E. Anchor in Immanuel Kant, *On History*, ed. Lewis White Beck (Indianapolis: Bobbs-Merrill, 1963), pp. 37–38. In fact, Herder presents his poetic figure of Jupiter's throne—the figure that Kant singled out for ridicule (p. 46)—to represent the self-generating *Kraft* that interknits mind and body. I mentioned Kant's ridicule of Herder's image in Chapter 2. In Chapter 6 I will briefly turn to Kant's possible response, in the third *Critique*, to Herder's representation of the idea of *Kraft* in the Jupiter image.

9. Rudolf Haym, *Herder nach seinem Leben und seinen Werken dargestellt*, 2 vols. (Berlin, 1877–85; reprinted Berlin: Aufbau Verlag, 1958), II.136–141.

vitalist theorizing of power, but the indispensable use of analogy and inherited literary representations. For Kant, however, this had to be a use of poetic figures within a Miltonic sublime that Herder did not comprehend despite his attempts to invoke the Miltonic sublime against Kant. Beiser has pointed out that for Herder, following Hamann, the use of analogy and literature in philosophical writing was part of his reaction "against the individualistic anthropology of the Enlightenment" so that rationality is understood by him as "the internalization of the traditions of a culture." Herder's "recognition of the role of analogy," says Beiser, leads him "to a striking conclusion about the importance of literature. Literature . . . is more important than philosophy for an understanding of life."[10] My proposal that in the second *Critique* Kant was already engaged in a procedure of succession to *Samson Agonistes* (and its procedure of succession) carries this further implication: that Kant in this way represented his own form of a more than individualistic anthropology in which literature, incorporated *within* philosophy, has an indispensable role. Unwittingly Herder had here, too, helped lead Kant to an extraordinary opportunity.

∼

In disclosing the maxims—the *a priori* moral principles—of the *Critique of Practical Reason*, Kant necessarily also discloses the predicates of his procedure of succession to an earlier procedure of succession. Kant found this earlier procedure of succession, including a host of its predicates and ideas, in Milton's *Samson Agonistes*. In the second *Critique* these predicates and ideas are deeply embedded in Kant's own storytelling, but it is more than possible to perceive their Miltonic provenience. In the procedure of succession, provenience is precisely that which provides the sublime impact that, in turn, enables Kant's originality and leap to exemplarity. The Kantian-Miltonic predicates within the storytelling of the second *Critique* are:

1. an individual has been unable to resist his lustful inclination
2. he has been unable to let any personal insult go unpunished
3. he has had his secret betrayed by someone he trusted "blindly" (*blindlings*)

10. Beiser, *The Fate of Reason*, pp. 140, 148.

4. he suffers a series of humiliations of self-conceit
5. he no longer wishes to live, yet persists in life as a duty
6. as a result of that series of humiliations, he achieves "liberty" or freedom as well as
7. the transfer of his standpoint, in the condition of outward blindness, to inward seeing of the disposition to the highest good, which is to say to the categorical imperative
8. for this highest good, he sacrifices his life for the preservation of his country, that is, when to do so is "an essential duty, transgression of which violates the moral law in itself" (*CPrR*, 5:158) [what Milton calls "the ends / For which our country is a name so dear" (*Samson Agonistes*, 893–894)]
9. his sacrifice is done (after considerable rational "scruple," *CPrR*, 5:158) in obedience to a vocation that must be identical with the moral law (as indicated below, this cannot be the behavior of a terrorist)
10. the good at which his sacrifice aims is expressed by Kant's term for the greatest possible good, *God's glory*.

To be sure, a number of these predicates are to be found, even several at a time, in other well-known storytellings of world literature—in *Oedipus at Colonus* or *Hamlet* or *King Lear*, for example. In fact, groupings of numbers of these predicates identify the tragic condition in the tragic literature of Western culture and beyond. Kant was surely counting on this commonality in expecting that we would recognize the inevitability, if not even the *a priori* status, of these predicates. And it is undoubtedly true that in *Samson Agonistes* Milton self-consciously follows a number of these predicates directly from works such as, indeed, *Oedipus at Colonus*. Yet, for all that, in the *Critique of Practical Reason* we have a singular case of the procedure of succession in the extensiveness and sum total of Kant's predicates. In accordance with the theory of the succession procedure that Kant would soon make explicit in the *Critique of Judgment*, we can already see that a "particular representation" must have "evoked" his heteronomous succession procedure (5:250) in the *Critique of Practical Reason*. This heteronomous succession is traced by the storytelling predicates that constitute an experience of the sublime and that enable the disclosure of moral reason in the autonomous succession procedure. Kant could only have found all of these storytelling predicates, in one integral representation, in the storytelling that is *Samson Agonistes*. The moral personality of Milton's Samson in *Samson Agonistes* is the sum total, or impact, of this storytelling. We see that this is unmistakably the case if we are viewing *Samson Agonistes* with Kant's eyes for Miltonic sublimity and Miltonic aesthetic ideas. (I will return below to the topic of aesthetic ideas.)

In the remainder of this chapter I propose to show that the specificity of Kant's intermittent storytelling in the second *Critique* is not only in its agglomeration of examples that recalls Milton's telling of the Samson story, but in the transfer, effected in this storytelling, between his empirical, heteronomous *firsts* and his *a priori*, autonomous *seconds*. This achieved transfer is a crucial part of Kant's work of philosophy in this *Critique*. Here, too, Kant confronts the problem that, even if his exposition is true, it is only an example for mere imitation. In other words, imitative servility was one inevitable effect on his readers of his own theorizing and his own use of examples. He could overcome this danger only if he could achieve a condition of exemplarity for the representations that constitute his exposition. This he attempts to attain for himself and for his philosophy in the succession procedure of his storytelling in the second *Critique*. This is to say that Kant's empirical and heteronomous storytelling is, in his terms, a necessary "preparation" that itself follows, in a procedure of succession, the preparation and procedure of succession within *Samson Agonistes*. And *Samson Agonistes* in turn follows, among others, Job's and Christ's (the archetype's) own agonizing, awe-inspiring preparations, thus adding yet another dimension to the effectively endless progression to which Kant succeeds in following Milton's tragedy. Kant's procedure of succession to *Samson Agonistes* (or, alternatively, if we could find such a thing, to some exact equivalent of the Kantian predicates and ideas that can be found in *Samson Agonistes*) occurs in the *Critique of Practical Reason* itself, that is, in the integral relation of poetry to philosophy. An essential point about what I am claiming here is that the specificity and concreteness of poetry and its storytelling are indispensable to Kant's work of moral philosophy. Although this kind of concreteness and this condition of storytelling are possible in arts other than poetry, they are preeminently achieved in poetry. This is likely one of the considerations that led Kant to rate poetry as the highest of the arts and to lay out both the procedure of succession and aesthetic ideas in relation to poetry—even and especially in response to Milton's aesthetic ideas. As one offshoot of this set of relations in Kant's thought, the heteronomous procedure of succession to *Samson Agonistes* in the second *Critique* produces freedom and the transfer. Freedom and the transfer then open the way to the autonomous, *a priori* procedure of succession, that is, with its inner transfer and its maxim of the categorical imperative. We need to see how at least the heteronomous part of this process works in practice.

Samson Agonistes and Preparation

Samson Agonistes is wholly preparation of the Kantian kind. The controlling irony, and the principal disclosure, of Milton's representation of Samson's activity of being *agonistes*, wrestling, is that his principal heroic action, his central agon, is already achieved in what seems to be mere prelude. This prelude is only his wrestling with his own moral consciousness, his overcoming of his outward self. Well before the catastrophe, that is, his serial humiliations of self-conceit have allowed him to escape the mere "inclination" that, in Milton's no less than in Kant's terms, can only be "blind and servile" *(blind und knechtisch)* (*CPrR*, 5:118). Samson's opening condition of being "Eyeless in *Gaza* at the Mill with slaves" (41) first and foremost represents the personality condition of being blind and servile.[11] Samson will increasingly real-

---

11. It seems possible that Kant's famous instance, in the *Critique of Judgment*, of the *Handmühle* as a symbol or metaphor of the *despotischen Staat* ruled by the *einzelnen absoluten Willen* (individual absolute will) (5:352) owes something to Milton's equally famous image, that is, of Samson and the slaves being used as beasts of burden to push the millstone with their hands—which, indeed, depicts a usual meaning of the term hand mill. In fact, although Kant's symbol or metaphor here is usually referred to as the despot's hand mill, this would seem to be a misnomer. Although Kant's metaphor is left too spare to allow one to feel secure in a reading, it seems odd to assume that the metaphor describes how the despot single-handedly (using his hand- or handy-size mill) grinds the citizens to powder between the millstones. This would tend to make the metaphor incoherent, since, ground to powder, the citizenry cannot even serve as the running parts of the despot's machine (parallel to the parts of a "living body" in the constitutional monarchy that Kant instances in the same passage). Rather, Kant focuses here on the functioning of "the despotic state." The primary signification of the hand mill, then, is that of large-scale enslavement of the citizens' free hands to the despot's private, absolute will, which means forcing their free

ize that, compared to that condition, his physical blindness and his servitude to the Philistines are trivial afflictions. So, too, as Milton presents it, the violent action which takes place after Samson's final exit is extraneous to Samson's independent moral achievement. Samson's *agonistes* method (exercised exhaustively before the catastrophe) is Kant's model for "the method of moral cultivation and exercise" that is indeed "only preparatory" (the *Methodenlehre einer moralischen Bildung und Übung* that is *nur Vorübung*). The progression and the procedure of succession in *Samson Agonistes*—which constitute its activity of being *agonistes*—unfold continually from the tragedy's first verses, "A little onward lend thy guiding hand / To these dark steps, a little further on" (1–2). These guided, preparatory steps in darkness (apparently leading nowhere in particular) seem to be only marking time or building suspense before the main course of *Samson Agonistes* is revealed. Yet these dark steps, one by one, are a symbol of the preparatory encounters that turn out to be, one by one, the main business of Samson's moral development. The reformation in his will or disposition—not his actions—is "what counts" (*GMM*, 4:407), for Kant as well as for Milton. Kant's procedure of succession to *Samson Agonistes* is for him, in turn, the "preparatory guidance" that puts him on "the track of the morally good in the first place" (*CPrR*, 5:152), which is to say in his own thinking of the progression and the procedure of succession. Kant's procedure and exposition of this Miltonic method is thus at the heart of his *immediately enacted* achievement of moral reason in the second *Critique*.

Like Job, Milton's Samson is finally a hero of faith, not of force. Some readers resist Milton's fictive predicates that the Philistines are the oppressors and enslavers and that Samson's act of violence, which closes the play, is therefore fully just. If we ignore these predicates we

---

hands to become mere instruments turning the machine or millstone of tyranny, as do Samson and his fellow slaves. For a recent essay that assumes that the hand mill meant by Kant is turned by the despot himself, see Kirk Pillow, "Jupiter's Eagle and the Despot's Hand Mill: Two Views on Metaphor in Kant," *Journal of Aesthetics and Art Criticism* 59 (2001): 193–209, where, interestingly enough, Pillow elaborates the view that "the key issue in assessing the cognitive status of the Kantian metaphors embodied in aesthetic ideas is their strong creativity" (203–205). Since, as we have seen, Kant thought of aesthetic ideas and Milton's poetry in close proximity, or even identity, this may be another reason for supposing that he was thinking of the Miltonic hand mill.

may reflect on another story that we find more pleasing, but we are no longer talking about the moral scenario of *Samson Agonistes*.[12] Milton makes clear that Samson does not kill indiscriminately. The amphitheater has been filled with those who have come to celebrate Samson's blinding and enslavement. The national significance of the event for "the people" assembled here is clearly its confirmation of the Philistine imposition of "servitude" (269) on the Hebrews:

> At sight of him the people with a shout
> Rifted the Air clamoring thir god with praise,
> Who had made thir dreadful enemy thir thrall. (1620–1622)

Whether mass collaboration justifies the killing of this crowd can certainly still be questioned, though if we transpose these circumstances to other, equivalent scenes of bloodthirsty rallies, and/or of crowds cheering for the enslavement of whole populations, many or most of us would usually say, I believe, that it does justify it. Milton's representation provides no persuasive reason to doubt that Samson's final (and, in effect, only) act in the tragedy is in the service not of his own but of God's "glory," which means (since God needs nothing), God's plan for justice and perfection in His creation. Upon listening to Samson's predictions of God's ultimate triumph over Dagon and his followers, Manoa is comforted by the thought, which he understands only imperfectly, that "God . . . will not long defer / To vindicate the glory of his name" (473–475). This is what the chorus finally understands to be the purpose of Samson's service at the climax of his moral development when they send him off, saying,

> Go, and the Holy One
> Of *Israel* be thy guide
> To what may serve his glory best. (1427–1429)

Kant's comment in the second *Critique* on the meaning of "the glory of God" is wholly apposite here. In this comment he unravels the inner

---

12. Resistance of this kind is prominent in Joseph Wittreich's *Interpreting* Samson Agonistes (Princeton: Princeton University Press, 1986), where, in part, Wittreich argues for a different fictive predicate.

logic of the term within the Judeo-Christian tradition in general and, indeed, in accord with Milton's play specifically:

> Those who put the end of creation in the glory of God [*die Ehre Gottes*] (provided this is not thought anthropomorphically, as inclination to be praised) perhaps hit upon the best expression [for *"the highest good"*]. For, nothing glorifies God more than what is most estimable in the world, respect for his command, observance of the holy duty that his law lays upon us, when there is added to this his magnificent plan of crowning such a beautiful order with corresponding happiness. (*CPrR*, 5:131)

Kant and Milton both believed that the world contains persons who perpetrate extreme evils. Neither Kant nor Milton would have thought that God's plan of crowning a beautiful order with corresponding, deserved happiness—in sum, with His glory—should hesitate before the resulting unhappiness of those who manifestly perpetrate evil.

Samson discovers that his service and his repentance are in obeying the moral law expressed by God's will. Samson's way to "repent the sin" (504) of revealing the secret that was entrusted to him will be in discovering for himself the secret incentive for living and acting—the noumenon—that eludes all material or sensory inclinations, such as those that earlier caused him to reveal his secret. Kant makes a similar point about his nameless protagonist in the second *Critique:*

> Even the whole sequence of his existence as a sensible being . . . is to be regarded in the consciousness of his intelligible existence as nothing but the consequence and never as the determining ground of his causality as a *noumenon.* . . . This is also the ground of repentance for a deed long past at every recollection of it. (*CPrR*, 5:98)

Kant, whose principal subject here is the disclosure of this noumenon in human personality, expounds the meaning of God's glory as an end of the noumenon. For both Kant and Milton, human reason has a capacity for achieving the good because of the goodness of the creator. At the same time, however, for both Milton and Kant the manifestations of moral reason can be seen, first and foremost, in a disclosure of the highest good within human reason, and then, secondarily, in a confirmation (if it is granted) of that good in God's revelation of His will. For both Milton in *Samson Agonistes* and Kant in the second *Critique,* the human achievement of moral reason is in procedures of succession within the experience of the sublime.

Kant's and Milton's Preparatory Guidance

Immediately before the conclusion of the second *Critique,* Kant says the following about the role of *exercise (Übung)* in moral reason in general and the role of *preparatory exercise (Vorübung)* in his present unfolding of moral reason:

> And now the law of duty, through the positive worth that observance of it lets us feel, finds easier access through the *respect for ourselves* in the consciousness of our freedom. When this is well established, when a human being dreads nothing more than to find, on self-examination, that he is worthless and contemptible in his own eyes, then every good moral disposition can be grafted onto it, because this is the best, and indeed the sole, guard to prevent ignoble and corrupting impulses from breaking into the mind.
>
> I have intended, here, only to point out the most general maxims of the doctrine of the method of moral cultivation and exercise [*Übung*]. Since the variety of duties requires further determinations for each kind of duty and would thus constitute a lengthy affair, I shall be excused if in a work such as this, which is only preparatory [*die nur Vorübung ist*], I go no further than these outlines [*Grundzügen*]. (*CPrR,* 5:161)

This language follows closely the method of "preparatory guidance" *(vorbereitenden Anleitungen),* centered in storytelling, which Kant at the beginning of the *Methodenlehre* says should be used in moral education:

> It certainly cannot be denied that in order to bring either a mind that is still uncultivated or one that is degraded onto the track of the morally good in the first place some preparatory guidance [*vorbereitenden Anleitungen*] is needed to attract it by means of its own advantage or to alarm it by fear of harm; but as soon as this machinery, these leading strings have had even some effect, the pure moral motive must be

brought to bear on the soul, the motive which—not only because it is the only one that can ground a character (a consistent practical cast of mind in accordance with unchangeable maxims), but also because it teaches the human being to feel his own dignity—gives his mind power, unexpected even by himself, to tear himself away from all sensible attachments so far as they want to rule over him and to find a rich compensation for the sacrifice he makes in the independence of his rational nature and the greatness of soul to which he sees that he is called. (*CPrR*, 5:152)

The parallelisms of these two passages suggest (more than Kant is willing to acknowledge except distantly) that in the *Critique of Practical Reason* as a whole he has himself engaged in a preparatory guidance of the storytelling kind. He engages in this preparatory storytelling, that is, not merely in the *Methode* section, but in much that has led up to, and prepared the way for, the conclusion of this work. This relation of *preparatory exercise* to *exercise proper* also suggests that Kant's lyrical personalization in the peroration has as its predicate the *story* of another specific personality.

At this point in my piecing together of Kant's storytelling, it is important to recall the close linkage between the terms *succession* and *endless progress (Nachfolge* and *Progressus ohne Ende)* that is operative in Kant's accounts of the experience of the sublime. His idea of the *endless progress (unendlichen Progressus)* of representations in the *Critique of Practical Reason* (5:83) or *progress without ending (Progressus ohne Ende)* of representations in the *Critique of Judgment* (5:255) is the same for him as the *progress ad infinitum (Fortschritte ins Unendliche)* of representations, which he names in his first formal definition of the sublime (*CJ*, 5:250). In addition, as we have noted earlier, these terms can be equated in the *Critique of Practical Reason* with the procedure of succession that provides access to the archetypal or exemplary (5:85). This procedure, which requires an endless progress of representations or examples (*CPrR*, 5:83), closely anticipates the succession to an endless line of representations or examples that discloses exemplarity in the *Critique of Judgment* (5:309, 318). Within the dynamics of the second *Critique* we can now see the vital role of Kant's identification of the endless progression with the procedure of succession:

[This is] the archetype which we should strive to approach and resemble in an uninterrupted but endless progress. (*CPrR*, 5:83)

[das Urbild ist, welchem wir uns zu näheren und in einem ununterbrochenen, aber unendlichen Progressus gleich zu werden streben sollen.]

But if one wants to represent these to someone as examples for <u>succession,</u> respect for duty (which is the only genuine moral feeling) must be used as the incentive—this earnest, holy precept that does not leave it to our vain self-love to dally with pathological impulses (as far as they are analogous to morality) and to credit ourselves with *meritorious* worth. . . . This is the only way of representing them that educates the soul morally. (*CPrR*, 5:85; underlining added)

[Will man jemanden [*sic*] aber sie als Beispiele der <u>Nachfolge</u> vorstellen, so muß durchaus die Achtung für Pflicht (als das einzige ächte moralische Gefühl) zur Triebfeder gebraucht werden: diese ernste, heilige Vorschrift, die es nicht unserer eitelen Selbstliebe überläßt, mit pathologischen Antrieben (so fern sie der Moralität analogisch sind) zu tändeln und uns auf *verdienstlichen Werth* was zu Gute zu thun. . . . Das ist die einzige Darstellungsart, welche die Seele moralisch bildet.] (underlining added)

Kant's failure to make explicit the relation of the succession to the endless progression is no doubt in part a function of his waffling on the question of whether the objects of heteronomous sublime experience can only be objects of nature, or both objects of nature as well as works of art, or, as his discussions in the *Critique of Judgment* often seem to suggest, primarily works of art, especially poetry. Yet it would seem clear that where the teaching of moral philosophy is concerned (the "teaching" [*Belehrung*], say, of the *Groundwork*) the philosopher must employ a representation of examples; and where the individual mind's work of moral reason is concerned, the activity that Kant is recommending equally entails an autonomous, inner representation of examples.

Indeed, in the *Critique of Practical Reason* we can feel the force of

Kant's detailed description in the *Critique of Judgment* of how the procedure of succession is achieved by "going to the same sources for a creative work"—the same sources from which the "exemplary *author* [originator]" (and his followers) created: "This means . . . learning from one's predecessor no more than the mode of availing oneself of such sources" (*CJ,* 5:283).[13] In both the second and the third *Critiques* this following of an endless progression made up of other individuals' examples, rather than just an endless progress generated solely from oneself (e.g., humiliations of self-conceit), leads to the transfer from heteronomous to autonomous procedures of succession. The latter culminate in the categorical imperative and perhaps even something very like a kingdom of ends. A kingdom of this kind is constituted by plural activities of disclosing *a priori* categorical imperatives from sources held in common with others. Thus even when Kant is speaking merely of the enactment of an endless progression, he is actually speaking of a representation of a known or recognizable or commonplace progression (in part, because a commonplace is always already an effectively endless progression of the given item), which is to say a succession of examples, as in a line of storytelling of a repeated or recurring story.

I am not suggesting that the humiliation of self-conceit becomes unimportant for Kant (i.e., that it could be replaced by any item whatsoever as long as the endless series is constituted). On the contrary, the goal of the succession of examples in moral reason is especially the humiliation of self-conceit that coincides with, or is even completed by, the experience of the sublime (i.e., the check to the vital forces). This is strongly suggested by Kant's saying, "Humiliation . . . comes upon us through such an example. [It] imposes on us the following [*die Befolgung*] of such an example" (*CPrR,* 5:77–78). Interestingly enough, the implication of these statements is that it is in the *Methode* and its direct specification of storytelling, which seems merely propaedeutic, rather than in the pre-*Methode* largest part of the *Critique of Practical Reason*—which would seem to be more serious or more purely philosophical—that this indispensable activity of Kant's moral philosophy is described.

Indeed, the passage quoted above from the beginning of the

13. For my departures from Meredith's translation in this passage, see Chapter 6.

Methode section, specifying the "preparatory guidance," contains the outlines of the principal story that Kant is continually re-telling in the *Critique of Practical Reason*. Instead of instancing Samson's story as an example of *Kraft*, as Herder recommends in his *Methode* of moral education, Kant *succeeds to*, namelessly but intensely, a Samson-like, and Miltonic, archetype or exemplarity. The power that interests Kant is first disclosed by Samson's heteronomous procedure of succession. Kant's storytelling is a re-telling of that which gives the "mind" of the protagonist "power, unexpected even by himself, to tear himself away from all sensible attachments so far as they want to rule over him, and to find a rich compensation for the sacrifice he makes in the independence of his rational nature and the greatness of soul to which he sees that he is called" (*CPrR*, 5:152). Kant's comment here is a highly precise description and explanation of the climax of *Samson Agonistes* (reached much before the catastrophe) in the otherwise rationally inexplicable accession of unexpected power within Samson's own "thoughts." With Kant's insight we can see that Samson's preparatory progression (which is in fact typologically endless) and his own procedure of succession have brought him to this extraordinary moment:

> I begin to feel
> Some rousing motions in me which dispose
> To something extraordinary my thoughts. (1381–1383)

In this emergence of the unexpected, there is more than a little that may remind us of parallels in the book of Job that provide Kant and Milton with some of their "same sources."

Herder, Job, Kant

In the first volume of *The Spirit of Hebrew Poetry* (1782), Herder lavished particular praise on Milton's invocation to light and acceptance of blindness (*Paradise Lost*, III.1–55). We should recall here Herder's claim, in the same volume, that the spirit of the poetry of Job (manifested also in the Prophets and in the Psalms) established the characteristic panegyric tone of modern European poetry that is achieved above all by Milton in *Paradise Lost*. As noted in Chapter 2, while Herder identifies the stylistic element of Job's tone as a "silent sublimity," he shows little or no understanding of how a poetics of negation might have a characteristic structure of representation, let alone how it might be part of a procedure of succession, in aesthetic light and shadow, for transfer between the empirical and the *a priori*.[14]

Kant would have felt that Herder misses what is most important here with regard to the poetics of both Job and Milton. Yet Herder deepens the parallelism between Job and *Paradise Lost*, the greatest of all modern poetic theodicies, by asserting that Job is the first work to represent "the true theodicy," "an epic representation of [the epic dimensions of] humanity [*die wahre Theodicee*, an *Epopee der Menschheit, Theodicee Gottes*]" which is on that account a "theodicy of God" or a moral justification of God's action in creation.[15] Kant would have recalled these Herderian connections (in one of Herder's most highly regarded works) when he came to write his "On the Miscarriage of All Philosophical Trials in Theodicy" (1791). There Kant argues, among other things, that an authentic theodicy must be built around the representation of something *soul-uplifting* or *sublime (seelenerhebend)*, which God has created as an "implanted inclination" *(eingepflanzte Neigung)* in the character of humanity (*AA*, 8:269, 271). Kant's substantive exemplification of such a theodicy is the book of Job (*AA*, 8:264–267). In his laudatory comments on Kant's essay, *"Ueber Hrn. Kants Aufsatz, in Betref* [*sic*] *der Theodicee,"* Kant's close friend J. E. Biester called Kant's analysis "sublime . . . divinely beautiful" *(erhaben . . . göttlichschön)* and made explicit the hovering relevance of Milton's theodicy by quoting—in English—*Paradise Lost,* II.557–567, where Milton consigns "false Philosophie," that is, the misconceived theologizing that Kant's essay comes to defeat, to the fallen angels in Hell.[16]

Biester and Herder were likely both influenced, directly or indirectly, by the work of Longinus commentators like William Smith. The

14. Herder, *Vom Geist der ebräischen Poesie*, 2 vols. (Dessau, 1782–83), I.85–88, 137; *SW*, XI.277, 312.

15. Herder, *Vom Geist der ebräischen Poesie*, I.147–148; *SW*, XI.319.

16. *Berlinische Monatsschrift* 2 (1791): 411–421. The cited comments appear on pages 420–421. We might note incidentally that since Kant is here Biester's principal addressee and since Biester was in frequent contact with Kant at this time, Biester's choosing to quote Milton in English—when a variety of German translations was readily available—is one more indication, even if an indirect one, that Kant was probably quite comfortable reading Milton in English.

linkage of the poetry of Milton with that of Job became commonplace around the time of—and no doubt partly because of—the publication of Smith's widely read translation and edition of Longinus, which both continues Addison's identification of the modern sublime with Milton and anticipates Lowth's extensive exposition of the sublime in Job. Smith even gives examples of the sublime of Milton and of Job on facing pages.[17] After Addison's essays on Milton's sublime, followed by Smith's *Longinus,* and after Albert Schulten's great edition of Job, *Liber Jobi . . . Commentario Perpetuo* (Leiden, 1737)—used by Lowth and every other serious scholar, Herder included—which frequently emphasized the sublimity of Job's imagery, this connection between Milton and Job, specifically with regard to the experience of the sublime, became obvious. It was self-evident, that is, even without anything like full awareness of the extent of Milton's profound emulations of the book of Job in all his major works—and, as we have seen, in "On His Blindness" as well.

Job, *Progressus,* Samson

In *Samson Agonistes,* Samson, like Job, achieves his moral personality in the *Progressus* of humiliations of self-conceit. With regard to Job, Kant explicitly recorded his deep interest in what he called "the difficulty associated with a purification of the dispositions in human beings even when they *want* to act according to duty." My proposal concerning Kant's tracing, in the *Critique of Practical Reason,* of the *Progressus* of humiliations of self-conceit in *Samson Agonistes* is that it includes (as does *Samson Agonistes*) retrospective tracing of Samson's humiliations to those of Job (and beyond, as I will soon note). In the book of Job, Kant found the "authentic interpretation" of an "*efficacious* practical reason . . . expressed allegorically."[18] In Kant's theory of succession this kind of allegorical or storytelling *Progressus* of humiliations is explicitly tied, in a circle, to the succession of examples that leads to exemplarity of human and human-divine archetypes. These archetypes themselves

17. William Smith, *Dionysius Longinus on the Sublime,* 2nd ed., London, 1742; 1st ed. 1739), pp. 118–119, 126–127, 155, et al.

18. Kant, "On the Miscarriage of All Philosophical Trials in Theodicy" (1791), in *Religion and Rational Theology,* trans. and ed. Allen W. Wood and George di Giovanni (Cambridge: Cambridge University Press, 1996), pp. 34, 31–32 (*AA,* 8:268, 264).

strive, using this method or procedure, to achieve a purification of the dispositions according to the propositions that we have seen: "Humiliation . . . comes upon us through such an example. [It] imposes on us the following [*die Befolgung*] of such an example" (*CPrR*, 5:77–78); this is "the archetype . . . we should strive to approach and resemble in an uninterrupted but endless progress [*unendlichen Progressus*]" (*CPrR*, 5:83). Each archetype or example that Kant would have us follow is engaged, indeed, in following out his own *Progressus* of humiliations. The intensity with which Kant hammers home the moral necessity for the incremental and finally decisive humiliation of self-conceit could not be more resolute. This necessity is for him the unique case of the bonding of cognition to sensation or feeling, *Erkennen* to *Empfinden:*

> The moral law, as the determining ground of the will, must by thwarting all our inclinations produce a feeling that can be called pain; and here we have the first and perhaps the only case in which we can determine a priori from concepts the relation of a cognition (here the cognition of a pure practical reason) to the feeling of pleasure or displeasure. . . . Pure practical reason . . . *strikes down* self-conceit [*Eigendünkel*]. . . . The moral law strikes down self-conceit. . . . In opposition to its subjective antagonist, namely the inclinations in us, it . . . *strikes down* self-conceit, that is, humiliates it. (*CPrR*, 5:73; the emphases are Kant's)

Samson Agonistes is a tragedy that takes place in the mind of the hero. The play is without doubt one of the most purely mental tragedies ever written, taking as its models Aeschylus's *Prometheus Bound* and Sophocles' *Oedipus at Colonus,* two plays that exemplify the rare class of tragedy that Aristotle calls *oikeon.* During the entire time that Samson is before us, until he exits and the catastrophe is reported by the messenger, the focus on his mind is intense and exclusive. The chorus accurately observes, to Samson, more than it understands:

> This Idol's day hath bin to thee no day of rest,
> > Laboring thy mind
> More than the working day thy hands (1297–1299)

> [Dieser Götzentag war kein Tag der Ruhe für dich; dein Geist arbeitet mehr, als an den Werktagen deine Hände. (*Simson*, p. 181)]

What the chorus calls Samson's "plain Heroic magnitude of mind [*aufrichtige heroische Großmuth*]" (1279; *Simson*, p. 180) becomes more and more freestanding as the play progresses.[19] Many readers—but not Kant, I am proposing—have been at a loss to see that anything actually happens in this restrictively mental activity. To take one famous instance, Dr. Johnson thought he could build on Aristotle's rules for the action of a tragedy to complain that *Samson Agonistes* "has a beginning and an end . . . but it must be allowed to want a middle, since nothing passes between the first act and the last, that either hastens or delays the death of Samson" (*Rambler,* 139).[20] Indeed, the more radical and more appropriate form of Dr. Johnson's remark, put as a question, is this: In this tragedy what is it that causes the turn or upturn—the inner *peripeteia* and *anagnorisis—solely in Samson's mind?* The answer to this question, I submit, is the self-regenerating process or procedure that gives Samson the new, deeper secret within his moral reason. This is now the secret of his life, as well as of *Samson Agonistes* as a work of tragedy. No one besides Milton, I propose, has had greater wherewithal to understand this secret than Kant in the *Critique of Practical Reason.*

The first condition of this Miltonic and Kantian secret is the affliction experienced by the honest person *in extremis* who, in Kant's storytelling, is ripe for discovering "something quite different from life, something in comparison and contrast with which life with all its agreeableness has no worth at all. He still lives only from duty, not because he has the least taste for living" (*CPrR,* 5:88). In the storytelling of the *Methode* this same story is told as "the story of an honest man . . .

19. Quite possibly, that is, this economy of intellectual effort was once recognized as the defining feature of a distinct genre of Greek tragedy. Aristotle, whose *Poetics* Milton echoes both in his preface and in the concept of catharsis expressed in the last lines of the play itself, mentions a class of tragedies called *oikeon* or the tragedy of "Appropriate Expression," of which *Prometheus Bound* appears to be the only complete example that has survived. F. J. H. Letters suggests that with regard to such a classification there seems to be an important similarity between Prometheus bound to his rock and Oedipus confined to the rock ledge at Colonus: "Only superhuman, semi-divine personages could direct the movement of classic tragedy from beginning to end while themselves thus physically impotent and immobilized." (See F. J. H. Letters, *The Life and Work of Sophocles* [London: Sheed and Ward, 1953], pp. 110 and 294.) Samson, merely conducting his interviews on "yonder bank" (3), would thus be in parallel with these Greek heroes. What comes after the interviews, I am arguing, is as far as Samson is concerned, God's will and work, not Samson's.

20. *Works of Samuel Johnson*, 12 vols. (London, 1823–25), III.436.

at a moment when he wishes that he had never lived to see the day that exposed him to such unutterable pain and yet remains firm in his resolution" (*CPrR*, 5:155–156). In the Kantian marriage of poetry and philosophy even the mere template of a story is already storytelling because it tells the skeletal tale of that story, which is its line of repeatability, its commonplaceness that can ultimately be grasped *a priori*. In *Samson Agonistes* Samson's immensely powerful recounting of his condition of being *in extremis* sets off a chain reaction of such stories, inevitably reaching back to something like an archetype (Christian or otherwise) in the innermost mind of the reader:

> Scarce half I seem to live, dead more than half.
> O dark, dark, dark, amid the blaze of noon,
> Irrecoverably dark, total Eclipse
> Without all hope of day! (79–82)

> Nor am I in the list of them that hope;
> Hopeless are all my evils, all remediless;
> This one prayer yet remains, might I be heard,
> No long petition, speedy death,
> The close of all my miseries, and the balm. (647–651)

Although Kant generally avoids metaphors, he formulates the idea of a personality escaping the mechanism of nature precisely as transcending the calculability of a "lunar or solar eclipse":

> If it were possible for us to . . . know every incentive to action . . . we could calculate a human being's conduct with as much certainty as a lunar or solar eclipse [*Mond- oder Sonnenfinsterniß*] and could nevertheless maintain that the human being's conduct is free. (*CPrR*, 5:99)

In Kant's terms, Samson's lament of the total eclipse of his physical sight is evidence, as indeed it is for Milton's storytelling, of Samson's ripeness for transfer away from every heteronomous incentive to recognition of his inner noumenon and what Kant calls "freedom and independence from the mechanism of the whole of nature" (*CPrR*, 5:87).

Here it is worth recalling that when Kant introduces his exposition of aesthetic ideas in §49 of the *Critique of Judgment* he writes, "The poet essays the task of interpreting to sense the rational ideas of invisible beings, the kingdom of the blessed, hell, eternity, creation, &c." (5:314). I pointed out in Chapter 1 that this description of "the poet" fits Milton most fully. I note now that the very next sentence in §49 fits Milton's *Samson Agonistes* quite remarkably. Kant writes, "Or, again, as to things of which examples occur in experience, e.g. death, envy, and all vices, as also love, fame, and the like, transgressing the limits of experience he ['the poet'] attempts with the aid of an imagination which emulates the display of reason in its attainment of a maximum, to body them forth to sense with a completeness of which nature affords no parallel; and it is in fact precisely in the poetic art that the faculty of aesthetic ideas can show itself to full advantage" (*CJ,* 5:314). It is difficult to think of a more apt description of Milton's invention of the ratiocinative drama of *Samson Agonistes* than "an imagination which emulates the display of reason." The same applies to Kant's phrases "to body them forth to sense with a completeness of which nature affords no parallel." In Milton's play, Samson from the beginning declares himself to be in the condition of virtual death. Again and again he wishes for the finality of "speedy death" (650). The words "death" and "dead" resound (two dozen times) throughout this tragedy to such an extent that we experience Samson bodied forth to sense, as Kant says, precisely within the pale of death.[21] In addition, Milton's usages of the

---

21. Lest one fail to see that the usages of "death" and "dead" are truly exceptional in *Samson Agonistes* and indeed constitute what Kant terms "a completeness of which nature affords no parallel," I offer here a partial iteration of those usages. These are all spoken by Samson, except for the penultimate one, by the chorus, and the final one, by Manoa: "Scarce half I seem to live, dead more than half" (79), "To live a life half dead, a living death, / And buried; but O yet more miserable! / Myself my Sepulcher, a moving Grave, / Buried, yet not exempt / By privilege of death and burial" (100–104), "and oft-invocated death / Hast'n the welcome end of all my pains" (575–576), "Sleep hath forsook and giv'n me o'er / To death's benumbing Opium as my only cure" (629–630), "This one prayer yet remains, might I be heard, / No long petition, speedy death, / The close of all my miseries, and the balm" (649–651), "But come what will, my deadliest foe will prove / My speediest friend, by death to rid me hence, / The worst that he can give, to me the best" (1262–1264), (Chorus:) "Noise call you it or universal groan / As if the whole inhabitation perish'd? / Blood, death, and deathful deeds are in that noise, / Ruin, destruction at the utmost point" (1511–1514), (Manoa:) "Nothing is here for tears, nothing to wail / Or knock the breast, no

words *envy, love,* and *fame*—and even of *vices* ("Nations . . . by thir vices brought to servitude" [268–269])—are also remarkably salient in this play.

In any case, what is certain is that Milton's representation of "total Eclipse" anticipates the full check to the vital forces (not just of eyesight) that will ultimately confer freedom in the endless progression of humiliations of self-conceit and the procedure of succession. This Miltonic "total Eclipse" was well-known to Kant's contemporaries. In Handel's oratorio *Samson,* which was monumentally reared on Milton's text and which was already famous in Germany by the late 1750s, the single best-known moment was Samson's aria "Total Eclipse."[22] It is possible that Kant's remark in the *Critique of Judgment* that "even the representation of the sublime, so far as it belongs to fine art, may be brought into union with beauty in a *tragedy in verse,* a *didactic poem,* or an *oratorio*" (5:325) in part flows from his awareness that Milton's *Samson* was in itself the first and (being closet drama) the second of these artistic kinds, and that it became the third kind as well.

---

weakness, no contempt, / Dispraise, or blame, nothing but well and fair, / And what may quiet us in a death so noble" (1721–1724).

22. On Handel's oratorios in Kant's world, especially in the Keyserling circle where those oratorios figured and where Kant's attendance is specifically noted, see Hermann Güttler, *Königsbergs Musikkultur im 18. Jahrhundert* (Königsberg, 1925), pp. 161, 210. Herder, we should note, wrote the German libretto for the first production of Handel's *Messiah* at Weimar, in 1780–81. Handel's relation to *Samson Agonistes* deserves emphasis. Handel was encouraged to compose an oratorio based on *Samson Agonistes* by James Harris (mentioned in Chapter 3) and his circle, and was inspired to proceed by hearing a reading of the whole of Milton's play. The libretto was composed by Newburgh Hamilton using an enormous part (almost half) of the text of *Samson Agonistes* and utilizing much else in Milton's poetry to stitch the whole together. Winton Dean, *Handel's Dramatic Oratorios and Masques* (London: Oxford University Press, 1959), p. 330, has listed the verses of fourteen of Milton's poems that Hamilton incorporated into the libretto, to which Dean adds that "the immense trouble taken, and the scrupulous reverence for the poet's text, must be unique at this period." An incident that became a famous part of the Handelian lore is that at his last revival of *Samson,* in 1753, the blind Handel was carried into the audience on a stretcher and "at the Total Eclipse . . . cry'd like an infant": see Donald Burrows and Rosemary Dunhill, *Music and Theatre in Handel's World: The Family Papers of James Harris 1732–1780* (Oxford: Oxford University Press, 2002), p. 291.

Succession upon Succession

As I began to suggest earlier, Kant's storytelling in the second *Critique* is especially intense because it is, in the wake of Milton's storytelling, a succession to a series of successions. That is, Kant's immediate succession procedure, I am proposing, is of Milton's *Samson Agonistes,* which is itself a representation of Samson's and Job's, and also of Christ's, succession procedures. In Milton's telling, Samson's awareness of his own participation in a *Progressus* of what he calls "examples" is a remarkable aspect of his self-consciousness. The extremity of Samson's case early leads him to sense that he will be, and already is, part of a typology of examples. Part of his agony is that he only does not know which typology. Bemoaning his disastrous capitulation to his inclinations, he says, "Of such examples add mee to the roll" (290). He will be, he laments, "to Ages an example" (765). His story, however, will not remain in the phase of one who has been undone by shameful inclinations, but will instead join the rolls of Job's trials and Christ's temptations, with their supersensible outcomes. (Milton printed *Samson Agonistes* twinned with *Paradise Regained,* his telling of Christ's temptations. The two German translations of these compositions that were produced in Kant's lifetime also printed them together.) In other words, in Milton's telling, Samson becomes someone in a line of those who have left behind all sensory incentives to life. He achieves this in the progressive humiliations of self-conceit, directly linked to the succession procedure which opens for him freedom and moral feeling in the experience of the sublime. Since each such humiliation of self-conceit can already summon up a memory of a progression of such representations, each can (to varying degrees) already give the hero a foretaste of the "inner freedom" (*CJ,* 5:271) that results from giving up sensory incentives to life. Kant, too, is a successor to this line of successions.

I have noted repeatedly that Kant makes clear that he requires a specific exemplum to initiate a succession procedure. In the second Critique, *Samson Agonistes* provides this exemplum. We may at first think that it is merely coincidental that many little things in the *Critique of Practical Reason* seem to recall the Samson story, as when Kant writes,

[1] For example, someone can make it his maxim to let no insult pass unavenged and yet see that this is no practical law but only his maxim—that, on the contrary, as being in one and the same maxim a rule for the will of every rational being it could not harmonize with itself. (5:20)

or

[2] Suppose someone asserts of his lustful inclination that, when the desired object and the opportunity are present, it is quite irresistible to him. (5:30)

or

[3] Suppose that an acquaintance . . . reveals [your] secret . . . [an acquaintance] to whom you could blindly [*blindlings*] trust all your affairs. (5:35)

If we note the parallel passages in Milton's text, it is difficult to think here in terms of coincidence. Corresponding to Kant's examples [1], [2], and [3] above, I quote *Samson Agonistes* first from the 1781 Mannheim translation, then directly from Milton:

[1] Gleich einem kleinen Gott umhergieng, bewundert von Allen und gefürchtet im Lande der Feinde, und keiner es wagte mich zu beleidigen. (*Simson*, p. 138)

> Like a petty God
> I walk'd about admir'd of all and dreaded
> On hostile ground, none daring my affront. (529–531)

[2] Von dem was ich itzt leide, war sie [Dalila] nicht die Hauptursach, sondern ich selbst (*Simson*, p. 122)

> of what now I suffer
> She was not the prime cause, but I myself. (233–234)

So laßt sie gehen. Gott sandte sie mich zu demüthigen, und meine Thorheit tiefer fühlen zu lassen, daß ich sein heilig anvertrautes Geheimniß, meine Sicherheit und mein Leben, einer solchen Natter dahingeben können! (*Simson*, pp. 163–164)

> So let her go, God sent her to debase me,
> And aggravate my folly who committed
> To such a viper his most sacred trust
> Of secrecy, my safety, and my life. (999–1002)

[3] Geheimniße der Menschen verrathen zu haben, Geheimniße eines Freundes, wie schändlich wäre schon diese That, wie sehr verdiente sie Spott und Verachtung Aller, von aller Freundschaft ausgeschlossen, als ein Plauderer vermieden, mit dem Wahrzeichen des Thoren gebrandmarkt zu werden! Aber ich habe Gottes Rathschluß nicht bewahrt, sein heiliges Geheimniß vermessen, gottlos, schwach wenigstens und mir zur Schande, geoffenbaret! (*Simson*, p. 136)

> To have reveal'd
> Secrets of men, the secrets of a friend,
> How heinous had the fact been, how deserving
> Contempt, and scorn of all, to be excluded
> All friendship, and avoided as a blab,
> The mark of fool set on his front? But I
> Gods counsel have not kept, his holy secret
> Presumptuously have publish'd, impiously,
> Weakly at least, and shamefully. (491–499)[23]

For Kant as well as for Milton what is most significant are the principal phenomenon and noumenon that issue from the series of humiliations of self-conceit. Even if the above examples are not fully identical in Kant and Milton, these three parallel moments mark, for both

23. Until just before the end of this chapter I will cite Milton's tragedy only in English, since it should be clear from the above samplings that, in fact (in all but a few instances), the 1781 Mannheim text provided the German reader with an accurate translation.

Kant and Milton, very much the same points in that series. In *Samson Agonistes,* that is, these examples or instances are principal parts of the *Progressus* of humiliations of self-conceit that Samson (exemplifying the Kantian formula) follows—both in his experience and in allusive following of other texts—in achieving personality. Now Kant follows this line of following. As I have suggested, the series of humiliations of self-conceit in *Samson Agonistes* stands in clear apposition with the series of humiliations of Job (himself understood to be a type of the archetype and antitype Christ). Samson's humiliations take the form of responses to successive encounters with the criticisms or verbal attacks on Samson by the chorus, by Manoa, by Dalila, and by Harapha. Job's humiliations are at the hands of his supposed comforters. In *Samson Agonistes* the series of humiliations of self-conceit provides the entire structure of the hero's dramatic development, *agonistes.* In lines 30–62 Samson even anticipates and details, without understanding its character or purpose, the unfolding line of these humiliations of self-conceit; and he even unwittingly hints there that his humiliations will issue in "ends above my reach to know" (62). In each scene of humiliation he will duly acknowledge his "shame" (457) and "hopeless . . . remediless" state (648), even granting to Dalila the "bitter reproach, but true, / I to myself was false ere thou to me" (823–824), and even insisting that he deserves to suffer Harapha's insults. Samson says to Harapha,

> All these indignities, for such they are
> From thine, these evils I deserve and more,
> Acknowledge them from God inflicted on me
> Justly. (1168–1171)

Clearly the prison house, with the encounters that take place there, is the main arena of his agonizing or wrestling—with himself—not the Philistine temple where the catastrophe, reported by the messenger, takes place, and where we learn nothing further of Samson's inner development. In the second *Critique,* Kant's instancing of examples [1], [2], and [3] is part of his storytelling in succession to all these stories, prompted and sustained, I propose, by Milton's *Samson Agonistes.*

Why the Hero Has Not Committed Suicide

After Samson has brought about the catastrophe, the chorus explains why in its view his violent act was God's will and that Samson's self-murder was not suicide:

> O dearly bought revenge, yet glorious!
> Living or dying thou hast fulfill'd
> The work for which thou wast foretold
> To *Israel*, and now li'st victorious
> Among thy slain self-kill'd
> Not willingly, but tangl'd in the fold
> Of dire necessity, whose law in death conjoin'd
> Thee with thy slaughter'd foes. (1660–1667)

Kant comments directly on the question of the moral meaning of a hero's sacrifice of his life for his country in an act which may seem to be suicide. In *Samson Agonistes* Samson's readiness for this act emerges as the specific answer to the question that principally torments him. This question mirrors the central question of Milton's talent sonnet and of Kant's example of the talent in the *Groundwork:*

> by which means,
> Now blind, disheart'n'd, sham'd, dishonor'd, quell'd,
> To what can I be useful, wherein serve
> My Nation, and the work from Heav'n impos'd [?] (562–565)

Manoa specifies that the use and service that are sought here are for Samson's "gift" or talent. He is confident of God's

> purpose
> To use him [Samson] further yet in some great service,
> Not to sit idle with so great a gift
> Useless. (1498–1501)

Here, from the second *Critique,* is Kant's elaborate claim that the will to sacrifice one's life for the preservation of one's country fulfills the requirements of a categorical imperative, but only under one condition:

> Let us now see in an example whether there is more subjective moving force as an incentive if an action is represented as a noble and magnanimous one than if it is represented merely as duty in relation to the earnest moral law. . . . [Kant first gives a shipwreck example that he finds clearly inadequate.] More decisive is someone's magnanimous sacrifice of his life for the preservation of his country; and yet there still remains some scruple as to whether it is so perfect a duty to devote oneself to this purpose of one's own accord and unbidden, and the action has not itself the full force of a model and impulse to imitation. But if it is an essential duty, transgression of which violates the moral law in itself and without regard to human welfare and, as it were, tramples on its holiness (such as are usually called duties to God because in him we think the ideal of holiness in a substance), then we give the most perfect esteem to compliance with it at the sacrifice of everything that could ever have value for our dearest inclinations, and we find our soul strengthened and elevated by such an example when we can convince ourselves, in it, that human nature is capable of so great an elevation above every incentive that nature can oppose to it.[24] (*CPrR*, 5:158)

Continually woven into this passage is the need to isolate the disposition to a moral action. Expressed as a distinction, this is the internalized "great . . . elevation [*Erhebung*]" of "such an example" that would give this "action . . . the full force of a model and impulse to imitation," that is, that would make it an "exemplary originality" *(musterhafte Originalität)* (*CJ*, 5:318). This *originality* that expresses the spontaneity, freedom, and moral feeling of the individual can at the same time be offered as an *exemplary* representation for all humankind. As such it is identical with the *a priori* categorical imperative that is expressed in the maxim of a "perfect" and "essential duty." This achievement of elevation or sublimity must always entail "the sacrifice of . . . our dearest inclinations" as when "the imagination by its own act

24. The passage continues, "Juvenal presents such an example" and quotes *Satire*, 8.79–84, verses which have nothing to do with sacrifice for the preservation of one's country. This may be another instance of Kantian distancing when he felt that his Miltonic debts would be taken to indicate influence of an imitative kind.

of depriving itself of its freedom . . . gains an . . . inner freedom" (*CJ*, 5:269–271). The clearing away of "every incentive" of sensible "nature" leaves the individual with the one supersensible incentive. For Kant this can only be achieved in the categorical imperative, which Rawls has argued is actually a "procedure for applying the categorical imperative."[25] I am proposing that underlying this procedure in the second *Critique* (and elsewhere in Kant's moral philosophy) is the procedure of succession in storytelling. Effected, at first, heteronomously, this succession procedure discloses the moral force of "such an example" as "someone's magnanimous sacrifice of his life for the preservation of his country" (*CPrR*, 5:158). Only when such an example achieves exemplary originality within an autonomous succession procedure can it be a categorical imperative, that is, in the formulation "*Act only in accordance with that maxim through which you can at the same time will that it should become a universal law*" (*GMM*, 4:421). The action of a suicide bomber who kills indiscriminately cannot meet this test since willing the maxim of his action as a universal law would entail willing that those whom his action was allegedly intended to preserve should be killed indiscriminately. Kant's claim is that applying the succession procedure that produces inner freedom in the experience of the sublime also discloses, inwardly, the moral feeling that must meet the requirement of universal consistency (for all humanity) in the categorical imperative. Without this consistency the hero who violently sacrifices his life could not be doing it for the preservation of his country and would indeed be no more than the equivalent of an indiscriminate terrorist. He would be endorsing the indiscriminate murder not only of others but also of his countrymen. We have seen that in the case of *Samson Agonistes* Milton makes clear that Samson does not kill indiscriminately. The specific circumstances of this moral recourse to the exercise of force are such that they might even be thought to require— *only in these circumstances*—that this exercise of force "*should become a universal law.*"

It is thus difficult not to be struck by the extent of correspondence between *Samson Agonistes* and Kant's choice of example: the justifica-

---

25. John Rawls, "Themes in Kant's Moral Philosophy," in *Kant's Transcendental Deductions: The Three Critiques and the Opus postumum,* ed. Eckart Förster (Stanford: Stanford University Press, 1989), p. 81.

tion for an individual's sacrifice of his life for his country in that individual's obedience, in the sacrifice, to an "essential duty" or, what is the same for Kant, "duties to God." For both Kant and Milton what come first are the succession procedures that subjectively disclose the "essential duty" to the individual moral reason. A divine revelation that declares or confirms that this essential duty, disclosed by moral reason, is among the "duties to God" is not essential to moral reason. I suggest that the situation here is closely parallel to what Milton asserts in the sonnet on his blindness when he concludes with the verse "They also serve who only stand and wait" or what Kant asserts in the *Groundwork:*

> Even the Holy One of the Gospel must first be compared with our ideal of moral perfection before he is cognized as such; even he says of himself [Matthew 19:17]: why do you call me (whom you see) good? none is good (the archetype of the good) but God only (whom you do not see). But whence have we the concept of God as the highest good? Solely from the *idea* of moral perfection that reason frames a priori and connects inseparably with the concept of a free will. (4:408–409)

> . . . Even this sole absolute lawgiver would . . . have to be represented as appraising the worth of rational beings only by their disinterested conduct. . . . That which . . . alone constitutes the worth of a human being is that in terms of which he must also be appraised by whoever does it, even by the supreme being. (4:439)

In expanding the storytelling of the book of Judges in order to unfold the development of Samson's moral reason—in the succession procedure—Milton weights the balance of human and divine will in the same way. Given the detailed appositeness of Milton's undertaking to Kant's aims, *Samson Agonistes* can serve Kant as the specific representation which he requires for the experience of the sublime and for everything that issues from the sublime in his theory, all centered in the procedure of succession. In this way Kant is engaged here in disclosing the freedom of his autonomous moral reason and personality in his own transfer from the tragic sublime to philosophy. In each example, or fragment of the puzzle-picture of an example, which he represents in his unobtrusively continual storytelling of his Samson-like story, he joins himself to the force of change that is made available by his Miltonic procedures of succession.

The Transfer from Blindness to Inner Sight

Indeed, to grasp the work of moral philosophy in the *Critique of Practical Reason* in the terms that I am proposing, we should be able to see how Kant's storytelling effects the transfer between the "two standpoints," the heteronomous and the autonomous. In the case of the procedures of succession employed in this work, I propose that Kant has in fact left traces that suffice for an identification of the more or less precise moment, or leap, from the sensible to the supersensible, that is, in the heteronomous succession procedure that is isomorphic with his autonomous succession procedure. I will set the stage for this identification and then present it *in concreto*.

We recall that in the *Groundwork of the Metaphysics of Morals* Kant explains that in the first standpoint "we represent ourselves in terms of our actions as effects that we see before our eyes." We transfer ourselves into the second "different standpoint when by means of freedom we think ourselves as causes efficient a priori" (4:450). We do not see the objects of thinking from this second standpoint: "When moral worth is at issue, what counts is not actions, which one sees, but those inner principles of actions that one does not see. . . . The insightful . . . avert their eyes" (*GMM*, 4:407, 409).

We have also seen that in the *Critique of Judgment* Kant will say clearly, even if without direct elaboration of the idea, that each representation in the procedure of succession must represent "its own inadequacy" to represent (5:252–253). Something very like this conviction of the indispensability of deficited representation is, I propose, reflected in the *Critique of Practical Reason*. We see this in Kant's saying,

> The governor of the world allows us only to conjecture his existence and his grandeur, not to behold them. . . . The inscrutable wisdom by which we exist is not less worthy of veneration in what it has denied us than in what it has granted us. (5:147–148)

Here, as in all the Miltonic moments of Kant's moral reason that I have surveyed, the saliency of the blind poet's—Milton's—poetics of blindness is vital for Kant. Although Kant here presents the stages of his heteronomous and autonomous procedures of succession in reverse order, thus obscuring his actual working procedures, we can derive from his text how his autonomous transfer to inner seeing, which is a not-seeing, in fact works. He has left strong, even if convoluted, evidence of his actual procedures.

I note, first, that in his heteronomous and autonomous procedures he employs virtually identical terms in describing the scene of inner seeing, that is, in the second standpoint that is achieved both in autonomy and in heteronomy. In autonomy he sees

> in his own eyes . . . the inward view of self-examination. (*CPrR*, 5:88)
> [in seinen eigenen Augen . . . den inneren Anblick der Selbstprüfung].

In heteronomy he sees the honest person *in extremis* seeing

> on self-examination . . . in his own eyes. (*CPrR*, 5:161)
> [in der inneren Selbstprüfung in seinen eigenen Augen].

In accordance with Kant's own theory, I have proposed that for him, too, the heteronomous procedure of succession must have come first as the "preparatory guidance" that put him "onto the track" of the autonomous procedure of succession. And, also in accordance with Kant's theory, I have proposed that even his preparatory guidance had to have been "evoked" by "a particular representation" of this scene of inner seeing.

I am now proposing that the inner sight that Kant describes from his own experience or that he records in the experience of the honest person *in extremis* is the effect of the sublime transfer between the two standpoints in procedures of succession. That is, the inner sight is the effect of the transfer from (a) the first standpoint in the realm of the sensible, where we see outwardly to (b) the second standpoint in the realm of the supersensible or intelligible, where we do not see outward things. Kant, moreover, posits a doubling of this transfer in isomorphic heteronomous and autonomous procedures of succession (*Nachfolgen* or *Befolgungen*) and their self-examinations *(Selbstprüfungen)*. In the autonomous procedure of succession we finally disclose the noumenon or unconditioned causality of moral personality. One of the invariable characteristics of this noumenon, which is otherwise individual in each personality, is the willing of external blindness, or dispensing with external seeing, and the transfer to inner seeing of freedom and moral feeling or the categorical imperative.

We may resist the idea of these transfers and isomorphisms as a cumbersome and unnecessary conceptual burden. Yet, here as elsewhere, it becomes clear from Kant's various presentations of these matters that the procedure of succession of which he speaks is actually two different procedures, both of succession. The transfer that is achieved in the heteronomous procedure of succession of examples and exemplarity discloses the condition of freedom and the supersensible, where the individual then experiences the autonomous procedure of succession that creates, in its inner transfer, pure moral feeling. Thus when in the scene of heteronomy of the *Methodenlehre* Kant describes the falling away of the sensible incentives as the removal of obstacles that is itself the beginning of moral feeling, he is not merely giving us something propaedeutic to moral feeling. In the second *Critique* this removal is an integral part of his two-stage account of how moral feeling is disclosed in the autonomy of moral reason.

To see this more clearly, it is worth refreshing our memories of that two-stage account. Kant here provides his most direct answer to the question of how moral feeling is disclosed after the check to the vital forces in the experience of the sublime:

> *Moral feeling* . . . is effected as follows: the representation of the moral law deprives self-love of its influence and self-conceit of its illusion . . . through the removal of the counterweight. And so respect for the law is not the incentive to morality; instead it is morality itself subjectively considered as an incentive inasmuch as pure practical reason, by rejecting all the claims of self-love in opposition with its own, supplies authority to the law, which now alone has influence. . . . This feeling (under the name of moral feeling) is therefore produced solely by reason. It does not serve for appraising actions and certainly not for grounding the objective moral law itself, but only as an incentive to make this law its maxim. (*CPrR*, 5:75–76)

Kant provides this answer within his explanation of how the autonomous succession to a series of representations—of humiliations of self-conceit—is "effected" by the honest person *in extremis*. Taken together with its placement within the Kantian theory of the sublime procedure of succession, the above passage implies neither that the sublime blackout leaves the individual helpless nor that he or she (thereafter) discovers a preformed moral feeling. Rather it suggests that the procedure of the removal of obstacles already has in it something vital for disclosing what is formally inherent to moral feeling. Within the context of the procedure of succession, it especially suggests that this procedure is conditioned, though only in freedom, by the recurring *form of removal* of each of the representations within the series. In each such representation the check to the vital forces is represented by the dimension of form that is the showing of inadequacy to represent. This structure is replicated, as well, in the overall form of both the heteronomous and the autonomous procedures of succession, that is, by their checks to the vital forces and their cancellations of sensible incentives. Kant emphasizes that this process of removal is not merely negative: "In the judgment of reason this removal of a hindrance is esteemed equivalent to a positive furthering of its causality" (*CPrR,* 5:75)—"namely the form of an intellectual causality, that is, of freedom" (*CPrR,* 5:73).

In the second *Critique* Kant has left us enough evidence to infer that his autonomous representations of what he calls the individual's and his own *(eigenen)* inner seeing *(inneren Anblick der Selbstprüfung)* have been made possible and readied for disclosure by his own work of preparatory guidance. This is his "preparation" in a heteronomous procedure of succession, in this case in his storytelling successions to Milton's storytelling. His inner seeing is the morally decisive second standpoint to which he is finally transferred by the autonomous *Progressus* and procedure of succession. This is to say, once again but now more fully, that the condition of the second standpoint that Kant represents, at *CPrR,* 5:87–88, as the autonomous tragic condition of the honest person *in extremis* can only have occurred or, rather, *happened—to* him—*after* the heteronomous procedure of succession that he places in a late position in the second *Critique,* at 5:161. Here is the procedure of succession in autonomy of the second *Critique* at 5:87–88:

> This idea of personality, awakening respect by <u>setting before our eyes the sublimity of our nature (in its vocation)</u> while at the same time showing us the want of accord of our conduct with respect to it and <u>thus striking down self-conceit,</u> is natural even to the most common human reason and is easily observed. Has not every even moderately honourable man sometimes found that he has abstained from an otherwise harmless lie by which he could either have extricated himself from a

troublesome affair or even procured some advantage for a beloved and deserving friend, solely in order not to have to despise himself secretly in his own eyes? When an upright man is in the greatest distress, which he could have avoided if he could only have disregarded duty, is he not sustained by the consciousness that he has maintained humanity in its proper dignity in his own person and honored it, that he has no cause to shame himself in his own eyes and to dread the inward view of self-examination? (underlining added)

[Diese Achtung erweckende Idee der Persönlichkeit, welche uns die Erhabenheit unserer Natur (ihrer Bestimmung nach) vor Augen stellt, indem sie uns zugleich den Mangel der Angemessenheit unseres Verhaltens in Ansehung derselben bemerken läßt und dadurch den Eigendünkel niederschlägt, ist selbst der gemeinsten Menschenvernunft natürlich und leicht bemerklich. Hat nicht jeder auch nur mittelmäßig ehrliche Mann bisweilen gefunden, daß er eine sonst unschädliche Lüge, dadurch er sich entweder selbst aus einem verdrießlichen Handel ziehen, oder wohl gar einem geliebten und verdienstvollen Freunde Nutzen schaffen konnte, blos darum unterließ, um sich ingeheim in seinen eigenen Augen nicht verachten zu dürfen? Hält nicht einen rechtschaffenen Mann im größten Unglücke des Lebens, das er vermeiden konnte, wenn er sich nur hätte über die Pflicht wegsetzen können, noch das Bewußtsein aufrecht, daß er die Menschheit in seiner Person doch in ihrer Würde erhalten und geehrt habe, daß er sich nicht vor sich selbst zu schämen und den inneren Anblick der Selbstprüfung zu scheuen Ursache habe?] (underlining added)

Kant almost fully dispenses with expedients of distancing from his sources when he shows us how much his autonomous achievement of inner seeing is a function of his storytelling procedure of succession to another storytelling. He shows us this *only after,* that is, he has completed his exposition of storytelling, in heteronomy, in the *Methode* section, where the parallels with his autonomous procedure of succession are pointed and distinctive:

The heart is freed and relieved of a burden that always secretly presses upon it, when in pure moral resolutions, examples of which are set before him, there is revealed to the human being an inner capacity not otherwise correctly known by himself, the *inner freedom* to release himself from the impetuous importunity of inclinations. . . . And now the law of duty, through the positive worth that <u>observance of [Befolgung]</u> it lets us feel, finds easier access through the *respect for ourselves* [i.e., that which is achieved in the experience of the sublime, which is intrinsic to the achievement of respect] in the consciousness of our freedom. When this is well established, <u>when a human being dreads nothing more than to find, on self-examination [in der inneren Selbstprüfung], that he is worthless and contemptible in his own eyes [in seinen eigenen Augen],</u> then every good moral disposition can be grafted onto it, because this is the best, and indeed the sole, guard to prevent ignoble and corrupting impulses from breaking into the mind. (*CPrR*, 5:161; underlining added)

[Das Herz wird doch von einer Last, die es jederzeit ingeheim drückt, befreit und erleichtert, <u>wenn an reinen moralischen Entschließungen, davon Beispiele vorgelegt</u> werden, dem Menschen ein inneres, ihm selbst sonst nicht einmal recht bekanntes Vermögen, *die innere Freiheit,* aufgedeckt wird, sich von der ungestümen Zudringlichkeit der Neigungen dermaßen loszumachen. . . . Und nun findet das Gesetz der Pflicht durch den positiven Werth, den uns <u>die Befolgung</u> desselben empfinden läßt, leichteren Eingang durch die *Achtung für uns selbst* im Bewußtsein unserer Freiheit. Auf diese, wenn sie wohl gegründet ist, <u>wenn der Mensch nichts stärker scheuet, als sich in der inneren Selbstprüfung in seinen eigenen Augen geringschätzig und verwerflich zu finden,</u> kann nun jede gute sittliche Gesinnung gepfropft werden: weil dieses der beste, ja der einzige Wächter ist, das Eindringen unedler und verderbender Antriebe vom Gemüthe abzuhalten.] (underlining added)

These parallels, which Kant does not disguise, require an explanation, which he does not directly supply. Once again, we may imagine that the reason for his hesitancy was his concern that the foregrounded, direct explanation would be misunderstood as the "blind and servile" imitation that he himself contemned. The autonomous achievement of inner seeing must not be blurred. Yet the isomorphism in these procedures of succession is vital and unmistakable.

～

Finally, it will help us see that something very like these isomorphic procedures of succession are occurring in Kant's writing if we identify here one concrete, highly specified aspect of his heteronomous procedure of succession. In accordance with his theory that the sublime succession procedure, in its heteronomous form, must be "evoked by a particular representation" (*CJ*, 5:250), Kant's own transfer from external seeing to inner seeing can begin to be willed only when he encounters an exemplary example of that transfer. This particular representation (in its specificity of language) must be part of the larger representation, in a procedure of succession, which is made up of the predicates of his storytelling and which themselves form his heteronomous procedure of succession. If my proposal of the relation of the *Critique of Practical Reason* to *Samson Agonistes* is justified, this must mean that in the *Critique of Practical Reason* the representation which, in heteronomy, evokes Kant's heteronomous succession procedure and transfer is some starting point in Milton's procedure of succession and transfer within *Samson Agonistes* itself. I now offer, in conclusion, one such starting point that Kant closely follows in Milton's text. This is a starting point for the final stage of the heteronomous procedure of succession that will prepare for the autonomous procedure of succession and its final transfer between Kant's standpoints.

In *Samson Agonistes* the impact of Samson's *Progressus* of humiliations of self-conceit already effects the transfer between the two standpoints that Milton locates in different representations of the power of seeing. Here, in the 1781 Mannheim translation, is the first standpoint, in which Samson knows that his external seeing has been moral blindness, even though he does not yet have inner moral seeing:

> O Schimpf, o Schande für Ehre und Religion! Sklavische Seele, mit sklavischer Strafe würdig belohnt! Der tiefe Abgrund, worein ich itzt herabgefallen bin, diese Lumpen, diese Arbeiten in der Mühle, sind nicht so niedrig, so schimpflich, als meine <u>vormalige Sklaverey, unedle, unmännliche, schmähliche, warhafte Sklaverey! und jene Blindheit, wie viel schlimmer war sie als diese, denn sie sah nicht wie verächtlich, wie niederträchtig, ich diente!</u> (*Simson*, p. 132; underlining added)

> O indignity, O blot
> To Honor and Religion! servile mind

Rewarded well with servile punishment!
The base degree to which I now am fall'n,
These rags, this grinding, is not yet so base
As was my former servitude, ignoble,
Unmanly, ignominious, infamous,
True slavery, and that blindness worse than this,
That saw not how degenerately I serv'd. (411–419; underlining added)

Here is Milton's second representation in which the Philistines are now represented as the embodiment of that *external seeing which is inner moral blindness,* while Samson, *still externally blind, has now achieved inner moral seeing:*

Halber Chor. . . . [the Philistines are] mit innerer Blindheit geschlagen. Aber er, obgleich äusserlich blind, obgleich geringgeschätzt und für nichts geachtet, entzündete, durch innere Augen erleuchtet, seine feurige Tapferkeit . . . (*Simson,* p. 205; underlining added)

Semichorus. . . . [the Philistines are] with blindness internal struck. But he though blind of sight, Despis'd and thought extinguish't quite, [is] With inward eyes illuminated His fiery virtue rous'd (1686–1690; underlining added)

Only the endless *Progressus* of humiliations of self-conceit and the endless procedure of succession (which for Milton already includes the procedures of succession of Job and Christ—and of Oedipus at Colonus and Prometheus bound—as exemplary examples) have intervened in Samson's moral reason to disclose this difference.

When Kant speaks of that which "has the greatest force on the mind of a spectator [auf das Gemüth des Zuschauers die größte Kraft habe]" in seeing the scene of moral near-perfection of the honest person *in extremis* (*CPrR,* 5:157), he is not speaking of a mere bystander *within* the scene. The fact that he is unmistakably speaking here of a storytelling strongly suggests both that he himself is specifically thinking of, and succeeding to, a dramatic representation of this tragic scene (even if in closet drama), and that he, too, is at this moment one such "spectator."

Thus I do not think it is mere coincidence that the language of Kant's "wenn der Mensch nichts stärker scheuet, als sich in der inneren Selbstprüfung in seinen eigenen Augen geringschätzig und verwerflich zu finden" (*CPrR*, 5:161) follows Milton's language in the 1781 Mannheim translation: "er, obgleich äusserlich blind, obgleich geringgeschätzt und für nichts geachtet, entzündete, durch innere Augen erleuchtet, seine feurige Tapferkeit . . ." (*Simson*, p. 205; underlining added). This passage in *Samson Agonistes* is the commencement of the tragedy's resounding rhetorical climax, that is, in the moment of transfer after its *Progressus* and procedure of succession. Nothing else in the play so completely represents blind Samson's achievement of insight into what—eluding the mechanism of all of nature and the conditioning by any empirical causality—gives him moral personality. This unconditioned noumenon can give meaning to his life because it is not under the control of any of the forces and inclinations which define the individual's mere desire for life. This noumenon is "something quite different from life, something in comparison and contrast with which life with all its agreeableness has no worth at all" (*CPrR*, 5:88). Perhaps we must say, here, too, that according to Kant's ideas of the purity of moral autonomy it must be impossible for an outsider to ascertain, or know, the scene of transfer in the autonomous procedure of succession that discloses Kant's moral feeling or categorical imperative. Yet if we are willing to do the work of tracing the side-by-side unfoldings of the forms of his heteronomous and autonomous procedures of succession he seems to make us at least partially privy to his own moment of final illumination. Within its unique web of Miltonic concepts, Kant's climactic placement of this passage, derived from his procedure of succession to Milton's storytelling in *Samson Agonistes* (with all its Miltonic-Kantian predicates), eerily lights up the scene of his unseen, autonomous disclosure of moral reason in the second standpoint.[26] This is the instant of transfer, achieved in the following of language,

---

26. Even here one is still left, equally, with the possibilities that Kant read Milton primarily in translation or in English: that is, the correspondences before us show either that he read *Samson Agonistes* mostly in translation or, equally possible, that he consulted the translations when, as in this instance, it was particularly important to make certain that he did not misunderstand Milton's verse.

when a human being dreads nothing more than to find, on self-examination, that he is worthless and contemptible in his own eyes. (*CPrR*, 5:161)

[wenn der Mensch nichts stärker scheuet, als sich in der inneren Selbstprüfung in seinen eigenen Augen geringschätzig und verwerflich zu finden.]

At this instant, this placement concretely represents Kant's heteronomous, then autonomous, procedures of succession to Milton's sublime poetry. No doubt there is much more that needs to be understood about these procedures. Yet we can at least see that in the *Critique of Practical Reason* these procedures are the working condition of Kant's moral reason and of his theorizing of moral reason.

CHAPTER 6

Kant's Miltonic Procedure of Succession in a Key Moment of the *Critique of Judgment*

My argument in this chapter is that all the features of Kant's Miltonic theory of the procedure of succession finally crystallized for him in composing §49 of the *Critique of Judgment*. Building upon and augmenting propositions that I have laid out in earlier chapters, I will propose that this crystallization took place in Kant's procedure of succession to a particular representation that is firmly located within a progression of representations in *Paradise Lost*. I begin by outlining my argument and my proposal:

1. For Kant the "aesthetic idea" is the means by which we disclose freedom and moral feeling. According to his account in §49, only a certain kind of "presentation" or "representation of the imagination . . . induces" the aesthetic idea (5:314).[1] His explanation of the elements of that representation in §49 is closely interconnected with other parts of the "Analytic of the Sublime." From these elements and their interconnections, we see that the requisite representation described in §49 is a procedure of succession to a virtually infinite progression of representations in the experience of the sublime. Each of the representations in this progression shows its inadequacy to represent.

2. In Kant's Elsner lecture comment on the *Folge von Gedanken*

---

1. In the present chapter, page references to Kant's works that are not attached to abbreviations are to the *Critique of Judgment*.

nach sich ziehen, he shows how this succession is achieved—how, in fact, he himself is achieving it—in a procedure of succession to verses of Milton. In other Kantian documents from immediately before and soon after the composition of §49, we have additional evidence that Kant was now especially thinking of the representation of the succession procedure in exemplifications of Milton's poetry.

3. In §49 Kant's example of a representation that produces the aesthetic idea is "Jupiter's eagle, with the lightning in its claws, . . . and the peacock of [heaven's] stately queen [Juno]" (5:315). Yet Kant by no means makes clear here how this representation can by itself induce the effects by which he is defining the aesthetic idea.

4. We can begin to reconstruct the specific supporting framework of Kant's representation of Jupiter and Juno from his engagement with the constellation of German Miltonism. I propose that in §49 Kant induces his aesthetic idea from his succession procedure to a specific Miltonic joint representation of Jupiter's eagle with Juno's peacock. This representation, to which G. F. Meier had drawn attention, was at the center of a variety of reflections on representations of Jupiter and Juno, and their birds, in their Miltonic connections.

5. Kant's achievement in §49 is distinctly Miltonic. His Miltonic procedure of succession to a representation of poetry of the sublime is an indispensable part of the workings of Kant's moral reason as he himself has defined those workings. He clearly indicates that following the progression in the experience of the sublime is always occasioned by a specific representation. For all the elements of such a representation that induces the aesthetic idea, and particularly for Kant's inheritance of those elements, a specific representation in *Paradise Lost* is uniquely illuminating of this Kantian necessity and its fulfillment.

∿

Long recognized as pivotal to the "Analytic of the Sublime" and even to the *Critique of Judgment* as a whole, §49 is titled "*The faculties of the*

mind which constitute genius." I noted in Chapter 1 that "the poet" of ge-
nius for the sublime to whom Kant refers in this section required no
naming. Milton was Kant's and his age's exemplary genius specifically
of the sublime, and the gathering of subjects which Kant itemizes here
is for the German reader the handprint of the author of *Paradise Lost.*
"The poet," Kant writes, "essays the task of interpreting to sense the ra-
tional ideas of invisible beings, the kingdom of the blessed, hell, eter-
nity, creation, &c." The philosophical core of §49 is the presentation of
"aesthetic ideas." Poetry and philosophy are intertwined at this core.
"It is in fact precisely in the poetic art," Kant specifies, "that the faculty
of aesthetic ideas can show itself to full advantage" (5:314). We have
seen that something like a virtual proof of the Miltonic identity of the
poet in this passage is available in Kant's 1781–82 direct comment on
aesthetic ideas in Milton's poetry: "Poetry offers many materials in the
world of invisible beings, so that Milton in his *Paradise Lost,* one of the
most magnificent poems, has delivered such things, about which one
would otherwise know nothing. When one [otherwise] tries to think
of a sublime invisible being or of a malevolent character opposing the
Lord of the world and the supreme governor, what kind of ideas can
emerge?"[2] (*AA,* 25.2:991) We have further seen that, in the Elsner
transcript of Kant's anthropology lectures given two years after the
publication of the *Critique of Judgment,* the example that Kant brings of
the presentation of "aesthetic ideas" is a passage of "Milton" from *Para-
dise Lost* (*AA,* 25.2:1561).

In §49 Kant builds on the unique status of Milton's poetry in con-
temporary German culture. In this section he emphasizes that the very
clarity of the aesthetic idea is dependent on representing the incapac-
ity of conceptual language to name that which "induces" the aesthetic
idea: "By an aesthetic idea I mean that representation of the imagina-
tion which induces much thought, yet without the possibility of any
definite thought whatever, i.e. *concept,* being adequate to it, and which
language, consequently, can never get quite on level terms with or ren-

2. "In der Welt der Geister giebt die Poesie vielen Stoff, so daß Milton in seinem
verlorenen Paradiese Eines [*sic*] der herrlichsten Gedichte geliefert hat, weil man
von solchen Sachen nichts weiß. Wenn man sich einen erhabenen Geist denkt, und
einen andern mit einer feindseeligen Gesinnung gegen den Regierer der Welt, und
gegen den obersten Beherrscher, was können da für Ideen hervorgebracht werden!"
(*AA,* 25.2:991).

der completely intelligible" (5:314). This means that Kant must find a way to effect the aesthetic idea while avoiding a conceptual translation of that which induces it. To do this he must *follow* the "representation of the imagination" rather than characterize it or, what would amount to the same thing (or less), merely name it. Yet he leaves definite traces of the representation of imagination that induces his thought. For the modern reader of Kant those traces have become almost invisible. They consist of elements of Milton's poetry, set within the constellation of German Miltonism, which we must now labor to reconstruct and make visible. The visibility of these largely unnamed elements is central, not marginal, to Kant's achievement in §49. It is possible that regaining this visibility may entail retrieval of dimensions of these elements of which Kant himself was at this same moment not fully conscious. Yet, whatever the degree of Kant's consciousness of these elements may have been, my proposal is that *from these elements* he at this moment discloses key features of his moral reason, especially his access to originality. He does this in a procedure of succession. I will now bring together previously ignored comments that Kant made just before and soon after his completion of the *Critique of Judgment*. I will show how these comments point clearly to a particular Kantian-Miltonic succession procedure. I will then adduce the specific passage of Milton's poetry, set within the constellation of German Miltonism, that, I propose, is the object of Kant's succession procedure in §49; and I will explain why this particular succession procedure (or its equivalent) is a philosophical necessity for Kant's presentation of moral reason.

∽

In §49 Kant's principal aim is to show how aesthetic ideas enable a free and original procedure of succession, a *Nachfolge* that is utterly distinct from mechanical imitation, *Nachahmung*. In the year before the composition of §49, Kant made at least two comments on the relation of Milton's poetry to the special kind of imitation that must transcend *Nachahmung*.

1. In the *Logik-Bauch* transcription of lectures from the winter semester of 1788–89 (which is to say, just months before the composition of §49), a passing comment indicates the apparently strange fact that Kant was thinking about Milton's poetry as a way of confronting basic

questions of philosophy. In the company of Leibniz and Wolff, Kant's greatest predecessors in German philosophy, he cites Milton's poetry as an exemplification of how we can either be tempted to mere imitation or use that exemplification for an "other way" that would be the *philosophical* antithesis of imitation:

> There are . . . rules whose use precedes cognition—this is *imitation* [*Nachahmung*]. . . . This imitation is very harmful. As long as one is taught by imitation in the schools and left to the natural disposition of any given teacher, there will be produced no geniuses, only imitators, because the spirit of imitation seriously damages natural talent. Great men, e.g., Leibniz, Wolff, Milton have, to be sure, brought about great benefits, but for that reason—because they were great—one imitated [*nachgeahmt*] them and, as a result, they are in this way as disadvantageous as in the other way they brought about benefits.[3]

> [Es giebt also Regeln, deren Gebrauch vor d. Erkentniß vorhergeht— d. ist *Nachahmung*. . . . Diese Nachahmung ist sehr schädlich. So lange man in Schulen durch Nachahmung gelehrt wird u. eines jeden Lehrers s. natürl. Disposition überlassen ist; solange werden keine Genis [*sic*], sond. Nachahmer seyn; denn d. Geist d. Nachahmung verdirbt sehr d. natürl. Talent. Große Männer z. B. Leibniz, Wolf [*sic*], Milton, haben zwar großen Nutzen gestiftet, aber darum, weil sie groß waren, hat man sie nachgeahmt u. folglich sind sie auf dieser Seite so nachtheilig, als sie auf d. andern Seite Nutzen gestiftet haben.]

Kant often noted that even if Milton's genius cannot be imitated, the outward features of his poetic subject can indeed be imitated harmfully. As we have seen, he insists on this by citing the superficial nature of Klopstock's apparently Miltonic renditions in the *Messias*. Kant's repetitions of this point are recurringly a way of focusing the difficult question of what an original kind of imitation (Milton's or of Milton) might be, since for Kant Milton is the exemplary modern original genius of the sublime. In the terms of the passage above, we can say that providing a model for original genius was the specific "great benefit" that Milton "brought about." Kant may even have expected more of

3. *Logik-Bauch* (Marburg Kant Archiv), 2.

Milton in this "other way" than of the philosophers themselves, since, as he said in one mood, even Leibniz (let alone Wolff) was "no original genius."[4] (We will see below, however, that he could change his mind about whether philosophers can be geniuses.) The "other way" is made clear by Milton's poetry when "natural disposition" and "natural talent" are allowed free reign, both in the teacher and in the disciple. A few pages later in the same *Logik-Bauch* lecture, Kant moves in the direction of specifying the concrete means of this other way that is more than imitation, that is, in a way of teaching how to produce, or *bring out,* the "aesthetic" of original genius:

> It is no good to teach someone the aesthetic according to rules, rather one should lay out for him pieces [i.e., works, artistic examples]. Rules can constitute a critique of aesthetics but they destroy natural genius because the natural product [of genius] must indeed be brought out. (*Logik-Bauch,* 6)

> [Es ist nicht gut jemanden in d. Aestetik <nach Regeln> zu unterrichten, sond. ihn [*sic*] lieber Stücke vorzulegen. . . . Die Regeln machen d. Kritik u. rotten dadurch d. natürl. Genie aus: denn d. natürl. Product muß zwar herausgebracht werden.]

Kant may here be on the way to saying that Milton's poetry offers the escape route—from imitation—in succession to a progression of *laid out* "pieces" or examples.

2. In the Busolt transcript of Kant's anthropology lectures (likely those of the same winter semester of 1788–89), we observe Kant already deploying almost all of the chief terms that he would shortly set down in §49. Here Kant explicitly places Milton "preeminently" (*vorzüglich*) at the center of these terms. The following is a paraphrase of the argument of the extended passage from Busolt (*AA,* 25.2:1492–1495) organized as a listing of its principal terms:

a. Genius is the vivid case of "the unique spirit" of each human being.

b. In genius is "originality of imagination."

---

4. *Matuszewski* (Marburg Kant Archiv), 270.

c. This makes genius capable of being a "model" for others.
d. Genius is manifested especially in the "arts."
e. Among the arts, "poetry" requires particularly large measures of talent.
f. "Freedom of imagination" is a chief ingredient of genius.
g. "The power of invention is opposed to imitation [*Nachahmung*]."
h. "Freedom and originality of imagination" go together in genius.
i. "Genius is attended by the expression of spirit."
j. "Spirit" is that which "animates" through "pure ideas."
k. The "representations" of such ideas are "original" and "a priori."
l. "Genius has the capacity of imagination to animate ideas" in a "play of all the mental powers."
m. "Such a painting, designed with freedom, is cause for admiration. This, Milton executes preeminently. [Ein solch mit freyheit entworfenes Gemälde, bewundert man. Das thut Milton Vorzüglich.]" (*AA*, 25.2:1494)

Two terms of §49 that are missing here are *sublime* and *procedure of succession*. In his Elsner anthropology lecture (1792–93), Kant would soon identify the latter term, directly and exemplarily, with Milton. So, too, in the same place he would at least implicitly identify the experience of the sublime with Milton by tracing in his verses the infinite progression that was for Kant (remembering the *Critique of Judgment*) the central structural feature of the sublime.

I have shown that in the second *Critique* Kant first employed the term *succession* as the antithesis of *imitation* and that he already glimpsed there that what it denoted was directly related to the experience of the sublime (*CPrR*, 5:85). In the *Groundwork of the Metaphysics of Morals* as well, I have argued, this relation is already strongly indicated.[5] Yet it was only in the course of composing §49 in the third *Cri-*

5. In the context of my discussion of passages of the *Critique of Judgment*, I will be elucidating below, again and more fully, the bond between the procedure of succession and the transcendental dimensions of the sublime. But it is worth saying here that this chronology of Kant's naming of the *Nachfolge* and incipient understanding of its significance is different from, even if consonant with, Zammito's and others' arguing that the event which "launched" the third *Critique* was "the breakthrough to a

tique that Kant finally crystallized and brought together all the parts of his explanation of the non-mechanical imitation that can transcend imitation. Even in the early stages of the composition of the third *Critique*, Kant haltingly grasped the interconnections of the parts of his explanation of the term *succession*. In the Busolt transcription we see his struggle to find and clarify a single term for this special kind of imitation. He flounders confusedly among *nachahmen, nachmachen,* and *nachäffen* (imitating, copying, aping). It is thus not surprising that in §47 of the third *Critique* he mis-wrote that the genius provides a model *nicht der Nachahmung, sondern der Nachahmung* ("not for imitation, but for imitation") which Johann Kiesewetter (Kant's editorial assistant) unhelpfully emended by changing the first *Nachahmung* to *Nachmachung*. As Meredith indicates in the notes to his translation, it was only in §49 that the term *Nachfolge* was fully and stably settled for the third *Critique*.

In the Busolt passage the ingredient of freedom is the vital partner of originality and *somehow* distinguishes the special kind of imitation that is Kant's organizing concern. It is *somehow* the sum total of this "painting, designed with freedom" that Kant says is especially "cause for admiration" and which he sees working in "Milton preeminently." But in the Busolt transcription the whole of Kant's account of the causes and effects of freedom is purely and repetitiously circular.

In §49 of the *Critique of Judgment* Kant put together the succession procedure with the impact of the experience of the sublime. The freedom within cognition thus produced was logically and philosophically answerable to the "painting, designed with freedom" that, in the Busolt lecture, Kant claimed "Milton executes preeminently" (*AA,* 25.2:1494). Together these comments of Kant suggest that in the period immediately leading up to §49 Kant was thinking about the succession procedure of Milton's poetry in all these ways simultaneously.

---

transcendental grounding of aesthetics, which occurred in the summer of 1787, during, and on the basis of, Kant's work on the *Second Critique*": John H. Zammito, *The Genesis of Kant's Critique of Judgment* (Chicago: University of Chicago Press, 1992), p. 7. What we have seen of the workings of a transcendental aesthetics of the sublime in the *Groundwork of the Metaphysics of Morals* suggests that this breakthrough was occurring, in practice, in 1785. In fact, the evidence of the *Groundwork* that we have seen also suggests that "the ethical turn" which Zammito dates with Giorgio Tonelli "after spring 1789" (p. 276) is also continually occurring, in practice, beginning in 1785.

I propose further that in §49 Kant was not only *thinking about* the Miltonic succession procedure, that is, in theory, but *thinking from the Miltonic* procedure of succession *in which he was here immediately engaged,* that is, in practice. As a way of opening this proposal, I will now try to establish that Kant's *Folge von Gedanken nach sich ziehen* of Milton's verse in the Elsner lecture in 1792–93 (in all its complexity of interconnections) is not invented on the spot but rather remembers Kant's own carefully executed succession procedure—designed with freedom—of Milton's verse two years earlier, that is, within §49. Establishing these connections is not of mere anecdotal interest but rather shows how deeply the idea of the procedure of succession ran for Kant in these years.

∼

As we have said more than once, a partnership of philosopher and poet is demonstrated *in concreto* in Kant's remark in Elsner concerning a succession or *Folge von Gedanken nach sich ziehen:*

> Aesthetic ideas are those representations that contain a wealth of thoughts which *ad infinitum* draw after it a succession of thoughts. Such ideas draw us into an immeasurable prospect, e.g. Milton's saying, "Female light mixes itself with male light, to unknown ends." Through this soulful [ingenious] idea the mind is set into continuous motion [*in einen continuierlichen Schwung*]. (*AA*, 25:1561)

It is noteworthy that Kant recurred to the same citation from Milton two years later in a letter to Schiller dated 30 March 1795.[6] (I discuss the letter as a whole in the appendix.) By collating the terms that Kant uses in these two passages, which cite the same verses of Milton, and then comparing them with Kant's terms in §49, we can clarify and even extend the meaning of Kant's representation of aesthetic ideas in §49. Here is the most relevant part of Kant's letter:

> I received the plan for a periodical that you sent me last summer and also the two first monthly issues. I found your *Letters on the Aesthetic Edu-*

---

6. Kant, *Correspondence*, trans. and ed. Arnulf Zweig (Cambridge: Cambridge University Press, 1999), pp. 497–498.

cation of Mankind splendid, and I shall study them so as to be able to give you my thoughts about them. The paper on sexual differences in organic nature, in the second issue, is impossible for me to decipher, even though the author [Wilhelm von Humboldt] seems to be an intelligent fellow. There was once a severely critical discussion in the *Allgemeine Literaturzeitung* about the ideas expressed in the letters of Herr Hube of Thorn concerning a similar relationship extending throughout nature. The ideas were attacked as romantic twaddle. To be sure, we sometimes find something like that running through our heads, without knowing what to make of it. The organization of nature has always struck me as amazing and as a sort of chasm of thought; I mean, the idea that fertilization, in both realms of nature, always needs two sexes in order for the species to be propagated. After all, we don't want to believe that providence has chosen this arrangement, almost playfully, for the sake of variety. On the contrary, we have reason to believe that propagation is not possible in any other way. This opens a prospect on what lies beyond the field of vision, out of which, however, we can unfortunately make nothing, as little as out of what Milton's angel told Adam about the creation: "Male light of distant suns mixes itself with female, to unknown ends" [*Paradise Lost*, VIII.148–152].[7]

The citation from Milton seems trivial and perfunctory. It even seems to issue in an acknowledgment of poetry's pointlessness. But the reality, for Kant, was very different. We can be sure of this by applying to evidence from another quarter.

It has not been noted before that Kant had encountered these particular verses of Milton in Part V of Hume's *Dialogues Concerning Natu-*

---

7. Like Hume, though somewhat differently (see below), Kant compresses these verses of Milton. As we have seen, in *Paradise Lost* they appear as follows: "Other Suns perhaps / With thir attendant Moons thou wilt descry / Communicating Male and Female Light, / Which two great Sexes animate the World, / Stor'd in each Orb perhaps with some that live" (VIII.148–152). Here is Bodmer's quite accurate prose translation (Zürich, 1742), p. 340: "Vielleicht wirst du dereinst auch andere Sonnen entdecken, denen ihre Monden aufwarten, die das männliche und das weibliche Licht mit einander vermischen, denn diese zwey grössen Geschlechtsarten geben der Welt das Leben, die vielleicht in allen Kugeln mit etwas, das lebet, versehen ist." Kant more than likely noticed that Bodmer here provides footnote commentary particularly (*only*, in fact) on the "Lebhaftigkeit," liveliness, of the representation of "die das männliche und das weibliche Licht mit einander vermischen."

ral Religion.[8] Hume assigned a specific philosophical valence to these verses by citing them in order to exemplify a particular view of natural theology—a view against which, we know, Kant directly struggled. We know that this was the case with Kant because in the *Critique of Judgment* (5:420–421) he explicitly attempts to refute the view for which Hume brings this quotation from Milton as support. Thus these particular verses are for Kant linked to two of the leading topics in the *Critique of Judgment,* one in each of its two parts: aesthetic ideas in the "Critique of Aesthetic Judgment" and natural teleology in the "Critique of Teleological Judgment." And finally, and more important, we will see that this quotation of Milton's verses, on the subject of light, is closely, even intimately, parallel to another citation of Milton's verses on light placed by Kant in precisely the same context of philosophical discussion, in §49 of that same work.

There are deep, partly hidden, homologies among [1] the letter to Schiller, [2] the passage from the lecture on anthropology, and [3] §49 of the *Critique of Judgment.* (The appendix offers a highlighting of the parallelisms among these passages together with, in the notes, fuller transcriptions of the passages.) All three texts contain the same pictorial outline of mental processes: in a *continuous swing* the mind *follows* an *endless* series of *thoughts* or representations to the point of such *mental fullness* that the overload *opens* a *chasm* or *abyss,* which is also an *immeasurable prospect.* In the case of [1] and [2], the picture is filled in or realized by *following Milton's representation of following* an endless series of thoughts or representations, in this case of the cross-gendered propagation of light for cosmic ends to which the mind cannot reach.

We should note that in Kant's brief restatement of the procedure of succession in the anthropology lecture [2] he explicitly names the "succession" (the *Folge von Gedanken nach sich ziehen]*) in "aesthetic

8. David Hume, *The Natural History of Religion,* ed. A. Wayne Colver, and *Dialogues Concerning Natural Religion,* ed. John Valdimir Price (Oxford: Clarendon Press, 1976), p. 193: "The two great Sexes of Male and Female, says *Milton,* animate the World." Hume's *Dialogues* had been published in English in 1779 and the German translation, *Gespräche über natürliche Religion,* already appeared in 1781 in Leipzig. Arthur Warda, *Immanuel Kants Bücher* (Berlin: Martin Breslauer, 1922), p. 50, lists this volume in Kant's personal library and adds that Kant's copy has been lost. Hume's citation of Milton is translated in *Gespräche über natürliche Religion* as follows: "Die zwey großen Geschlechter der männlichen und weiblichen Gattung, beleben nach **Miltons** Ausdrucke die Welt" (p. 104).

ideas." He is here observing the heteronomous half of the formal isomorphism that, in its two halves, constitutes the full procedure of succession: "Aesthetic ideas are those representations that contain a wealth of thoughts which *ad infinitum* draw after it a succession of thoughts" (*AA*, 25.2:1561). This restates his comment in the *Critique of Judgment*, §49, where he had focused on the heteronomous succession to the examples and exemplarity of predecessors which, in the full procedure of succession, yields a new "exemplary originality" in aesthetic ideas (5:318).

A slightly later passage of the third *Critique*, in §53, confirms that Kant sought this efficacy of moral reason especially in poetry:

> *Poetry* [*Dichtkunst*] (which owes its origin almost entirely to <u>genius</u> and is least willing to be led by precepts or example) holds the first rank among all the arts. It expands the mind by giving <u>freedom</u> to the imagination and by offering, from among the <u>boundless multiplicity</u> of possible forms accordant with a given concept, to whose bounds it is restricted, that one which couples with the <u>presentation</u> [*Darstellung*] of the concept <u>a wealth of thought</u> [*Gedankenfülle*] to which no verbal expression is completely adequate, . . . <u>thus rising aesthetically to ideas</u> [*<u>sich also ästhetisch zu Ideen erhebt</u>*]. (5:326; underlining added)

From the correspondences between this and earlier passages in the *Critique of Judgment* and with Kant's way of describing Milton's poetry, specifically with regard to sublimely rising to aesthetic ideas, it is clear that Kant allowed himself to think of *"poetry"*—*Dichtkunst*—as the kind of poetry that fulfills the special conditions of the Miltonic sublime.

If we now put together the points of convergence that we have gathered from Kant's Bauch (1788–89), Busolt (1788–89), and Elsner (1792–93) lectures and from his letter to Schiller (1795), we are almost in a position to locate the precise place in §49 of the *Critique of Judgment* where it would have made the greatest sense for Kant to have enacted a procedure of succession to Milton's poetry—and where, I propose, he does just that, even if with careful distancing. Only a few more preparatory steps are necessary to render that succession procedure immediately intelligible and credible.

~

I now take up a point of view internal to §49. My aim is to explain the "animating" *(belebende)* act of moral reason that Kant executes in his procedure of succession to Milton's poetry.

Kant indicates in the opening of §49 that he is now in quest of something of great importance but also of great difficulty. He seeks "that whereby" the "faculty of presenting *aesthetic ideas*" *(das Vermögen der Darstellung ästhetischer Ideen)* "animates" *(belebt)* the mind, "the material which it employs for that purpose." This material is "that which sets the mental powers into a swing [*Schwung*] that is final, i.e. into a play which is self-maintaining" (5:313–314). This quest is fraught with danger for Kant because the something that he seeks does that which is apparently antithetical to the critical philosophy: it bridges heteronomy (the empirical encounter of some "material") and autonomy (the mind's "self-maintaining" activity). Without cancelling the critical philosophy, it must achieve exactly that which Kant had warned, in 1785, is the impossible thing that Herder was claiming for the use of analogy (and of poetry) in philosophy: it must fill the "immense void between the contingent and the necessary" *(AA, 7:57).*[9]

Near the end of §49 Kant reveals, without fanfare—and apparently without immediate exemplification or application—what he has found: this is the procedure of succession to a progression of representations that issues in the transformative experience of the sublime and that can, on that account, bridge the individual material example and the archetypical or universal. This act of succession relates to the contingent in a way that discloses "not . . . imitation" *(nicht . . . Nachahmung)* of the merely empirical but an "exemplary originality" *(musterhafte Originalität),* which is in the condition of the *a priori* (5:318). Kant's manner of proceeding from the opening to the close of §49 is left somewhat disjointed, so that the work of piecing together partly falls to the reader. Nevertheless, Kant has left the items for assembly ready to hand.

For this work of assembly we need to keep clearly in mind the link we have shown (most recently in the last chapter) between the "succession" *(Nachfolge)* and the "progression without end" *(Progressus ohne*

9. The translation is from Kant, *On History*, ed. Lewis White Beck, trans. Lewis White Beck, Robert E. Anchor, and Emil L. Fackenheim (Indianapolis: Bobbs-Merrill, 1963), p. 41.

Ende) in Kant's accounts of the sublime.[10] Kant lays down the ground-work of connections among succession, progression, and the "aes-thetic estimate" *(ästhetische Beurtheilung)* (5:258–259), the last of which closely resembles the aesthetic idea. It is clear that there is a close par-allelism between these connections and Kant's explicit association—in the anthropology lecture—of a "succession" with the "aesthetic ideas" of Milton's sublime poetry. In that place, the procedure of succession is described as being both *to* and *in* Milton's poetry.

We need to recall here, as well, the principal things that we learn from Kant's account of the succession procedure and its element of *Progressus:*

1. In a heteronomous succession procedure the mind is located in an effectively endless progression of existing representations, al-ways "evoked by a particular representation" (5:318, 250).[11]

2. Each representation in the progression that admits of this pro-cedure of succession (as opposed, Kant specifies, to a

10. As we have seen in both Chapters 4 and 5, the identification of *Progressus* with *Nachfolge* in the *Critique of Practical Reason* is already subtle and profound. For the reader's convenience, I cite the core passages of that identification once again: "das Urbild ist, welchem wir uns zu nähern und in einem ununterbrochenen, aber unendlichen <u>Progressus</u> gleich zu werden streben sollen"—"The archetype which we should strive to approach and resemble in an uninterrupted but endless <u>progress</u>" (*CPrR,* 5:83; underlining added); "Will man jemanden [*sic*] aber sie als Beispiele der <u>Nachfolge</u> vorstellen, so muß durchaus die Achtung für Pflicht (als das einzige ächte moralische Gefühl) zur Triebfeder gebraucht werden: diese ernste, heilige Vor-schrift, die es nicht unserer eitelen Selbstliebe überläßt, mit pathologischen Antrie-ben (so fern sie der Moralität analogisch sind) zu tändeln und uns auf *verdienstlichen* Werth was zu Gute zu thun. . . . Das ist die einzige Darstellungsart, welche die Seele moralisch bildet"—"But if one wants to represent these to someone as examples to be imitated [<u>followed</u>], respect for duty (which is the only genuine moral feeling) must be used as the incentive—this earnest, holy precept that does not leave it to our vain self-love to dally with pathological impulses (as far as they are analogous to mo-rality) and to credit ourselves with *meritorious* worth. . . . This is the only way of repre-senting them that educates the soul morally" (*CPrR,* 5:85; underlining added).

11. At 5:255 Kant refers to this effectively endless progression as a *Progressus ohne Ende.* Other instances of this *ins Unendliche gehenden Progressus* occur in the *Critique of Practical Reason,* 5:32, 83, 122, 123, and in the *Critique of Judgment,* 5:258, 259. To be sure, succession to (as opposed to imitation of) a progression of representations can also be effected with art forms other than poetry, though Kant makes clear that po-etry is the preeminent vehicle for the sublime (5:314–317 and especially 326–327).

Nachahmung, imitation) is partially negative or represents "its own inadequacy" to represent (5:252–253).

3. The individual's act of following this given progression issues in the experience of the sublime (5:255).
4. The specific heteronomous succession procedure discloses to the individual, or transfers the mind into, an isomorphic, autonomous ("self-maintaining") succession procedure that also issues, for that individual, in the experience of the sublime, hence in freedom and moral feeling (5:313, 318).

Between the opening and close of §49 Kant provides concrete examples of what the "material" might be that occasions these things. Indeed, material instances or examples of some kind are logically required here, since, according to the principles that Kant is at this moment presenting, he, too, can reach his recognition of this process only through a procedure of succession to a progression of examples that begins, for him, with a particular example. Yet the examples that he cites from Friedrich Wilhelm II and Philip Lorenz Withof partly obscure what his own material—in his presently enacted succession procedure—actually is.

I propose that in §49 Kant's faculty of aesthetic ideas *follows* a passage in Milton's poetry, significant traces of which are directly in evidence here. At this moment, in this instant, this procedure of succession to Milton's poetry animates Kant's mind and sets it into a swing that is final and self-maintaining. With this succession procedure in view we can see that which Kant's examples from Friedrich and Withof partly obscure. Within the contexts in which Kant encounters them, the principal elements of Milton's poetry, and of this passage specifically—elements that are hardly to be seen, if at all, in Friedrich's or Withof's verses—are these: (a) the typology that is a following of an effectively endless progression in the experience of the sublime (of the exemplary poet of sublime exemplarity), (b) the constituting of the typological progression with representations that show us their own inadequacy to represent, (c) the representation (by that progression) of aesthetic light, genius, respect, freedom, and moral feeling.

A paradox, linking heteronomy and autonomy, is implicit in all these operations. This paradox is bound up with one of Kant's most difficult claims in the *Critique of Judgment,* namely, that aesthetic judgment—about which it is usual to think, at least partly, in terms of aesthetic experience—determines moral feeling *a priori*. I suggest that Kant's laying out of the elements of this paradox is part of the epistemological change that Dieter Henrich has registered in Kant's new way of using the term *Darstellung, presentation,* in the *Critique of Judgment. Darstellung,* Henrich explains, for Kant now comes to mean the "*arrangement*" and "exhibition of concepts that are derived from perceptions in a general and formal way."[12] In my view, the *a priori Darstellung* to which Henrich calls attention is the autonomous procedure of succession that produces the experience of the sublime, freedom, and moral feeling. The autonomous procedure of succession, in this view, is at the core of Kant's "aesthetic ideas" and is disclosed to us only through the formal isomorphism of, or transfer between, the heteronomous and autonomous succession procedures. This means that a heteronomous succession procedure always precedes the disclosures of autonomy in moral reason. In fact, Kant's heteronomous succession procedure, leading to his autonomous succession procedure, is presently performed *within* §49 of the *Critique of Judgment.* I propose that this performed heteronomous succession is to Milton's poetry of the sublime.

~

It may at first seem implausible to expect to locate a crystallization of such far-reaching importance in the half-dozen pages that make up §49 (5:313–319). But aside from the fact that, as we say and as Kant will show us more than metaphorically, insight often comes in lightning flashes, there are strong reasons for supposing that, measured even by Kantian orders of philosophical magnitude, something extraordinary suddenly became clear to Kant during the composition of §49.

Among those who have studied the order of composition of the parts of the *Critique of Judgment,* there is a fairly strong consensus that the composition of §49, together even with the decision to include the "Analytic of the Sublime" (most of which had been written considerably earlier) in the "Critique of Aesthetic Judgment," constituted the very last stage—in fact, the stage beyond what was supposed to be fin-

---

12. Dieter Henrich, *Aesthetic Judgment and the Moral Image of the World: Studies in Kant* (Stanford: Stanford University Press, 1992), pp. 47–49.

ishing touches—of Kant's work on the third *Critique*.[13] It is reasonable to suppose that it was these final additions and changes in particular that left the third *Critique* in a condition of emergence and incompleteness, even of partial disorder. This condition obtains with regard to all the key terms of §49 and impinges in ever widening circles on the *Critique of Judgment* as a whole. These new or revised terms are: *aesthetic ideas, exemplary originality, succession, genius, representation, poetry, the sublime,* and *freedom.*

Kant's final burst of composition was unforeseen even by himself. Before writing §49 he had twice written to his publisher, François Lagarde, saying that the book was entirely finished, requiring only final checking, collation, and transcription. He had even pressured Lagarde to clear a press so that the book could be printed in time for the upcoming Leipzig book fair. It was at this point, with Lagarde now breathing down his neck, that Kant's thinking on a chain of key issues achieved its decisive crystallization.

The catalyst for this crystallization was the new role of exemplarity—in fact, of Miltonic exemplarity—in Kant's theory of aesthetic ideas. The same constellation of German Miltonism that gave Kant the elements of his theory of the procedure of succession, and with it the foundation of aesthetic ideas, also revealed to him the incomparable value of *exemplarily* exemplifying aesthetic ideas in a *succession* to Milton's poetry. That German Miltonist line flowed (with the many reinforcements that we have seen) from Addison's exemplification of the Longinian sublime by Milton's genius and poetry of the sublime. As prologue to my concluding proposal for Kant's implemented procedure of succession to that poetry, and therefrom his achievement of aesthetic ideas, I turn now to the chief features of Kant's theory of aesthetic ideas.

∼

Recent commentary has shown the centrality of Kant's exposition of aesthetic ideas to his claim for the *a priori* determination of moral feeling by aesthetic judgment. Yet the same commentary has also shown

13. Zammito, *The Genesis of Kant's Critique of Judgment*, pp. 1–2, puts together and augments the work of Michel Souriau, Gerhard Lehmann, James Meredith, and Giorgio Tonelli on "the genetic development of Kant's versions of the *Third Critique* . . . at their more problematic junctures."

that, no less than the larger claim, his exposition of aesthetic ideas seems, in Allison's words, "cryptic and incomplete."[14] One of the elements of Kant's exposition that may seem especially cryptic and incomplete, if not deeply confusing, is that he speaks of an equivalent to a completed idea that resides *a priori* in the mind of the reader or spectator, yet as an integral part of that idea he includes an activity of "representation" as well as an after-effect of that activity. The after-effect is "induced" in the mind of the reader or spectator by the aesthetic idea itself. The circularity of these elements seems to defeat comprehension. I am proposing that Kant's theory of the activity of succession is an integral part of his theory of the aesthetic idea. We need to untangle the relation between these two theories. The former decodes and completes the latter.

Kant sets out the faculty of aesthetic ideas not only "on its own account" within the imagination but in its partnership with reason's faculty of "intellectual ideas." Indeed, as a whole, Kant's exposition of aesthetic ideas in §49 works to bridge the terms *Vorstellung, sensuous representation,* and *Darstellung, logical presentation* (e.g., 5:317–318). Consonant with this bridging, his explanation of aesthetic ideas emerges side by side, I propose, with his enacted procedure of succession to Milton's poetry. Here is Kant's explanation of aesthetic ideas in the *Critique of Judgment,* beginning with the passage that I cited a bit earlier:

> By an aesthetic idea I mean that representation of the imagination which induces much thought, yet without the possibility of any definite thought whatever, i.e. *concept,* being adequate to it, and which language, consequently, can never get quite on level terms with or render completely intelligible. . . . It is in fact precisely in the poetic art that the faculty of aesthetic ideas can show itself to full advantage. This faculty, however, regarded solely on its own account, is properly no more than a talent (of the imagination).
>
> If, now, we attach to a concept a representation of the imagination belonging to its presentation, but inducing solely on its own account such a wealth of thought as would never admit of comprehension in a definite concept, and, as a consequence, giving aesthetically an unbounded expansion to the concept itself, then the imagination here

14. Allison, *Kant's Theory of Taste,* p. 260.

displays a creative activity, and it puts the faculty of intellectual ideas (reason) into motion—a motion, at the instance of a representation, towards an extension of thought, that, while germane, no doubt, to the concept of the object, exceeds what can be laid hold of in that representation or clearly expressed. (§49, 5:314–315)

To date, Allison has made the fullest sense of Kant's aesthetic ideas. He explains that Kant's main reason

> for characterizing these products of the imagination as "ideas" . . . may be described as their transcendent pretensions. Kant puts the point by stating that, though they are inner intuitions, they share with ideas of reason the feature of not being completely determinable by a concept . . . [§49, 5:314]. The latter is because they either attempt to depict something explicitly supersensible (such as [as Kant says] the poet's depiction of heaven, hell, eternity, creation, and the like) or they emulate ideas of reason in striving for a maximum, that is, for a completeness [that they cannot attain] in the representation of something sensible. . . . Aesthetic ideas . . . indirectly exhibit ideas of reason (in virtue of their analogous ways of gesturing to the supersensible) . . . by means of an analogy.
>
> . . . The key point is that aesthetic ideas involve a striving toward transcendence or a gesturing to the supersensible, either through the depiction of something inherently supersensible (for example, God, freedom, or immortality) or through their endeavor to express a totality or completeness that exceeds what is exhibitable in experience. Moreover, it is in virtue of this formal feature, which pertains to aesthetic ideas as such, that they "serve as a substitute for a logical exhibition". . . . In expanding the mind and "prompting much thought," (albeit of an indeterminate kind) aesthetic ideas lead the mind . . . from something sensible to the supersensible.

All this is not optional or incidental for Kant's moral thought. Allison emphasizes that "aesthetic ideas . . . remain an essential presupposition" of Kant's entire account of the moral dimension of aesthetic judgment:

> An appeal to aesthetic ideas is necessary precisely in order to understand how there could be an isomorphism between a reflection [on the

beautiful, Allison says] based on an intuition and one [a reflection on the good] on a concept. . . . Kant cannot spell out the formal analogy between these two qualitatively distinct species of liking without appealing (at least implicitly) to his doctrine of aesthetic ideas.[15]

In my view Allison's insistence that we ignore Kant's placement of aesthetic ideas within his explanation of the sublime, rather than of the beautiful, where Allison wants to relocate them, is unnecessary and mistaken. In fact, Allison himself notes the striking formal resemblances between Kant's account of the sublime and his account of moral respect, but Allison calls this only a "significant analogy".[16] We must entertain the possibility that Kant's succession procedure for producing exemplary originality in the experience of the sublime is for him the formal ground of an extended complex of highly significant formal analogies, a nesting of what Allison would call isomorphisms. These isomorphisms—embracing the double standpoints inherent in aesthetic ideas, aesthetic judgment, moral judgment, the sublime, ge-

15. Ibid., pp. 256–261.

16. Ibid., p. 324. Allison explains his devaluation of the feeling of the sublime compared with moral feeling in this way: "The analogy is merely the consequence rather than the ground of the liking for the sublime. Assuming the correctness of Kant's analysis, the reason one likes something deemed sublime (in spite of its manifest counterpurposiveness for our sensible cognition or interests as a sensible being) is that it brings with it an awareness of our supersensible nature and vocation, in short, of our moral autonomy. Consequently, it is the *ground* of this liking that both explains the analogy and licenses the demand for universal agreement. The underlying assumption is simply that one ought to like something that functions in this way, at least if one values appropriately one's moral autonomy. . . . It must also be kept in mind that the judgment of the sublime (like that of taste) is *aesthetic;* that the feeling is merely analogous to (not identical with) moral feeling; that the respect it involves is both causally and phenomenologically distinct from respect for the moral law. . . . A judgment of sublimity is neither equivalent to nor entails moral approval. More generally, it is crucial to Kant's moral theory to keep these two feelings apart, since the failure to do so would undermine the rational foundations of morality. . . . The sublime (like the beautiful) is viewed by Kant merely as a preparation for morality and is, therefore, without any *direct* moral significance" (pp. 335–336 and 341–342). Lewis White Beck, *A Commentary on Kant's* Critique of Practical Reason (Chicago: University of Chicago Press, 1960), pp. 220–221, spells out the formal symmetry of Kant's accounts of the sublime and of respect. He, too, does not regard the formal symmetry as significant for Kant's moral philosophy.

nius, respect, the Typic, and exemplary originality—issue in aware-
ness of, or transfer to, the faculty within us for recognition of
the supersensible. I am proposing that Kant carries out this transfer
in §49.

We should not be misled by the way Kant seems to restrict the opera-
tions of the succession procedure to the genius, which could be taken
to mean that he excludes the philosopher—which would mean Im-
manuel Kant—from participation in the succession procedure. In §47
he does say that we must not call "a man of *brains,* and often great
brains, a *genius.*" This exclusion applies, he adds, even to so "great a
mind" as the natural philosopher "Newton" (5:308–309). Indeed, in
an anthropology lecture of 1791–92 Kant specifically makes the same
point by differentiating Newton from Milton and Shakespeare: "New-
ton was a great mind, but no genius. . . . Milton, Shakespeare are ge-
niuses [Newton war ein großer Kopf, aber kein Genie. . . . Milton,
Shakespeare sind Genies]."[17] Kant, however, had articulated a differ-
ent view of the philosopher in his lectures on Meier's *Auszug aus der
Vernunftlehre,* beginning around 1770. There Kant firmly puts the phi-
losopher in the same category of genius as the artist while also making
the different though closely related point that genius, in this case
in the "art of philosophizing," is beyond the reach of *Nachahmung/*
imitation: "Philosophy and the art of philosophizing cannot possi-
bly be learned. Philosophy requires more genius than imitation [Die
Philosophie und die Kunst zu philosophieren kann unmöglich erlernt
werden. Zur Philosophie gehört mehr Genie, als Nachahmung]."
With regard to this remark, Schlapp notes too hastily that Kant later
excluded philosophy from the sphere of activity of genius.[18] In the late
1780s Kant indeed prefers to "decline" the "honor" and "manner of a
genius"; yet at the same time he describes the "academic" work that he
aims at in philosophy as follows:

> When the labor, the consistent application and caution which this re-
> quires has succeeded, there remains for the true genius (not the sort
> who try to make everything out of nothing) to provide it with a sublime

---

17. *Matuszewski,* 269:32–51; Schlapp, *Kants Lehre vom Genie und die Entstehung der
'Kritik der Urteilskraft'* (Göttingen: Vandenhoeck & Ruprecht, 1901), p. 392.

18. Schlapp, *Kants Lehre vom Genie,* p. 50.

turn of spirit and so to set in motion the use of the dry principles.
(*Reflection* 990; *AA*, 15:435)[19]

It is plausible to suggest that in the 1780s Kant could very well have
worked for the possibility of a philosopher's—even his own—partici-
pation in a succession procedure of true geniuses that included Mil-
ton, *the* modern poetic genius of the sublime.

⁓

The new concept of *Darstellung* that Dieter Henrich has located in the
Critique of Judgment illuminates, I suggest, the setting of Kant's develop-
ment of his idea of the procedure of succession. Henrich attempts to
fill out Kant's "move from an ultimately empirical aesthetics to an aes-
thetics founded upon transcendental principles" with "a priori status."
This transcendental aesthetics must make it possible to "conceive of a
cooperation between the faculty of combination (imagination) and
the faculty of concepts (understanding) that takes place *prior* to the
employment of any particular concept." Henrich believes that in the
Critique of Judgment the "key term" in Kant's "advanced view on
the *possession* and the *usage* of concepts" in aesthetics is "'exhibition'
(*'Darstellung,'* traditionally translated as 'presentation')," which now
means "producing instances" of concepts "in intuition." "To exhibit a
concept means to associate with it in intuition a manifold of a distinc-
tive unitary (temporal and/or spatial) shape. . . . If the understanding
operates in the aesthetic situation as the power of exhibiting concepts,
it must do so by virtue of a feature distinctive of the exhibition of con-
cepts that are derived from perceptions in a general and formal way.
This can only be the unity and the precision of the *arrangement* of a
perceived manifold in space and time."[20] Henrich's concern here is
with the *a priori* and autonomous in Kant's usage of *Darstellung* in the
Critique of Judgment; and he does not identify a special role of the expe-
rience of the sublime in this usage. Yet for Kant in the *Critique of Judg-
ment,* this *a priori Darstellung* is, I am proposing, closely connected with
the autonomous succession procedure that issues in the experience of

19. Cited by Zammito, *The Genesis of Kant's Critique of Judgment,* p. 187. Zammito ar-
gues that Kant's parenthetical reference to the false kind of genius is part of his battle
against Herder.
20. Henrich, *Aesthetic Judgment and the Moral Image of the World,* pp. 34–38, 41, 47–
49.

the sublime. And, further, this *a priori,* autonomous exhibition or succession procedure is formally isomorphic with an empirical, heteronomous exhibition or succession procedure. My contention is that the ground of the symmetrical transfers in this formal isomorphism—the basis of the "move" that Henrich describes—is the aesthetics of *ästhetisches Licht* that Kant inherited in combination with a Miltonic exemplarity and that he amplified greatly.

In fact, in the same essay in which Henrich describes Kant's *a priori Darstellung,* he calls attention to Kant's debt to Meier's fluid movement among aesthetics, ethics, and metaphysics.[21] Henrich, however, does not mention the aesthetics of *ästhetisches Licht* (and *Licht und Schatten, light and shadow*)—or of aesthetic *Klarheit,* clarity. That aesthetics is for Meier the core of "the animation of thoughts" *(die Lebhaftigkeit der Gedanken).* Kant was to develop the aesthetics of light and shadow in extraordinary ways, but he learned the outline of this aesthetics most directly from Meier's *Anfangsgründe.* There, we have seen, the exemplary power of Milton's poetry of aesthetic light is given a prominent, even unique place.

I have suggested in earlier chapters that for Kant, advancing on Meier, the *a priori* procedure of succession to aesthetic light becomes the core of Kant's presentation of aesthetic ideas in the *Critique of Judgment.* Within those ideas themselves, as Kant conceives them, an autonomous procedure of succession to aesthetic light is prepared by the formal isomorphism of a heteronomous procedure of succession to representations of aesthetic light. In Kant's individual case in the *Critique of Judgment,* his heteronomous succession procedure—following Meier and others in this, as well—is to the line or typology and the archetype *(Urbild)* of Milton's poetry, especially the succession to aesthetic light within that poetry, specifically its *following of following* and *its arrangements of light and shadow.* By the end of this chapter the integral relation of Kantian-Miltonic succession to aesthetic light and shadow will, I hope, be substantially clarified.

～

I wish to describe, next, Kant's practice of his succession procedure within his presentation of aesthetic ideas in §49 of the *Critique of Judgment.* To do this I will first begin to reconstruct the relevant supporting

21. Ibid., pp. 31–33.

framework of Kant's example—"Jupiter's eagle, with the lightning in its claws, . . . and the peacock of [heaven's] stately queen [Juno]"—from his engagement with the constellation of German Miltonism. Here are the sub-steps (of items 4 and 5 at the beginning of this chapter) in my argument for this reconstruction:

a. One of the reasons that Kant turned to a representation of Jupiter in 1790, in the *Critique of Judgment,* was that in his 1785 reviews of Herder's *Ideen* he had himself placed a representation (by Herder) of Jupiter at the center of discussion of the role of analogy and poetry in philosophy.

b. Kant could not have failed to see that the specific topic of representing Jupiter had been directly connected with the issue of originality in Milton's poetry by Meier, Herder, and Christian Adolph Klotz.

c. In the *Anfangsgründe* Meier specifically identified Milton's representation of "Jupiter's eagle"—and of Jupiter and Juno together—with a series of representations in *Paradise Lost.*

d. We know that at the moment of composing §49 of the *Critique of Judgment* Kant had the *Anfangsgründe* open before him. The comments with which he surrounds "Jupiter's eagle, with the lightning in its claws, . . . and the peacock of [heaven's] stately queen [Juno]" correspond in detail (as Schlapp noted, without elaboration) to another passage from the *Anfangsgründe* (i.e., a passage in addition to the one in which Meier calls attention to Milton's representation of Jupiter's and Juno's birds). This other passage accompanies Meier's long citation of Milton's representation of the journey of the angel Raphael (*Paradise Lost,* V.247–287), which Kant in his lectures (likely following Meier, as Schlapp noted) referred to as "Milton's journey of the angel."[22]

e. In the *Anfangsgründe* Meier observes that Milton's representation of Jupiter's and Juno's birds gains its power from being part of *a series*—Kant would say *Progressus*—of representations in *Paradise Lost.* Parts of this extensive, intensely interconnected series in *Paradise Lost* are cited by both Meier and Kant.

22. For Schlapp's notes, see *Kants Lehre vom Genie,* pp. 337n and 177n.

f. I propose that Kant discloses his aesthetic idea and the form of his moral will in procedures of succession to the aesthetic light and shadow of this representational *Progressus*.

～

a. Contrary to the impression that Kant seems to create, his choice of "Jupiter's eagle, with the lightning in its claws, . . . and the peacock of [heaven's] stately queen [Juno]" as his major representation of aesthetic ideas in §49 is hardly offhand. Indeed, given the demanding work that Kant envisions for this representation, it was impossible that this choice could be anything but discriminated with the greatest possible care. Neither Kant nor any of his serious readers could have forgotten that in his 1785 reviews of Herder's *Ideen* he had especially ridiculed the use of a simile of "the throne of Jupiter" (and of erotic "communion"). Kant pronounced that "critics of discriminating philosophic style" must agree that such "excursions out of the area of the philosophic into the sphere of poetic language . . . conceal the corpus of thought as under a farthingale."[23] Beginning in 1785 much changed in Kant's thinking about these matters. Now, in 1790, in the *Critique of Judgment,* he chooses his own representation from the same sphere of poetic language, that is, to meet the most rigorous demands of "discriminating philosophic style." It cannot be accidental that from the infinite possibilities for such a choice he hits upon a representation of Jupiter paired with his consort. Clearly he is persuaded that he has developed a philosophical lexicon, and "style," which correlates with the characteristics of that specific representation. He is not doing public penance for his rough handling of Herder but rather, typically for Kant, learning from his opponents and finally, systematically, going beyond them.

The burden that Kant lays on the representation of Jupiter and Juno is indeed enormous. It is presented not only to explain but to perform, or achieve instantaneously, the impact of a key moment in Kant's aesthetic-moral philosophy: the emergence of the aesthetic idea. The "proper function" of the aesthetic idea, he says, is "animating the mind by opening out for it a prospect into a field of kindred representations stretching beyond its ken." The aesthetic idea, evoked by the

23. Kant, *On History,* ed. Beck, pp. 41, 45–46; *AA,* 8:57, 60–61.

Jupiter-Juno representation, must give "the imagination an incentive to spread its flight over a whole host of kindred representations that provoke more thought than admits of expression in a concept determined by words." In response to this representation, Kant is sure, "the imagination here displays a creative activity, and it puts the faculty of intellectual ideas (reason) into motion—a motion, at the instance of a representation, toward an extension of thought, that, while germane, no doubt, to the concept of the object, exceeds what can be laid hold of in that representation or clearly expressed" (§49, 5:315). Yet Kant does not spell out how his chosen representation—with its unspecified "whole host of kindred representations"—can accomplish all this. It seems inescapable to suppose that Kant expected his informed readers to be able to fill in the blanks concerning his citing of the Jupiter-Juno representation.

~

b. In 1789 Kant's initial prompting for his focus on a Jupiter representation was, as I have said, likely his own earlier ridicule of Herder's Jupiter simile. Yet when he came to place his Jupiter representation within the problematics of distinguishing originality from imitation, he could not have failed to recall, in addition, the ways in which Herder and other well-known writers specifically placed representations of Jupiter—indeed, specifically Milton's representations of Jupiter and Juno—within that problematics. In the second part of the *Kritische Wälder* (1769), Herder extensively and heatedly responded to Christian Adolph Klotz's dismissive remarks on the use of classical mythology in modern poetry. A long run of Klotz's remarks not only centered on the representation of Jupiter and Juno but included harsh criticism of Milton's incorporation of pagan mythological images into his Christian epic.[24] The question that Klotz and Herder were fighting out with considerable visibility was directly related to Meier's:[25] "Whether in a Heroic Poem Made by a Christian the Angels and the Devil Can and Must Replace the Pagan Gods?"[26] I repeat here, from

---

24. See, for example, Klotz, *Epistolæ Homericæ* (Altenburg, 1764), pp. 78–80.

25. Johann Gotthelf Lindner, *Kurzer Inbegriff der Aesthetik, Redekunst und Dichtkunst,* 2 vols. (Königsberg, 1771–72), I.227, is among those attending to Klotz's and Herder's encounters.

26. "Untersuchung der Frage: Ob in einem Heldengedichte, welches von einem

Chapter 2, Meier's remarks in that essay on the need to differentiate the originality of a modern (and Christian) poet from harmful imitation. Meier locates such originality in an act of imaginative "succession" *(nachfolgen):*

> My inquiry is into a source of many significant effects [*eine Quelle vieler wichtigen Folgen*] with which our contemporary poets might be served, insofar as they learn a manly way of succeeding the ancients [*auf eine männlichere Art den Alten nachfolgen*], as the majority of them [meaning, he says, Milton, as well as Tasso and Voltaire][27] are accustomed to do. But it will be possible to show this more meaningfully at the end of this investigation.

> One may be permitted only to put oneself in the place of a pagan, and read *Homer,* in order to be able to contemplate *Jupiter, Juno,* etc. with deference. . . . We cannot be struck with wonder by any deed of Jupiter's because we regard him and his deeds as a chimera. . . . A Christian poet proceeds artlessly, and does not achieve his goal, if he brings forward the pagan gods [*"Mars, Bellone, Jupiter, Juno"*] as did *Homer* and *Virgil.*[28]

At the end of the essay Meier tries to spell out what this activity of "succeeding"—*nachfolgen*—might be. He tells us that the modern Christian poet, who avoids mere imitation,

> succeeds [*nachfolgt*] the ancients in a rational and manly way . . . as *Milton* has sometimes done in an irreproachable way.[29]

Christen verfertiget wird, die Engel und Teufel die Stelle der heydnischen Götter vertreten können und müssen?" The essay was published in the *Critischer Versuch zur Aufnahme der Deutschen Sprache* 15 (1746): 179–200.

27. Tasso in *Jerusalem Delivered* and Voltaire in *Henriade.*

28. Meier, "Untersuchung der Frage," pp. 180 and 184, 187. I cite the essay from the reprinting in *Georg Friedrich Meier, Frühe Schriften zur ästhetischen Erziehung der Deutschen in 3 Teilen,* ed. Hans-Joachim Kertscher and Günter Schenk (Halle: Hallescher Verlag, 1999–2002), I.126–140. The page numbers are those of the 1746 printing. In Chapter 2 the German texts are given in footnotes.

29. Ibid., pp. 197–198.

Herder and Klotz were formulating their answers, in their different ways, in relation to the same Miltonic usage of Jupiter and Juno that Meier had instanced. Yet neither Herder nor Klotz applies to the considerable resources for answering such a question that Meier had made available not only in the essay that asks their question in its title but also, in the same year, in the *Anfangsgründe*.

Herder, we should note, discourses at length on this subject. Not surprisingly he seizes the opportunity to expound his relativistic historicism. It is surprising, however, that he altogether misses the possibilities of the negative poetics that is contained in Meier's exposition of "aesthetic light" and "aesthetic shadow." It is surprising because the supporting examples of Milton's poetry that Herder brings here to counter Klotz are strongly of the negating kind. Here are Herder's English citations (as he gives them) from Milton:

> ——while *universal Pan*
> Knit with the Graces and the Hours in dance
> Led on th' eternal spring. Not that fair field
> Of Enna, where Proserpin gathering flowers
> Herself a fairer flowr etc.———
> ————nor that sweet grove
> Of Daphne by Orontes, and th' inspir'd
> Castalian spring, might with this Paradise
> Of Eden strive; nor that Nyscian ile
> Girt with the river Triton etc.——[*Paradise Lost*, IV.266–276]
> ——as Jupiter
> On Juno smiles, when he impregns the clouds
> That shed May flow'rs——[*Paradise Lost*, IV.499–501]
> ——in shadier bower
> More sacred and sequester'd, though but feign'd
> Pan or Sylvanus never slept, nor Nymph
> Nor Faunus haunted. [*Paradise Lost*, IV.705–708] (*SW*, III.235–236)

Both directly in connection with these citations and later, Herder comments principally on the Jupiter and Juno passage brought also by Meier. Herder's immediate commentary on his assembly of passages does indeed begin to formulate an insight into the power of negation, and of sublimation toward higher ends, in these various verses. Yet, as I have said, he fails to apply this insight even to the beginnings of a theory of aesthetic light and shadow such as Meier had provided. (I will return to Meier's theory of aesthetic light and shadow near the end of this chapter.) I quote Herder here especially to suggest what Kant, if he needed it, would have read as additional incentive for presenting his far more advanced, systematic view of these matters. Herder comments,

> So writes Milton: his secular similes are nothing but auxiliary representations in the service of his sacred representations: he has recourse to them when words in the orbit of his religion lack the mainspring to put his idea into play at the level he wishes: and only then does his fancy wander in the magical regions of Greek poetry when he indeed satisfies our senses and now gives our soul time to collect the pictures of its youth. Being a poet [of religion], could he not do this? Just in that way he sets our spirit vibrating truly, so that, so to speak, it [our spirit] itself poetizes. Otherwise surely not as a poet of religion? What is worthier of religion than the use of such similes for its exaltation? The Bible, Jehovah Himself in the Bible, speaks in that way. (*SW*, III.236–237)[30]

> [So dichtet Milton: seine profanen Gleichnisse sind nichts als Hülfsvorstellungen zum Dienste seiner heiligen Vorstellungen: er nimmt zu ihnen seine Zuflucht, wenn Worte innerhalb dem Kreise seiner Religion nicht Triebfedern geben, seine Idee so hoch zu spielen, als er sie haben will: und nur dann irret seine Phantasie in diese Zaubergegenden der Griechischen Dichtung, wenn er schon unsre Sinne erfüllet, und jetzt der Seele Zeit läßt, die Bilder ihrer Jugend zu sammeln. Konnte er dies nicht thun, als Dichter? Eben dadurch schlägt er ja an unsern Geist, daß er gleichsam sich selbst dichte. Oder etwa nicht als Dichter der Religion? Was ist der Religion würdiger, als solche Vergleichungen zu ihrer Erhöhung? Die Bibel, ja Jehovah selbst in ihr spricht also.]

Herder emphasizes the negating force of these passages in a footnote, where he castigates Klotz for citing but not reading or understanding

30. Herder's response to Klotz about Jupiter and Juno is already well under way on pp. 208–211. Herder responds to remarks in Klotz's *Epistolæ Homericæ* as well as in his *Beytrag zur Geschichte des Geschmacks und der Kunst aus Münzen* (Altenburg, 1767). In the latter Addison is of central importance.

Milton's phrase "though but feign'd." Yet Herder takes this negative poetics no further, not with regard to Milton, nor with regard to a general theory of what makes such passages, as he there exclaims, *wie erhaben!*—"how sublime!"

~

c. In connection with Kant's choice of a representation of Jupiter's and Juno's birds, it has not been noted before that in the second volume of the *Anfangsgründe* Meier specifically cites—in Bodmer's 1742 translation—Milton's representation of the eagle of Jupiter, together with the peacock of Juno, in *Paradise Lost:*

> Zuerst gab die Natur verschiedene Zeichen, die sie in Vögel, Thiere und Luft einprägte; die Luft ward nach einer kurzen Morgenröthe plötzlich verdunkelt. Nahe vor ihren Augen schoß der Vogel Jupiters aus seinem Luftkreise herunter, und verfolgte zwey Vögel von den zierlichsten Federn. . . . Sie richteten ihre Flucht gerade nach dem östlichen Thore zu.[31]

Bodmer's translation is extremely faithful to Milton's text, except for the fact that, indeed, Bodmer and Meier—like Kant—call the eagle *Jupiter's* rather than Jove's. Here is Milton:

> Nature first gave Signs, imprest
> On Bird, Beast, Air, Air suddenly eclips'd
> After short blush of Morn; nigh in her sight
> The Bird of *Jove*, stoopt from his aery tow'r,
> Two Birds of gayest plume [i.e., peacocks] before him drove:
> . . . . .
> Direct to th' Eastern Gate was bent thir flight. (*Paradise Lost*, XI.182–190)

Even taken alone, Meier's citing of this passage is of substantial interest. It ratifies his view of a Miltonic aesthetic of light and shadow and of animation of thought *(Lebhaftigkeit der Gedanken)*, such as we have seen that Kant learned from Meier. With Kant's own sensitivity to deficited images and to Milton's sublime, he could not have failed to see how the passage is a brilliant play of paradisal light and tragic shadow. No

---

31. *Anfangsgründe aller schönen Wissenschaften*, 3 vols. (Halle, 1754–59), II.597–598.

sooner has the morning shone than it is "eclips'd" *(verdunkelt)*. But the importance of Meier's citation of this passage is greater than this. Its significance must be measured within the Miltonic progression, and the idea of such a progression, that Meier provided to Kant.

∼

d. Before returning to this passage from Book XI and to its place within its progression stretching the length of *Paradise Lost,* we must register the special quality of attention that Kant brought to Meier's *Anfangsgründe* at the time he was completing the *Critique of Judgment.* The extent and depth of that attention is well seen in Kant's account of aesthetic ideas in §49, where he attends closely to Meier's explanation of "energetic concepts" *(nachdrückliche Begriffe)* and of the "attention" *(Achtung)* one "must give them." (I cited phrases from this explanation in Chapter 2.) Meier writes as follows shortly after his long citation of what Kant calls "Milton's journey of the angel":

> All concepts that contain much, and on that account are to be contemplated as a whole consisting of many parts, are called *energetic concepts* (conceptus praegnantes) and to that heading also belong those concepts (conceptus complexi) that are composed of a principal concept and secondary concepts. *The principal concepts* are those which command the most attention, the remaining being called *the secondary concepts.* All energetic concepts are vital because they contain a great multiplicity. . . . Every luminous concept conjointly spreads its light over those concepts which are connected to it. . . . In that they at the same time represent a great deal to us, they afford us a broader prospect. And those in particular that contain many secondary concepts besides the principal concept represent, as it were, the principal concept proximately and the secondary concepts distantly, which produces in the soul an extraordinarily agreeable prospect. (*Anfangsgründe,* I.270–271)[32]

> [Alle Begriffe, die vieles in sich enthalten, und also als ein Ganzes zu betrachten sind, welches aus vielen Theilen besteht, heissen *nachdrückliche Begriffe* (conceptus praegnantes) und es gehören hieher

32. Schlapp, *Kants Lehre vom Genie,* p. 337, calls attention to this passage in Meier but does not discuss its possible significance or ramifications for Kant.

auch diejenigen, welche aus einem Hauptbegriffe und aus Nebenbe-
griffen zusammengesetzt sind (conceptus complexi). *Die Hauptbegriffe*
sind diejenigen Begriffe in einem andern, auf welche man am meis-
ten Achtung geben muß, die übrigen heissen *die Nebenbegriffe.* Alle
nachdrückliche Begriffe sind lebhaft, weil sie eine grosse Mannigfaltig-
keit enthalten. . . . Ein jeder heller Begriff [breitet] sein Licht zugleich
über diejenigen aus . . . , welche mit ihm verbunden werden. . . . Indem
sie uns vieles mit einemmale vorstellen, so geben sie uns eine weitere
Aussicht. Und diejenigen insonderheit, welche ausser dem Hauptbe-
griffe viele Nebenbegriffe enthalten, stellen uns gleichsam den ersten
in der Nähe vor, und die letztern von ferne, welches der Seele einen
ungemein angenehmen Prospect verursacht.]

In the famous paragraph of §49 in which Kant discusses the represen-
tation of Jupiter's and Juno's birds, he writes,

Those forms which do not constitute the presentation of a given con-
cept itself, but which, as secondary representations of the imagination,
express the successions [series, *Folgen*] connected with it, and its kin-
ship with other concepts, are called (aesthetic) symbols [emblems,
Attribute][33] of an object, the concept of which, as an idea of reason, can-
not be adequately presented. In this way Jupiter's eagle, with the light-
ning in its claws, is a symbol [*Attribut*] of the mighty king of heaven,
and the peacock of its stately queen. They do not, like *logical attributes,*
represent what lies in our concept of the sublimity and majesty of cre-
ation, but rather something else—something that gives the imagina-
tion an incentive to spread its flight over a whole host of kindred repre-
sentations that provoke more thought than admits of expression in a
concept determined by words. They furnish an *aesthetic idea,* which
serves the above rational idea as a substitute for logical presentation,
but with the proper function, however, of animating the mind by open-
ing out for it a prospect into a field of kindred representations stretch-

33. Meredith gives "derivatives connected with it" for *die damit verknüpften Folgen*
and "*attributes*" for *Attribute.* My translations of these words are meant to bring out the
connections between "expressing [*ausdrücken*] the successions [series, *Folgen*]" and
(aesthetic) special symbols [Fr. *Attribute,* emblems] of an object in the *Nachfolge.* In
5:312, just two pages before the usage of *Attribute* in §49, it is clear that the term
makes more sense in its meaning as "symbol" than as mere "attributes."

ing beyond its ken. But it is not alone in the arts of painting or sculpture, where the name of attribute is customarily employed, that fine art acts in this way; poetry and rhetoric also derive the soul that animates their works wholly from the aesthetic symbols [*ästhetischen Attributen*] of the objects—symbols which go hand in hand with the logical, and give the imagination an impetus to bring more thought into play in the matter, though in an undeveloped manner, than allows of being brought within the embrace of a concept, or, therefore, of being definitely formulated in language.—For the sake of brevity I must confine myself to a few examples only. When the great king expresses himself in one of his poems by saying. . . . (5:315; underlining added)

[Man nennt diejenigen Formen, welche nicht die Darstellung eines gegebenen Begriffs selber ausmachen, sondern nur als Nebenvorstellungen der Einbildungskraft die damit verknüpften Folgen und die Verwandtschaft desselben mit andern ausdrücken, *Attribute* (ästhetische) eines Gegenstandes, dessen Begriff als Vernunftidee nicht adäquat dargestellt werden kann. So ist <u>der Adler Jupiters mit dem Blitze in den Klauen ein Attribut des mächtigen Himmelskönigs und der Pfau der prächtigen Himmelskönigin.</u> Sie stellen nicht wie die *logischen Attribute* das, was in unsern Begriffen von der Erhabenheit und Majestät der Schöpfung liegt, sondern etwas anderes vor, was der Einbildungskraft Anlaß giebt, sich über eine Menge von verwandten Vorstellungen zu verbreiten, die mehr denken lassen, als man in einem durch Worte bestimmten Begriff ausdrücken kann; und geben eine *ästhetische Idee,* die jener Vernunftidee statt logischer Darstellung dient, eigentlich aber um das Gemüth zu beleben, indem sie ihm die Aussicht in ein unabsehliches Feld verwandter Vorstellungen eröffnet. Die schöne Kunst aber thut dieses nicht allein in der Malerei oder Bildhauerkunst (wo der Namen der Attribute gewöhnlich gebraucht wird); sondern die Dichtkunst und Beredsamkeit nehmen den Geist, der ihre Werke belebt, auch lediglich von den ästhetischen Attributen der Gegenstände her, welche den logischen zu Seite gehen und der Einbildungskraft einen Schwung geben, mehr dabei, obzwar auf unentwickelte Art, zu denken, als sich in einem Begriffe, mithin in einem bestimmten Sprachausdrucke zusammenfassen läßt.—Ich muß mich der Kürze wegen nur auf wenige Beispiele einschränken.

> Wenn der große König sich in einem seiner Gedichte so ausdrückt:
> . . .] (underlining added)

Kant's numerous and obvious verbal echoes of Meier's language are sufficient to make us aware that Kant likely had Meier's text before him as he wrote this passage of §49. The core of Kant's presentation of the aesthetic idea is taken from the core of Meier's passage: "All energetic concepts are vital because they contain a great multiplicity. . . . And then every luminous concept conjointly spreads its light over those concepts which are bound up with it. . . . In that they all at once represent a great deal to us, they afford us a broad prospect." At the very center of this core are the "kindred" (or "secondary") embodied concepts or representations—Meier's *Nebenbegriffen* or Kant's *Nebenvorstellungen*—that constitute the great multiplicity and open up the broad prospect. We have seen that Kant was looking closely at other, closely related pages of the *Anfangsgründe*. Using Milton's poetry, these other pages point to the theory of that multiplicity of kindred representations and provide Miltonic exemplifications of their progression, not least with regard to Milton's representation of Jupiter's and Juno's birds, to which I now return.

～

e. Meier is profoundly aware that Milton's signifying of the expulsion (of the pair of peacocks) at the Eastern Gate and, simultaneously, the complex dissension between the sexes (Jupiter's eagle versus Juno's peacock) is a symbolic drama that is intensified by compression and juxtaposition. Indeed, Meier directly calls attention to this compression, saying, "The reader must read what comes before and what comes after to become aware of how charming and melancholy these portents are [Der Leser muß das vorhergehende und nachfolgende lesen, wenn er gewahr werden will, wie reitzend und wehmüthig diese Omina sind]" (*Anfangsgründe*, II.598). For "what comes before," Meier had himself earlier cited at length, from Book IV, Milton's description of the lovemaking of Adam and Eve, with its central simile of Jupiter and Juno (cited also by Herder). Here, amidst Eve's and Adam's shared passion, the simile tells of Jupiter's "superior love," and with it the germ of a problematic sexuality based on dominance and submissiveness. What is already problematic here subtly foreshadows Jupiter's raptorial eagle swooping down on, and *driving away,* Juno's birds after the fall:

> Unsre algemeine Mutter sagte so, und lehnte sich mit Augen eines ehelichen untadelbaren Reitzes und einer huldreichen Ergebenheit an unsren ersten Vater, sie umhalfete ihn halb, und halb fiel ihre aufschwellende Brust auf die seine, nackend, ausgenommen daß das fliessende Gold ihrer losgebundenen Haare sie verhüllete. Ihre Schönheit und ihm ergebene Pracht gebaren eine innerliche Wullust [*sic*] bey ihm, er lachte sie mit einer viel grössern Liebe an, als Jupiter die Juno anlächelt, wenn er die Wolken schwanger macht, welche die Mäyblumen ausstreuen, und küßte ihre keuschen Lippen mit einem reinen Kusse. (*Anfangsgründe,* I.313–314)

In Milton these are the verses:

> So spake our general Mother, and with eyes
> Of conjugal attraction unreprov'd,
> And meek surrender, half imbracing lean'd
> On our first Father, half her swelling Breast
> Naked met his under the flowing Gold
> Of her loose tresses hid: he in delight
> Both of her Beauty and submissive Charms
> Smil'd with superior Love, as *Jupiter*
> On *Juno* smiles, when he impregns the Clouds
> That shed *May* Flowers; and press'd her Matron lip
> With kisses pure. (*Paradise Lost,* IV.492–502)

Meier's reference point for "what comes after" the "Bird of *Jove*" that drives the pair of peacocks "direct to th' Eastern Gate" is obviously the scene of expulsion in Book XII, in which the winged angel of the Lord now does the office of the bird of Jove:

> In either hand the hast'ning Angel caught
> Our ling'ring Parents, and to th' Eastern Gate
> Led them direct, and down the Cliff as fast
> To the subjected Plain, then disappear'd. (637–640)

Even the implicit lightning bolts in the claws of Jove's eagle emerge here in transformed guise:

> They looking back, all th' Eastern side beheld
> Of Paradise, so late thir happy seat,
> Wav'd over by that flaming Brand, the Gate
> With dreadful Faces throng'd, and fiery Arms. (XII.641–644)

We may feel that these passages of *before* and *after* give us quite enough of what is painfully "charming and melancholy" in the human condition. This Miltonic progression, however, is built from far more than these three passages. The progression is constructed entirely of portents *(Omina)* or prolepses, which all contain elements of foreboding that are yet not entirely despairing. This includes the final scene of expulsion which itself portends the future of a humanity that will be excluded from the possibility of perfect happiness yet can redeem human love all the same. At whatever point we enter this progression in *Paradise Lost,* we encounter the harmony and/or disharmony of the "two great Sexes [that] animate the World" (VIII.151).

We see more evidence of the multiplicity of this progression in the passage from Book V that Kant calls "Milton's journey of the angel" and that Meier fully cites before his excursus quoted above. I repeat part of my earlier quotation from Kant to emphasize, now, how complementary and continuous are Meier's idea of the "great multiplicity" of the progression and Kant's exposition of the experience of "boundless multiplicity" that produces the "wealth of thought" in the aesthetic idea:

> *Poetry* (which owes its origin almost entirely to genius and is least willing to be led by precepts or example) holds the first rank among all the arts. It expands the mind by giving freedom to the imagination and by offering, from among the <u>boundless multiplicity</u> of possible forms accordant with a given concept, to whose bounds it is restricted, that one which couples with the presentation of the concept <u>a wealth of thought</u> [*Gedankenfülle*] to which no verbal expression is completely adequate, . . . <u>thus rising aesthetically to ideas</u> [*sich also ästhetisch zu Ideen erhebt*]. (5:326; underlining added)

With regard to my itemizations from Milton's boundless multiplicity of representations in the progression to and from Jupiter's and Juno's birds, it is not necessary to assume that Kant registered all of the links that I am spelling out here. At the same time, however, it is clear that Meier's as well as Kant's responses to any part of this Miltonic progression are framed by, and derive their depth from, awareness of the larger Miltonic phenomenon of proliferating progression. This is the métier of interconnected, radiating representation in *Paradise Lost* as a whole. Milton's density and range of poetic interconnection are so great that it is a rare reader who is equipped to take them in fully.[34] Yet it is obvious that Meier and Kant saw at least a considerable part of the endless multiplicity and continuity of interconnection that is characteristic of Milton's genius. Milton's Jupiter-Juno progression is a premier case of that métier. In *Paradise Lost* a vast multiplicity of associations (including the feminine and masculine character of the brooding, impregnating dove-like Holy Spirit: I.17–22) is one way or another linked to the harmony or the disharmony of male and female, Jupiter and Juno, eagle and peacock (itself a masculine symbol adopted by the female), sun and moon. This is the Miltonic resonating chamber that gives meaning to Kant's saying that the aesthetic idea, evoked by the Jupiter and Juno representations, must give "the imagination an in-

34. Here is another instance—not necessarily noticed by either Meier or Kant—of the overwhelming force of continuity that drives Milton's progression, such that, I suggest, a sensitive reader's conscious or unconscious mind is never far from contact with the force field of this continuity. In the verses of Book V that Kant cites, Milton anticipates the Jovian eagle's stooping "from his aery tow'r" (XI.185) to portend the tragic expulsion. In this passage Raphael is described on his journey to give Adam and Eve the tools that they need to be able to ward off that expulsion:

> Down thither prone in flight
> He speeds, and through the vast Ethereal Sky
> Sails between worlds and worlds, with steady wing
> Now on the polar winds, then with quick Fan
> Winnows the buxom Air; till within soar
> Of Tow'ring Eagles . . . he flies. (V.266–274; underlining added)

An eagle's "tower" is its spiral upward flight. In his downward flight the angel has reached this highest point that eagles reach. This, then, is a portent of a portent. It is precisely from this point (described in Book V) that the expulsion (described in Book XII) will begin in the Omina of Jupiter's eagle stooping "from his aery tow'r" and driving Juno's peacocks before him (described in Book XI).

centive to spread its flight over a whole host of kindred representations."

We have seen evidence that Kant was directly aware of at least one other link in the Miltonic progression to and from Jupiter's and Juno's birds. This is the passage from the angel's response to Adam, in Book VIII, cited by Kant in his Elsner lecture (and in his letter to Schiller):

> What if that light
> Sent from [Earth] through the wide transpicuous air,
> To the terrestrial Moon be as a Star
> Enlight'ning her by Day, as she by Night
> This Earth? reciprocal, if Land be there,
> Fields and Inhabitants: . . .
> . . . ; and other Suns perhaps
> With thir attendant Moons thou wilt descry
> Communicating Male and Female Light,
> Which two great Sexes animate the World,
> Stor'd in each Orb perhaps. (140–152)

In Book I Milton gives us a simile of the Sun's eclipse, which we can take as the beginning of the effectively endless *Progressus* that both Meier and Kant follow. As a prolepsis or portent of Adam and Eve's fall, Milton describes fallen Satan

> ruin'd, and th' excess
> of Glory obscur'd: As when the Sun new ris'n
> Looks through the Horizontal misty Air
> Shorn of his Beams, or from behind the Moon
> In dim Eclipse disastrous twilight sheds. (593–597)

If we lay the Jupiter and Juno passage of Book XI side by side with this, it is obvious that what comes later in this progression proceeds from these earlier verses:

> Nature first gave Signs, imprest
> On Bird, Beast, Air, Air suddenly eclips'd
> After short blush of Morn; nigh in her sight

> The Bird of *Jove*, stoopt from his aery tow'r,
> Two Birds of gayest plume before him drove:
>
> . . . . .
>
> Direct to th' Eastern Gate was bent thir flight. (182–190)

The "bird of Jove" passage in Book XI recalls from Book I the "Air" as well as the "Sun" in "Eclipse" immediately after it is "new ris'n." That is, these phrases in Book I are precise equivalents of "Air suddenly eclips'd / After short blush of Morn" in Book XI. The "disastrous twilight" or double light of dis-asters (stars that no longer propagate their light in creative unity) and the Sun hidden by the Moon are the total antithesis of the harmonious condition described by Milton (and cited by Kant) in Book VIII, that is, the angel's description of the sun and moon and "two great Sexes [that] animate the World." Thus the progression between the passages in Books I and XI also explains how the passage in Book VIII is an integral part of the same sustained progression. In the passage of Book VIII the angel suggests that the harmony of "Male and Female Light," as of the "two great Sexes" that "animate the World," has not yet been disrupted (140–152). In the passage cited by Meier from Book XI, the bird of Jove is seen *driving* away the peacock, sacred to Juno, in a state of a "disastrous twilight" where the double (twi-) light of male and female have been put internally asunder. This series of passages by no means exhausts this progression and its multiplicity of interconnections.[35] Yet once we have grasped the

35. In their order of appearance in *Paradise Lost,* the chief passages in the Miltonic progression to which both Meier and Kant paid special attention are the following: I.593–597, IV.492–502, V.266–274, VIII.140–152, XI.182–190, and XII.637–644. Although the passages from Books I and XII are not mentioned explicitly by either Meier or Kant, the direct linkage of these passages with the passage from Book XI is obvious to any reader of *Paradise Lost* whose interest is, as Meier puts it, to see "what comes before and after" that passage. In addition, it is worth mentioning a few more instances of this progression in which the element of light and shadow is especially vivid: Milton repeatedly draws his picture of Satan's fallen imagination as a projection of totalitarian egotism on the sun's (versus the moon's) role in the heavens and even uses this in Satan's double temptations (first in dream, then in waking) of Eve: see IV.27–35, V.41–47, IX.602–608. (I have commented on Milton's representation of this aspect of Satan's imagination in *The Dividing Muse: Images of Sacred Disjunction in*

continuity of this progression in Milton's poetry, we can begin to understand how Kant's encounter of a representation of the birds of Jupiter and Juno, cited by Meier specifically within this progression of aesthetic light and shadow—and of eclipse of aesthetic light and shadow—could serve as the trigger for Kant's procedure of succession.

⁓

f. In 1792–93 Kant's citation of the verses from *Paradise Lost,* VIII.140–152 within his Miltonic exposition of aesthetic ideas is an intense backward glance at an event of the deepest significance for his moral life: namely, the disclosure, *in concreto,* of his aesthetic idea and his moral will in the procedure of succession. Kant here recalls, perhaps even summons anew, the specific procedure of succession in §49 that was in that instance initiated by Milton's representation of Jupiter's eagle and Juno's peacock within that same progression. As we have seen repeatedly, the entirety of this progression in *Paradise Lost* is either an anticipation or a confirmation of the idea in Book VIII that the "two great Sexes animate the World" by harmoniously supplying the energy of aesthetic light and shadow. But what, more precisely, is this energy—or animation or impetus *(Schwung)*—of aesthetic light and shadow?

⁓

We can clarify what aesthetic light and shadow represent for Kant by revisiting his extensive concurrence with, but also decisive divergence from, Meier's closely related views. It is evident that at the moment of Kant's composition of §49 of the third *Critique,* Meier was one of the two central figures (the other being Herder) in the constellation of German Miltonism to whom Kant was most closely attending. At this

---

Milton's Poetry [New Haven: Yale University Press, 1985], pp. 102–103.) In tandem, when in Book VIII Adam "to the Nuptial Bow'r" leads Eve "blushing like the Morn," we hear that the "happy [i.e., favorable] Constellations on that hour / Shed thir selectest influence" (VIII.510–513), while after the fall and the falling out of Adam and Eve, the Moon and other heavenly bodies are "taught . . . Thir influence malignant when to show'r, / Which of them rising with the Sun, or falling, / Should prove tempestuous" (X.656–664). With Kant's deep interest in astronomy and constellations, the continuity of these details would probably have been apparent in a way that escapes most of us. For a taste of Kant's astronomical preoccupations that parallel some of Milton's (including what Kant calls "unending progression"), see Kant's *Universal Natural History and Theory of the Heavens, AA,* 1:256 and his n. 19.

moment in Kant's engagement with, or following of, Meier, he leapt to an entirely new understanding of the elements that Meier had foregrounded: namely, aesthetic light and shadow, Miltonic "energetic ideas," and Milton's representation of Jupiter and Juno in its progression.

Meier's explanation of "aesthetic shadow" is the meaningful heart of his otherwise mechanical exposition of "aesthetic light" and of his seemingly superficial requirement that "in an aesthetic construction light and shadow must succeed one another." He explains that "**aesthetic shadow** *(umbra æsthetica)*" is that which is achieved in "praiseworthy privation [*lobenswürdigen Mangel*] as distinct from the blameable kind." He adds that aesthetic shadow is "a place of rest where the spirit recuperates and rallies its powers in order to contemplate the subsequent brighter elements all the better" (*Anfangsgründe*, I.258, 264–265).

The contours of the Kantian sublime correspond suggestively to Meier's account. We see this in the phenomenon of a "deprivation" *(Beraubung)* (5:269) that Kant derives from the basic elements of a "check to the vital forces" and a subsequent "discharge [of energy] all the more powerful" (5:245). Yet Kant's replacement of an encounter with "privation" *(Mangel)* with the act of creating a "deprivation" *(Beraubung)* signals a sharp turn in a completely different direction. Meier highlights the "contemplation" of an observed, already represented "privation" that is found to be "praiseworthy" because it functions as an interval of rest for recuperating powers of appreciating "the subsequent brighter elements" of the representation. Meier's interest in privation, we may say, is passive; Kant's active. Kant's interest is not in contemplation of an existing representation, but in the mind's act of representation that is itself the form of moral will. (At least in the Miltonic case, the precedent procedure of succession pursues its own active *Beraubung*.) As in other instances of the Kantian procedure of succession, Kant exits the apparent circularity in this moral act of creating the moral will to act. This is achieved in the transfer from heteronomous to autonomous procedures of succession.

Kant's representation is of a procedure and disclosure of the moral will: of the "imagination by its own act depriving itself of its freedom [the *Beraubung der Freiheit der Einbildungskraft durch sie selbst*] . . . in the interest of inner freedom." Ultimately this representation is of the created form of that procedure, which, in its inner or autonomous manifestation, is the moral will acting in accord with the form of its maxim. In the mind's inner representation of this form the mind "gains an extension and a might greater than that which it sacrifices. . . . It is only through sacrifices that this might makes itself known to us aesthetically . . . and this involves a deprivation . . . though in the interests of inner freedom—whilst in turn it reveals in us an unfathomable depth of this supersensible faculty, the consequences of which extend beyond reach of the eye of sense [*ins Unabsehliche*]" (5:269–271). Kant explains that, as in the poetry that the mind follows actively in succession, the function of the aesthetic idea created by the sublime is "animating the mind [*das Gemüth zu beleben*] by opening out for it a prospect into a field of kindred representations stretching beyond its ken." This gives the imagination an "impetus" or *Schwung* (§49, 5:315) toward the supersensible. Kant succeeds to Milton's precedent procedure of aesthetic light and shadow in order to achieve this impetus. In *Paradise Lost* the Fall represents the loss of the harmony of alternate deprivations that are coordinated between the light and shadow of sun and moon, moon and sun, male and female, female and male. In the Kantian schema of this Miltonic succession, we transfer (following Milton) to inner sight and moral feeling. Here, too, Milton's poetry provides Kant with his "analogon veritatis."[36] It is possible that, in the abstract, Kant as well as Milton initially identify the empirical with the female and the *a priori* with the male. Yet the complementarity between the sexes that Milton and Kant emphasize in the "Male and Female Light" that "animate the World" pictures a shared mind of humanity that equally contains both genders. Whereas Herder portioned out the "masculine" muse to Milton and "the more delicate muse" to Klopstock (*SW,* XVIII.118), Kant sees a combination and mixing *(vermischen)* of male and female in Milton's muse of aesthetic light and shadow.

The momentousness of Kant's turn to the *animation of the mind* by its succession to aesthetic light and shadow is highlighted by his difference from Hume in citing Milton's verses on "Male and Female Light." Hume had written, "The two great Sexes of Male and Female, says *Mil-*

36. The phrase, which I discussed in Chapter 2, is from Kant's 1779 anthropology lecture (Marburg Kant Archiv, *Brauer,* 54).

ton, animate the World."³⁷ Kant's citation of Milton's verses seems to forget the phrase "animate the World," yet his citation and use of this passage of Milton actually engage with this phrase far more deeply than does Hume. Kant's point—echoing very much the same point in §49 of the third *Critique* about the representation of Jupiter and Juno—is that the poet's representation of the heavenly constellation (deployed "to unknown ends") and the reader's response (drawing the mind "into an immeasurable prospect") together animate "the mind." Through this animated mind, in Kant's view, the animated world makes its appearance. The Miltonic representations to which Kant applies thus give the mind "a continuous impetus" or set it "in continuous motion" *(in einen continuierlichen Schwung)* in the aesthetic idea.

It would be a mistake to think that Kant is here on the verge of propounding a genetic principle, of mind and world, of the kind that he had rejected in Herder. The "impetus" or force that, Kant says, animates the mind, and that he traces in a representation of Jupiter and Juno ("king" and "queen"), and in the mixing of male and female light within the mind, is pointedly different from Herder's idea of a self-generating *Kraft,* power, also represented in an erotic image of Jupiter's power. For Kant, poetic or any other images have meaning only when they become part of the mind's representational processing. Thus, starting with the superficial sameness of theme in Jupiter images of the kind that Herder and Kant (and others) employ, Kant builds a world of specified difference. Herder's Jupiter image, like his account of *Kraft,* led to his exposition of "The Genetic [Originating] Power" *(Die genetische Kraft),* which is the topic of section 4 of the seventh book of the *Ideen.* Kant duly notes this "genetic power" in his reviews.³⁸ Beiser observes that, for Kant, Herder's idea of "organic power" had nothing more than "pseudo-scientific status."³⁹ We should add that in

37. David Hume, *The Natural History of Religion,* p. 193.

38. Kant, "Reviews of Herder's *Ideas for a Philosophy of the History of Mankind,*" trans. Anchor, in Kant, *On History,* ed. Beck, pp. 44, 47.

39. Frederick C. Beiser, *The Fate of Reason: German Philosophy from Kant to Fichte* (Cambridge, Mass.: Harvard University Press, 1987), p. 156. My difference from Beiser's views of Kant and Herder is especially with regard to the relation of philosophy to literature. Beiser writes, "Kant would not dispute Herder's claim . . . that the best understanding of life is to be found in literature. . . . But, in Kant's eyes, we can-

the *Critique of Pure Reason* Kant analyzed at length the unprovability of just such a concept of *"fundamental power" (Grundkraft)* (A647–652/ B675–680).[40] In the *Critique of Judgment* he does not contradict that analysis even if, beginning in 1785, he significantly adopted Herder's advocacy of a necessary partnership between philosophy and poetry. Kant's way of locating poetry within the mind's procedures of succession gives us his conception of that working partnership. In his representation of Jupiter and Juno he traces the emergence of form within the procedure of succession of the aesthetic idea. He traces this form in the autonomous procedure of succession that has been prepared by the isomorphic heteronomous procedure of succession to Milton's *Progressus* of aesthetic light and shadow. In this mere form, which is equivalent or perhaps identical to the mere form of a law or the form of a moral will, the actualization of freedom takes place.

We have repeatedly seen (most extensively in Chapter 4) that Kant attaches a special significance to the role of form in the disclosure of moral will. Yet we, like Kant, do not cease to be amazed by this vital power of mere form—that is, either when we meet it in Kant's explanations or when we encounter it in our own everyday experience. I recall here what he says about one manifestation of such form:

> The will is thought as independent of empirical conditions and hence, as a pure will, as determined *by the mere form of law,* and this determining ground is regarded as the supreme condition of all maxims. The thing is strange enough, and has nothing like it in all the rest of our practical cognition. (*CPrR,* 5:31)

When we keep in mind the many points of parallelism between the procedure of succession (not least, succession to poetry of a certain

---

not do good natural science and good literature at the same time. It is the fatal flaw of Herder's philosophy that it tries to do both" (p. 158). Kant, we can see, found and followed a way in which philosophy and poetry become parts of the same activity.

40. For Kant the weakness of this idea is the apt illustration of the fact that "the hypothetical employment of reason, based upon ideas viewed as problematic concepts, is not, properly speaking, *constitutive,* that is, it is not of such a character that, judging in all strictness, we can regard as proving the truth of the universal rule which we have adopted as hypothesis. For how are we to know all the possible consequences which, as actually following from the adopted principle, *prove* its universality?" (A647, B675)

kind) and the procedure of the categorical imperative, we see how similar indeed, perhaps even identical, are the form of the aesthetic idea and the form of the law. In experiencing this parallelism, we attain to accustomed astonishment at the indispensable importance of something as merely formal as poetry of a certain kind. It follows that in the Kantian view we require such poetry in our lives in order to attain moral personality.

∼

By the time Kant reached §49 of the *Critique of Judgment,* he had traveled a long road from the insight that he had set out in the *Critique of Pure Reason:* "There . . . exists a relation and connection between reality and negation ['cessation in nothingness (=0=*negatio*)'], or rather a transition from the one to the other, which makes every reality representable as a quantum. The schema of a reality, as the quantity of something in so far as it fills time, is just this continuous and uniform production of that reality in time as we successively descend from a sensation which has a certain degree to its vanishing point, or progressively ascend from its negation to some magnitude of it" (A143/B182–183). This journey was enabled by his seeing that *poetry*'s—specifically, Milton's—representation of aesthetic light is a successive flaring out of *energeia* in an endless *Progressus.* Energy of this kind is represented in the continuous oscillation (descent and ascent) between light and shadow, between "reality" that is sensory content and "negation" of that sensory content. Exemplary form emerges from the relation, in oscillation, between that representation of reality and its negation. For Kant this aesthetic light and shadow are at the heart of the "aesthetic ideas" that in the Elsner lecture he explicitly identifies as Miltonic. In these ways Kant, following Milton's light and Milton's aesthetic idea, represents the procedure of succession to an infinite progression of representations, each of which represents negation within representation.

Kant was continually engaged with the constellation of German Miltonism, yet his achievement is unique within that constellation. He alone had the synthesizing power to see how Milton's representation of Jupiter's eagle and Juno's peacock was related to a productive, negative poetics in the procedure of succession. With Kant, and with Milton, we see the birds of Jupiter and Juno in their lightning and accompanying shadow, all the while hovering dangerously at the edge of eclipse. In the Kantian sublime manifold we observe the multitude of representations collocated here, their endless prospect, and the impetus of the animated mind that they engender. Kant would perhaps have considered it otiose, or inevitably enervating to his own and Milton's intensity of impact, to detail how this multiplex representation works concretely. What Kant sees dynamically is, among other things, occasioned by the metonymy of lightning that is the proliferating sign of the mind's transfer to *a priori* sublimity. This is at least part of what he means when he speaks of the "sublimity" that is not in nature "but rather" somewhere else, namely, in what he calls the mind's self-reflexive "something else": "Something that gives the imagination an incentive to spread its flight over a whole host of kindred representations that provoke more thought than admits of expression in a concept determined by words. They furnish an *aesthetic idea*" (5:315).[41] A densely populated, immensely powerful progression is telescoped here. The lightning bolts of retribution—in this configuration, also of desire and creativity—appear like claws of light against the darkness. The claws are the metonymic representation of the eagle. The eagle and the peacock are the symbolic representations of Jupiter and Juno. Jupiter and Juno are the mythic representations of heaven's king and queen. Heaven's king and queen are the periphrastic representation of God's creative presence in being. And in attempting to imagine God, necessarily as a representation of the invisible and ineffable, the human imagination gives out.[42] This, or something very like it, is a characteristic Miltonic and Kantian succession procedure constituting the aesthetic idea in its transferential complexity. This density is characteristic of Milton's poetry, especially in imbricating light with deep shadow and thereby constituting a kind of representation that shows its own inadequacy as representation. The verses of the "great king" and of Withof are strictly limited in poetic-philosophical value. Yet they, too, can appear to serve Kant's purpose because they exemplify,

41. Strictly speaking there is no equivalent to "its flight" in Kant's German. Whether Kant meant to continue the eagle imagery in his description of the mind responding to that imagery is an open question.

42. Meredith may obscure this effect by adding commas around "with the lightning in its claws," thus implying two separate images, while Kant's continuous German phrase allows an easier flow of metonymy from claw-lightning to Jupiter's bird: "der Adler Jupiters mit dem Blitze in den Klauen."

in a small way, the aesthetic light that Milton's poetry gigantically represents as exemplary genius.[43] The common denominator of Kant's examples of aesthetic ideas is the sublime representation of aesthetic light and aesthetic shadow.

Far more, however, than a few poignant verses (of Friedrich or Withof) is required for a succession procedure of Kant's kind. In fact, what such a succession procedure requires, and what Kant details in §49, are all the chief elements of the manifold that constitutes Milton's poetry. Guarded though he remains, Kant's following of Milton's unique representation of the commonplaces of Jupiter's eagle and Juno's peacock fulfills Kant's need to incorporate into his present "wealth of thoughts" the exemplary originality which only Milton's poetry both exemplifies and makes accessible to him. This (or something virtually identical with this) must be the case for Kant, in other words, in his present philosophical enactment of the procedure of succession. All the elements of §49 are Miltonic segments of the Miltonic succession procedure that Kant initiates with the representation of "Jupiter's eagle, with the lightning in its claws, . . . and the peacock of [heaven's]

43. A couple of bibliographical observations can be made here. It has not been noted before that Kant probably chose this one verse of Withof's because, in addition to filling the bill of verse (by a poet with no intellectual preeminence that could raise questions about heteronomous influence on Kant) on the dual subject of light and morality, it was the only verse (especially the simile that Kant expounds) that Mendelssohn had marked for praise in the course of a twenty-page review of Withof's *Aufmunterungen in moralischen Gedichten* (1755). Mendelssohn's review appeared in *Bibliothek der schönen Wissenschaften und der freyen Künste* 1 (1757): 86–106. On page 95 he exclaims, "What a great thought lies in the following description! [Welch ein großer Gedanke liegt in folgender Beschreibung!]," before quoting the verse quoted by Kant and the two preceding verses. About the verse quoted by Kant, Mendelssohn then adds, "The expression *die Sonne quoll* [the sun streamed forth] is hard and strange; only the following splendid simile [i.e., "as out of virtue rises peace"] makes good on this small defect [Der Ausdruck, *die Sonne quoll*, ist hart und ungewöhnlich; allein das folgende vortreffliche Gleichniß machet diesen kleinen Fehler wieder gut]". Incidentally, in the recent Cambridge edition of Kant's *Critique of the Power of Judgment,* p. 383, n45, the editors say that Kant misquoted Withof. Quoting from Withof's *Sinnlichen Ergötzungen* (Leipzig, 1782), they write, "Properly quoted, the line is 'The sun streamed forth, as tranquility flows from goodness' *(Die Sonne quoll hervor, wie Ruh' aus Güte quillt).*" But Mendelssohn and Kant both accurately quoted the line as it appears in the 1755 edition of Withof's *Aufmunterungen in moralischen Gedichten:* "Die Sonne quoll hervor, wie Ruh aus Tugend [virtue] quillt."

stately queen [Juno]." At this moment of finding the crowning touch of the *Critique of Judgment,* Kant gives us, in succession, the light and shadow of Milton's sublime—and of Milton's genius. This procedure of succession gives Kant access to the aesthetic idea and its transfer— and to his own experience of the sublime and his own genius. He was almost willing to acknowledge this provenience, or, better, this partnership, in his anthropology lecture two years later. The work of poetry and philosophy—and of geniuses in both realms—is seamlessly continuous here. Arranged as one effectively endless line of succession, these are the "sources," as Kant terms them, which have made possible the aesthetic light and aesthetic shadow of his procedure of succession. This presentation of a heteronomous procedure of succession discloses to him his autonomous and *a priori* procedure of succession as well as his freedom and moral feeling. Only lightning of this kind, this flash of formal symmetries, can disclose his moral reason.

Conclusion

Constellation, Succession, and Kantian Poetry

A final if still provisional reflection is in order here on the relation, and the difference, between constellation and succession, at least between Kant's engagement with the constellation of German Miltonism and Kant's Miltonic procedure of succession. Taking into account the various elements of these phenomena that we have seen, this reflection yields the inference that Kant's idea of poetry—preeminently represented by Milton's poetry—is grounded in the *a priori*.

In the foregoing chapters we have repeatedly been put on the track of Kant's procedures of succession to Milton's poetry by first following out Kant's embeddedness in the constellation of German Miltonism. This method of investigation is mandated by Kant's own placements of Miltonic succession. We have seen this most recently in the paragraph of §49 of the *Critique of Judgment* in which Kant explicates his chosen representation of aesthetic ideas (5:315). That paragraph is constructed from (a) opening and closing comments that he derives directly from comments of G. F. Meier and (b) Kant's centrally placed representation of a succession to Milton's *Progressus* (i.e., of Jupiter's and Juno's birds), which generates the aesthetic idea. In composing this paragraph Kant has in immediate view particular pages of Meier's *Anfangsgründe;* and, considering Kant's several foci here, it is impossible to imagine that he was not recalling, as well, Meier's emphases on the greatness of Milton's poetry, on "clarity" and aesthetic light and shadow, on the animation of the mind by energetic concepts, and on the concept of the procedure of succession itself (including even Meier's preoccupation with Matthew's parable of the talents as a para-

301

digm of *Nachfolge* or, indeed, what he has to say about representing Jupiter and Juno in general or about Milton's representations of Jupiter and Juno specifically, even in their *Progressus*). Kant no doubt encountered Meier's highlightings close to the organizing center of his experience of the constellation of German Miltonism. As we have also seen, the presence of Herder—Kant's antipole in this constellation—is strongly in evidence in Kant's choice of his chief exemplifying representation in §49. Kant's tracing of these elements of the constellation is indeed so intricate that his activity of following it is suggestive of succession itself, even, indeed, a Miltonic succession. After all, what makes the constellation of German Miltonism identifiable as a constellation is that its diverse participants are focused on trying to understand the aesthetic and moral impact of Milton's poetry, including (not infrequently) its endless progressions of representation. In addition, we have seen evidence suggesting that Kant developed principal ideas of the *Nachfolge* from his own early fascination with tracing astronomical constellations.

Yet, for all this, in all the texts of Kant that we have examined, the difference between the following of constellation and the procedure of succession remains decisive. The following of constellation, no matter how subtle and creative, always retains an element of what Kant regards as imitation. Perhaps we must say that the dangers of blindness and servility are even especially acute in constellation because of its almost invisible gravitational pull. To be sure, constellation may itself become part of the "preparation" that is also an aspect of succession; and for anyone experiencing the scenarios of constellation, there will inevitably be present a kind of unspoken storytelling in connecting the points of constellation. Finally, however, only succession can provide the experience of "influence" in freedom that Kant identifies; and only succession is viewed by Kant as an integral part of the aesthetic activity that discloses moral feeling. Succession alone entails the transfer from the heteronomous to the autonomous, and from the sensible to the supersensible, as well as the transformation of exemplification into exemplarity, so that a leap to the universal becomes possible. For Kant, poetry has a special capacity for representing exemplarity. "*Poetry* . . . which . . . is least willing to be led by precepts or example . . . holds the first rank among all the arts" (*CJ*, 5:326). As we have seen, Kant means by this that, in endless progressions and in procedures of succession, poetry uses examples to disengage the mind from what is empirical in examples, thus achieving exemplarity.

The features of succession that constellation does not share are disclosed in the aesthetic ideas that Kant directly links to his idea of poetry. "It is in fact precisely in the poetic art," he says in §49, "that the faculty of aesthetic ideas can show itself to full advantage." He may seem to disclaim this claim when he immediately adds, "This faculty, however, regarded solely on its own account, is properly no more than a talent (of the imagination)" (*CJ*, 5:314). Yet in the *Groundwork of the Metaphysics of Morals* and the *Critique of Practical Reason,* we have seen how much philosophical store Kant can set in mere "talent"; and even in the *Critique of Pure Reason* he speaks of "pure *a priori* imagination."[1] Especially in the way he invokes *"poetry"* in the *Critique of Judgment,* the inconsistencies in his account of the sublime suggest that here, too, he hesitated before, and partly covered up, the boldness of his philosophical claim for the unique capacity of "the poetic art" to "show"—or disclose—"the faculty of aesthetic ideas."[2]

The Kantian-Miltonic procedure of succession is distinguished from Kant's engagement with the constellation of German Miltonism in at least four ways, all of which are functions of the procedure of succession that he performs with regard to Milton's poetry of the sublime: (a) The lines of the Kantian-Miltonic succession are experienced by the viewer as an effectively endless line of representations, each representing—crucially—its representational inadequacy, its shadow with light. (b) The succession to this *Progressus* of aesthetic light and shadow produces another kind of light and shadow, a "discharge" of energy that follows a "check to the vital forces" in the experience of the sublime. (c) The movement or procedure of succession discloses a causality of freedom. (d) The act of experiencing the succession is a freely willed movement to moral reason.

1. Here is the phrase in context: "The *schema* of sensible concepts, such as of figures in space, is a product and, as it were, a monogram, of pure *a priori* imagination, through which, and in accordance with which, images themselves first become possible" (*CPR*, A141–142/B180–181).

2. In ways different from what I am describing, Sarah L. Gibbons, *Kant's Theory of Imagination: Bridging Gaps in Judgement and Experience* (Oxford: Clarendon Press, 1994), p. 143, attempts to distinguish inherent similarities and differences between the faculty of the sublime and the products of fine art.

Kant's Miltonic procedure of succession thus results in an accessing of practical freedom as well as an exercise of that freedom as an *a priori* causality. In *The Essence of Human Freedom,* Heidegger builds his discussion of freedom upon Kant's accounts of the causality of freedom. Yet Heidegger charges that Kant "completely fails" to provide "the clarification of movement" that is the "philosophical situation" of the causality of freedom. In light of Heidegger's obliviousness to Kant's clarification of movement in the procedure of the *Nachfolge*—which precisely discloses a causality of freedom—we may decide that the failure here is Heidegger's, not Kant's.[3]

Surprising—"strange," "singular," "unexpected"—as it may continue to seem, Kant found that the object that fully satisfied the conditions of the procedure of succession was poetry of a certain kind.[4] In Kant's individual case this kind of poetry was exemplified by Milton. Poetry of this Kantian kind is a representation and implementation of the transfer from the sensible to the supersensible, from heteronomy to autonomy, and from the empirical to the *a priori.* The form of this poetry is not an arbitrary invention. The procedure of succession, which gives form to this poetry, is the outward manifestation and disclosure of the mind's *a priori* activity of succession. Although we never forget that Kant is always journeying toward the *a priori,* we must equally recall his awareness of how all his journeys begin: "There can be no doubt that all our knowledge begins with experience" (*CPR,* B1). In Kant's recorded experience, the poetry that is grounded in the *a priori,* and that leads him back to the *a priori,* is Milton's poetry of the endless progression, of exemplarity, and of succession.

3. Martin Heidegger, *The Essence of Human Freedom: An Introduction to Philosophy,* trans. Ted Sadler (New York: Continuum, 2002), p. 22.
4. In citing, once more, the terms *strange, singular, unexpected,* I have recurred to Kant's discussion of the surprising but vital importance of "mere form" in moral reason (*CPrR,* 5:31, 79, 152).

APPENDIX

INDEX

Kant's Letter to Schiller, Citing Milton, and Its Parallelisms with Two Other Kantian Passages

Here is virtually the whole of Kant's letter to Schiller on 30 March 1795:

Esteemed Sir,

I am always delighted to know and engage in literary discussions with such a talented and learned man as you, my dearest friend. I received the plan for a periodical that you sent me last summer and also the two first monthly issues. I found your *Letters on the Aesthetic Education of Mankind* splendid, and I shall study them so as to be able to give you my thoughts about them. The paper on sexual differences in organic nature, in the second issue, is impossible for me to decipher, even though the author [Wilhelm von Humboldt] seems to be an intelligent fellow. There was once a severely critical discussion in the *Allgemeine Literaturzeitung* about the ideas expressed in the letters of Herr Hube of Thorn concerning a similar relationship extending throughout nature. The ideas were attacked as romantic twaddle. To be sure, we sometimes find something like that running through our heads, without knowing what to make of it. The organization of nature has always struck me as amazing and as a sort of chasm of thought; I mean, the idea that fertilization, in both realms of nature, always needs two sexes in order for the species to be propagated. After all, we don't want to believe that providence has chosen this arrangement, almost playfully, for the sake of variety. On the contrary, we have reason to believe that propagation is not possible in any other way. This opens a prospect on what lies beyond the field of vision, out of which, however, we can unfortunately make nothing, as little as out of what Milton's angel told Adam about the creation: "Male light of distant suns mixes itself with female, to unknown ends" [*Paradise Lost,* VIII.148–152]. . . .

. . . With regard to my small contribution to this journal . . . I must . . . beg a somewhat lengthy postponement. Since discussions of political and religious topics are currently subject to certain restrictions and there are hardly any other matters, at least at this time, that interest the general reading public, one must keep one's eye on this change of the weather, so as to conform prudently to the times [*man . . . muß, um sich klüglich in die Zeit . . . zuschicken*].[1]

Everything Kant says here is, in fact, organized around his seemingly offhand quotation from Milton. It is unmistakable in Kant's Elsner remark that the same verses of Milton exemplified for Kant something that was of primary significance. One must wonder what Schiller could have made of this strange, almost dark letter. The most significant of Kant's assertions is hidden in information to which Schiller had little or no access. Schiller must have wondered why Kant was quoting Milton at him in such an aggressive manner. When the full context of this quotation in both of these Kantian instances is taken together with precise parallels in the *Critique of Judgment,* §49, the import of this exemplification, and of what Kant was not willing to reveal to Schiller, only grows exponentially.

I suggest that Kant is here writing two letters simultaneously. One is a letter to Schiller, brimming with politesse, saying almost nothing. The second is a letter of deep reaffirmation, in the face of someone (though himself a poet of liberty) associated with dangers to Kant. The second letter, composed for Immanuel Kant, draws strength from its distancings, from disclosure (initially only to himself) within distancing, consolidating and preserving meanings for a better time and for more understanding and/or more sympathetic readers. My description of Kant's doubleness, or duplicity, certainly suggests a considerable anxiety, perhaps paranoia, on his part. Yet no one can doubt

1. Immanuel Kant, *Correspondence,* trans. and ed. Arnulf Zweig (Cambridge: Cambridge University Press, 1999), pp. 497–498; *AA,* 12:10–12.

that he and his system had innumerable real foes at this time. Kant's trauma at having received, just the previous year, a personal letter of warning from the king (regarding *Religion within the Boundaries of Mere Reason* and its claims for moral reason) could not have been far from his thoughts, not in eighteenth-century Germany—and certainly not in the years immediately following the fall of the Bastille (1789). During these years Kant did not hide his enthusiasm for the French Revolution.[2] For our present discussion what is important to recognize, specifically with regard to Kant's turning to Milton's poetry, about Kant's distancings—so marked in the letter to Schiller—is only that its antecedents significantly predate both the letter to Schiller and the king's censure concerning *Religion*. In other words, Kant's prudential strategies for quietly weathering the "restrictions" on his moral philosophizing, which inevitably had profound implications for "political and religious topics," became deeply ingrained. These strategies are, I am suggesting, continuous with the distancing in which he had long engaged—and in which he is engaged in the letter—in relation to the ideas and materials that he links specifically to Milton. Here we see again, concretely, that at least after 1789 Kant learned to keep half-hidden the ways in which he was actively following Milton's "painting, designed with freedom" (*AA*, 25.2:1494).

On this reading of the letter to Schiller, it may even have pleased Kant to imagine that his correspondent would think him doddering and incoherent. Kant is intent on inner consolidation. Here, as in his lectures, Milton is put forward as the standard-bearer of true poetic genius. For Kant, the genius must never be confused with the mere "talented and learned man," such as (in Kant's view) Schiller represents. In fact, as Schiller at least partially knew, Kant considered Schiller's reservations about Kantian moral philosophy to be the effect of his intellectual limitations. As Gerold Prauss has suggested, Kant probably thought that in the second *Critique* he had provided a strong refutation of Schiller's central ethical conceptions.[3] Moreover, Schiller has unforgivably associated himself with the *Schwärmerei* of people like

2. See Manfred Kuehn, *Kant: A Biography* (Cambridge: Cambridge University Press, 2001), pp. 340–343.

3. Gerold Prauss, *Kant über Freiheit als Autonomie* (Frankfurt am Main: Vittorio Klostermann, 1983), pp. 240–277, especially pp. 247–248. See Henry E. Allison, *Kant's Theory of Freedom* (Cambridge: Cambridge University Press, 1990), pp. 183–184, for a view of this matter that is complementary, though not identical, to Prauss's.

Humboldt, not to speak—Kant had spoken of it repeatedly—of Klop-stock (the touted "German Milton" whose achievement must not be confused with that of the real Milton), or of Schiller's intimate associate Goethe (who Kant thought had not the highest kind of genius), or of Goethe's intimate associate Herder, and, indeed, of the entire *Sturm und Drang* (which, in Kant's view, was dragging German culture down the road to fanatical emotionalism). Some part of this background noise must have been audible to Schiller. Yet Kant's comments on the "two sexes" that are needed "in order for the species to be propagated," preparing and leading up to the quotation from Milton, must have bewildered Schiller totally.

To be sure, the tone of Kant's letter is meant to suggest, to Schiller, an ironic trivialization of just these things. But once we adduce Kant's previous usage of the Milton citation and reconstruct around it the framework of Miltonic ideas that he assembled in the *Critique of Judgment,* we understand that he secretly mocks Schiller with what is in fact an irony-clad formula of the succession procedure, with its mental "continuous motion" and "wealth of thoughts," as well as its resultant (in this case, mocking) overload: "To be sure, we sometimes find something like that running through our heads, without knowing what to make of it." The same camouflage is applied to the philosophical import of the "abyss of thought" that precisely "opens a prospect on what lies beyond the field of vision." Kant's saying that "out of" this "we can unfortunately make nothing" is an attenuated, ironic, and veiled restatement of the "inability" of the mind to grasp an endless totality (*CJ,* 5:250) that is at the same time the awakening of the mind's "ability" for the "infinite of supersensible intuition" (*CJ,* 5:254–255). In other words, it is a restatement of the heart of Kant's theory of the sublime, which is, in turn, at the heart of the succession procedure, aesthetic ideas, and the moral efficacy of autonomous aesthetic judgment. The phrase *so little—so wenig*—with which, by analogy, Kant seems to belittle Milton's verses is thus the sure sign of Kant's claim for the colossal moment of knowing nothing in the procedure of succession and its "immeasurable prospect" *(unabsehbaren Prospekt),* its "prospect into a field stretching beyond its ken" *(Aussicht in ein unabsehliches Feld).*[4] Having reversed the signs on Kant's statements to Schiller, we can see that the phrase "abyss of thought" *(Abgrund des Denkens)* in the letter is logically

4. See Chapter 2 for Herder's hostile attention to this phrase.

amplified by Kant's observations in the *Critique of Judgment* that "the mind feels itself *set in motion* in the representation of the sublime in nature. . . . The point of excess for the imagination . . . is like an abyss [*Das Überschwengliche für die Einbildungskraft . . . ist gleichsam ein Abgrund*] in which it fears to lose itself" (5:258); to "look . . . into the infinite . . . is an abyss [*auf das Unendliche hinaussehen . . . ein Abgrund ist*]" (5:265).

∼

I believe that the parallelisms among these texts virtually speak for themselves in the way that I am proposing. At the very least they must challenge us to explain what Kant was thinking when he created these symmetries. Here, in conclusion, is a highlighting (in underlining) of parallelisms among [1] Kant's letter to Schiller, 30 March 1795, [2] the passage from his lecture on anthropology, 1792–93, and [3, a, b, c] §49 of the *Critique of Judgment* (1790). The passages are reproduced more fully in the notes:[5]

5. [1] "Die im zweyten M. Stück enthaltene Abhandlung, über den Geschlechtsunterschied in der Organischen Natur kann ich mir, so ein guter Kopf mir auch der Verfasser zu seyn scheint, doch nicht enträtzeln. Einmal hatte die A. L. Z. sich über einen Gedanken in den Briefen des Hrn. Hube aus Thorn (die Naturlehre betreffend), von einer ähnlichen durch die ganze Natur gehenden Verwandtschaft, mit scharfem Tadel (als über Schwärmerey) aufgehalten. Etwas dergleichen läuft einem zwar bisweilen durch den Kopf; aber man weiß nichts daraus zu machen. So ist mir nämlich die Natureinrichtung: daß alle Besaamung in beyden organischen Reichen zwey Geschlechter bedarf, um ihre Art fortzupflanzen, jederzeit als erstaunlich und wie ein Abgrund des Denkens für die menschliche Vernunft aufgefallen, weil man doch die Vorsehung hiebey nicht, als ob sie diese Ordnung gleichsam spielend, der Abwechselung halber, beliebt habe, annehmen wird, sondern Ursache hat zu glauben, daß sie nicht anders möglich sey; welches eine Aussicht ins Unabsehliche eröfnet, woraus man aber schlechterdings nichts machen kann, so wenig wie aus dem, was Miltons Engel dem Adam von der Schöpfung erzählt: 'Männliches Licht entferneter Sonnen vermischt sich mit weiblichem, zu unbekannten Endzwecken'" (*AA,* 8:11).

[2] "Ästhetische Ideen sind solche Vorstellungen, die eine Fülle von Gedanken enthalten, die bis ins Unendliche eine Folge von Gedanken nach sich ziehen. Solche Ideen ziehen uns in einen unabsehbaren Prospekt, z. E. Milton's Ausspruch: Weibliches Licht vermischt sich mit männlichem Licht zu unbekannten Endzwecken. Durch diese geistvolle Idee wird das Gemüt in einen continuierlichen Schwung versetzt" (*AA,* 25.2:1561).

[3a] "Geist in ästhetischer Bedeutung heißt das belebende Princip im Gemüthe. Dasjenige aber, wodurch dieses Princip die Seele belebt, der Stoff, den es dazu

from the letter to Schiller, 1795:

[1] Die . . . Abhandlung, über den <u>Geschlechtsunterschied in der</u> <u>Organischen Natur</u> [in the next sentence, "einer ähnlichen <u>durch die</u> <u>ganze Natur gehenden</u> Verwandtschaft"] kann ich mir . . . nicht enträtzeln. . . . <u>Etwas dergleichen läuft einem zwar bisweilen durch den</u>

anwendet, ist das, was die Gemüthskräfte zweckmäßig in Schwung versetzt, d. i. in ein solches Spiel, welches sich von selbst erhält und selbst die Kräfte dazu stärkt.

Nun behaupte ich, dieses Princip sei nichts anders, als das Vermögen der Darstellung ästhetischer Ideen; unter einer ästhetischen Idee aber verstehe ich diejenige Vorstellung der Einbildungskraft, die viel zu denken veranlaßt, ohne daß ihr doch irgend ein bestimmter Gedanke, d. i. Begriff, adäquat sein kann, die folglich keine Sprache völlig erreicht und verständlich machen kann. . . .

Wenn nun einem Begriffe eine Vorstellung der Einbildungskraft untergelegt wird, die zu seiner Darstellung gehört, aber für sich allein so viel zu denken veranlaßt, als sich niemals in einem bestimmten Begriff zusammenfassen läßt, mithin den Begriff selbst auf unbegränzte Art ästhetisch erweitert: so ist die Einbildungskraft hiebei schöpferisch und bringt das Vermögen intellectueller Ideen (die Vernunft) in Bewegung, mehr nämlich bei Veranlassung einer Vorstellung zu denken (was zwar zu dem Begriffe des Gegenstandes gehört), als in ihr aufgefaßt und deutlich gemacht werden kann" (5:313–315).

[3b] "Man nennt diejenigen Formen, welche nicht die Darstellung eines gegebenen Begriffs selber ausmachen, sondern nur als Nebenvorstellungen der Einbildungskraft die damit verknüpften Folgen und die Verwandtschaft desselben mit andern ausdrücken, *Attribute* (ästhetische) eines Gegenstandes, dessen Begriff als Vernunftidee nicht adäquat dargestellt werden kann. So ist der Adler Jupiters mit dem Blitze in den Klauen ein Attribut des mächtigen Himmelskönigs und der Pfau der prächtigen Himmelskönigin. Sie stellen nicht wie die logischen Attribute das, was in unsern Begriffen von der Erhabenheit und Majestät der Schöpfung liegt, sondern etwas anderes vor, was der Einbildungskraft Anlaß giebt, sich über eine Menge von verwandten Vorstellungen zu verbreiten, die mehr denken lassen, als man in einem durch Worte bestimmten Begriff ausdrücken kann; und geben eine *ästhetische Idee,* die jener Vernunftidee statt logischer Darstellung dient, eigentlich aber um das Gemüth zu beleben, indem sie ihm die Aussicht in ein unabsehliches Feld verwandter Vorstellungen eröffnet. Die schöne Kunst aber thut dieses nicht allein in der Malerei oder Bildhauerkunst (wo der Namen der Attribute gewöhnlich gebraucht wird); sondern die Dichtkunst und Beredsamkeit nehmen den Geist, der ihre Werke belebt, auch lediglich von den ästhetischen Attributen der Gegenstände her, welche den logischen zu Seite gehen und der Einbildungskraft einen Schwung geben, mehr dabei, obzwar auf unentwickelte Art, zu denken, als sich in einem Begriffe, mithin in einem bestimmten Sprachausdrucke zusammenfassen läßt" (5:315).

[3c] "Nach diesen Voraussetzungen ist Genie: die musterhafte Originalität der

Kopf; aber man weiß nichts daraus zu machen. So ist mir nämlich diese Natureinrichtung . . . wie ein Abgrund des Denkens für die menschliche Vernunft aufgefallen, . . . welches eine Aussicht ins Unabsehliche eröfnet, woraus man aber schlechterdings nichts machen kann, so wenig wie aus dem, was Miltons Engel dem Adam von der Schöpfung erzählt: "Männliches Licht entferneter [sic] Sonnen vermischt sich mit weiblichem, zu unbekannten Endzwecken."

The paper on sexual differences in organic nature [in the next sentence, "a similar relationship extending throughout nature"] . . . is impossible for me to decipher. . . . To be sure, we sometimes find something like that running through our heads, without knowing what to make of it. . . . as a sort of chasm [abyss] of thought. . . . This opens a prospect on what lies beyond the field of vision, out of which, however, we can unfortunately make nothing, as little as out of what Milton's angel told Adam about the creation: "Male light of distant suns mixes itself with female, to unknown ends." [*Paradise Lost*, VIII.148–152]

from the lecture on anthropology, 1792–93:

[2] Ästhetische Ideen sind solche Vorstellungen, die eine Fülle von Gedanken enthalten, die bis ins Unendliche eine Folge von Gedanken nach sich ziehen. Solche Ideen ziehen uns in einen unabsehbaren Prospekt, z. E. Milton's Ausspruch: Weibliches Licht vermischt sich mit männlichem Licht zu unbekannten Endzwecken. Durch diese geistvolle Idee wird das Gemüt in einen continuierlichen Schwung versetzt.

Aesthetic ideas are those representations that contain a wealth of thoughts which *ad infinitum* draw after it a succession of thoughts. Such ideas draw us into an immeasurable prospect, e.g. Milton's saying, "Fe-

---

Naturgabe eines Subjects im freien Gebrauche seiner Erkenntnißvermögen. Auf solche Weise ist das Product eines Genies (nach demjenigen, was in demselben dem Genie, nicht der möglichen Erlernung oder der Schule zuzuschreiben ist) ein Beispiel nicht der Nachahmung (denn da würde das, was daran Genie ist und den Geist des Werks ausmacht, verloren gehen), sondern der Nachfolge für ein anderes Genie, welches dadurch zum Gefühl seiner eigenen Originalität aufgeweckt wird, Zwangsfreiheit von Regeln so in der Kunst auszuüben, daß diese dadurch selbst eine neue Regel bekommt, wodurch das Talent sich als musterhaft zeigt" (5:318).

male <u>light</u> mixes itself with male <u>light,</u> to unknown ends." Through this <u>soulful</u> [ingenious] idea <u>the mind</u> is set into a <u>continuous motion.</u> (*AA,* 25.2:1561)

from §49 of the Critique of Judgment (1790)

[3a] <u>Geist in ästhetischer Bedeutung</u> . . . heißt . . . das, was <u>die Gemüthskräfte zweckmäßig in Schwung versetzt,</u> . . . ; unter einer ästhetischen Idee aber verstehe ich <u>diejenige Vorstellung</u> der Einbildungskraft, die viel zu denken veranlaßt, <u>ohne daß ihr doch irgend ein bestimmter Gedanke, d. i. Begriff, adäquat sein kann, die folglich keine Sprache völlig erreicht</u> und verständlich machen kann.

<u>*Soul*in an aesthetical sense,</u> signifies . . . that which <u>sets the mental powers into a swing that is final,</u> . . . ; by an aesthetic idea I mean <u>that representation</u> of the imagination which induces much thought, yet <u>without the possibility of any definite thought whatever, i.e. *concept,* being adequate to it, and which language, consequently, can never get quite on level terms with</u> or render completely intelligible. (5:313.30–314.5)

[3b] Man nennt diejenigen <u>Formen, welche nicht die Darstellung eines gegebenen Begriffs selber ausmachen,</u> sondern nur als <u>Nebenvorstellungen der Einbildungskraft</u> die damit <u>verknüpften Folgen</u> und die Verwandtschaft desselben mit andern ausdrücken, *Attribute* (ästhetische) eines Gegenstandes, dessen Begriff als Vernunftidee nicht adäquat dargestellt werden kann. So ist der Adler Jupiters mit dem Blitze in den Klauen ein Attribut des mächtigen Himmelskönigs und der Pfau der prächtigen Himmelskönigin. Sie stellen nicht wie die *logischen Attribute* das, was in unsern Begriffen von der <u>Erhabenheit</u> und Majestät der Schöpfung liegt, sondern etwas anderes vor, was <u>der Einbildungskraft Anlaß giebt, sich über eine Menge von verwandten Vorstellungen zu verbreiten, die mehr denken lassen, als man in einem durch Worte bestimmten Begriff ausdrücken kann;</u> und <u>geben eine *ästhetische Idee,*</u> die jener Vernunftidee statt logischer Darstellung dient, eigentlich aber um <u>das Gemüth zu beleben, indem sie ihm die Aussicht in ein unabsehliches Feld verwandter Vorstellungen eröffnet. Die schöne Kunst aber thut dieses nicht allein in der Malerei oder Bildhauerkunst (wo der Namen der Attribute gewöhnlich gebraucht wird); sondern</u>

die Dichtkunst und Beredsamkeit nehmen den Geist, der ihre Werke belebt, auch lediglich von den ästhetischen Attributen der Gegenstände her, welche den logischen zu Seite gehen und der Einbildungskraft einen Schwung geben, mehr dabei, obzwar auf unentwickelte Art, zu denken, als sich in einem Begriffe, mithin in einem bestimmten Sprachausdrucke zusammenfassen läßt.

Those forms which do not constitute the presentation of a given concept itself, but which, as secondary representations of the imagination, express the successions connected with it, and its kinship with other concepts, are called (aesthetic) *attributes* of an object, the concept of which, as an idea of reason, cannot be adequately presented. In this way Jupiter's eagle, with the lightning in its claws, is an attribute of the mighty king of heaven, and the peacock of its stately queen. They do not, like *logical attributes,* represent what lies in our concepts of the sublimity and majesty of creation, but rather something else—something that gives the imagination an incentive to spread its flight over a whole host of kindred representations that provoke more thought than admits of expression in a concept determined by words. They furnish an *aesthetic idea,* which serves the above rational idea as a substitute for logical presentation, but with the proper function, however, of animating the mind by opening out for it a prospect into a field of kindred representations stretching beyond its ken. But it is not alone in the arts of painting or sculpture, where the name of attribute is customarily employed, that fine art acts in this way; poetry and rhetoric also derive the soul that animates their works wholly from the aesthetic attributes of the objects—attributes which go hand in hand with the logical, and give the imagination an impetus to bring more thought into play in the matter, though in an undeveloped manner, than allows of being brought within the embrace of a concept, or, therefore, of being definitely formulated in language. (5:315.9–31)

Der Dichter wagt es, Vernunftideen von unsichtbaren Wesen, das Reich der Seligen, das Höllenreich, die Ewigkeit, die Schöpfung u. d. gl., zu versinnlichen; oder auch das, was zwar Beispiele in der Erfahrung findet, z. B. den Tod, den Neid und alle Laster, imgleichen die Liebe, den Ruhm u. d. gl., über die Schranken der Erfahrung hinaus vermittelst einer Einbildungskraft, die dem Vernunft-Vorspiele in

Erreichung eines Größten nacheifert, in einer Vollständigkeit sinnlich zu machen, für die sich in der Natur kein Beispiel findet; und es ist eigentlich die Dichtkunst, in welcher sich das Vermögen ästhetischer Ideen in seinem ganzen Maße zeigen kann. Dieses Vermögen aber, für sich allein betrachtet, ist eigentlich nur ein Talent (der Einbildungskraft).

The poet essays the task of interpreting to sense the rational ideas of invisible beings, the kingdom of the blessed, hell, eternity, creation, &c. [These items, taken separately and together, describe no other major poem so obviously as *Paradise Lost.* To some extent they could be taken to apply as well to Klopstock's *Der Messias,* itself directly emulating *Paradise Lost,* but we know the disesteem in which Kant held Klopstock's poetry, precisely in comparison with Milton's.] Or, again, as to things of which examples occur in experience, e.g. death [Milton's famous allegory of Death and Sin], envy [Milton's central characterization of Satan's envy of God and then of Adam and Eve], and all vices, as also love, fame, [these items as well are typical of Milton's descriptions but less uniquely so] and the like, transgressing the limits of experience he attempts with the aid of an imagination which emulates the display of reason in its attainment of a maximum, to body them forth to sense with a completeness of which nature affords no parallel; and it is in fact precisely in the poetic art that the faculty of aesthetic ideas can show itself to full advantage. This faculty, however, regarded solely on its own account is properly no more than a talent (of the imagination). (5:314.26–36)

[3c] Nach diesen Voraussetzungen ist Genie: die musterhafte Originalität der Naturgabe eines Subjects im freien Gebrauche seiner Erkenntnißvermögen. Auf solche Weise ist das Product eines Genies (nach demjenigen, was in demselben dem Genie, nicht der möglichen Erlernung oder der Schule zuzuschreiben ist) ein Beispiel nicht der Nachahmung (denn da würde das, was daran Genie ist und den Geist des Werks ausmacht, verloren gehen), sondern der Nachfolge für ein anderes Genie, welches dadurch zum Gefühl seiner eigenen Originalität aufgeweckt wird, Zwangsfreiheit von Regeln so in der Kunst auszuüben, daß diese dadurch selbst eine neue Regel bekommt, wodurch das Talent sich als musterhaft zeigt.

Genius, according to these presuppositions, is <u>the exemplary origi-</u><u>nality of the natural endowments of an individual in the</u> *free* <u>employ-</u><u>ment of the cognitive faculties.</u> On this showing, the product of a ge-nius (in respect of so much in this product as is attributable to genius, and not to possible learning or academic instruction,) is <u>an example,</u> <u>not for imitation [Nachahmung] (for that would mean the loss of the</u> <u>element of genius, and just the soul of the work), but to be succeeded</u> <u>[Nachfolge] by another genius—one whom it arouses to a sense of his</u> <u>own originality in putting freedom from the constraint of rules so into</u> <u>force in his art, that for art itself a new rule is won—which is what</u> <u>shows a talent to be exemplary.</u> (5:318.6–15)

Index

Abbt, Thomas, 54, 114n68, 153, 164; and genius and talent, 128–133, 129nn17–18, 130–132nn20–23, 140, 140n31, 145, 153, 164; mentioned by Kant, 130–131; and Baumgarten and Meier, 140n32

Abraham, 151

Adam, 18, 39, 74, 262, 286, 289, 290, 292n, 308, 311, 313, 316

Adams, Robert Merrihew, 207n37

Addison, Joseph: and Longinus, 4, 102, 110, 114; and Young, 16n, 36, 101, 101n52; impact of his Milton essays in Germany, 18n11, 21n13, 229; and Miltonic negation and succession, 67, 67n19, 68–70; on Milton and the sublime, 70, 70n, 76n, 99n, 269

Aeschylus, 101, 230; *Prometheus Bound*, 231n19

Aesthetic ideas: in the *Critique of Judgment*, 9, 10n11, 21n13, 67, 148, 233, 255–256, 265; in Milton's poetry, 10, 13, 19, 26, 31, 36, 43, 79, 87, 261, 266–272; and aesthetic light and shadow, 36; and Baumgarten, 57; and Meier's energetic ideas, 57, 58, 60, 62–63, 63n12, 64, 70; and Breitinger, 59; in succession in §49 of the *Critique of Judgment*, 61, 116, 275, 277, 283, 292, 297, 299; and un-

conditioned negativity, 87; and succession, 114, 116, 301, 303; and the *Groundwork,* 123; in the second *Critique,* 218; and *Samson Agonistes,* 218, 219. *See also* Allison, Henry E.; Jupiter and Juno; Sublime, the

Aesthetic light and shadow: and the constellation of German Miltonism, 7, 22, 31, 34; in Milton's poetry, Kant on, 9, 36, 43, 56, 124–125, 293–294, 296–297; and the sublime, 9–10, 27, 31, 44; in succession, 27, 33, 43, 79, 277, 294, 300; and Milton, Meier on, 36, 57, 58, 59, 59n, 63, 63n12, 64, 66, 67, 70, 73, 275, 292, 301; in the second *Critique,* 44; and Addison, 70; and Lowth, 73; and *energeia,* 125; in the *Critique of Judgment,* §49, 267, 275, 277, 299; in the *Progressus,* 297, 303

Allison, Henry E.: isomorphism, 37, 37n23; impersonal standpoint, 118n1; test of universalizability, 147; freedom of heteronomous actions, 147, 207n36; direct ethical (in)significance of the sublime, 147n39, 272, 272n16; activity of "taking as," 166n2; concept of the person and procedures of the categorical imperative, 169,